LEADERSHIP

A REFLECTIVE AND STUDENT FOCUSED APPROACH

ANDREI LUX

s

1 Oliver's Yard
55 City Road
London EC1Y 1SP

2455 Teller Road
Thousand Oaks
California 91320

Unit No 323-333, Third Floor, F-Block
International Trade Tower
Nehru Place, New Delhi – 110 019

8 Marina View Suite 43-053
Asia Square Tower 1
Singapore 018960

Editor: Emma Yuan
Editorial assistant: Charlotte Hegley
Production editor: Sarah Cooke
Marketing manager: Lucia Sweet
Cover design: Hayley Davis
Typeset by: C&M Digitals (P) Ltd, Chennai, India
Printed in the UK by Bell & Bain Ltd, Glasgow
BB0347308

© Andrei A. Lux 2025

Apart from any fair dealing for the purposes of research, private study, or criticism or review, as permitted under the Copyright, Designs and Patents Act, 1988, this publication may not be reproduced, stored or transmitted in any form, or by any means, without the prior permission in writing of the publisher, or in the case of reprographic reproduction, in accordance with the terms of licences issued by the Copyright Licensing Agency. Enquiries concerning reproduction outside those terms should be sent to the publisher.

Library of Congress Control Number: 2024936859

British Library Cataloguing in Publication data

A catalogue record for this book is available from the British Library.

ISBN 978-1-5296-0348-4
ISBN 978-1-5296-0347-7 (pbk)

Reader, this book is dedicated to you, so that you may go further than I ever could.

BRIEF CONTENTS

Online Resources — xix

1. Introduction to Leadership — 1
2. Global Leadership Context — 23
3. Personality, Traits, and Psychopathy — 45
4. Situational, Servant, and Authentic Leadership — 69
5. Charismatic and Transformational Leadership — 95
6. Culture, Diversity, and Inclusive Leadership — 123
7. Values, Integrity, and Ethical Leadership — 149
8. Self-Awareness and Leadership Development — 177
9. Power, Influence, and Communication — 201
10. Practical Leadership Skills — 227
11. Leading Teams and Managing Conflict — 253
12. Leading People through Change — 279

Author's Note — 307
Biography — 309
Index — 311

CONTENTS

Online Resources   xix

1 Introduction to Leadership   1
  Overview   1
  So, what is leadership anyway?   2
  What is leadership to you?   3
    Share your ideas, learn about others'   4
    Where did you get these ideas?   5
    Are leaders born special?   6
  Finding your own way   6
    Personal reflection   7
    Everyday leadership   8
  What leadership isn't   8
    Leadership vs management   9
    Doing both jobs well   10
    Over-managed and under-led   11
  Evolution of leadership   12
  Defining leadership   13
    Academic definitions   16
    Current leadership definition   17
  What is influence?   18
    Inspiring others   19
  Summary   20
  References   20

2 Global Leadership Context   23
  Overview   23
  Revolutionary change   24
    Geopolitical conflicts   24
    Technological advancements   25
    Social movements   26
  Volatile, uncertain, complex, and ambiguous   26
  Contemporary leadership challenges   27
    It's happening now, in real time   28

Increasingly international	29
Cross-cultural collaboration	30
Accountability and intolerance	31
Inversion of expertise	32
Flexible and remote work	33
Advantages	34
Disadvantages	34
So is flexible work good, or bad?	35
Leadership challenges	35
Traditional leadership challenges	36
Overcoming leadership challenges	37
Megatrends	38
Developed nations	38
Developing nations	38
Economic dominance	39
Urbanisation	39
Fourth Industrial Revolution	40
Future leaders	41
Summary	42
References	42

3 Personality, Traits, and Psychopathy — 45

Overview	45
Psychology	46
Your unique traits and personality	46
Personality profiling	47
Where did my personality come from?	48
Hereditary genetics – 45%	48
Childhood environment – 15%	49
Your choices – 40%	49
Context matters	50
The Big Five	51
Extroversion	52
Agreeableness	52
Emotional stability	53
Conscientiousness	54
Openness	54
There's no good or bad, it's about fit	55
Personalities and leadership	56
Guide your development	56
Understand your followers	57
Cognitive style	58

	Carl Jung	59
	Myers–Briggs Type Indicator	60
	Limitations of the MBTI	61
	Commercially motivated pseudoscience	61
	The Dark Triad	62
	Means, motive, and opportunity	63
	Leadership is the long game	64
	Summary	65
	References	65
4	**Situational, Servant, and Authentic Leadership**	**69**
	Overview	69
	Leadership behaviour	70
	Task focused	70
	Relationship focused	71
	What's more important?	71
	Situational leadership	73
	Contingency model	73
	Leadership style	73
	Situational control	74
	Leadership fit for context	75
	Situational leadership theory	77
	Four leadership styles	77
	Academic background	79
	Advantages and challenges	80
	Situational leadership overview	80
	Servant leadership	81
	Six dimensions	82
	Creating long-term value	83
	It comes back to why you lead	84
	Challenges that remain	85
	Authentic leadership	86
	Four dimensions	87
	Your journey inspires others	88
	Ongoing controversy	90
	Summary	90
	References	91
5	**Charismatic and Transformational Leadership**	**95**
	Overview	95
	Charisma	96
	Charismatic leadership	97

Emotional basis		98
Signalling		100
Stable appearance		101
Personality traits		102
Behaviour		103
Sources of charisma		103
Sending charismatic signals		105
Nonverbal charismatic signals		107
Context		108
Outcomes		110
Amorality		111
Transformational leadership		111
Transformational vs transactional		112
Four dimensions		112
Charismatic and transformational?		114
How are followers changed?		114
Challenges that remain		116
Summary		116
References		117

6 Culture, Diversity, and Inclusive Leadership — 123

Overview		123
Growing complexity		124
Culture		125
Cultural values		126
Leadership perceptions		126
Six layers of values		128
Stereotypes and myths		130
Hall		131
High- vs low-context		131
Monochronic vs polychronic		132
Hofstede		132
Individualism vs collectivism		132
Power distance		133
Masculinity vs femininity		133
Uncertainty avoidance		134
Long- vs short-term orientation		134
Trompenaars and Hampden-Turner		135
Universalism vs particularism		135
Neutral vs emotional		135
Specific vs diffuse		136
Achievement vs ascription		136

Cultural profiles	137
Containers of culture	138
Cultural cognition	139
Analytic vs holistic thought	139
Diversity and inclusion	141
Multiculturalism in organisations	142
Inclusive leadership	142
Five dimensions	143
Belongingness	143
Uniqueness	143
Everyone can contribute	144
Challenges in practice	144
Summary	145
References	146

7 Values, Integrity, and Ethical Leadership   149

Overview	149
Values	150
Instrumental and terminal	151
Where values come from	153
Discover your values	155
Self-accepting leaders	155
Ethics	156
Hedonism, stoicism, and other -isms	157
Moral principles	157
Unethical behaviour	159
Ethical climate	159
Integrity	161
Conflicts of responsibility	162
Ethical dilemmas	163
Human resources	163
Conflicts of interest	164
Organisational resources	164
Balancing act	165
Pressure changes everything	166
Why bother? Isn't it hard enough	166
Followers' commitment	167
Positive leadership	167
Ethical leadership	168
Dual responsibilities	169
Four dimensions	169

	Effects on followers and performance	170
	Challenges that remain	171
	Your perfect life	172
	Summary	172
	References	173
8	**Self-Awareness and Leadership Development**	**177**
	Overview	177
	Self-awareness	178
	Self-concept	180
	Self-knowledge	181
	Self-aware leadership	182
	Reflective learning	183
	Double-loop learning	183
	Single-loop learning	184
	Double-loop learning	184
	Learning from setbacks	185
	Reflective journal	186
	Event	186
	Reaction	187
	Reflection	187
	Realisation	188
	Reflection-in-action	189
	Personal mastery	189
	Personal vision	190
	Current reality	191
	Creative tension	192
	Self-limiting beliefs	193
	Leading with mastery	194
	Leadership development	196
	Summary	197
	References	198
9	**Power, Influence, and Communication**	**201**
	Overview	201
	Power	202
	Positional sources of power	203
	Coercive	203
	Legitimate	203
	Reward	204
	Information	204
	Connection	205

Personal sources of power	205
Expert	205
Referent	206
Using power appropriately	207
Workplace bullying	208
Influence	209
Traditional influence tactics	209
Rational persuasion	209
Consultation	210
Inspirational appeal	210
Collaboration	210
Apprising	211
Ingratiation	211
Personal appeal	212
Exchange	212
Legitimising	212
Pressure	213
Coalition	213
Psychological empowerment	215
Meaning	215
Competence	216
Self-determination	216
Impact	217
Motivation at work	217
Communication	218
Written and oral	219
Non-verbal	220
Active listening	221
Summary	222
References	223
10 Practical Leadership Skills	**227**
Overview	227
Critical thinking	228
Identifying	228
Analysing	229
Reflecting	230
Evaluating	231
Reasoning	231
Decision-making	232
DECIDE model	233
Maximising vs satisficing	234

Cognitive biases 235
    Confirmation bias 236
    Groupthink 237
    Attribution asymmetry 237
    Sunk cost fallacy 238
Goal setting 238
Stress 239
    Pressure vs performance 240
    Managing stress 241
Emotional intelligence 243
    Perceiving emotions 244
    Using your emotions 244
    Understanding emotions 245
    Managing emotions 245
Positive psychology 246
    The happy secret 247
    Power of storytelling 248
Summary 250
References 251

11 Leading Teams and Managing Conflict   253

Overview 253
Groups vs teams 254
Types of teams 255
    Functional 255
    Cross-functional 256
    Self-managed 257
    Global or virtual 257
Team development 258
    Forming 259
    Storming 259
    Norming 260
    Performing 260
    Shifting responsibilities 261
Team vital signs 262
    Teams in decline 262
    Teams progressing 263
    Every team is different 264
Types of conflict 264
    Constructive conflict 265
    Destructive conflict 266
    Active vs passive conflict 266

Constructive conflict: active vs passive		267
Destructive conflict: active vs passive		267
Conflict resolution		268
Five resolution styles		269
Assertive vs cooperative		269
When to use each style		271
Competing		271
Avoiding		272
Accommodating		273
Compromising		273
Collaborating		274
Summary		275
References		276

12 Leading People through Change — 279

Overview		279
What is change?		280
Why do organisations need to change?		281
Four types of organisational change		282
Process		282
Functional or structural		283
Cultural		283
Distribution of power		284
Change models		284
Kurt Lewin		284
Driving forces		284
Restraining forces		285
Enabling change		286
Three phase process		286
Lewin's force-field analysis		286
John Kotter		287
Eight stage process		288
Organisational change		289
Beware generic solutions		289
Thinking it through		290
Crafting smart plans		290
Purpose		290
Objectives		291
People		291
Resources		292
Timeframes		292

Leading change	293
Personal change	293
Change vs transition	294
Transition cycle model	294
Denial	295
Resistance	296
Exploration	296
Commitment	297
Transition cycle	297
Resistance to change	298
Why do people resist change?	298
What does resistance look like?	299
Defensive thinking	300
Resistant behaviour	300
Emotional resistance	300
Leaders can resist change too	301
Responding to resistance	301
Empathy	302
Communication	302
Participation	302
Safety climate	303
Summary	304
References	305
Author's Note	307
Biography	309
Index	311

ONLINE RESOURCES

This textbook is accompanied by online resources to aid teaching and support learning. To access these resources, visit: **https://study.sagepub.com/Lux**. Please note that lecturers will require a Sage account in order to access the lecturer resources. An account can be created via the above link.

FOR LECTURERS

PowerPoints

This book is accompanied with a set of comprehensive Microsoft PowerPoint slides for each Chapter. The slides include web links and QR Codes for the 34 online Activities and the 12 Videos that are embedded throughout the text. The PowerPoints can be downloaded and adapted to suit individual teaching needs.

Teaching Guide

This book also comes with a Teaching Guide that provides practical guidance and support for lecturers using this textbook in their teaching. The Teaching Guide explains how to prepare for and deliver the content in class, and includes a Quick-Start Guide that outlines simple steps to easily deploy this material to get started.

Alongside the book, you now have everything you need to start teaching contemporary leadership.

1
INTRODUCTION TO LEADERSHIP

--- Overview ---

The chapter starts with two reflective exercises, asking you first to explore some of the ideas that you already have about leadership, and then to consider where you absorbed these ideas (e.g. from your parents, social groups, school, work, media).

You're then introduced to the concept of everyday leadership, the notion that we are all leaders to one another, and that every single social interaction is a leadership intervention where we have the capacity to make a significant, positive impact on each other's lives.

We'll then distinguish leadership from analogous concepts such as command, governance, and management, exploring how our understanding of leadership has evolved, before focusing in on a contemporary definition of leadership and then unpacking how leaders inspire people with purpose.

The chapter concludes with a reflective exercise that gets you to start developing your own personal vision.

Exercise 1.1: What is leadership to you?

Exercise 1.2: Who or what shaped your ideas?

Video 1.1: Drew Dudley - Everyday leadership

Video 1.2: Simon Sinek - How great leaders inspire action

Exercise 1.3: Start with why

SO, WHAT IS LEADERSHIP ANYWAY?

Leadership is a complicated process and there's no one right way to do it. In part, that's because we have all already absorbed plenty of ideas about what is good leadership before we've even opened this book. These ideas make up your implicit leadership theory (Lord et al., 2020). That's not the case with many other topics. If I was going to talk to you today about astrophysics, most of us would know very little to begin with, and we'd be like a relatively blank slate ready to receive information.

Leadership is a little bit different. Over the course of our lives we have all absorbed lessons in leadership from our environment, primarily through our personal experiences, in both the formal and informal sides of our lives. In the informal side, this is first through our family, interacting with our parents, watching them interact with our siblings, with each other, with others in the community, and later interacting with our friends and colleagues.

Likewise with religious groups, during community activities, participating in sports teams, etc. All the time we are like little sponges, picking up information from these myriad interactions. Whether consciously or not, we're watching how people influence one another, how groups work together, towards what kinds of goals, set by whom, and of course, what outcomes result from these leadership interactions.

We do the same thing through the formal side of our personal experiences. First in school, then in university, and then in the workplace. Our teachers, lecturers, our bosses are all giving us examples to learn from by demonstrating certain leadership competencies, behaviours, attitudes, and skills. Meanwhile we are forming our own ideas about what good leadership looks like and, as you can imagine, this can get very, very diverse.

If you are brought up in a strict religious household, your idea of good leadership is likely to be different from someone who has been bought up in a secular or more open kind of family. If you went to boarding school your perception may be different from those who stayed with their parents, and so on.

Another way that we absorb ideas about leadership is through secondary sources, like the media – watching the news, television, scrolling through your Facebook, Reddit, Twitter, or TikTok feed, etc. Think about all of the ways that you consume media and the kinds of leadership behaviours and attitudes that are portrayed as desirable, effective, or appropriate.

The types of leaders that we watch in the media will influence our ideas significantly. Are you watching people like Vladimir Putin or Donald Trump, and are you thinking, 'Yeah, this is a great leader!', or are you watching people like Pope Francis, Barack Obama, and Jacinda Ardern? All are prominent leaders in our time, but they demonstrate very different ideals, different attitudes and behaviour.

As we process personal primary experiences and consume secondary sources, we are comparing the interactions against this picture in our mind about what good leaders are supposed to be like and we are constantly revising and adapting our ideas as new information becomes available.

WHAT IS LEADERSHIP TO YOU?

Before I start sharing my ideas or those that others have come up with, we are going to explore some of the ideas that you already have about leadership. You have all opened this book with some pretty interesting thoughts about this topic and we are going to start by unpacking what those are to create a baseline that will serve as a platform for you to build on.

I want you to transform as you work through this text and one of the best ways to do that is through personal reflection. You will notice that reflection is a theme that we keep coming back to over and over in this text because it's one of the best ways, and maybe one of the only ways, for you to learn to be better leaders.

Let's work through the first activity (Exercise 1.1), which asks what leadership means to you. People have come up with many leadership theories, each with different ideas about what good leaders do, what is effective and what isn't, so there are no right or wrong answers at this stage. Think about what is true for you. Aim for a couple of sentences that capture your main ideas.

Exercise 1.1

What is Leadership to you?

Image Alt Text: https://ecuau.qualtrics.com/jfe/form/SV_9nr5cZZlSexBUyi

---

Over the years I've heard many different ideas from my students. However, a few themes come up time and time again.

Goals/Vision. Goals are a destination of sorts, something to move towards. The best goals are those shared by the team; it's not just about what I want as a leader, it's about what we want to achieve as a team.

Delegating. Leadership enables people to come together and achieve more than we ever could by working alone. We all have unique strengths and weaknesses. You don't have to do it all alone – organise tasks around individuals' talents so that they can each contribute meaningfully.

Empowering. Great leaders don't micromanage; they trust their team to do good work and they inspire others by giving away their own power and control. Give your team as much autonomy as you can over what they do and how they do it, as long as it moves you towards your goals.

Supporting. Leadership is about facilitating; it's about helping other people to be stronger, more successful, and to reach their potential. Understand what kind of support your team needs and work to ensure that they get it, whether that's more resources and training or encouragement and emotional support.

Responsibility. Becoming a leader is essentially saying that I have enough capacity to not only take care of myself but to also take care of others. That means taking on some of their responsibility for doing the right thing and making it my responsibility.

Depending on what you came up with, some of the theories that we will encounter in this text may resonate with you more, and others less. I want you to cherry-pick – that is, to take the best bits of everything and make them your own, an authentic expression of who you are as a leader.

Share Your Ideas, Learn About Others'

Leaders meet a lot of people. The more senior you are as a leader the more people you will meet, every day, every week. It's important for leaders to have clear goals to work towards, but you also need to be able to share your ideas with others to inspire them to join you on your journey.

You need followers to believe in your vision, so a lot of what you will do is actually explaining, articulating your ideas to other people. I want you to get as comfortable as you can at meeting new people and striking up a conversation to explain your ideas to people you don't know.

If you're reading this text as part of a leadership-related class, talk to some of the other students. Preferably pick someone new that you haven't met before and start a conversation about leadership; share your definition from Exercise 1.1 and find out their definition in return. If you're working through this on your own, talk to a friend, colleague, or family member.

The more people you talk to about leadership the more you will discover how diverse our ideas can be. Hearing a bit about what other people think is an important first step to becoming a leader yourself, because it's other people who will ultimately determine whether or not you are an effective leader.

It's not so much about what you think of your own leadership skills but rather what other people think of you and your leadership skills. Whether or not you think you're doing all the right things doesn't matter, it's what your followers think about your leadership that will decide if they are motivated and inspired to pursue your shared goals.

Herein lies the challenge: everyone has very different ideas about what good leadership is and so every one of your followers will decide for themselves whether or not you are effective based on what they think about leadership. Part of becoming a good leader therefore means clarifying those ideas and expectations with your team so that you come to some mutual understanding of what they need and expect from you as a leader.

Some people may be motived by having a challenge to overcome, others may need more emotional support, some will need access to additional training and resources, others might prefer that you just tell them what needs doing and then get out of their way. It will be different for different people and there is no shortcut; you have to take the time to get to know your team.

Where Did You Get These Ideas?

Now that you've written down a few of your ideas about leadership and shared them with others, the next big question is where did you get them?

I mentioned earlier that you have absorbed leadership lessons throughout your life from your experiences. Some of your ideas will be anchored in personal experiences, interactions that you have had or witnessed firsthand. Other ideas you may have picked up from secondary sources, like media, books, and stories. All the while you are implicitly drawing knowledge about what leaders do and what is good leadership and what is not.

Often you will find that you have already had far more leadership experience than you might think – for example, being an older brother or sister. Whether you know it or not, this is a leadership position; you're taking responsibility for younger siblings, helping to guide and support them. The same goes for playing team sports, being involved in community groups, and working in teams at school or in the workplace.

I want you to view as many of your past experiences as possible through a leadership lens. As long as you have helped clarify a shared vision, or helped guide, motivate, inspire, and support others, you've been a leader. Some of your experiences will be more significant than others and a handful of incidents in particular might stand out.

We can either mimic what we see and experience – for example, replicating the kinds of good leadership behaviours that our parents, coaches, or teachers might have demonstrated – or we can form our ideas in contrast to what we've experienced or seen out in the world.

Sometimes we can learn the most from bad leaders. Have you ever had a really horrible boss at work? When you were watching them lead, surely you thought to yourself, 'Later on when I have my own team that I am supervising, I'm not going to be like that, I will never treat anyone like that.' The same process is taking place but in reverse; we form ideas about what is good leadership and at the same time form ideas about what is bad.

Think about it now, where did you get your ideas about leadership? See if you can narrow it down to a few key sources, whether you've been influenced by a particularly important person in your life, a specific incident, or something else entirely.

I would like you to work through Exercise 1.2, which will ask you to consider where you got your ideas about leadership from and write down a few of the most influential sources (e.g. your parents, friends, school, work, media, books, specific incidents).

Exercise 1.2

Who or What Shaped Your Ideas?

Image Alt Text: https://ecuau.qualtrics.com/jfe/form/SV_6D1u4uiQeAt2L3w

Are Leaders Born Special?

A question that regularly comes up in any leadership discussion is whether leaders are born with special abilities that enable them to lead and be effective, or if anyone can develop these skills.

Having certain characteristics and qualities might make it easier for some people to step into leadership roles. If you are sociable, charismatic, and like to focus on the big picture, that can make it easier for you to move into a leadership role.

But leadership is definitely something that you can develop; it's a set of behaviours learnt from a journey of personal growth and development. Now that's super exciting, because I can teach this stuff to you, you can embrace it and make it part of who you are and become leaders in your own right.

I believe that leadership is for everybody, and I believe in you. If you want to be a leader, you can be, and working through this text will help you to aspire towards leadership roles. Some of you are leaders already in different spheres of your life, and we are going to unpack some of those experiences so you can learn from them, gain as much information from personal tacit knowledge as you can, and then develop yourselves further.

FINDING YOUR OWN WAY

The more you read about leadership, the more you practise and reflect on your experiences, the more you digest, interpret, and internalise these ideas for yourselves, the better you will get. That's because there is not only one way to lead well. I'm not going to tell you, 'Here, this is how you to do it' and then you simply go out follow my instructions and get easy wins – that's not how it works.

Instead, I'm going to help you understand how you can lead well. Each and every one of you will lead differently through your character. In this text you will encounter some approaches that speak to you more than others, they'll resonate with who you are and your own experiences, and there will be some approaches that just won't work for you at all.

One of the challenges of leadership development is letting go of some of the intellectual baggage that we bring with us from previous generations, ideas that may have reflected leadership in parts of the world at certain times but that no longer serve us today.

Over the course of my own research I have started to challenge some of the implicit ideas that we have about leadership, For example, we often think that good leaders have to be confident and charismatic and outspoken. But that's not necessarily always the case. I am a lot of those things, so it's easy for me to agree because it reflects well on me, but I have met other good leaders who are none of those things.

One leader who I admire is nothing like me at all. She is very quiet, shy and reserved. She doesn't thrive in public situations or formal social settings, but she has something else that I don't have, a warmth and an honesty and a transparency. She reveals some of her vulnerability to the people around her and they open up in return.

I have seen people contribute much more with her than they ever do with me. Because I have strong, well-articulated opinions and don't avoid difficult conversations, I can come across as overbearing or confrontational in some situations, whereas she is very much about bringing people out, helping them feel safe enough to share their ideas with the team. Both approaches have their place.

There are many paths to leadership, and you will need to find your own way.

Personal Reflection

The first two exercises asked you to explore what ideas you had already formed about leadership and where you may have picked them up from. The process of thinking back over what you thought, how you felt, what you did, or what interactions you witnessed firsthand is called personal reflection.

Your past experiences are not just a bunch of stuff that's happened to you, they're treasure troves of valuable self-knowledge. Please don't dismiss your experiences by thinking, 'Well I played a team sport once, so what?' You don't have to run a company to have leadership experience.

All of these interpersonal interactions contain valuable leadership lessons, and when you think back on them, you give yourself an opportunity to learn something about yourself and about leadership. You don't even have to go anywhere; you can reflect while sitting on the couch at home and it costs you nothing.

What I'm going to do in this text is enable you to access that information. We'll work through reflective exercises in a structured way, and we'll keep doing this over and over until it becomes second nature, until the reflection cycle is automatic so that you are learning from every single leadership interaction that you have.

Self-reflection is particularly powerful because the insights that you get are not going to be something that I've told you, they're going to be deeply personal, connected to who you are and the experiences that have shaped you. No one else can give you that, it's something that you have to give yourself; but I'll provide you with the tools to help dig that treasure out.

Everyday Leadership

Video 1.1 introduces the idea of everyday leadership and in it Drew Dudley talks about leading in a completely different way to what we might imagine leadership to mean. Every time I watch this, I am amazed by how powerful an agent for change we can be in each other's lives.

Video 1.1

Drew Dudley – Everyday Leadership

Summary

Everyday leadership is the idea that we are all leaders to one another, and that every single social interaction is a leadership intervention where we have the capacity to make a significant positive impact on each other's lives.

Image Alt Text: https://www.ted.com/talks/drew_dudley_everyday_leadership

I want to teach you to become leaders who can positively influence the experiences of the people around you. If one kind word to a stranger can change their whole day, imagine what we can achieve when we apply this mindset to our teams and organisations. Think about how your actions can affect your followers and colleagues.

Every time you lend others strength by sharing a little bit of your own kindness, every time you inspire others to reach higher than they thought they could before, you are a leader. These are things that we have probably been doing for a while without giving ourselves much credit, but they can make all the difference.

Every quiet act of encouragement and support counts and can reshape how people think of themselves, about how valuable they are and how much they have to offer. These transformative interactions capture how I want to frame leadership in this text.

WHAT LEADERSHIP ISN'T

The other challenge for understanding leadership is that we discuss it in many different fields or parts of our world. For example, dialogues about leadership persist in the armed forces, in politics, in business organisations, and in relation to social movements. It's useful for us now to consider what leadership is not: it's not command, governance, management, or influence alone.

When we study leaders in a military context, their primary concerns are command and control, giving orders to achieve objectives. In business their primary concern is management, administering operations that achieve organisational goals. In political discourses their primary concern is governance, creating policy to advance state interests, and in social movements their primary concern is to influence, reshaping the values or behaviour of others.

So leadership itself is not core to these various functions, but rather it's something that runs parallel to the primary concern within each of these different spheres. Alongside command, we have leadership, alongside management, we have leadership, etc.

We then award leadership to people who are particularly successful in each of those roles, we grant them the title of being a leader. When politicians see their nations to prosperity, we praise their leadership qualities. When managers build profitable companies, we say it's their leadership that's responsible. Commanders who win many battles, the same thing again.

What we're not doing is specifically invoking any kind of distinct behaviour to explain what leadership is. So is it enough that political leaders have enacted beneficial policies that have helped their nations to prosper? Or is there something else at work here, and at what tipping point or threshold does effective policymaking and governance suddenly become leadership? That's not always very clear.

Leadership vs Management

The difference between leadership and management is more nuanced. We often see these two terms used interchangeably, but they are not the same.

The notion of management comes from the British and American industrial revolutions of the 19th century, starting around the 1880s with Fredrick Taylor's idea of scientific management. Taylor's thinking was consistent with the dominant scientific paradigm of the time and emphasised analysis, empiricism, standardisation, and efficiency.

At the time, factory owners would break production processes down into their constituent parts, use measurement to quantify the tasks, and discover through analysis more efficient ways to conduct each task, thereby improving the overall production process. By standardising processes factory owners were able to minimise production waste and improve efficiency.

When business owners acquired more than one factory, they quickly realised that they couldn't handle running multiple factories on their own and they appointed agents to fulfil this function. The people they chose were knowledgeable in the production process, but unable to establish their own factories. These agents became the first professional managers (Tucker, 1981).

Leadership on the other hand emerged around the start of the third industrial revolution in the 1970s and it's something very different. Before the 1970s business schools largely ignored the concept of leadership; they taught industrial management, often employing experienced managers to deliver courses.

In the booming post-World War 2 global economy the third industrial revolution started to rapidly change the business landscape. In the span of a few decades the environment shifted from relatively stable manufacturing that prioritised production volume and efficiency towards knowledge economies where business success was determined by human capital and intellectual property.

Add globalisation and we have the hyper-competitive environment that we know to be the norm today. In this environment the principles of scientific management were no longer teaching us how to build and operate competitive businesses. So in response to these changes, business schools started to think about leadership almost as an antidote to the shortcomings of management.

So, what is management? It's a set of tools and techniques that derive from formal authority in an organisational hierarchy, from positional power that gives you control over your subordinates. Managers spend their time planning, setting budgets and organising resources, assigning staff and delegating responsibilities, maintaining control, and then solving any problems that arise along the way.

Let's be clear, we need good managers in our organisations because they can take a specific goal or an objective, get the right people together, negotiate an appropriate budget, work within the allocated resources, put it all into an action plan, control the process and deliver results. Managers therefore thrive in predictable environments, achieving short- to mid-term goals that maintain the ongoing operations of an organisation; managers preserve the status quo.

Leadership is something that comes from who you are, your behaviour, your character, your values, and your mindset. It derives from personal influence, and not formal authority. So in addition to your followers, you can also lead your peers, you can lead your superiors, and you can lead others outside of your organisation.

What leaders do is establish the direction, creating a vision that inspires others to work and persevere until it is realised. Leaders align people behind that vision, helping them understand how they fit into that greater picture so that everyone can contribute their unique talents to advance the team towards that vision. Leaders therefore confront uncertainty to ensure that organisations stay relevant and competitive into the future; leaders create positive change.

Doing Both Jobs Well

The 2008 Global Financial Crisis (GFC) pushed many organisations around the world to de-layer their management hierarchy – that is, reduce their employment of middle managers as a way to cut costs and improve agility in decision-making (Hassard & Morris, 2021). As a side-effect, de-layering reduced the distance between the roles of leaders and managers.

Before the 2008 GFC, we had leaders at the most senior levels of our organisations setting the vision, inspiring, motivating, and empowering others. Then we had a hierarchy of middle and frontline managers who were implementing and planning and organising and controlling, to deliver on that vision. Once we lost the middle management tier, both the leadership and the management functions were compressed into every level of management.

Managers today have to do both roles well, but the problem is that these two functions pull us in very different directions. Management ensures relative stability and enables organisations to achieve specific objectives, whereas leadership creates turbulence, empowering positive change to secure the future of our organisations. How then, do we reconcile the need for stability and change?

When you are facing dozens of decisions and interactions every day, approach each one from both perspectives and ask yourself, 'Should I be a manager in this moment – does this situation need resource control, planning and oversight? Or should I be a leader – is this an opportunity to promote change, offer support to help my team grow, to transform aspects of the organisation?' Then you can make an informed decision about which part of your role you'll emphasise in your response.

It's disastrous when you get it wrong. Imagine an employee approaches you for managerial support. They need additional resources, training, or role clarity, but you misread the situation and offer them leadership support instead – that is, encouragement and empathy. How will they feel? Frustrated and let down; they needed help, not a dose of confidence. The same thing happens the other way around; more resources won't be much use to someone who can't find meaning in their work and needs inspiration from their leader to help them get engaged.

Over-managed and Under-led

Most organisations and countries today are over-managed and under-led, and that's because management is easier than leadership. Management is about applying the toolkit; we can easily teach people the necessary skills for planning and budgeting and controlling workloads, and they can take those skills and frameworks, apply them to their organisations, work through the steps, and successfully achieve short- to mid-term goals.

Leadership is more abstract, and it depends in part on who you are, how you conduct yourself and how far along you've come on your journey of personal growth and development. And it depends in part on whether people trust and believe in you, and if you have a vision that's worth following. There are no easy shortcuts for how to develop that, which is why business schools create many good managers and few good leaders.

But interest in leadership is growing fast, and as a concept, leadership is starting to overtake management. If we look at research publications, grants, the number of university courses, business school programmes, vocational education training, textbooks, and popular literature, leadership is on the rise, and we are now at a tipping point where leadership studies will surpass management studies.

As a global society we've understood that leadership is essential. Something about this role is so fundamental, so critical, that without it we cannot build successful and enduring organisations of any kind, including for-profit businesses, public sector, not-for-profit, and non-government organisations, regional and national governments, armed forces, or religious and social movements.

Scholars have made great progress in developing contemporary leadership theories that help explain this elusive phenomenon, providing us with practical guidance and enabling professional development. Empirical research testing these modern approaches reveals strong positive relations with desirable organisational outcomes, including profitability, employees' satisfaction, engagement, commitment, and trust, as well as pro-social outcomes such as well-being and social responsibility.

EVOLUTION OF LEADERSHIP

Let's go back a little and look at how we got to this modern idea of leadership.

If we consider the history of the world and of leadership knowledge, stories about leaders come from the earliest human writings. We have accounts from several thousand years about the lives of leaders, their great feats, and teachings about leadership (cf. *The Art of War* by Sun Tzu, circa 500 BCE; *The Education of Cyrus* by Xenophon of Athens, circa 370 BCE).

Naturally no historical account is without bias, so we must read them with a grain of salt, becoming critical and analytic, rather than passive, consumers of literature.

For example, take Alexander the Great, one of the most successful and renowned military commanders of all time, undefeated in battle throughout a decade-long campaign. What isn't as well known is that he inherited both a strong kingdom and an experienced army from his father. His leadership position was given to him, and this was not an exception but rather the norm in our history.

So in the historical context over the last few thousand years, leaders inherited their status. Certain people were granted leadership positions either by birth, marriage, or were appointed to leadership roles by virtue of their social class membership. Such roles typically could not be challenged and were therefore accepted by the subordinate followers. Without opportunities for social mobility, power was consolidated into noble houses and passed on through lineages.

Hereditary power structures have therefore shaped leadership thinking throughout history. Historical leadership behaviour typically resembled command, demonstrating absolute control over subordinates, who could neither refuse nor challenge their leader's position without personal consequences.

Niccolò Machiavelli compiled the kind of leadership mindset and behaviours that work well in this context in his treatise titled *The Prince*, published posthumously circa 1514. Machiavelli advocated using whatever means necessary to achieve your ambitions, including immoral behaviour – for example, being cruel rather than merciful, cultivating a grand and favourable reputation, and breaking promises that would otherwise compromise your interests. His focus was on building and maintaining power.

Similarly entrenched power structures persist today in many parts of the world. Consider some of the developing nations, where opportunities for social mobility are rare and people born into particular castes or classes are often restricted to certain professions and roles. It may come as no surprise, then, that many leaders would consider Machiavelli's treatise to be just as relevant today as it was in 1514, and in a context where your power is absolute, perhaps they are right.

Fast forward to today, the modern leadership context is above all characterised by choice. In much of the developed world, we no longer have to do as we are told, we do not have to follow where others lead, we have a choice. With unparalleled personal agency to pursue our own adventures, we can pick careers that capture our interests and harness our talents, or choose to start our own businesses.

We're no longer tied to place, we have freedom of movement and can choose to relocate to another region, city, or country if it suits us. We can choose if we want to lead ourselves and we can choose if we want to follow someone else. We can choose who we follow and why: if we share their values and we believe in their vision. Such liberties were unheard of in centuries past.

I work at this university because I like my leaders; I share the values of the Dean of the business school, I aspire to the Vice Chancellor's vision, and I believe in the purpose of this university. But there are over 800 accredited business schools around the world that I could apply to instead; I am not bound to be here, I choose to be here, I am here doing this work because I want to.

Given that context, how the Vice Chancellor and the Dean have to lead me is very different from what we've seen throughout history. Imagine if they tried to command me, or manipulate me through deceit, or coerce me by intimidation as Machiavelli recommended. Not only would they fail to secure my engagement, but I'd likely leave the organisation entirely. Why would I put up with that kind of treatment? I don't have to, so I wouldn't.

We've reshaped the world, granting people new liberties that enable us to choose our own path and, as a result, our thoughts about leadership have been turned completely upside-down. We don't teach command in business schools any more. Instead, in our study of leadership we now look towards influence, inspiration, and values. We need people to willingly choose to follow their leaders, and that requires a significant departure from earlier approaches.

DEFINING LEADERSHIP

In this section we're going to look at some leadership definitions to help us understand what it means, to see how those ideas have changed over the years, and to outline what we think about it today. Definitions are useful because they help us to identify who or what we're studying or trying to understand. A good definition of leadership should enable us to determine if someone is a leader or not.

First let's look at the *Oxford English Dictionary*. If you look up 'leadership', it will say that it's a 'position of being a leader'. If we keep going, a 'leader' is then 'someone who leads', and 'to lead' is either 'to go with someone to show them the way', 'to make someone go in the right direction', or 'to be in control of something'. So leadership, according to this definition, is about being in a position to show people the way or to be in control of something.

The first part seems to be about a destination of some sort, which could be either a specific physical place or a more abstract vision of the future. 'The way' also suggests a process or a manner of doing things. The leader is then someone who by virtue of their position can direct people towards this destination or guide them in this way of doing things.

The second part is about control, using power or authority to make decisions and shape what and how things are done, which echoes the earlier section about making people go in the right direction. The definition therefore presumes that leaders have knowledge about what is 'right' that they use to dictate the direction and conduct of their followers.

Let's look at two people who might fit some of these definitions, to see if we can identify whether these people are leaders according to the Oxford Dictionary definition. First up we have Napoleon Bonaparte, depicted crossing the French Alps in this lovely oil painting. What do you think? Is he a leader here?

Jacques-Louis David (1801). *Napoleon crossing the Alps* (CC0 1.0).

Is he in control of something? Yes, he is a General in command of an army and the First Consul of France. Is he directing people towards a specific destination? Certainly, his troops are crossing the Alps into Italy to reinforce the besieged city of Genoa in a campaign against the Austrians. So according to the Oxford English Dictionary definition,

Napoleon is clearly a leader here, and you can imagine that this definition fits most military commanders well.

That was a warm-up question. Let's consider someone a bit different: Stefani Germanotta, known professionally as Lady Gaga. Gaga is a popular American singer, songwriter, and actress. What do you think, is she a leader?

Carlos Vazquez (2021). *Lady Gaga enters the inauguration platform* (CC BY 2.0).

Gaga is an influential person, but is she directing people towards a specific destination or is she in control of something? From the perspective of her fans, no, there's no clearly defined purpose beyond entertainment and no, she isn't in direct control of them. From the perspective of her stage crews, music producers, event organisers, etc., yes, she is in control of them and may direct them towards certain objectives.

Gaga also founded the Born This Way Foundation and cosmetics brand Haus Laboratories. The non-profit is led by co-founder and President Cynthia Germanotta and the cosmetics brand by CEO Ben Jones. Gaga likely retains an interest as a founder of these organisations and yet her direct control of them may be limited. However, these organisations have clearly defined objectives that they are moving people towards.

So it looks like Gaga satisfies some of the criteria for being a leader in certain aspects, but not in others. On the balance of things, if we strictly apply the Oxford Dictionary definition, no, Gaga is not a leader, except to her own production team. But I hope you're getting a sense that there is something else here as well that the definition does not quite capture, some quality that makes her influential, which is why we can't just stop at the Oxford Dictionary.

Academic Definitions

Let us now consider some academic definitions of leadership, starting with ideas from the 1940s and progressing through to our current understanding. We'll use our two examples to see how these definitions may help us determine who is and isn't a leader.

Copeland (1942) defined leadership as 'the art of influencing a body of people, by persuasion or example, to follow a line of action. It must never be confused with drivership [...] which is the art of compelling a body of people, by intimidation or force, to follow a line of action' (p. 77).

Copeland makes a clear distinction between what he calls drivership – which is essentially command – and influencing by persuasion, which is then the domain of leadership. So at this early stage in modern leadership knowledge we are already seeing a schism between command and leadership as two discrete concepts or functions.

But where does this leave someone like Napoleon? Is he a leader according to Copeland's definition? On the face of it, no. As an army General, Napoleon best fits the definition of drivership: he was in command of his legions, they were compelled and could not resist that compulsion, which is therefore a case of intimidation. So if we apply Copeland's definition, Napoleon wasn't a leader. But that doesn't seem right; it can't be the whole story.

Accounts of Napoleon's behaviour on campaign paint a different picture (cf. Lynn, 1989). For example, he camped in the midst of his army and shared some of their hardships, and inspired his troops with clever persuasive techniques, such as being highly visible in battle, promoting soldiers on their merit, and awarding medals for valour. These influential actions better fit with Copeland's description of leadership, so some of Napoleon's behaviour was leadership, and some was not.

What about Gaga, did she influence people by persuasion or example to follow a line of action? Yes, in starting the Born This Way Foundation, soliciting support and inspiring others to work towards her vision, she was clearly a leader. As an entertainer from her fans' perspective, no, because there is no line of action attached to her influence, and for her production team, maybe, depending on whether she inspires or compels them.

Even with Copeland's definition we can see that it's too simplistic to try and determine if certain people are leaders or not in their entirety. Rather, leadership is something that we must study in context – different people may exhibit leadership behaviour at different times or in some situations, and not in others. Academic definitions are therefore useful for us to better understand what is, and isn't, effective leadership behaviour.

Let's set aside Napoleon and Gaga as our two examples and look at another definition, onwards to the 1950s. Stogdill (1950) defined leadership 'as the process (act) of influencing the activities of an organised group in its efforts toward goal setting and goal achievement' (p. 4).

For Stogdill, the purpose of leadership is not in producing 'a line of action' as Copeland suggests, but about influencing others to set and work towards specific goals. He shifts the focus from compliance – getting people to do what you want – to achieving outcomes. The 'organised group' for the first time has a role in setting goals. The approach is participative, a group process that leaders help guide, which is a radical departure from leaders unilaterally setting the direction.

Let's look at one more historical definition. Seeman (1960) defined leadership as 'acts by persons which influence other persons in a shared direction' (p. 53). A shared direction seems self-explanatory, but contains an important truth: I cannot lead you somewhere that you don't want to go; I can compel you, but I cannot lead you. Seeman's ideas reflect the emerging counterculture of the day: a revolution in social norms at a time of prosperity and cultural exploration.

Seeman's definition would seem to fit a great many people. For the first time it resembles the notion of 'everyday leadership' that Drew Dudley introduced us to earlier, and captures the sort of positive influence that we can have on one another in our daily interactions. But if we try to apply this definition to our own leadership development, it isn't very instructive about what is, and isn't, effective leadership behaviour. Perhaps it's a little too broad to be useful.

Current Leadership Definition

Fast-forward to today's best definition. Yukl and Gardner (2020) define leadership as 'the process of influencing others to understand and agree about what needs to be done and how to do it, and the process of facilitating individual and collective efforts to accomplish shared objectives' (p. 26).

Yukl and Gardner combine some of the best parts of the earlier definitions that we've encountered into one coherent whole. The most interesting addition is that the people we are leading need to understand and agree with what they're doing, and how they're doing it. Such notions rarely feature in prior leadership scholarship and mark a radical advance in our thinking.

Yukl and Gardner restyle the role of leaders as facilitating others' efforts. Facilitating is a supportive role, it's about helping people to succeed in their endeavours; so effective leaders today are no longer directing, but enabling and empowering. Both the language we use to describe good leadership and the ideas behind that language have evolved considerably as we have grown as a society.

One concept has stood the test of time and remains in this latest iteration of leadership: influence. Recall that having shared objectives means that I cannot lead you somewhere that you don't want to go, which is why our followers must understand and agree – herein is the domain of influence. So while leaders cannot compel, for that ceases to be leadership, they can influence you to engage of your own volition.

WHAT IS INFLUENCE?

Influence is the ability to have an effect on people, situations, or processes, to help shape or change them in some way. When we talk about influence in a leadership context, we tend to mean your intentional ability to have an effect on other people's behaviour, values, attitudes, or decisions.

There are only four ways to get people to do what you want (Parsons, 1963). You can: offer an incentive; threaten them with negative consequences; invoke an obligation by highlighting why they should do as you ask; or you can persuade them to do what you ask for their own reasons, because they want to.

However, if you offered me an incentive, I'd do the work because I want the incentive, but not because I want to do the work, and there's a huge difference in performance between the two. People who work not only because they have to, but because they want to, are far more engaged and committed (Lux et al., 2023), and that's what creates extraordinary organisations.

Incentives, consequences, and obligations can only produce compliance; people will do the bare minimum necessary to secure incentives, to avoid repercussions, or to fulfil their obligations. These three approaches to influence are therefore rarely useful for leadership; we must focus our efforts on persuasion, which enables us to motivate followers to go above and beyond compliance.

The best way to motivate people is to inspire them by giving their work meaning. Connect what they're doing with a greater purpose so that they get a sense that their work is important, it matters and has an impact on the world and on the lives of others. But we must first understand what that purpose is before we can help articulate it for others. The effect is profound and the difference between working purely for the money and working with purpose cannot be overstated.

For example, I'm not writing this book just to fulfil my academic performance requirements, or to get rich or famous. I'm giving you what I have discovered about leadership, sharing what I have read, and passing on what others have thought, so that you can apply these lessons and make them your own, reaching further than I ever could and spreading positive leadership to others with whom you interact. That gives me a sense of meaning and purpose, I want to be here; I'm writing this line in my office late at night, long after everyone else has left, and it barely feels like work at all.

As leaders, it is our role to inspire our followers so that they can find meaning in their work and that our organisations can benefit from their superior performance. Organisations made up of people who only do the base level of work are not competitive against those with capable leaders who inspire their people to believe in what they're doing – that's where we come in.

Inspiring Others

Video 1.2 discusses where inspiration comes from and in it Simon Sinek talks about how great leaders inspire their followers to achieve exceptional results. So far, we're explored why it's important for us to influence others by inspiring them; Simon tells us how to actually do it.

Video 1.2

Simon Sinek – How Great Leaders Inspire Action

Summary

Inspiration comes from your purpose; people aren't inspired by what you do, but by why you do it. To inspire others, start by telling them why you're doing what you do, and work with people who share your cause, who believe what you believe.

Image Alt Text: https://www.ted.com/talks/simon_sinek_how_great_leaders_inspire_action

---

Here's my 'why', the reason why I'm doing this work: I believe that shaping the leaders of tomorrow is the most positive impact that I can have on the world. How do I do it? I apply a student-centric transformative pedagogy to promote contemporary positive leadership practices. What do I do? I publish leadership research, I teach leadership at undergraduate, postgraduate, and executive MBA levels, and I supervise doctoral students studying leadership.

My purpose is what gets me up in the morning and it drives everything else that I do in my teaching-related work. It's also why I'm perfectly happy to write a textbook, publish media releases, to present keynotes and workshops at other organisations, to talk about leadership on the radio, etc. What I do isn't nearly as important as why I'm doing it, as long as it's advancing my overall purpose.

Now I would like you to come up with one sentence that captures your purpose (Exercise 1.3). Consider what gets you up in the morning, why you're working on your leadership skills, what thoughts or ideas help you to persevere when the going is slow and hard – in short, what do you believe?

Write down one reason why you're doing what you're doing as a leader, or as an aspiring leader. Keep your answer to one sentence, starting with 'I believe that…'.

Exercise 1.3

Start With Why

Image Alt Text: https://ecuau.qualtrics.com/jfe/form/SV_0j3Zyws5fRFRezs

---

Your purpose will be a powerful source of inspiration for both you and your followers as you progress on your leadership journey.

SUMMARY

I believe that leadership is for everybody, but it's a complicated process and there's no one right way to do it. Depending on your past experiences and existing ideas, some of the theories that we will encounter in this text may resonate with you more, and others less. I want you to take the best bits of everything, make them your own, an authentic expression of who you are as a leader. There are many paths to leadership, and you will need to find your own way.

Your past experiences are not just a bunch of stuff that's happened to you, they're treasure troves of valuable self-knowledge. Often you will find that you have already had far more leadership experience than you might think – you don't have to run a company to have leadership experience. I want you to view as many of your past experiences as possible through a leadership lens.

Everyday leadership is the idea that we are all leaders to one another, and that any social interaction can be an opportunity to make a positive impact on others' lives. Every quiet act of encouragement and support counts and can reshape how people think of themselves, how valuable they are and how much they have to offer.

The current definition of leadership describes it as 'the process of influencing others to understand and agree about what needs to be done and how to do it, and the process of facilitating individual and collective efforts to accomplish shared objectives' (Yukl & Gardner, 2020, p. 26).

The best way to motivate people is to inspire them by giving their work meaning. Connect what they're doing with a greater purpose so that they get a sense that their work is important, it matters and has an impact on the world and on the lives of others. To inspire others, start by telling them your purpose; people aren't inspired by what you do, but by why you do it.

> 'I believe that the world is a fine place, and worth fighting for.'
>
> Paraphrased from *For Whom the Bell Tolls* by Ernest Hemingway (1940).

REFERENCES

Copeland, N. (1942). *Psychology and the soldier*. The Military Service Publishing Company.

Hassard, J., & Morris, J. (2021). The extensification of managerial work in the digital age: Middle managers, spatio-temporal boundaries and control. *Human Relations*, 1–32. https://doi.org/10.1177/00187267211003123

Lord, R. G., Epitropaki, O., Foti, R. J., & Hansbrough, T. K. (2020). Implicit leadership theories, implicit followership theories, and dynamic processing of leadership information. *Annual Review of Organizational Psychology and Organizational Behavior, 7*, 49–74. https://doi.org/10.1146/annurev-orgpsych-012119-045434

Lux, A. A., Grover, S. L., & Teo, S. T. T. (2023). Reframing commitment in authentic leadership: Untangling relationship–outcome processes. *Journal of Management & Organization, 29*(1), 103–121. https://doi.org/10.1017/jmo.2019.78

Lynn, J. A. (1989). Toward an army of honor: The moral evolution of the French Army, 1789–1815. *French Historical Studies, 16*(1), 152–173.

Parsons, T. (1963). On the concept of influence. *Public Opinion Quarterly, 27*(1), 37–62. https://doi.org/10.1086/267148

Seeman, M. (1960). *Social status and leadership: The case of the school executive.* Bureau of Educational Research and Service.

Stogdill, R. M. (1950). Leadership, membership and organization. *Psychological Bulletin, 47*(1), 1–14. https://doi.org/10.1037/h0053857

Tucker, B. M. (1981). The merchant, the manufacturer, and the factory manager: The case of Samuel Slater. *Business History Review, 55*(3), 297–313. https://doi.org/10.2307/3114126

Yukl, G. A., & Gardner, W. L. (2020). *Leadership in organizations* (9th ed.). Pearson Education.

2
GLOBAL LEADERSHIP CONTEXT

Overview

The chapter starts by looking at some of the revolutionary changes that have reshaped our industrial and civil landscape to create a vivid picture of the global leadership context as perpetually volatile, uncertain, complex, and ambiguous.

We'll then explore six new challenges that today's leaders have to face. You'll be asked to consider which of these issues might be the most difficult for you to navigate, and then outline personal focus areas to help guide your own leadership development.

Next, we'll look to the future by exploring some of the global megatrends that are driving future changes, including demographic, economic, and sociocultural shifts, as well as what the fourth industrial revolution promises to bring.

You're then asked to consider what kind of leadership qualities and behaviour the world will need in future, and the chapter culminates by explaining how these changes are forcing us to rethink leadership.

Video 2.1: Stanley McChrystal – Listen, learn … then lead

Exercise 2.1: Overcoming leadership challenges

Video 2.2: World Economic Forum – What is the fourth industrial revolution?

Exercise 2.2: What kind of leaders do we need?

Now that we've had a broad introduction to leadership, let's focus in on the organisational context. Leaders don't operate in a vacuum; their actions are inherently tied to the context where they are embedded.

REVOLUTIONARY CHANGE

If we look back throughout our history, much of it is marked by revolutionary change. By that I mean significant developments that rapidly reorganised the industrial and civil landscape; with each advance creating a turbulent wake of follow-on effects that forced organisations to either rethink their prior practices, or face obsolescence.

To better understand the role of leaders within organisations today, we first need to consider some of the major upheavals of our age.

As you can imagine, what companies do to stay competitive today is very different to what they did one hundred years ago. Likewise, the role of leaders and what kind of behaviours are useful have changed with the times – to understand where we're going, we must learn about where we've come from. Let's look at some of the landmark events that have affected the business world.

Geopolitical Conflicts

Our world is near-perpetually engulfed in armed conflict in one place or another. Plenty of examples come to mind immediately: World Wars One and Two, the Cold War, the Vietnam War, wars in Iraq and Afghanistan, the War on Terrorism, the Syrian civil war, and now the invasion of Ukraine – just to name a few. There are unfortunately many more.

In addition to armed conflict, geopolitical tensions likewise affect organisations. Consider, for example, the deteriorating relations between North Korea and the United States or between China and Australia. Changes in the geopolitical landscape happen quickly and have far-reaching effects on organisations and, by extension, on leaders and leadership.

The implications of geopolitical conflict on organisations include opening and closing trade opportunities through sanctions, tariffs, or trade agreements, dramatically altering the supply of and demand for certain goods and services. Some people think that armed conflicts fuel economic activity, and in a few isolated cases they'd be right, but it's a fallacy to think that conflict brings a net benefit to any society.

Frédéric Bastiat (1801–1850) tells a parable of the broken window to explain: say a playing child accidentally breaks a window. A glazier is hired and paid $100 to repair the damage. We might mistakenly conclude that breaking the window added $100 worth of economic activity to the local economy. Such arguments are often made in favour of spending on active armed conflict or peace-time defence building.

What's missing from this picture is that which isn't as easy to see: the opportunity cost of employing that original $100 more constructively (Carabini, 2007) – for example, using it to buy a new book or jacket. The glazier's time and materials could also be better spent installing a window for a new house. Together these actions could have provided a net benefit to the community, but are lost, and instead we're forced to spend our resources only to restore the community to its prior state before the damage.

Beyond the destruction of tangible assets like buildings and infrastructure is the erosion of trust in democratic and financial institutions. Why would I acquire a factory or lease office space if I can't be sure that it won't be seized by the state or bombed by an aggressor? Why bother to earn, save, and invest money when its value may quickly evaporate from hyperinflation? Such productive economic activities are often disrupted, or cease altogether.

Technological Advancements

The next most visible changes are innovations in technology. Over the last few centuries we made landmark advances when we invented the steam engine, cotton loom, vaccination, telegraphs, electricity, fertiliser, plastics, petroleum, the internal combustion engine, the ballpoint pen, computers, the Internet, and smartphones. Consider the immense disruption caused by each of these inventions to existing markets at the time of discovery.

Vaccinations are still one of our most potent ways to save lives, significantly altering our mortality rate and contributing to marked population growth in many developed nations (Bonanni, 1999). Population growth means more people entering the workforce, more people consuming products and generating economic activity, increasing the wealth and prosperity of nations. Of course access to vaccines is not ubiquitous and developing nations are often still plagued by preventable disease.

Fritz Haber and Carl Bosch invented fertiliser and revolutionised agriculture, doubling how much we could produce and enabling us to feed our rapidly growing populations. Automation and robotics changed the pace and scale of manufacturing, fuelling consumption of commodities and creating a growing middle class. Advances in telecommunications connected people around the world, creating new markets and globalising production, marketing, and sales.

The digital age is changing the core nature of products, moving from tangible goods towards digital services (Kannan & Li, 2017): for example, Spotify instead of physical CDs, Netflix instead of cinemas. Online rental network platforms like Airbnb and Uber let us reap the dormant value from owned products such as housing and cars. The gig economy is changing employment relations, with organisations shifting towards contract workers to shirk the associated costs and risk of employees.

Each one of these developments – among many others – have had significant effects on industries and organisations. Imagine if you were weaving fabrics by hand when Edmund Cartwright invented the powered loom and others soon automated the textile industry. Your business would have faced a significant threat to its survival. Why would I pay you to make textiles so slowly, expensively and inefficiently, when I could have a much greater volume cheaper and faster?

Industries and businesses using outdated technology at every point in history would fall behind competitors and lose profitability if they could not quickly adopt new technologies.

Social Movements

Socio-political movements are the result of a values shift across populations and they reshape how our societies are organised. Consider a selection of the advancements that we've made: we abolished slavery and child labour, introduced contraception and family planning, gave women the right to vote, formed the United Nations and European Union, wrote the Universal Declaration of Human Rights and the Paris Climate Accords.

With the 1926 Slavery Convention we began abolition in earnest, freeing millions to pursue self-determination. Yet similar practices persist in contemporary forms, such as debt bondage. After our discussions about the productivity advantages of freely willing followers, I hope it comes as no surprise that slavery is bad for business. Beyond being immoral, both traditional and modern forms of slavery are objectively harmful to total economic output and social development (Datta & Bales, 2013).

Modern contraception and family planning enabled more women to enter the workforce and pursue careers, increasing national productivity and dramatically changing the demographic profile of our organisations. The women's suffrage movement grew in parallel, with the majority of nations granting women the right to vote in parliamentary elections by the end of the 20th century, bringing women's perspectives into governance and policymaking. A movement towards equitable opportunities and outcomes for women and other minorities remains underway.

International organisations like the United Nations and World Trade Organisation, treaties like the Universal Declaration of Human Rights and Paris Climate Accords, and trade agreements have enabled global commerce and dismantled inefficient protectionist policies, helping bring the world closer together to address problems of global concern, such as food insecurity.

The notion of a European Union was a distant dream even fifty years ago. Now unified by treaty, people can move freely across the continent without having to stop at every border, produce visas, and change currency. Businesses can move money, goods, and offer services without paying additional tariffs. The region has since enjoyed peace, stability, and prosperity unlike any other point in the history of the continent.

Each of these radical advances, and countless others, upended many existing markets and business practices. Alongside these changes and values shifts, we have been forced to rethink what it means to be a leader and what kind of leadership behaviours are effective and appropriate. What I see is a trend toward the rule of law, freedom, self-determination, and the meaningful inclusion of everyone in work and society.

VOLATILE, UNCERTAIN, COMPLEX, AND AMBIGUOUS

Many scholars and industry leaders alike consider today's business environment to be far less predictable than it was a few hundred years ago and, as a result, much more difficult for leaders to navigate successfully. We've borrowed an acronym from the armed forces to describe the current environment as VUCA: volatile, uncertain, complex, and ambiguous (Bennett & Lemoine, 2014).

Volatility. The environment is volatile when there are frequent, irregular changes of unknown magnitude or duration. For example, the stock market is volatile with prices sometimes changing by 30% or more overnight, and other times remaining relatively stable with only minor fluctuations for long periods.

Uncertainty. The environment is uncertain when the implications of current and pending changes are unknown; the issue is a lack of information. For example, the existence of cyber-security threats to business is fairly well known, but when, how, and on what scale would a breach affect your organisation remains unknown.

Complexity. The environment is complex when there are so many interconnected variables that modelling their interactions becomes impractical and overwhelming. For example, the Internet has created an accessible surplus of information and leaders in the public domain are expected to behave with perfect knowledge.

Ambiguity. The environment is ambiguous when the cause-and-effect relationships are not yet well understood and so there are no precedents for making future predictions. For example, many organisations that moved to flexible and work-from-home arrangements during the COVID-19 pandemic are now wondering whether to return to traditional offices as the effects on performance remain unclear.

VUCA proponents readily label the business world as far more volatile, uncertain, complex, and ambiguous today than ever before. In my opinion, this is false, it's simply not true at all. As you can see from a quick look through our history earlier in the chapter, radical advances are not new, they are the norm of our world. I'm not saying that we're not in a 'VUCA world' – we certainly are – but that it's nothing new, the world has always been volatile, uncertain, complex, and ambiguous.

If the VUCA environment isn't a new leadership challenge, then what is?

CONTEMPORARY LEADERSHIP CHALLENGES

Video 2.1 serves as a platform for us to consider the modern global leadership context. In it Stanley McCrystal highlights some of the ways that he's had to change his approach to leadership in response to various changes in the environment. He paints a powerful picture of the immense challenges facing contemporary leaders.

Video 2.1

Stanley McChrystal – Listen, Learn ... then Lead

Summary
Leaders today are confronted with new difficulties, particularly around long-distance collaboration, cross-cultural interaction, and the pace of change. Forming positive relationships is more important now than ever before to help us overcome these barriers.

Image Alt Text: https://www.ted.com/talks/stanley_mcchrystal_listen_learn_then_lead

---

It's fascinating to hear that in the military, leadership isn't focused on command any more. It's been the traditional approach for over 2000 years, but now, even in our armed forces, there's a proliferation of followers' choice and that's changing everything. Of course leaders must be able to give orders in combat, but for those orders to be followed commanders first have to build relationships characterised by trust and shared purpose with their team outside of combat – and that's the real leadership challenge.

Stanley McCrystal is talking about leadership in a military context, but the same kinds of situations are arising all the time in the business world, and so we can also directly transpose his insights to organisational settings. Stanley highlights some of the major developments in the external environment and that is what I want to focus on in this section, because that's what is creating new challenges for leaders today; the world is changing and it's forcing us to rethink how we lead each other.

Let's look at a few of the major changes that are creating new challenges for leaders.

It's Happening Now, in Real Time

One of the stories that Stanley tells is about a senior officer watching his son in a firefight on a monitor in real time and he can't do anything about it right now; it always hits me hard to think about leaders facing situations like that today.

A business example that comes to mind is the 2010 Deepwater Horizon oil rig fire and the Gulf of Mexico oil spill that followed. The disaster became an instant news story around the world and, as with everything, there were leaders overseeing those operations when it happened.

Can you imagine what that must be like? Perhaps you're the wife of one of the key leaders. Your husband is working offshore and you're having your breakfast, scrolling through random news feeds on your phone, and then you see a Twitter post – last night 11 dead, 17 injured, oil pouring out into the sea – on a rig that your husband is in charge of right now.

The public is outraged, the news media are having a field-day. The tweets and re-tweets keep flooding in, it's on the local news, and you're just in shock. You get off Twitter and call your partner; they're in crisis mode, no time to talk, the rig is sinking, and all of this is taking place in real time and there's nothing you can do to help.

Now imagine being the leader. People in your charge are dead, others wounded. Company assets have been destroyed; reputational damage is only just beginning. Reefs, beaches, birds, and marine life irreparably damaged. The public witch-hunt is on; we all want to know who's responsible for this horror. And as a leader, that's you, it's your responsibility.

The chief executive Tony Hayward calls you himself, he's standing up in front of the press in half an hour and wants to know what happened. You've got the crisis to manage, ongoing spill to stop, people to take care of, and we already want to know what happened and why. You've barely had time to think about starting the investigation, but as the leader, it's all on you, and it's happening now.

The organisations all around us may seem amorphous, enigmatic and obscure; I often hear people refer vaguely to 'the government', 'Apple', 'big pharma', etc. We bring them to life as legal persons, but they're not really. It's real people making real decisions that govern the actions of these organisations; they're leaders with names, and faces, and addresses.

It wasn't just BP as some unknowable and remote entity that was responsible for the oil rig deaths and the Gulf of Mexico oil spill. It was Robert Kaluza and Donald Vidrine, two senior officers on the Deepwater Horizon oil rig, who were later charged with manslaughter for their involvement (among others) in a complex web of culpability, negligence, and mistakes.

Let this stand as an example of how leadership can all go horribly wrong. Leaders not only have to do what's right, but often at short notice with little time to make well-informed decisions, and they carry the responsibility for far-reaching consequences. It can feel like it's 'always on'; you don't often get time to rest and recharge, and this new pace has created additional pressure on leaders.

Increasingly International

New organisations today are increasingly what we call 'born global' in the sense that they have an international business focus from their very inception (Knight & Cavusgil, 2004).

Companies used to be created to fulfil a specific need in a particular place, usually in a small geographic area like a community, town, or city; your local grocery store, cinema, or car mechanic come to mind. Even most multinational companies like Toyota, Microsoft, and Coca Cola first spent decades expanding across their domestic markets before venturing overseas.

For now the majority of organisations remain domestic; relatively few companies export anything and fewer still are export-intensive (Ferguson et al., 2021). Only around 20–30% of people in developed countries work for a multinational organisation. But the focus on early and widespread internationalisation is growing fast.

Today entrepreneurs routinely target markets across the whole planet, often by offering unique products that cater to specific market segments in multiple locations (Knight & Cavusgil, 2005). Supply chains regularly span national borders and production facilities aren't always co-located with raw materials or end users.

Competitive organisations make the most of the advantages offered by many different countries: sourcing raw materials and manufacturing in China, distributing from London, Toronto, New York and Hong Kong, developing software in Poland, offsetting tax with headquarters in Ireland, and hiring the best talent from around the world to provide products and services to dozens of locations, often with local distributors, outlets, and support offices.

The shift towards a global business mindset means that many parts of our organisations might be operating across different time zones and currencies, and working within different legal and regulatory frameworks.

Navigating the myriad complexities created by these differences is a new and significant challenge for contemporary leaders. You'll often find yourself coordinating with people working in different locations and having to overcome the limitations of distance and digital communication.

Cross-cultural Collaboration

International mobility has also already radically diversified even domestic workplaces. On average around 15% of the population of OECD countries was born overseas. In Australia, it's almost 30%, and another 20% are second generation migrants with at least one parent born overseas; that's half the country with a foreign background.

As people move between cities, countries, and social groups, they pick up and share their cultural outlook along the way. The interactions create complex 'third culture' identities that are a mixture of international heritages and domestic influences (Pollock et al., 2017). Individual people are more diverse than ever before and within organisations it's now the norm to see heterogeneous constellations of people working together.

Appreciate that every person you're leading is from a different background to you and the others in your team, embedded with different cultural values, practices, beliefs, and ethical ideals. These different opinions, experiences, and perspectives are a critical asset that can strengthen your team through diversity, but only when people feel valued and safe enough to contribute. It's your job as a leader to enable everybody to bring their own unique talents to the advantage of the team.

Cultural differences can also be a fount of conflict and sometimes you'll feel like you've confronted an impossible task. How can we hope to create a shared sense of purpose, build trust, and inspire people to work towards a common goal when there's just so much that's different between us? It's actually an opportunity to appeal to the things we have in common, and there's a lot more than you might think.

We'd like to imagine ourselves as unique snowflakes, no two alike, and maybe on the surface that's true, but our core values are rarely all that different. We all want to be treated with respect, to feel valuable and know that what we're doing matters, to have a sense of control over our lives, and we all want trustworthy leaders who act with integrity.

The increasing cultural diversity of workplaces offers both significant challenges and opportunities for leaders in modern organisations. See the value in everyone's unique differences and build stronger teams through complementary diversity.

Accountability and Intolerance

The widespread access to high-speed Internet and social media, with an emphasis on video and photo sharing, is making leadership behaviour more visible, and with more exposure comes greater accountability.

Let's say I'm managing your local McDonald's. I'm having a rough day; there's drama at home and I'm feeling rather worn down, just trying to keep it together. Then one of my employees makes a mistake, again, for the third time today. It's dangerous, they're a menace, people could get hurt. Against my better judgment I lose my temper and yell at them; this is the last straw and I really let them have it, venting all my own frustrations.

Standing just behind the counter is a customer with their smartphone up, filming the whole scene as it unfolds. By the time I notice, they've already posted it on Twitter and tagged it #mcdonalds. McDonald's corporate social media team see the post, flag it, and escalate the issue to management.

That afternoon I'm pulled into a virtual meeting with the regional manager, the HR manager, and a media relations adviser. They say my behaviour was completely unacceptable and that it doesn't align with our organisational values. I'm fired on the spot and publicly denounced on Twitter to mitigate reputational damage to the company.

Pretty soon it feels like everyone in town has seen the video; I can't show my face in public without being ridiculed. Would you hire me for another leadership role now? Unlikely. Why would anyone want to work with someone who treats their employees like that? I'm completely tainted; a leadership career has been destroyed in the space of an afternoon.

The heightened visibility of leadership behaviour is a radical departure from prior norms, and it's happening at all levels of the leadership hierarchy. Just two decades ago only top tier managers (CEOs, Directors, etc.) were so exposed to public opinion, and with their every action laid bare they were compensated accordingly.

Few of us might feel like we're on the global stage – I'm certainly not as exposed as some political leaders who appear constantly on the news – but, in a sense, every leader today is acting on the world stage, and every action must be with the knowledge of that potential exposure and in the context of an international audience.

Expect that everything you do as a leader will be seen and scrutinised. With more of our leadership interaction taking place over digital platforms, very detailed records are retained. Most large organisations store vast amounts of digital data; every keystroke in every document, every email, phone call, MS Teams message, reaction, note, and comment is backed up – and can be recalled.

Don't get me wrong, this is a good thing. I'm a strong advocate for transparency in all our interactions and exposing the deplorable behaviour of some so-called leaders is just and right. But it also sets an insanely high standard. Because information is so readily available on the Internet, we expect our leaders to have perfect knowledge and act with flawless grace.

Anything you do, anything you say or don't say, and how you say it, might be offensive to a particular group that you might not even know existed, and if that behaviour was captured and posted to social media you would immediately be held to account. Why didn't you know better, why were you not sensitive to the needs of that group? How could you be so ignorant or callous?

I believe that most people – and by extension, most leaders – are trying to do their best. Sometimes our best isn't all that great, but we can't possibly know everything and always act in perfect cognisant harmony with that knowledge. Yet that is the standard that we're holding our leaders to.

Today there's little tolerance for intolerance; leaders must be respectful of countless differences, appreciating the value of that diversity and tailoring their behaviour accordingly. It may seem like yet another insurmountable demand and will require you to take proactive steps to learn about yourself and others, and always be mindful of your behaviour.

The proliferation of high-speed Internet and social media therefore adds a new and cumulative pressure on leaders with increased visibility and accountability for their behaviour.

Inversion of Expertise

Stanley McChrystal also talks about an inversion of expertise as a new challenge for leaders. Before now you'd be promoted to a leadership role because you were particularly good at doing the job, you were the star performer, and in a way that legitimised your leadership position – you knew best.

The pace of development is now so fast that what frontline staff do in their roles is often radically different to what their leaders grew up doing during the early stages of their careers. How then can leaders stay credible and legitimate when they've never done what their staff are doing? It might seem like they have few relevant skills and no job-specific expertise to pass on.

I'll give you an example. Teaching is one of the core academic functions at a university, but most senior university leaders today (e.g. the Deans, Vice-Chancellors, etc.) haven't taught in years, and when they did, it was with handwritten overhead transparencies, photocopied paper handouts, and rote learning textbook chapters for exams.

Meanwhile I spend most of my teaching time creating digital content, built into interactive and intuitive websites. In addition to face-to-face teaching, I often deliver video lectures and engage with students in live virtual classrooms. Even my in-class exercises are hosted online and embedded in our learning management system; students bring Internet-enabled smart devices to their classes to interact with the material.

Our university assessments today are authentic and applied, in that they directly resemble the kinds of work that you'll be doing in industry, and in that they ask you to solve real problems that organisations are facing rather than hypothetical ones. I've long ago removed exams from every course that I coordinate.

Few of my senior university leaders have ever delivered this kind of teaching and learning experience. But that's okay, because I don't need them for their job-specific expertise, I need them to inspire me, to enable me, and to support me so that I can do the job well. Frontline staff are the experts now and this inversion of expertise is a new challenge for leaders today.

Successfully navigating this new landscape requires leaders to be more transparent, more willing to listen, and more willing to learn from their team – we don't have to have all the answers; we hire talented staff so that they can do amazing work and it's our job as leaders to bring out the best in them.

You are legitimate then, not because of your work-related expertise, but because of your leadership skills, and that's not actually about doing the work. If we go back to Yukl and Gardner's definition of leadership from Chapter 1, nowhere does it say that I need to be an expert in the work itself – your leadership role is about helping your team to do their jobs well.

The more senior a leader you become the more you realise that your role is less about the work itself, and more about building positive relationships, enabling and inspiring your team, and attracting more talented people to join your cause; these skills rarely come easily and being a good leader is hard work.

Flexible and Remote Work

Organisations are increasingly moving towards flexible and remote work arrangements, also known as flexible working practices (Soga et al., 2022); that is, allowing their employees to work whenever and wherever they want, as long as the work gets done.

The COVID-19 pandemic dramatically accelerated the trend towards flexible work, primarily as a result of the lockdowns and self-isolation protocols imposed by many governments around the world. Organisations quickly turned to flexible work as a solution to maintain business continuity while large portions of their workforce were confined to their homes for extended periods, often with little warning or consistency.

Estimates vary, but in 2022 around 30% of employees in developed countries worked remotely all the time, and another 30% worked remotely at least some of the time, while only around 40% of workplaces weren't offering flexible work options. Flexible work arrangements as part of the 'new normal' are here to stay, but the ramifications will take us years to fully appreciate while we reimagine the nature of work and strive to get it right.

We'll focus our discussion on the implications for employees and the subsequent leadership challenges; the practice has known advantages, disadvantages, and offers new difficulties for leaders to navigate.

Advantages

Autonomy is a major benefit of flexible work arrangements (Johnson et al., 2020); people typically have more control over when and how they complete their work. Being in control of our own work feels good and communicates a sense of trust from our leaders.

Given the freedom to make their own schedules, people can also better align their work hours with personal, social, and familial commitments, so that they can do more of the things they want in life and don't have to feel like they're compromising or missing out. It's particularly helpful for those with carer responsibilities.

People in flexible work therefore tend to have a better work–life balance, which in turn makes them more satisfied and productive in their work, and more committed to the organisation (Bloom et al., 2015). Working from home also saves a significant amount of time, expense, and stress by not having to commute to and from work.

Flexible arrangements are typically advantageous for employers too, who get a more productive workforce that needs less office space and is cheaper to house. It sounds fantastic, a win–win for everybody, but is it all too good to be true?

Disadvantages

Unfortunately there's also a host of risks and disadvantages associated with flexible and remote work, including social isolation, blurred work–life boundaries, and asymmetric demands.

Working remotely from home can be a lonely and socially isolating experience with fewer opportunities to connect with colleagues, making it harder to form new meaningful relationships and weakening pre-established social ties (Bloom et al., 2015). Remote workers often feel like they're excluded from important decisions and miss out on career-advancing opportunities.

Being 'at work' in a dedicated location separates our personal and professional lives by creating a physical and psychological boundary between the two. Ironically, flexible work can therefore exacerbate work–life conflicts because it blurs the lines between work and home life (Bellmann & Hübler, 2020); it becomes less clear where work ends and home starts, and issues from one readily spill over into the other.

Flexible work can feel constantly on-demand, interrupting your leisure time and creating stress that disrupts your personal life. Likewise personal issues (e.g. relationships, finances, health, etc.) can leave you feeling emotionally depleted while you're trying to work, which makes it harder to be productive (Peasley et al., 2020).

It can be difficult to mentally disconnect from work, especially if you haven't established clear boundaries on work-related technology use at home (Barber & Jenkins, 2014). Without proper recovery, people tend to burn out: they start feeling stressed, exhausted, and get cynical about the work, which severely reduces productivity.

Being at home comes with its own distractions and demands, and experiences vary significantly across the workforce. For example, parents with school-aged children at home in remote learning find it harder to focus on their work (Calear et al., 2022), compared to young professionals without dependants.

So is Flexible Work Good, or Bad?

Among the various stories about flexible and remote work, one narrative remains consistent – the experiences are different for different people, in different roles, across different organisations and sectors. So the answer to whether flexible work arrangements will be effective for your team is going to depend on your followers and on the context.

Experiences vary between organisations where remote work has been normalised and those where it's stigmatised, between people with children and carer responsibilities and those without. Even within the same organisation, for virtually identical employees in the same role: some people love it, and others hate it.

The overall effects of flexible work on organisational performance and employees' mental health, for example, remain unclear, chiefly because of the wide disparity of experiences. It will take time for us to understand when, where, for whom, and in what context remote work is appropriate and beneficial to organisations and for employees personally.

In the meanwhile, let's turn to the leadership challenges that flexible work is creating today.

Leadership Challenges

All of our leadership efforts are mediated through communication. Every way that we can try to influence others is contained and transmitted, either through something we say or do, or how we say and do it. The value of skilful and intentional communication for effective leadership cannot be overstated, and I have dedicated a whole chapter in this text to help you get it right, every time. For now, I'll just briefly discuss the new communication challenges associated with flexible work.

Flexible work arrangements mean that leaders are physically removed from their followers, which drastically alters our communication modes, and, as a result, directly affects our leadership interactions. Stanely McCrystal (Video 2.1) talks about now having to use a broad array of digital communication platforms like emails, phone calls, virtual meetings, text messages, and chat not just for communication, but for leadership – and that's a significant new challenge.

Communication is a process that takes place in context and includes not only the explicit content of a message but also the way that it's transmitted – for example, how you say it, and your body language (hand movements, facial expressions, and eye contact).

Being face to face with a person is the richest form of communication because you can observe all of the minutiae of their non-verbal and contextual messages, like where they're looking when they say certain things, how close they're standing to you, the tone and volume they're using. All of those things give us cues to help us better understand what they're trying to communicate.

Every other form of communication is less effective. In shorthand written communication like text messages and chat, there are very few contextual cues to help us decipher the intended meaning. Emails might have more detail, but they're often slower.

Phone calls are good because we can hear details from the other person's voice, and video calls are the best because we can also observe a lot of non-verbal facial expressions, but they're still contextually poorer than face-to-face conversations.

The leadership challenge is the same – to build trust, inspire, and forge a sense of shared purpose – but now we've got to do it over imperfect digital communication platforms where so much of our leadership is lost in translation. In person we can look each other in the eye, feel trust, sense confidence, show gratitude, and acknowledge respect – giving someone a 'thumbs up' emoji over chat is hardly the same.

Video communication platforms might be commonly available now, but not everyone is comfortable broadcasting their homelife to work colleagues; many people will routinely leave the microphone muted and camera switched off. You risk exposing your private life, and even if it's a perfectly ordinary life (if such a thing exists), your right to keep it private should remain.

For example, I think that my apartment is comfortable, classy, and well appointed. I strictly control the visible backgrounds for my virtual meetings, making sure that they're pleasing to look at, reflect my character and speak well of me. Consider how drastically different people's experiences will be here – what would I see in your background right now?

Giving leaders a window directly into the private lives of their followers raises complex ethical issues and blurs the boundaries of responsibility. Imagine the sheer breadth of what you might see in the video call background of your followers: frolicking naked children, dishevelled roommates, evidence of substance abuse, domestic violence, the list goes on.

Exposure to our followers' private lives further extends leaders' responsibilities and adds new job demands in the form of emotional labour in managing the experiences. Leaders aren't trained counsellors and it's not the same as offering a friend advice; this is part of your work role.

Building the kinds of close positive relationships that are essential for effective leadership is harder over long distance, and the increasing proliferation of flexible and remote work poses a significant new challenge for leaders.

Successfully navigating this new environment requires leaders to be more relationship oriented, promote higher-context communication modes, and be more mindful of the content of our messages – digital communication strips away contextual cues and forces us to rely primarily on the explicit content of our messages.

Our understanding about the demands of this new way of working is evolving as we learn more; leaders will need to stay agile in their approach and be ready to cater to different employees' needs. Remember, one size does not fit all when it comes to flexible work.

TRADITIONAL LEADERSHIP CHALLENGES

Leading others well is always a challenging experience. Above I've outlined some of the new issues that leaders today have to navigate, and these are in addition to a host of ongoing challenges that leadership roles entail.

Some of the routine difficulties that you'll encounter include motivating, enabling, and inspiring your team, dealing with the VUCA environment, building consensus, leading change, handling conflict, delegating and learning to trust your team, feeling confident and confronting imposter syndrome, staying humble when things go well, taking responsibility when things go wrong, and learning to keep going when the going is hard and slow.

Each of the traditional challenges gets exponentially more complicated when combined with one, or more, of the contemporary challenges. For example, inspiring people is tough at the best of times, but doing it with a diverse and cross-cultural team over a low-context digital communication platform is much harder; there are so many opportunities for miscommunication, for your confidence and values to be misinterpreted, such that you offend rather than uplift.

Over the remaining ten chapters I'll help you to find your own leadership style and develop relevant skills that will enable you to overcome these leadership challenges and become drivers of positive change in the world.

OVERCOMING LEADERSHIP CHALLENGES

Now that we've got a vivid picture of the current leadership landscape, I would like you to consider how you would deal with some of the challenges that you might face as a leader (Exercise 2.1). Write down which of these issues – traditional, contemporary, or both – might be the most difficult for you to navigate and why.

Once you've identified what might be your toughest hurdles, I want you to consider what you could do to help overcome these challenges. Think about whether you'll need to work on specific skills, address areas of weakness, get help, or plan to delegate and recruit followers with certain capabilities to complement your talents so that you can capitalise on your strengths. Aim to write down two or three specific actionable steps, which will be important areas of focus for your development.

Exercise 2.1

Overcoming Leadership Challenges

Image Alt Text: https://ecuau.qualtrics.com/jfe/form/SV_a3rryuUZkFgG6hg

---

This is where we are today. Next let's look to the future to see what changes, challenges, and opportunities are on the horizon.

MEGATRENDS

Our world is currently being reshaped by several well-known megatrends that encompass large-scale and interrelated demographic, economic, and social shifts. These changes span national borders to connect with and influence many different aspects of the world.

Each country has a different demographic trajectory – that is, how its population is changing into the future. Regional demographic changes, when viewed from a macro global perspective, have far-reaching social and economic implications.

Developed Nations

Many developed nations' populations are aging and shrinking; the average age is increasing and there are fewer and fewer people in total.

There are two main causes: advances in healthcare mean that people are living longer, and, as nations mature and more people are educated, they tend to have smaller families with fewer children, so the number of people entering those populations is reducing.

That means the workforce, or proportion of people in that population of working age, is getting smaller, but retirees are living longer. The working population is now facing a growing burden to maintain the rest of their society by paying tax to fund healthcare systems that were designed when the population looked very different, with a large workforce and a smaller aged population.

Older workers will need to stay employed longer to sustain themselves, and governments will need to rethink the retirement age. Imagine adding another generation to the workforce with people as old as 75 and as young as 18 working alongside one-another; they'll have grown up in different worlds – for perspective, compare today's university graduates to those from the 1970s.

One solution that developed nations will increasingly rely on is to import migrant workers from the fast-growing populations to sustain their own economies. Governments will compete to attract high-skilled migrants with lucrative opportunities, and we'll see a lot more international migration, which means more diversity for organisations and leaders to navigate.

Developing Nations

Developing nations' or emerging economies' populations are young and growing quickly; there are a lot more people having children, and having bigger families. Their workforces are increasing, and with more productive members in these societies, working, generating income and spending, their consumer markets are growing quickly too.

Asia, as an economic region in 2009, made up about a quarter of the world's middle-class population. Members of the middle class are particularly important because they're the largest consumers, so that's where most businesses make their profits.

Estimates suggest that by 2030 Asia will have two-thirds of the whole world's middle-class population and consumption – that's a massive and important shift. Organisations that once sold to Europeans and North Americans will need to realign their products and brand identities to target middle-class consumers in Asia, who have very different values and tastes.

The demographic shifts also create risk. Young growing populations need to be fed, housed, educated, and employed for us to reap the benefits and produce value for those societies. If there are no economic and educational opportunities for people, that's when we'll encounter problems in the form of social discontent, crime, and violence.

People without opportunities are much more susceptible to radical ideologies, to form secessionist movements, and cause civil unrest. The real concern is that the fastest growing populations are also in those nations that are least prepared to deal with these challenges.

For example, populations are growing fast in South America and sub-Saharan Africa, but opportunities for economic advancement and education aren't keeping up. We might find a group of young, willing, but unemployed and under-educated people in these regions who have nothing to do, and may well turn towards counterproductive social enterprises if we cannot address these gaps.

Economic Dominance

The demographic changes discussed above signal a significant impending shift in global economic power. The idea of Western economic dominance is fairly new. If we look back over the last 5000 years, Egypt reigned as the dominant power on the planet for 2100 years (3000–900BCE), followed by Greece and Rome for 1375 years (900–475BCE), and then China for 1125 years (475–1600); only in the last 420 years have Western Europe and the Americas taken centre stage.

Today the age of Western dominance is ending. The G7 (the United States, Japan, Germany, United Kingdom, France, Italy, and Canada) now face shrinking and aging populations, and will soon find GDP growth slowing and their economic power waning. At the same time the populations, the workforce, productivity, and consumer markets in China, India, Brazil, Indonesia, Mexico, and Turkey are growing quickly. The next few decades may bring colossal shifts in global economic dominance.

Urbanisation

In 1950 around 30% of people across the planet lived in cities, and 70% lived in rural areas outside of major cities; and some 200 years ago 90% lived in rural areas. As we automated agricultural and manufacturing systems, fewer people needed to live and work in rural areas, and so we've moved increasingly towards knowledge economies and urban city living.

In 2022 about 55% of the global population lived in cities and 45% in rural areas, but by 2050 estimates suggest that 70% of people will be living in cities. Within the span of a single century we will have reversed the proportions of our urban and rural populations.

Urbanisation has created a new phenomenon we call megacities – cities with more than 10 million inhabitants, and there are already more than 30 on the planet. Around two-thirds are in developing nations – that's how fast these countries are growing to surpass the developed world.

The challenge for developed nations is that their city infrastructures are already established, and they are increasingly strained as more people move into the cities. Many opted to build sprawling low-density suburbs, which proved a short-sighted and economically inefficient solution when you consider having to extend transport, power, water, Internet, policing, hospitals, and schooling.

Wealthy developing nations are investing heavily in brand new megacities that are built quickly to modern infrastructural specifications and are already designed for a 70% urban population. These new cities in many ways have an advatntage over the historical sites that we're slowly rebuilding to handle new growth.

The phenomenon is also changing how we see internationalisation; organisations are thinking about which cities, rather than just countries, to operate in as the new measure of global penetration. It's not enough to be in the right countries, we now need to be in the right cities to maximise growth – recall that few of these are in the developed Western world; are you ready to lead teams in Guangzhou?

These megatrends are changing the leadership landscape around us today and bringing us closer to the next industrial revolution. Let's see what that might look like and then consider what kinds of leadership challenges and opportunities these changes could create for us in the near future.

FOURTH INDUSTRIAL REVOLUTION

The World Economic Forum created a video (Video 2.2) to capture some of our aspirations for what the next, fourth, industrial revolution could include. In it various thought leaders discuss what changes are on the horizon across different industries and how they might reorganise our societies and reshape the nature of work.

Let's listen to what they have to say, and we'll use it as a starting point to consider how we might need to reimagine leadership in relation to some of these developments.

Video 2.2

World Economic Forum – What is the 4th Industrial Revolution?

Summary

We are on the cusp of the fourth industrial revolution, which will not only change what we do and how we do it, but it will change us by bringing together digital, physical, and biological systems. The values shift that will enable this revolution is triggered by a new story about how we want to live – focusing not on growth but on maximising well-being, shifting the narrative away from reducing harm and towards meeting the basic needs of every human being on the planet for all generations to come.

Image Alt Text: https://www.youtube.com/watch?v=kpW9JcWxKq0

I trust that by now you're starting to see how navigating the fourth industrial revolution will require skilled leaders to steer us through a myriad of potential social and economic catastrophes. Before I share my own thoughts on the matter, I want you first to think about what kind of leaders we will need to help us successfully navigate the challenges and embrace the opportunities. Try to picture these leaders in your mind and write down some of the behaviours, values, and attitudes that they might demonstrate (Exercise 2.2).

Exercise 2.2

What Kind of Leaders Do We Need?

Image Alt Text: https://ecuau.qualtrics.com/jfe/form/SV_b8CtjUEVDpWALci

FUTURE LEADERS

We're facing times of great difficulty, but also of great advancement and opportunity. What we'll need now is not more greed and selfishness, but wisdom, unity, and compassion towards one another. The changes unfolding across the world in the coming years will be as revolutionary and complex as any that we've encountered before, and we'll need leaders who are bold, courageous, authentic, inclusive, and selfless to help guide us:

Bold leaders who are agile and curious, ready to ask the difficult questions, to both initiate and embrace positive change for responsible progress.

Courageous leaders who stand firm to their values about what's right and just, instead of yielding to the easy route of popular opinion.

Authentic leaders who are strong enough, and vulnerable enough, to build open and honest relationships with others.

Inclusive leaders who know that everyone has something to contribute, and enable others by helping them to feel safe and valued.

Selfless leaders who think beyond their own ambitions, freely share their expertise, and can bring people together to address issues of global concern.

We must each of us strive to become the leaders that the world will need; let us dedicate ourselves to that.

SUMMARY

Leaders' actions are inherently tied to the context in which they are embedded. Our history is marked by revolutionary change, including geopolitical conflicts, technological advancements, and social movements that reorganised the industrial and civil landscape. The leadership environment is – and always has been – volatile, uncertain, complex, and ambiguous.

Recent changes in the external environment, however, are forcing us to rethink how we lead. Major developments include a new, faster pace as events unfold across digital platforms in real time, more international collaboration, radically diversified workplaces, increased accountability, an inversion of expertise, and more flexible work arrangements.

Leading others is always a challenging experience, and you'll encounter plenty of routine hurdles like motivating, enabling, and inspiring your team. But each of these traditional challenges gets exponentially more complicated when combined with one or more of the contemporary issues. For example, inspiring people is tough at the best of times, but doing it with a diverse and cross-cultural team via a low-context digital communication platform is much harder.

Looking to the future, megatrends are reshaping the demographic, economic, and social landscape of our world. Developed nations' populations are aging and shrinking, while developing nations' populations are young and growing quickly. These changes signal a significant impending shift in global power and the age of Western economic dominance is ending.

The next industrial revolution will occur alongside a new story about how we want to live, focusing not on growth but on maximising well-being, shifting the narrative away from reducing harm and towards meeting the basic needs of every human being on the planet for all generations to come.

The changes unfolding across the world in the coming years will be as revolutionary and complex as any that we've encountered before, and we'll need leaders who are bold, courageous, authentic, inclusive, and selfless to help guide us.

'There's hope in people, not in structures and systems, but in you, and in me.'

Paraphrased from *Think on These Things* by Jiddu Krishnamurti (1989).

REFERENCES

Barber, L. K., & Jenkins, J. S. (2014). Creating technological boundaries to protect bedtime: Examining work–home boundary management, psychological detachment and sleep. *Stress and Health, 30*(3), 259–264. https://doi.org/10.1002/smi.2536

Bellmann, L., & Hübler, O. (2020). Working from home, job satisfaction and work–life balance – robust or heterogeneous links? *International Journal of Manpower, 42*(3), 424–441. https://doi.org/10.1108/IJM-10-2019-0458

Bennett, N., & Lemoine, G. J. (2014). What a difference a word makes: Understanding threats to performance in a VUCA world. *Business Horizons, 57*(3), 311–317. https://doi.org/10.1016/j.bushor.2014.01.001

Bloom, N., Liang, J., Roberts, J., & Ying, Z. J. (2015). Does working from home work? Evidence from a Chinese experiment. *The Quarterly Journal of Economics, 130*(1), 165–218. https://doi.org/10.1093/qje/qju032

Bonanni, P. (1999). Demographic impact of vaccination: A review. *Vaccine, 17*, S120–S125. https://doi.org/10.1016/S0264-410X(99)00306-0

Calear, A. L., McCallum, S., Morse, A. R., Banfield, M., Gulliver, A., Cherbuin, N., Farrer, L. M., Murray, K., Rodney Harris, R. M., & Batterham, P. J. (2022). Psychosocial impacts of home-schooling on parents and caregivers during the COVID-19 pandemic. *BMC Public Health, 22*(1), 1–8. https://doi.org/10.1186/s12889-022-12532-2

Carabini, L. (2007). Bastiat's 'The Broken Window': A critique. *Journal of Libertarian Studies, 21*(4), 151–155.

Datta, M. N., & Bales, K. (2013). Slavery is bad for business: Analyzing the impact of slavery on national economies. *The Brown Journal of World Affairs, 19*(2), 205–223.

Ferguson, S., Henrekson, M., & Johannesson, L. (2021). Getting the facts right on born globals. *Small Business Economics, 56*(1), 259–276. https://doi.org/10.1007/s11187-019-00216-y

Johnson, A., Dey, S., Nguyen, H., Groth, M., Joyce, S., Tan, L., Glozier, N., & Harvey, S. B. (2020). A review and agenda for examining how technology-driven changes at work will impact workplace mental health and employee well-being. *Australian Journal of Management, 45*(3), 402–424. https://doi.org/10.1177/0312896220922292

Kannan, P. K., & Li, H. A. (2017). Digital marketing: A framework, review and research agenda. *International Journal of Research in Marketing, 34*(1), 22–45. https://doi.org/10.1016/j.ijresmar.2016.11.006

Knight, G. A., & Cavusgil, S. T. (2004). Innovation, organizational capabilities, and the born-global firm. *Journal of International Business Studies, 35*(2), 124–141. https://doi.org/10.1057/palgrave.jibs.8400071

Knight, G. A., & Cavusgil, S. T. (2005). A taxonomy of born-global firms. *MIR: Management International Review, 45*(3), 15–35.

Peasley, M. C., Hochstein, B., Britton, B. P., Srivastava, R. V., & Stewart, G. T. (2020). Can't leave it at home? The effects of personal stress on burnout and salesperson performance. *Journal of Business Research, 117*, 58–70. https://doi.org/10.1016/j.jbusres.2020.05.014

Pollock, D. C., Van Reken, R. E., & Pollock, M. V. (2017). *Third culture kids: The experience of growing up among worlds* (3rd ed.). Nicholas Brealey Publishing.

Soga, L. R., Bolade-Ogunfodun, Y., Mariani, M., Nasr, R., & Laker, B. (2022). Unmasking the other face of flexible working practices: A systematic literature review. *Journal of Business Research, 142*, 648–662. https://doi.org/10.1016/j.jbusres.2022.01.024

3
PERSONALITY, TRAITS, AND PSYCHOPATHY

Overview

This chapter explores the role of personality traits in shaping leadership interactions. It starts with the field of psychology, discussing the nature of traits and personality profiling, and then considering where our personality traits come from and how they change across different contexts.

Next, we introduce an influential personality framework known as the Big Five, where you'll work through a series of reflective exercises that reveal your overall personality profile. We discuss how personality dimensions affect leadership and how we can use personality profiles most effectively.

Afterwards we explore differences in cognitive style, considering how different people prefer to gather and analyse information. You'll discover your own preferred style and be challenged to recognise the advantages of leading diverse teams. We next study the Myers–Briggs Type Indicator (MBTI) as a popular but flawed personality framework to learn from its limitations.

The chapter concludes with a discussion of dysfunctional leadership using the Dark Triad personality framework, which includes narcissism, psychopathy, and Machiavellianism. We're much more likely to find a psychopath at the head of a major organisation than we are in the general population. Why is that, and what can we learn from their behaviour?

Quiz 3.1: Big Five personality profile

Quiz 3.2: Cognitive style instrument

Quiz 3.3: Revised psychopathy checklist

Who you are as a leader matters and will shape how others respond to your leadership, based on who they are and their perceptions of you; that's why it's so important to get to know yourself and your followers. We've borrowed some tools from the field of psychology that can help us to learn more about ourselves and others.

PSYCHOLOGY

Psychology is the study of people's behaviour and their mental processes. It's about trying to understand what people do, how they do it, and why, over time and in different contexts.

The modern field of experimental psychology started in Germany around the 1830s, then spread rapidly and was well underway across the world by the 1900s. To help us understand people in this way we've since studied their perception, cognition, attention, emotions, motivation, and of course, their personality, among many other factors.

Leadership as a field of research sits within the broader domain of organisational psychology and most of our theoretical frameworks and tools are grounded in applied psychology. You can see the connection; if we can understand how people think, feel, and behave, then we can anticipate their likely responses and influence them towards a specific purpose.

We'll therefore explore personality, traits, and cognition from a leadership perspective, using these concepts as tools that can help us learn more about ourselves and better understand others. Our goal is to better inform how we interact with our followers to become more effective leaders.

Your Unique Traits and Personality

Your traits are the personal characteristics that distinguish you from other people, things that are distinctive about you – the ways you behave, how you think, what you prefer, things that make you different – for example, being cheerful, organised, modest, competitive, outspoken, or clumsy, excitable, impulsive, and so on. There are easily more than 500 identified traits, and your personality is the unique combination of your many traits.

I like to picture our personalities as constellations in the night sky, made up of hundreds of bright stars that come together to form distinctive patterns; likewise, we each have a variety of different traits that fit together into our personality. Your personality is then the unique way you behave, think, and feel, over time and in different contexts, when taken in concert as a combined whole of who you are as a person.

The concept of having a 'personality' appeared early on in the study of psychology and became increasingly influential. Since its inception and through to the present day personality research has been applied extensively to business contexts. Organisations of all kinds want to achieve their goals effectively, and we know that we need people to help us do that – the best people, preferably – but how do we know who the best people are?

Such questions abound in organisations: how do we screen for the best employees to hire? Who are the best candidates for leadership development programmes and succession planning? What kinds of behaviours, mindsets, and emotions will enable our organisation to better achieve its goals, and how do we find people who exhibit these characteristics and encourage them in others? Enter the field of personality profiling.

Personality Profiling

Personality profiling is a way to classify and understand various dominant traits, to see how they coalesce into overarching personality 'dimensions' that are perhaps more generalisable. The process is essentially one of categorisation and simplification; you might wonder why we'd want to reduce the beauty and complexity of our diversity in this way.

If we accept that every single person is entirely unique, bearing no resemblance to anyone else, then none of our prior knowledge based on interactions with other people would be useful for informing our approach to new interactions. It then becomes much more difficult to predict how as yet unknown people might react to our leadership attempts and offers us no guidance on what we should do to influence them.

Fortunately, people aren't quite as unique as we might like to think and rather share many similarities. To better inform decision-making processes and enable further personality research we sought to classify groups of people into more manageable personality profiles based on the patterns of dominant traits that they have in common.

The first personality assessments were developed in the 1920s and used to guide personnel selection, primarily in the armed forces, by narrowing down potential job applicants and identifying employees who were more suitable for promotion. One example from this era that you've probably heard of before is the Rorschach inkblot test, which is still in popular use in some parts of the world.

Today there are dozens of personality profiling tools and they're used extensively in a variety of contexts, including clinical and forensic psychology, recruitment, marketing, consumer behaviour, customer relationship management, and employee testing. They're even used in couples counselling, on dating apps, and across pop culture – for example: 'Which Hogwarts house do you belong in?'. Some of these tests are more reliable than others.

When used appropriately, personality profiling can offer a reasonably robust, research-informed, and easy-to-use way to help understand people and social interactions that enable us to make better decisions; so it's not surprising that organisations have readily embraced the concept.

These ideas have permeated throughout our understanding of interpersonal interactions such that whenever we think about influencing another person, we might find that we're asking ourselves what kind of person they are to try and calculate what kind of influence tactic would work best.

WHERE DID MY PERSONALITY COME FROM?

Your personality is something that you develop; you're born with some of your personality traits and the rest you make up as you go along. Your personality is therefore not a static concept; rather, it's dynamic, constantly being developed and reshaped over your lifetime. Two factors that have influenced your personality are your genetics and the early childhood environment in which you were raised, but it doesn't stop there. Let's look more closely at these two sources first.

Hereditary Genetics – 45%

You genetically inherit some aspects of your personality from your biological parents. If you've ever heard the phrase 'the apple doesn't fall far from the tree', it's referring to the genetic components of personality and suggests that offspring are in some way close to, or resemble, the parent in their behaviour, preferences, mannerisms, or more specifically, their personality traits.

The field of behaviour genetics is highly contentious, mainly because we don't have single genes that are responsible for specific traits or behaviours; rather, these complex social processes are controlled by thousands upon thousands of different genes working together (Chabris et al., 2015). Predicting individual behaviour based on a DNA sequence is a thing of fiction, but we do know that genetics have a major influence on who we are today.

Of course, we cannot directly inherit distinct behaviours that depend on context because they're social constructs and must be learnt. For example, the language you speak, your religious beliefs, or your political ideology. But your propensity for language acquisition, your religiosity or tendency for political activism may be inherited. It's more accurate to say that we inherit traits, which might predispose us towards certain preferences, mannerisms, and behavioural patterns.

The first law of behaviour genetics is that all traits are heritable (Turkheimer, 2000), but that doesn't mean that you'll be exactly like your biological parents. It's better to think about genetics as accounting for a portion of the overall influence that determines your traits. Some things are more heritable than others. For example, your blood type and eye colour are upwards of 90% hereditary, your height is closer to 80%, raw intelligence is about 60%, and your personality is approximately 45% inherited (Harden, 2021, p. 42).

So where does the rest of your personality come from?

Childhood Environment – 15%

Another important influence on your personality is the environment in which you grew up. Each of us has been exposed to countless different experiences that inevitably shape a portion of who we become later in life.

When we're growing up, we see our parents and guardians behaving in certain ways and demonstrating various behaviours and interaction patterns among themselves and with others in different social contexts. Meanwhile we're constantly and often unconsciously absorbing cues about what's acceptable and desirable social conduct (and what isn't), and forming our personalities based on this information.

The second law of behaviour genetics, however, is that the family environment has a much smaller effect than hereditary genetics, and these environmental effects are also stronger for some things and weaker for others.

For example, around 35% of your intelligence and educational attainment are shaped by the family environment in which you were raised (Harden, 2021; McGue, 2010). The well-educated then tend to be employed in more prestigious occupations, have successful marriages, better well-being, and live longer; that's how families reproduce social privilege across multiple generations.

The early social environment is therefore clearly important in shaping your opportunities for success, but when it comes to your personality, the environment in which you grew up matters far less and accounts for only around 15% of the total effect (Mõttus et al., 2019; Turkheimer & Waldron, 2000).

Between hereditary genetics and our early childhood environment, we've explained up to around 60% of our personality so far, which still leaves a big portion unaccounted for: what is it?

Your Choices – 40%

Hereditary genetics and our early childhood environment play a formative role in shaping our personality, but they're only part of the story. The third law of behaviour genetics says that a large part of the differences in complex human behavioural traits are not accounted for by the effects of either genes or families.

Even identical twins who were raised together, who have exactly the same genetic heritage and share the same formative environment, still only have up to around 60% similarity across their personality traits (Mõttus et al., 2019). What this tells us is that the remaining 40% of our personality traits are explained by other influences.

We somewhat unhelpfully call the missing part of this story the effects of the 'non-shared environment' (Turkheimer & Waldron, 2000), which basically includes everything else that isn't genetic or early childhood upbringing. Some think that these differences are the product of chance (Plomin & Daniels, 1987).

I disagree. I believe that it's our choices that determine the remainder of our personalities. It's how we choose to respond to our experiences that shapes who we become; it's about choice, not chance – this remaining 40% is the manifestation of our free will over who we are (Turkheimer, 2011).

Personalities remain malleable well into adult life and continue to be shaped by critical life experiences (Bleidorn et al., 2018). After our childhood years we are more conscious and agentic in our interpretation, experience, and responses to the environment and life events.

Against the backdrop of these many different events and interactions, we're evaluating our experiences and deciding for ourselves how we choose to live them, what we believe, and that's what shapes who we become. We start to self-select the traits that then determine what kind of person we grow up to be, and that emerging identity gets clearer and more stable as we get older (Briley & Tucker-Drob, 2017).

Some life events seem so big that they'll determine the course of your whole life, but it's how we choose to experience these events that shapes who we become, for better or for worse.

Consider the influential people, events, and interactions that you've experienced, and how they have helped inform the kind of person you are today. But don't ever feel trapped by who you are or think that you're just a product of your genetic heritage, home environment, and life events; rather, your personality is what you make it.

Context Matters

Now that we know a little bit about where our personalities come from, let's consider the different contexts that we might find ourselves in and how they might affect the way we interact.

We typically don't behave in the same way at all times, with everyone, across all situations. That's not to say that we're sometimes putting on a false façade, misrepresenting or concealing our 'true' identity. Rather, different social contexts tend to invoke different aspects of our personalities to come to the forefront.

For example, think about how you behave at home with your parents, versus how you behave with your friends on the weekend, versus how you behave in professional settings like school, university, or the workplace, versus how you behave in a sporting or religious setting, or even how you behave when you're alone in a safe and familiar environment, versus someplace new.

With your friends you might find yourself being more open-minded and carefree, while at school or in the workplace you could conduct yourself more professionally, being mindful of details, deadlines, and responsibilities. Others could find the complete opposite, that they're more creative and interested in new possibilities at work, but take on a more responsible role in social settings with friends, planning activities and keeping everyone to schedule.

Even within the same context, specific aspects of our personality may be triggered by the presence or absence of certain people. Imagine what you're like in public alone, with family or close friends, with new acquaintances, or your work colleagues. It's likely that there will be a fairly stable pattern of differences in how you interact across the breadth of these various social contexts.

You're still the same person, you still have the same overarching and dominant personality traits, but different parts might come to the foreground to stand in the limelight of your conscious identity at different times – these are all authentic representations of who you are.

We tailor our personality to best suit the context that we're in, based on what we're trying to achieve in that situation, which is part of broader 'self-regulation' processes (Inzlicht et al., 2021). Contextual changes to our personality can happen consciously, when we intentionally alter which aspects of our character we emphasise, or subconsciously in response to our environment.

If you've ever heard someone say, 'I hate who they are when they're around person X', they're most likely referring to a subconscious personality shift that's triggered by the presence of another individual. Some people and situations can bring out the best, or the worst, in you. Take note of how your personality shifts according to your social context and think carefully about the kind of person you want to be.

As a leader you'll need to be mindful of how the dominant aspects of your personality affect your interactions with others. Work towards consciously, intentionally, bringing out your own best qualities, as is appropriate for the context, to help you positively influence others and build strong professional relationships.

THE BIG FIVE

The most popular and well-established personality framework is known as the 'Big Five' and it's been around since the 1980s. It categorises the vast array of possible personality traits into the following five groups, or 'dimensions': extroversion, agreeableness, emotional stability (also known as neuroticism), conscientiousness, and openness to experience; sometimes referred to using the OCEAN or CANOE acronyms.

The Big Five are interesting because the framework enjoys an unusual level of academic consensus and after hundreds of studies it's just as relevant today. Having survived for decades under the rigours of academic critique, the Big Five appear irrefutable and impervious to argument, which suggests to me that they're capturing a fundamental truth about the human condition.

If personalities are so multi-faceted and include hundreds of traits, why are there only five dimensions? In part it's about how many different concepts we can hold in our short-term memory when we're making decisions – the ideal number is seven, plus or minus two (Miller, 1956). Having five dimensions balances capturing the complexity of personality with brevity, so that we're not including so many categories that we start losing track and they cease to be useful to inform our decision-making.

The Big Five dimensions are not personality 'types', so you won't find yourself labelled as 'agreeable' or 'open to experience'; rather, these are coherent groups of traits that fit together into broader conceptual themes. For example, 'conscientiousness' will include traits like being organised and mindful of details. The dimensions aren't absolute, so you won't be either conscientious or not. Instead, think of them as a continuum where you'll have varying degrees of each dimension.

And it's particularly applicable to leadership as we'll see; but for now let's look at each of these five personality dimensions in more depth.

Extroversion

Extroversion is about sociability, excitability, and assertiveness; it captures how you approach the external world and conduct yourself in social interactions. It includes being more emotionally expressive, actively engaging with your environment, and being energised in social settings.

More extroverted people enjoy interacting with others and come across as being full of energy. They tend to be enthusiastic and action-oriented individuals. They like to speak up and tend to assert themselves early on in group environments, which might make them seem more confident and dominant.

Highly extroverted people will often seek out the company of others. They tend to be quite outgoing, competitive, and decisive; they know what they want, they're quick to make choices and confident in their decisions. Sometimes this can come across as bossy, confrontational or attention-seeking.

People who are low in extroversion, or 'introverts', tend to be more reserved. They prefer working alone and avoid competition. They're more independent of the social world and being around others can feel draining, so they need space to recharge. They're deep thinkers and need less external stimulus than extroverts, and they are often seen as quiet and low-key.

Agreeableness

Agreeableness is about empathy, kindness, and a general concern for social harmony; it captures how well you get on with other people. It includes being considerate, helpful, generous, trusting of others and trustworthy yourself, and willing to compromise for others' needs, benefit, and interests.

More agreeable people are approachable and tend to have a strong need for affiliation or connection with others; they're nice friendly people who come across as warm and personable. They usually have an optimistic view of human nature and want to see the best in others.

Highly agreeable people are supportive and thoughtful, often forming positive relationships. They're quick to empathise with others' feelings and to share their burdens, which can also make them quite sensitive to rejection. Highly agreeable people may come across as naïve or let others take advantage of their kindness.

People who are low in agreeableness, or are 'disagreeable', are insensitive and callous. They have a thicker hide, which is to say that they're more resilient and much less reliant on other people. They tend to keep themselves apart from others, preferring to remain more distant. They're the lone wolf, happy to take life on by themselves and they don't need anyone else's help. In some ways that makes them cold and hard, but it also makes them strong and independent.

Emotional Stability

Emotional stability is also known as neuroticism, and it's sometimes confused with neurosis, which is a class of mental disorder, or similar concepts like behavioural adjustment, which is about your ability to adapt to changes in your environment – you might have seen emotionally stable people referred to as being 'well adjusted'.

Emotional stability is about your tendency to get anxious, stressed, and upset; it captures how well you respond to adversity. It includes your emotional resilience and how much self-control you have over how you feel.

We all face challenges and setbacks during our lives; we find ourselves in stressful situations in both our personal and professional lives, and at times we fail and disappoint ourselves and others. There's no way to avoid all hardship and no one has a perfect charmed life, but it's how we experience these difficulties that can matter the most, and that's what emotional stability tries to capture.

Emotionally stable people tend to remain calm in adverse or difficult situations and instead process their emotions in constructive and positive ways – for example, when confronted with harsh criticism, first recognising and accepting their emotions, and then progressing quickly to see the opportunities for learning and growth. They're confident and resilient, spend less time worrying, and rarely get angry or depressed for long. Sometimes they can come across as detached or emotionally closed off.

Emotionally unstable people tend to experience more mood swings, anxiety, irritability, and sadness. They're prone to overthinking and often worry about how others perceive them. They tend to feel more vulnerable, self-conscious, and can get upset easily; when things go wrong, they often get frustrated and angry.

People who are more emotionally unstable tend to feel things very deeply. Instead of being calm and collected, they're intense and passionate, sometimes dramatic and tempestuous. They're driven by their emotions – both positive and negative – which makes them quick to anger, but quick to love too. Their emotional inconsistency can come across as wild, temperamental, and free.

Conscientiousness

Conscientiousness is about planning, determination, and working towards specific goals; it captures your approach to work and how much structure you prefer in your life. It includes being organised and self-disciplined, being mindful of your responsibilities, and striving for achievement with forethought and perseverance.

Conscientious people set themselves clear goals and they're strategic in how they pursue those goals, carefully planning and organising their activities with meticulous attention to detail. They have good impulse control such that their actions are intentional and designed to move them toward their goals.

Highly conscientious people are dependable and prudent. They tend to be well organised and methodical in their approach to work and life in general. They're great at following rules and well-established protocols. Having clearly defined structures and set schedules helps them to feel safe and in control.

Being very conscientious can also make some people more stubborn, inflexible, and focused to the point of being myopic, missing other opportunities that might arise to either improve their plans or take them in new directions. They can feel adrift and get overwhelmed without sufficient guidance, structure, or clarity.

People who are a low in conscientiousness tend to be more spontaneous and easy-going, preferring to let events unfold naturally. They're very flexible in their approach to life and work; they like to keep their options open to pursue new possibilities, readily embracing opportunities and not getting overly invested in specific plans or outcomes.

Less conscientious people can feel suffocated by too much structure and get bored easily when asked to do highly prescriptive or process-oriented work, which means that they sometimes come across as impulsive, capricious, and unreliable.

Openness

Openness to experience is about adventure, imagination, and curiosity; it captures your willingness to try new things. It includes preferring to engage in a diverse breadth of life and work-related experiences, having an appetite for change, intellectual stimulation, and learning.

People who are open to new experiences prefer variety and value independence. They are interested in their surroundings and enjoy travelling and learning new things. They're intellectually curious and tend towards abstract lateral thinking that's outside the box. They're unconstrained by conventional beliefs and more likely to entertain deviant and usual ideas.

People who are highly open to new experiences tend to have a broad range of interests; they'll dabble in many different hobbies, careers, and even relationships; they'll live in different places and meet new people because they're constantly seeking change, looking for something novel and exciting. They're original, daring, trailblazers who feel comfortable in new environments.

Having a high appetite for new experiences might mean that these people only accumulate many brief and superficial encounters without the depth of understanding acquired from long-term engagement. Lacking the commitment that it takes to develop significant expertise in any one thing, they'll start many different journeys but won't progress vary far down any road.

People who are instead less open to new experiences tend to develop mastery over a single specific skillset; they'll pick something that they enjoy and then keep practising and working on that one thing, perfecting their craft rather than splitting their attention with other interests.

People who are more closed to new experiences prefer the safety of routine and appreciate the familiar over the unknown. They're practical people who like to work with their hands and apply themselves to what they consider is the 'real world' rather than to abstract ideas, but this pragmatic approach can also come across as intolerant and closed-minded.

There's no Good or Bad, it's About Fit

If we only focus on the positive traits at one end of the Big Five personality dimensions you might feel like we should all strive to be agreeable extroverts who are conscientious, emotionally stable, and open to new experiences, but that's completely wrong and a waste of your unique and valuable character.

I hope that you've now got a more balanced perspective. For example, being more open or closed to new experiences both come with their own advantages and limitations, which isn't to say that one's good and the other's bad – quite the opposite. We're all different, and different people will fit better in different roles in a team where they can best draw on their unique personality traits to contribute the most value.

Let's work through an online quiz (Quiz 3.1) that will ask you a series of questions and then, based on your answers, calculate your scores on each of the Big Five personality dimensions. Looking at your results will reveal your 'personality profile'. We'll first see what scores you get and then discuss how knowing this can help us to become more effective leaders.

Quiz 3.1

Big Five Personality Profile

Image Alt Text: https://ecuau.qualtrics.com/jfe/form/SV_e5sZEcoq5JaiTbw

Adapted from Lussier and Achua (2004).

I do this same test every time with each new group of students that come through my class, and I always get roughly the same pattern of results. The specific numbers might vary a little, but the order from highest to lowest stays the same. I score highest on extroversion, conscientiousness, and emotional stability, around the lower middle on openness, and lowest on agreeableness.

My results intuitively align with what I'd consider to be my own personality profile; I'm confident and outspoken, diligent, well-organised, and emotionally resilient. I'm interested in new experiences and like to embark on new adventures, but I also need long periods of stability where I can focus on bigger projects that I feel are important; I'm strong and independent, but I know that I can also at times come across as confrontational, aggressive, and unsympathetic.

Reflect on what your personality profile reveals about your own behaviour, preferences, approach to work, to life in general, and about your interaction patterns with others. Accept your strengths, and flaws, in equal measure with both grace and humility.

Next let's consider how personalities intersect with leadership.

PERSONALITIES AND LEADERSHIP

We know that who you are as a leader matters and that the Big Five personality dimensions influence the likelihood that you will rise to leadership roles and whether or not you'll be effective (Judge et al., 2002), but that's an over-generalisation and what's missing is the nuance of context.

Who you're leading, in what kind of an organisation, of what size, in what industry, where in the world, and countless other factors will affect how personalities interact with leadership. Instead of trying to predict who will emerge as a leader and be successful, I believe that a more effective use for personality profiling is to help you to get to know yourself and others.

Now that you've worked through the Big Five framework to identify your own personality profile, there are two things that we can do: we can use the information to help guide our own development, and we can use the framework to help us better understand our followers. Let's consider our own professional growth first.

Guide your Development

Understanding our personality traits through frameworks like the Big Five helps us to further advance our self-awareness, and the more we know about ourselves the more intentional we can be with how we approach our leadership development. You can use your personality scores to identify situations where you're most likely to excel, to build on your character strengths, and offset your weaknesses.

Self-awareness is the extent and clarity of the factual knowledge you have about yourself, including details of your strengths, weaknesses, personality, feelings, values, motivations, and desires.

For example, I'm more extroverted, so I sought out a career where I would often interact with lots of people – teaching classes, presenting research, giving keynote lectures, hosting workshops, chairing boards and committees, knowing that I'm more likely to enjoy myself and using these interactions as opportunities to further develop my extroversion into a talent for public speaking.

Remember that aspects of your personality can be both strengths and weaknesses. For example, I know that I can be disagreeable, which allows me to make tough decisions and look after myself, but it also means that I sometimes struggle demonstrating kindness and empathy.

I've got two options: if I decide that agreeableness is particularly important to me, then I can work to cultivate a sense of kindness, be more considerate and sympathetic to others' concerns. Our personalities are not pre-determined; we can change them through our actions, acquiring new traits and removing old ones that no longer serve us. But you don't have to do everything yourself either.

Instead of trying to 'fix' the disagreeable side of my personality, I can also ask for help or better yet, delegate to others for whom this comes more naturally. For example, when supervising doctoral students, I prefer to partner with a more agreeable colleague so that they can contribute a nurturing aspect to our supervision team; we're more effective together because we can each make the most of our unique talents.

As a leader, think about what aspects of your personality you can draw on to add the most value to your team. If you're particularly emotive, perhaps it's inspiration that you can offer; if you're an excellent planner, then provide structure and guidance, etc. I recommend working to build on your strengths to develop these natural talents even further, rather than trying to mitigate your weaknesses.

Consider carefully what are the unique advantages and limitations of your personality profile. As we move on to discuss various leadership theories in the next few chapters, think about how your personality might fit better with certain approaches, and less well with others. Now let's look at how we can use personality profiles to inform our interactions with our followers.

Understand your Followers

Familiarising ourselves with the different personality dimensions helps us to see aspects of these traits in other people, and suddenly their behaviour, choices, and interaction patterns start to make more sense. We're essentially personality profiling them, and while our external perspective will rarely be perfect or complete, the more insight we have the better.

As leaders we're constantly seeking to influence followers towards our shared objectives, which can take many different forms, including inspiring, supporting, directing, empathising, and enabling. Personality profiling helps guide your leadership efforts by giving you cues about your followers' needs and preferences across different situations.

For example, when my team is faced with a significant setback, I can expect that those who are less emotionally stable will need more support to process the experience before they re-engage with our objectives. If I want my team to try a new way of working, I know that it will be easier for me to persuade those who are more open to new experiences first.

Personality profiling can also help you communicate more effectively by tailoring your approach to better suit your audience, irrespective of your own dominant traits. For example, if you're a particularly passionate person, communicating emotively might not appeal to someone who's more reserved. Rather, approach people in ways that they will find compelling.

An appreciation of personality differences can also help you to build more effective teams. As a leader, get to know your followers and help them find ways to contribute to the advancement of your shared objectives. Build strength through complementary diversity, so that we're always using everyone's best talents to their full potential and helping offset each other's limitations.

Our intention here is first to make personality knowledge explicit to directly inform our conscious leadership decision-making, and then to continue using these processes such that they become automatic – that is, fast, effortless, and subconscious – so that we're not only making better leadership decisions, but we're also making them quickly in the moment.

Consciously applying these ideas will make you more effective as a leader, and the more often you do it, the more natural it becomes, until it's an automatic part of your thought processes. For example, I know immediately who on my team would be best suited to an extroverted role where they need to engage a timid audience, and who'd be terrified by that prospect.

The Big Five framework is the most robust approach for understanding our personality differences that's supported by significant academic research. Another way to think about your personality is through the lens of 'cognitive style'. Let's see how this perspective can be useful.

COGNITIVE STYLE

Cognition is about acquiring knowledge and understanding through thought, experience, and the senses. It's typically discussed as a hierarchical set of processes starting with sensation, perception, motor skills, attention, memory, and then reasoning, problem-solving, and language (Harvey, 2022). Entire domains of research underpin and further expand each process.

How different people prefer to think varies, and the variety of approaches can be broadly categorised into 'cognitive styles', which can be thought of as aspects of our personality (Armstrong et al., 2012). Like the Big Five dimensions that we discussed previously, our natural cognitive style informs and shapes our behaviour.

One of the contemporary challenges facing leaders today is making justified decisions quickly, and amidst a surplus of information. More digital and international collaboration, greater visibility and accountability, and radically diversified workplaces have created a complex, high-stakes, and fast-paced decision-making context.

As leaders we need to sift through a surfeit of information to find what's relevant with confidence, knowing that we'll be held to account for the decisions that we make based on that information. But the quality of our decisions is bound by the constraints of time and the limits of reason; we can only access and digest so much information.

Understanding how you and others on your team prefer to gather, interpret, evaluate, and respond to information is therefore critical to effective leadership. When you're making decisions, your cognitive style influences the kind of information that you would usually look for, and how you analyse that information to form your judgment.

The goal is to build effective teams through diversity and synergy, drawing on a range of different but complementary approaches to collecting and analysing information to best inform your decision-making. You want people who will seek out different kinds of information and can analyse it in different ways to broaden your perspective; they'll find things you never thought to look for and make connections that you can't see, so that you can make better informed decisions.

There are many ways to categorise and measure cognitive style in organisational contexts (Armstrong et al., 2012), but most models explore how we gather and analyse information. Let's look at an influential approach developed by Carl Jung that can help make us better leaders.

Carl Jung

Jung (1923/1976) proposed that personalities are either introverted or extroverted, and are then defined by how we prefer to search for and analyse information. According to Jung, when searching for information we tend to apply either more 'sensing' or 'intuition', and when analysing information, we're either more 'feeling' or 'thinking'. The labels can be confusing, but here's what they mean.

> *Sensing* involves a focus on details and the properties of individual parts; people tend to approach the search more rationally, preferring to meticulously gather specific information, looking for reliable evidence in a structured way.
>
> *Intuition* involves a focus on similarities, patterns, and relationships; people tend to approach the search more holistically, preferring to gather more general information like values and perceptions, looking for possibilities in an unstructured way.
>
> *Thinking* is the more objective approach that's systematic, methodical, and empirical; it's based on logical reasoning, prioritises accuracy and truth, and values justice. It's about making deliberate decisions based on reason and conscious thought.

Feeling is the more subjective approach that's impulsive, compassionate, instinctive; it's based on personal values, prioritises people and perspectives, and values harmony. It's about making quick decisions based on past experiences and social norms.

The different approaches for gathering and analysing information are dimensions, not exclusive categories. For example, some people might be entirely 'thinking' in their decision-making, but most of us will have a preference that involves elements of both 'thinking' and 'feeling', with one that tends to be more dominant. Our approach can also be influenced by the nature of the task that we're working on.

None of these cognitive styles is inherently better or worse; it's about finding an appropriate fit between the situation, the person, and the purpose. That's not to say that some people won't be useful in certain situations; rather, everyone can contribute something valuable and it's up to us as leaders to find a way to bring out the best in them, such that diverse contributions are constructive and collaborative rather than hostile and destructive.

Let's start by finding out your cognitive style. The following quiz (Quiz 3.2) will ask you a series of questions and then based on your answers it will calculate scores to reveal your preferred approach to gathering and analysing information.

Quiz 3.2

Cognitive Style Instrument

Image Alt Text: https://ecuau.qualtrics.com/jfe/form/SV_0eplz6Wsl04kV2m

Adapted from Whetten and Cameron (1995).

Jung's work on cognitive styles has been adapted by a well-known personality framework called the Myers–Briggs Type Indicator (MBTI), but as we'll see over the next few sections, not all personality frameworks are reliable. Let's see what we can learn from the limitations of the MBTI.

Myers–Briggs Type Indicator

The MBTI is a popular personality framework that's based on the idea that people can be categorised into distinct personality 'types' instead of considering our differences as ranging in magnitude along dimensions that include coherent groups of traits as we saw in the Big Five.

Myers and Briggs borrowed the three dimensions from Jung's framework, which included introversion–extroversion, sensing–intuition, and thinking–feeling, and then added a fourth that they called judging–perceiving to capture whether a person prefers planning or being spontaneous, respectively.

The MBTI instrument classifies you according to these four pairs of dimensions, where each one is assigned a letter – for example, extroversion 'E'. The 16 possible combinations of categories then generate the personality types which are each represented by a four-letter acronym; for example, you could be labelled an 'ESTJ' for being extroverted, sensing, thinking, and judging.

It might sound reasonable to those uninitiated into the field of psychology, but let's unpack what's happening behind the scenes before we consider using the MBTI for personal development.

Limitations of the MBTI

Myers and Briggs created the MBTI instrument by watching their friends and family who, according to the authors, 'clearly' displayed each of the 16 personality types. Basically, they made it up based on some people they knew, with complete disregard for the well-established and rigorous process of psychometric scale development (Stein & Swan, 2019).

Myers and Briggs argue that people are born with a 'true' personality type that's captured by one of these 16 combinations. There are two issues here, first with where our personalities come from, and then with the idea of discrete categories.

Hereditary genetics certainly play a role in personality development, but that's only part of the story. Claims that personalities are assigned at birth and remain static throughout our lives and across contexts seem absurd given what we know now, and the MBTI authors' case for the existence of a 'true' personality is based on anecdotal observation rather than systematic, empirical evidence.

Individual differences in personality and cognitive style make sense as dimensions, but not categories. Our personalities are complex and vary in magnitude along the various dimensions that we've identified; we don't fit neatly into boxes. It's remains unclear why the MBTI authors chose these dimensions and not others to exclusively capture all the possible complexity of personality.

The resulting MBTI survey has significant psychometric deficiencies that render it virtually unusable for scientific research, which is why you'll struggle to find it applied in reputable academic journals. Major issues include limited theoretical validity, poor reliability, and categories that aren't independent (Gardner & Martinko, 1996). If it's that bad, why then is the MBTI so popular?

Commercially Motivated Pseudoscience

Sometimes the concepts that grip public interest lack theoretical rigour, and distinguishing valid science from pseudoscientific fluff can be difficult in the post-truth era of misinformation. The MBTI is a part of a billion-dollar personality testing industry and several million people take the test each year, including many employees from Fortune 500 companies.

The MBTI therefore exists in a 'parallel universe' that's governed by commerce rather than the methodological constraints and theoretical scrutiny required of rigorous science (Stein & Swan, 2019). It's not surprising then that the MBTI prioritises revenue-generating hype over the often messy and complicated substance of truth.

If you read descriptions of MBTI personality types online, you'll find examples of famously successful people representing each category alongside broadly positive statements. We see aspects of our character resonating with these descriptions and want to associate ourselves with some of their greatness.

The MBTI gives us the illusion of control and makes us feel special; we want to believe in it and that's no accident – it's exactly what's intended behind the scenes. The overall experience can feel rather profound, but in showing us a categorical caricature of what we want to believe it offers us no knowledge, or truth.

People tend to agree with personality descriptions that seem to be specifically tailored to them, and yet are vague enough to apply to most people; the process is known as the Forer effect (Forer, 1949). That's what's happening with the MBTI, and it puts this framework into the same realm as astrology, numerology, fortune telling, and aura reading.

As leaders we can't afford the luxury of making naïve decisions based on pseudoscience. Our choices matter and affect the lives of many people who depend on us. Great leaders act on reliable research-informed evidence, striving for knowledge and truth.

Let's stick to real science and look at another personality framework called the 'Dark Triad' that's reliably grounded in clinical psychology.

THE DARK TRIAD

Not all personality dimensions are good, and the following three are together known as the 'Dark Triad': narcissism, psychopathy, and Machiavellianism. Let's explore where these terms come from, what they mean, and how they're connected to leadership.

We've borrowed the first two from clinical psychology; the *Diagnostic and Statistical Manual of Mental Disorders* includes 'narcissistic personality disorder', and 'antisocial personality disorder' which was previously called psychopathy (American Psychiatric Association, 2013). Christie and Geis (1970) originally proposed Machiavellianism as a personality dimension by distilling the philosophy and recommendations from Machiavelli's original text and named it after him.

Narcissism is about being self-obsessed, overly conscious of your appearance, and needing admiration; it captures how important you think you are relative to others. It includes feeling highly entitled, superior to others, and having a tendency towards interpersonal dominance. Narcissists are pretentiously imposing in their appearance or style and exaggerate their achievements and talents.

Psychopathy is about being bold, socially disinhibited, and lacking empathy; it captures how you behave in social contexts. It includes being fearless, self-confident, and socially assertive, but also having reckless and impulsive behaviour, defying authority, and thrill-seeking destructively. Psychopaths disdain close connections with people and tend towards cruelty and exploitation.

Machiavellianism is about being manipulative, callous, morally indifferent, and driven by self-interest; it captures how you pursue your personal goals and ambitions. It includes meticulous long-term planning, calculated behaviour, a disregard for others except insofar as they can be valuably used, and a willingness to engage in immoral behaviour like lying, cheating, and deceit.

As personality dimensions, narcissism, psychopathy, and Machiavellianism are 'subclinical', which means that the behaviour severity is below a threshold to be diagnosed and for the individual to be committed into psychiatric care. However, people who score highly on these dimensions are disruptive and harmful; they're more likely to be counterproductive at work, to cheat in academic settings, be unfaithful in romantic relationships, commit crime, and display antisocial behaviour (Furnham et al., 2013).

Sounds bad, right? And yet, we're much more likely to encounter a psychopath or narcissist at the head of a major organisation as compared to the general population – why is that? Let's look again at the Dark Triad personality dimensions, this time from a more cynical leadership perspective.

Means, Motive, and Opportunity

Narcissists are quick to self-promote, they're adept at impression management, and capable of effectively navigating organisational politics. Psychopaths are bold and self-confident, they've got a clear vision and pursue their goals relentlessly, they're willing to take risks and make pragmatic, dispassionate decisions. Machiavellians are ambitious and calculating, they can establish powerful social networks, gain co-workers' trust, and extract desired outcomes from clients.

Suddenly these qualities might appear to be the assets of ruthless, powerful, corporate leaders; these behaviours might even be consistent with their organisations' mission and culture, particularly in publicly listed for-profit companies that emphasise quarterly returns. That's why we tend to see more people with these qualities in some leadership roles, because the Dark Triad can help them to achieve organisational goals in the short term.

Narcissistic, psychopathic, and Machiavellian leaders can intimidate, manipulate, bully, and scheme to squeeze every ounce of performance out of their subordinates, and it often works in the short term. They do it because they can; they have the means, the motive, and some organisations provide them the opportunity by applauding their outcomes, but it's not effective leadership as we know it. So, what happens next?

Leadership is the Long Game

The social and organisational problems associated with Dark Triad leaders quickly start to accumulate and soon lead to an inevitable collapse. The narcissistic, psychopathic, and Machiavellian qualities that can sometimes extract high performance in the short term, also sow the seeds of their leadership failure.

In leadership contexts, the kinds of behaviours perpetrated by Dark Triad leaders are broadly known as 'abusive supervision' (Tepper, 2000) and can manifest in a variety of harmful interactions with followers including verbal abuse, demeaning remarks, bullying, gaslighting, coercion, and sexual harassment.

The tendency to mistreat colleagues and followers, to circumvent policies, and to promote their own interests undermines Dark Triad leaders' overall effectiveness; they're toxic people who damage relationships, systems, and organisations (O'Boyle et al., 2012).

Aspects of the Dark Triad dimensions can help people rise to leadership roles, but they're soon met with scepticism and dissatisfaction because they're ineffective and harmful (Brunell et al., 2008; Leckelt et al., 2020). Dark Triad leaders might portray themselves as considerate and capable, often believing it to be true, but the evidence reveals the opposite.

Dark Triad leaders rarely form the kinds of positive, collaborative relationships that enable people and organisations to achieve their long-term goals. Manipulation, deception, and abuse will always come to light and cannot create sustained energy and commitment towards a shared purpose over the long term.

Truly effective leadership is about the long game, building enduring positive relationships that create lasting value for people and organisations. Be wary of leaders who may appear successful but have many short stints of six months or less in different organisations throughout their career.

To finish off this section, let's work through our last quiz (Quiz 3.3) for the chapter: a psychopathy test. You'll be asked to rate the degree to which a series of behaviours are present from 0 'definitely absent', to 1 'possibly present', or 2 'definitely present'. You can test yourself or think of someone else who you know well. The quiz will calculate your total score out of 40.

Quiz 3.3

Revised Psychopathy Checklist

Image Alt Text: https://ecuau.qualtrics.com/jfe/form/SV_cT7Vl2mx6NYcilC

Adapted from Hare et al. (1990).

To give you some perspective on your results, around 80% of the general population will score less than five and fewer than 1% will score above the diagnostic threshold of 30; the average score for incarcerated offenders is around 22 and approximately 15% of them will score above 30 (Babiak et al., 2010).

SUMMARY

Who you are as a leader matters and will shape how others respond to your leadership. The concept of personality comes from the field of psychology, which is about trying to understand what people do, how, and why, over time and in different contexts. Personality profiles are useful tools to help us learn more about ourselves and others to become more effective leaders.

Your personality is the unique combination of your many traits, which are the characteristics that distinguish you from other people. You inherit around 45% of your personality traits from your biological parents, absorb another 15% from your early childhood environment, and you determine the remaining 40% for yourself based on your choices. Different social contexts also invoke different aspects of our personalities to come to the forefront.

The Big Five personality framework categorises traits into five coherent dimension groups: extroversion, agreeableness, emotional stability (neuroticism), conscientiousness, and openness to experience. Being higher or lower on these dimensions isn't inherently good or bad; everyone can contribute something valuable and it's up to us as leaders to bring out the best in people, where they can draw on the advantages of their unique personality such that their diverse contributions are constructive and collaborative.

The Dark Triad, on the other hand, includes three dysfunctional personality dimensions: narcissism, psychopathy, and Machiavellianism. People who score highly on these dimensions are harmful and disruptive. In leadership contexts, the kinds of behaviours perpetrated by Dark Triad leaders are broadly known as abusive supervision and will inevitably fail to produce positive long-term outcomes.

Leadership isn't only about who you are; it's what you do that can matter most. There are no personality traits that will define whether or not you'll be successful, and I believe that anyone can become an effective leader if they dedicate themselves to the task.

'It is our choices that show us what we truly are.'

Albus Dumbledore, in *Harry Potter and the Chamber of Secrets* by Joanne Rowling (1998).

REFERENCES

American Psychiatric Association. (2013). *Diagnostic and statistical manual of mental disorders: DSM-5* (5th ed.). American Psychiatric Association.

Armstrong, S. J., Cools, E., & Sadler-Smith, E. (2012). Role of cognitive styles in business and management: Reviewing 40 years of research. *International Journal of Management Reviews*, *14*(3), 238–262. https://doi.org/10.1111/j.1468-2370.2011.00315.x

Babiak, P., Neumann, C. S., & Hare, R. D. (2010). Corporate psychopathy: Talking the walk. *Behavioral Sciences and the Law*, *28*(2), 174–193. https://doi.org/10.1002/bsl.925

Bleidorn, W., Hopwood, C. J., & Lucas, R. E. (2018). Life events and personality trait change. *Journal of Personality*, *86*(1), 83–96. https://doi.org/10.1111/jopy.12286

Briley, D. A., & Tucker-Drob, E. M. (2017). Comparing the developmental genetics of cognition and personality over the life span. *Journal of Personality*, *85*(1), 51–64. https://doi.org/10.1111/jopy.12186

Brunell, A. B., Gentry, W. A., Campbell, W. K., Hoffman, B. J., Kuhnert, K. W., & DeMarree, K. G. (2008). Leader emergence: The case of the narcissistic leader. *Personality and Social Psychology Bulletin*, *34*(12), 1663–1676. https://doi.org/10.1177/0146167208324101

Chabris, C. F., Lee, J. J., Cesarini, D., Benjamin, D. J., & Laibson, D. I. (2015). The fourth law of behavior genetics. *Current Directions in Psychological Science*, *24*(4), 304–312. https://doi.org/10.1177/0963721415580430

Christie, R., & Geis, F. L. (1970). *Studies in Machiavellianism*. Academic Press.

Forer, B. R. (1949). The fallacy of personal validation: A classroom demonstration of gullibility. *Journal of Abnormal Psychology*, *44*(1), 118–123. https://doi.org/10.1037/h0059240

Furnham, A., Richards, S. C., & Paulhus, D. L. (2013). The dark triad of personality: A 10 year review. *Social and Personality Psychology Compass*, *7*(3), 199–216. https://doi.org/10.1111/spc3.12018

Gardner, W. L., & Martinko, M. J. (1996). Using the Myers-Briggs Type Indicator to study managers: A literature review and research agenda. *Journal of Management*, *22*(1), 45–83. https://doi.org/10.1016/S0149-2063(96)90012-4

Harden, K. P. (2021). 'Reports of my death were greatly exaggerated': Behavior genetics in the postgenomic era. *Annual Review of Psychology*, *72*, 37–60. https://doi.org/10.1146/annurev-psych-052220-103822

Hare, R. D., Harpur, T. J., Hakstian, A. R., Forth, A. E., Hart, S. D., & Newman, J. P. (1990). The revised psychopathy checklist: Reliability and factor structure. *Psychological Assessment*, *2*(3), 338–341. https://doi.org/10.1037/1040-3590.2.3.338

Harvey, P. D. (2022). Domains of cognition and their assessment. *Dialogues in Clinical Neuroscience*, *21*(3), 227–237. https://doi.org/10.31887/DCNS.2019.21.3/pharvey

Inzlicht, M., Werner, K. M., Briskin, J. L., & Roberts, B. W. (2021). Integrating models of self-regulation. *Annual Review of Psychology*, *72*, 319–345. https://doi.org/10.1146/annurev-psych-061020-105721

Judge, T. A., Bono, J. E., Ilies, R., & Gerhardt, M. W. (2002). Personality and leadership: A qualitative and quantitative review. *Journal of Applied Psychology*, *87*(4), 765–780. https://doi.org/10.1037/0021-9010.87.4.765

Jung, C. G. (1923/1976). *Collected works of C. G. Jung, Vol 6: Psychological types* (H. G. Baynes, Trans.; R. F. C. Hull, Ed.). Princeton University Press.

Leckelt, M., Geukes, K., Küfner, A. C. P., Niemeyer, L. M., Hutteman, R., Osterholz, S., Egloff, B., Nestler, S., & Back, M. D. (2020). A longitudinal field investigation of narcissism and popularity over time: How agentic and antagonistic aspects of narcissism shape the development of peer relationships. *Personality and Social Psychology Bulletin*, *46*(4), 643–659. https://doi.org/10.1177/0146167219872477

Lussier, R. N., & Achua, C. F. (2004). *Leadership: Theory, application, skill development* (2nd ed.). Thomson/South-Western.

McGue, M. (2010). The end of behavioral genetics? *Behavior Genetics*, *40*(3), 284–296. https://doi.org/10.1007/s10519-010-9354-0

Miller, G. A. (1956). The magical number seven, plus or minus two: Some limits on our capacity for processing information. *Psychological Review*, *63*(2), 81–97. https://doi.org/10.1037/h0043158

Mõttus, R., Sinick, J., Terracciano, A., Hřebíčková, M., Kandler, C., Ando, J., Mortensen, E. L., Colodro-Conde, L., & Jang, K. L. (2019). Personality characteristics below facets: A replication and meta-analysis of cross-rater agreement, rank-order stability, heritability, and utility of personality nuances. *Journal of Personality and Social Psychology*, *117*(4), 35–50. https://doi.org/10.1037/pspp0000202

O'Boyle, E. H., Forsyth, D. R., Banks, G. C., & McDaniel, M. A. (2012). A meta-analysis of the dark triad and work behavior: A social exchange perspective. *Journal of Applied Psychology*, *97*(3), 557–579. https://doi.org/10.1037/a0025679

Plomin, R., & Daniels, D. (1987). Why are children in the same family so different from one another? *Behavioral and Brain Sciences*, *10*(1), 1–16. https://doi.org/10.1017/S0140525X00055941

Stein, R., & Swan, A. B. (2019). Evaluating the validity of Myers-Briggs Type Indicator theory: A teaching tool and window into intuitive psychology. *Social and Personality Psychology Compass*, *13*(2), 1–11. https://doi.org/10.1111/spc3.12434

Tepper, B. J. (2000). Consequences of abusive supervision. *Academy of Management Journal*, *43*(2), 178–190. https://doi.org/10.2307/1556375

Turkheimer, E. (2000). Three laws of behavior genetics and what they mean. *Current Directions in Psychological Science*, *9*(5), 160–164. https://doi.org/10.1111/1467-8721.00084

Turkheimer, E. (2011). Genetics and human agency: Comment on Dar-Nimrod and Heine (2011). *Psychological Bulletin*, *137*(5), 825–828. https://doi.org/10.1037/a0024306

Turkheimer, E., & Waldron, M. (2000). Nonshared environment: A theoretical, methodological, and quantitative review. *Psychological Bulletin*, *126*(1), 78–108. https://doi.org/10.1037/0033-2909.126.1.78

Whetten, D. A., & Cameron, K. S. (1995). *Developing management skills* (3rd ed.). HarperCollins.

4
SITUATIONAL, SERVANT, AND AUTHENTIC LEADERSHIP

Overview

This chapter begins by examining leadership as a set of behaviours. Behavioural theories are a landmark advance over trait-based approaches because behaviours can be taught and leaders are therefore made, not born. Leaders can focus their behaviour in varying degrees on either the task at hand, or on the relationships with and among their followers.

Quiz 4.1: Task vs relationship focus

Quiz 4.2: Servant leadership

You'll discover your own natural leadership behavioural tendencies through a reflective exercise.

However, no single leadership trait or behaviour is effective in every context with every follower; rather, the notion of 'fit' determines successful leadership. You are therefore introduced to two situational leadership theories: Fiedler's contingency model and situational leadership theory, and we work through examples to see how the models apply to different contexts.

Quiz 4.3: Authentic leadership

Afterwards the chapter moves on to discuss two contemporary integrative leadership approaches, beginning with servant leadership and then authentic leadership. You'll complete exercises to see how your own leadership behaviour aligns with these styles. Discussion of each theory includes its unique benefits and challenges so that you can develop a balanced perspective.

The true measure of a leader is in what they do, more than who they are, what they believe, or intend to do. Your actions and behaviour determine how you influence people and events, living on in history as the account of your leadership.

There's no one right way to lead, but we've come up with a few leadership theories that explain what kind of approaches might be more effective. Each leadership theory will give you a different perspective that you can combine into your own unique style that resonates with your character.

In this chapter we'll first talk about leadership behaviour and consider where we can focus our energy and attention. Then we'll explore four leadership theories, starting with two situational leadership models, followed by servant and authentic leadership.

LEADERSHIP BEHAVIOUR

Another way for us to understand what is and isn't good leadership is to look at leadership behaviour, what leaders actually do, and then consider how and when specific behaviours can make them more effective.

Approaching leadership from a behavioural perspective is an exciting improvement on personality and trait-based frameworks because behaviour can be taught. Discovering what kinds of leadership behaviour are most effective lets us train you to become better leaders; and what you do as a leader is much more important than who you are (DeRue et al., 2011).

Thousands of discrete actions could be considered within the scope of leadership behaviour. Trying to catalogue each specific action and decide whether it's arbitrarily effective or not would be futile. Instead, we've tried to understand the focus of leadership behaviour, looking more broadly at where leaders are directing their energy and attention, towards what purpose.

At the core of leadership there are three entities: the leader, the task to be accomplished, and the followers who invest their efforts. And so we can think about all leadership behaviour as focusing on either the task at hand, or on the relationship with and among followers.

Behrendt et al. (2017) outline the kinds of leadership behaviours included in each of these two 'meta-categories'. Let's take a closer look.

Task Focused

Task-focused leadership behaviours are those that support others in accomplishing shared objectives, and include clarifying, motivating, and facilitating.

> *Clarifying* is about building a deeper and more comprehensive understanding. It includes sharing ideas, beliefs, and information; finding out what's been done

before, why it was done that way and what were the results; assessing the present situation, its opportunities, challenges, and identifying relevant stakeholders or interested parties.

Motivating is about creating enthusiasm and determination. It includes considering various different possibilities, the costs of their pursuit, and likely outcomes; finding those preferences and aspirations that we share; and securing a firm sense of commitment to work towards common goals by focusing on the benefits of positive outcomes.

Facilitating is about enabling others to succeed in their efforts. It includes strategic planning, guiding, and focusing their work such that every action is meaningful and moves them closer toward their objectives; providing valuable resources, and training to help develop individual competencies; attracting external support and identifying opportunities for improvement and growth.

Relationship Focused

Relationship-focused leadership behaviours are those that enable others to come together effectively as a team, and include promoting coordination, cooperation, and positive reinforcement.

Coordination is about creating structures that help people work together. It includes setting communication norms about the preferred medium, frequency, purpose, and tone; creating consistency by standardising who does what, when and how; guiding individual contributions to align with and support team efforts; and creating systems that help the team stay well organised without direct supervision.

Cooperation is about encouraging people to get more engaged with the team. It includes making people feel valued; assigning tasks to people that best fit their interests, skills, and values; giving people autonomy over their own work; and recognising the value of their unique individual contributions to our shared progress.

Positive reinforcement is about promoting desirable behaviour to continue. It includes building up people's sense of self-efficacy such that they believe in their own ability to succeed; highlighting positive experiences, past successes, and future ambitions; helping others to see the best in people and in the team; acknowledging, upholding, and rewarding valuable contributions.

What's More Important?

Both task- and relationship-focused leadership behaviours are important and affect whether leaders will be successful overall, but they're each better suited to different outcomes (DeRue et al., 2011). Task-focused behaviours tend to improve team performance now, while relationship-focused behaviours improve group cohesion, which helps build stronger teams and thereby improves future performance (Braun et al., 2020).

In an attempt to provide leaders with some guidance, non-academic frameworks like the 'leadership grid', which was previously known as the 'managerial grid', somewhat unhelpfully suggest that we should simultaneously focus on both task and relationship-oriented behaviour (Blake & Mouton, 1964). I'm not sure they know what 'focus' means.

The two meta-categories describe distinct and often competing behaviours; we can't do both at the same time. Choosing to focus on any one thing also carries with it the opportunity cost of what else you could have been doing instead: when you're improving a task, you're likely to be less attentive to developing relationships. So how are we supposed to do both?

Such paradoxes make sense when we consider leadership behaviour as alternating between the two areas of focus over time (Zhang et al., 2015). For example, we can set challenging goals and then provide more support and lessen the requirements when our followers meet obstacles; we can standardise the overall workload but assign different parts of tasks to align with individuals' skills and interests.

The effects of leadership behaviour on team performance and cohesion aren't linear and more isn't always better; we can focus either too much or too little on task- or relationship-oriented behaviour. For example, over-clarifying tasks will stifle your followers' ability to be innovative in their approach, and too much autonomy can create problems with coordination.

The timing of leadership behaviour is also critical; there's no point doing the right thing at the wrong time. For example, praise should be offered promptly and alongside the achievement or it will lose its effect.

It's straightforward then that we must find a balance between directing our energy and attention towards improving tasks and relationships. What remains unclear is when, with whom, in what context, and to what extent we should focus our behaviour on either tasks or relationships (Yukl, 2012).

Consider how we've been talking about leadership and all the different contexts: everyday interactions, politics, business, sports, families, communities. It's unlikely that there's one set of behaviour that will define you as a good leader and be universally effective in all of these situations. Banking firms, social media marketing start-ups, weekend soccer clubs, and church groups might need different approaches.

Neither task- nor relationship-focused behaviours alone are consistently effective across all leadership situations and must be applied in consideration of the leadership context. Let's see how situational leadership theory can help us to reconcile what kind of behaviour can be most effective in these different settings.

SITUATIONAL LEADERSHIP

The main idea underpinning situational leadership theories is that no one leadership style or approach is universally effective across all contexts and with all followers, and therefore, finding the right fit between leadership style and the situation will determine your success.

The process requires you to first diagnose relevant aspects of the leadership environment, including the nature of the work and the relationships with and among followers, and then select a leadership style that will be most effective based on our situational leadership framework. Which aspects we include in our diagnosis of the environment and what we do with that information to inform our leadership style varies between different situational leadership models.

Two prominent situational leadership frameworks are known as the 'contingency model' and 'situational leadership theory'. Let's look at each of these theories in more depth to see what they can offer us to further develop our leadership perspective.

Contingency Model

Fiedler (1964) introduced the contingency model to explain what kind of leadership style works best across a range of different organisational contexts. The model first looks at your natural leadership style and how much control is available in the situation, and then maps out which style fits best with each type of situation.

Leadership Style

Fiedler proposed that we each tend towards either a more task-oriented or relationship-oriented leadership style, which correspond with the two categories of leadership behaviour that we outlined earlier in this chapter; our preference is also known as our 'motivational orientation'.

We can all perform both task- and relationship-oriented leadership behaviour, but one may come easily to us, while the other is more challenging to enact, even when the situation calls for it. To figure out your preferred leadership style, Fiedler created a survey called the least preferred co-worker (LPC) scale. Let's work through it (Quiz 4.1) and find out your results.

Think of everybody who you've ever worked with in any context, including in the workplace, social settings, sports, community groups, etc., and identify the one person with whom you had the most difficulty getting the job done. The person could have been your peer, supervisor, or subordinate.

It's not necessarily the person that you liked the least, but with whom you had the hardest time working together effectively and successfully. You'll be asked to describe this person as they appear to you on a set of bipolar scales; for example, gloomy–cheerful, boring–interesting, tense–relaxed, and so on.

The test will calculate whether you're naturally a more task or relationship-oriented leader based on your answers.

―――― Quiz 4.1 ――――

Task vs Relationship Focus

Image Alt Text: https://ecuau.qualtrics.com/jfe/form/SV_6zOWlXcvzD0alF4

Adapted from the least preferred co-worker scale (Fiedler, 1967).

Describing your least preferred co-worker in mostly negative terms suggests that you're driven by a need for accomplishment and can get frustrated when unable to effectively complete the task at hand, which means that you're a more task-oriented leader. Whereas mostly positive terms suggests that you can find and focus on positive qualities even in difficult relationships and have a stronger need for developing and maintaining cohesive relationships with your colleagues, which shows that you're more of a relationship-oriented leader.

If you find that your score is very close to 50/50, within 5 points above or below, it means that you tend to straddle the two leadership styles and it may be easier for you to change your approach depending on the demands of the leadership situation that you're currently facing.

The LPC scale is a robust and reliable measure of your preferred leadership style that's been supported by decades of academic research (Ayman et al., 1995). Your actual LPC score might vary between tests, but the overall interpretation of your results is unlikely to change dramatically over time; you'll consistently score as either a more task-oriented leader or a more relationship-oriented leader or, more rarely, in the middle of the two categories.

Now that we've identified your preferred leadership style, let's see what Fiedler considered in his model to evaluate the nature of the leadership context.

Situational Control

Fiedler's contingency model next assesses how much influence and control leaders have over the situation by measuring three components: the quality of leader–member relations, the degree of structure inherent in the task, and the extent of the leader's positional power.

The quality of leader–member relations is about how much team members respect their leader and how well they can work together. When leaders don't have the support of their team, or if the team doesn't get along, you'll have to dedicate your energy and attention towards controlling the group, rather than planning, problem-solving, and productivity.

The degree of structure in the task is about whether the work includes clearly prescribed steps, known requirements, and easily measured objectives; or if the work is more ambiguous and creative with broad objectives and many potential solutions. Highly structured tasks are therefore more predictable and allow leaders to confidently direct team efforts.

Leaders' positional power is about the authority granted by virtue of their role within an organisation. It includes whether they can legitimately punish and reward followers by hiring and firing staff, promoting or transferring, assigning tasks and responsibilities, or controlling pay directly by changing hourly rates and salaries or indirectly by controlling working hours for shift and contract workers.

The three dimensions of the situation are each divided into two categories: the quality of leader–member relations is classified either as 'good' or 'poor'; the tasks are either 'structured' or 'unstructured'; and leaders' positional power is either 'strong' or 'weak'. Different combinations of these categories give us eight different leadership contexts or environment 'types'.

Leaders have the most influence and control in 'type 1' environments where you have good relations, a structured task, and strong positional power, and the least in 'type 8' environments with poor relations, an unstructured task, and weak positional power; the remaining environment types range between these two extremes.

For example, a well-liked general manager in an established manufacturing facility has much more influence and control compared to the distrusted chair of a volunteer organisation who is faced with a vague policy-making task. It follows that the most effective leadership style varies depending on the nature of the situation. Let's see what kind of leadership works best in each environment.

Leadership Fit for Context

Leaders of every kind are retained and rewarded for making productive teams that achieve organisational goals, from chief executive officers to sports team coaches and elected local officials. But neither leadership style nor aspects of the leadership environment alone are enough to predict group performance; what matters most is the fit between these two elements.

Ample research using Fiedler's contingency model (Strube & Garcia, 1981) shows that task-oriented behaviour is most effective in situations where leaders enjoy strong influence and control (types 1, 2, and 3) or else have very little control (type 8), and that relationship-oriented leadership behaviour tends to work best in situations with moderate levels of control (types 4, 5, 6, and 7); see Table 4.1.

Table 4.1 Contingency Model

Situation type	Quality of relations	Task structure	Positional power	Leadership focus – Task	Leadership focus – Relationship
Type 1	Good	Structured	Strong	—X—	
Type 2	Good	Structured	Weak	—X—	
Type 3	Good	Unstructured	Strong	—X—	
Type 4	Good	Unstructured	Weak		—X—
Type 5	Poor	Structured	Strong		—X—
Type 6	Poor	Structured	Weak		—X—
Type 7	Poor	Unstructured	Strong	—X—	
Type 8	Poor	Unstructured	Weak	—X—	

Adapted from Fiedler (1971, p. 131).

For example, I led a team of 20 academic staff who taught management, international business, and human resource management in our Bachelor of Commerce course. I had the team's trust and the team members worked well together. Our task was unstructured – although we had policies that set out how we scaffolded our teaching and assessed students' learning, the content was entirely up to my team who were all subject-matter experts in their field, and I had relatively weak positional power.

According to Fiedler's model, I was in a type four situation and I therefore primarily focused on relationship-oriented leadership behaviour to be most effective: I enabled coordination by creating structures that helped people work together, promoted cooperation by giving people autonomy, and offered positive reinforcement.

When dealing with the more strictly prescribed elements of teaching pedagogy, my context shifted to a type two environment; at those times I adopted a task-focused leadership style and prioritised clarifying, motivating, and facilitating behaviour. Our team consistently received high scores across all teaching metrics and the model worked well to predict our performance.

The contingency model can help you anticipate how effective your leadership style will be in a particular situation or suggest if another approach would be better. At the organisational level, the model can also help us make better decisions about recruitment, team composition, work design, training, and succession planning.

Consider your own leadership context along these three dimensions of control, identify the type of situation that you're in, and decide whether more task- or relationship-focused leadership behaviour will be most effective in that environment – does it align with your own natural leadership style that we discovered using the LPC scale? If not, you've got some work to do.

When your natural leadership style doesn't fit your current context, you can either change your leadership style or change aspects of the environment to better suit your preferred approach – for example, improving relationships with and among the team or clarifying ambiguous tasks to add more structure.

Next, we'll look at another approach to situational leadership that's based primarily on your followers' developmental needs.

Situational Leadership Theory

Hersey and Blanchard (1969) first introduced a model called the 'life cycle of leadership' and later renamed it 'situational leadership theory,' as it's known today. The model outlines another way to decide when either task- or relationship-focused leadership behaviour is more effective, this time from the followers' perspective rather than the leadership context more broadly.

The core concept of situational leadership theory is that the most effective leadership style varies depending on the development level of individual followers and your team as a whole, that people at different stages of professional growth need different kinds of leadership behaviour to best enable their performance. That makes sense. We probably wouldn't lead a highly skilled and experienced worker the same way as someone who's just started the job this week.

Followers' development level is about how ready they are to be self-directed in their work, it's also known as their 'task-related maturity' and includes their competence and commitment. Competence is about having the task-specific knowledge, skills, and experience that you need to perform well in your job. Commitment in the context of situational leadership theory is about being motivated, confident in your abilities, and willing to accept responsibility.

Highly developed followers and teams have demonstrated competence and commitment, they're able to work effectively on their own and complete their work to a high standard. Someone who's new to their role will take time to learn what's required and build confidence before they're ready to assume responsibility for their work – effective situational leadership can support them in their development to progress faster towards self-directed high performance.

Four Leadership Styles

Situational leaders improve team performance by focusing on their followers' growth needs to help the team advance to the highest level of development. There are four leadership styles that we can use to be most effective at each stage of the process: starting with directing, then coaching, supporting, and finally delegating.

Each leadership style involves different levels of focus on task- and relationship-oriented behaviour. Figure 4.1 illustrates the four stages, starting with directing in the lower right quadrant.

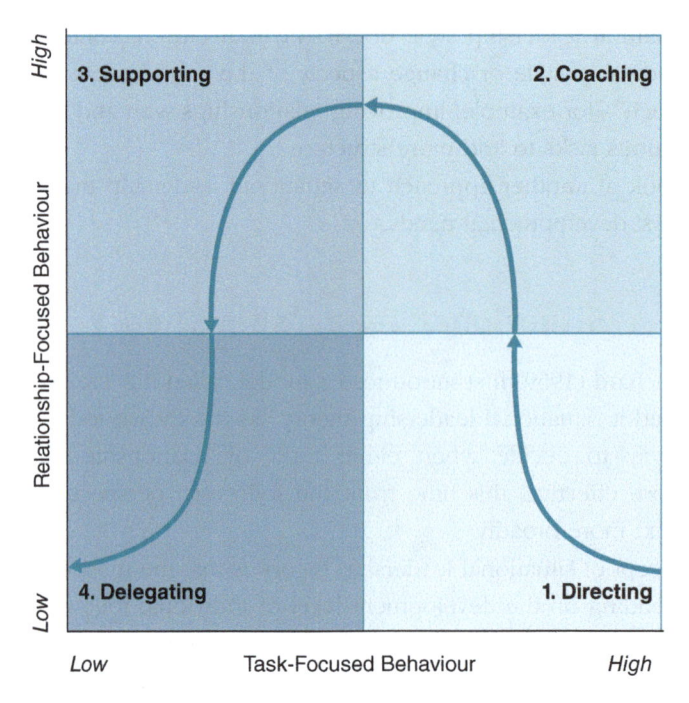

Figure 4.1 Situational leadership model (Hersey et al., 2012).

Directive leadership is most useful when a team first comes together; it includes high task- and low relationship-oriented behaviour. Your role is to clarify the task by providing information and giving instructions, identifying performance metrics and relevant stakeholders, sharing core values, motivating your team by finding common goals, securing a firm sense of commitment, and starting to develop individual competencies with personalised training.

Coaching leadership is most useful when a team has started working together; it includes moderate task- and high relationship-oriented behaviour. Your role is to encourage productive relationships among the team by setting communication norms, aligning tasks with individuals' emerging areas of ability, standardising processes, and building competence through continuous improvement and by focusing individual efforts onto high value-adding tasks.

Supportive leadership is most useful when a team gets more confident with the work; it includes low task- and high relationship-oriented behaviour. Your role is to build their confidence by upholding valuable contributions, and solidifying team structures to ensure that individual efforts support shared progress – granting access to valuable resources, guiding their own independent strategic planning, and creating systems that will enable effective behaviour to continue unsupervised.

Delegating leadership is most useful when the team has fully matured into a capable and high-performing unit; it includes very low task- and low relationship-oriented behaviour.

Your role is to get out of the way and give your team autonomy over their own work and decisions. You're now primarily the figurehead of the team, promoting their capabilities to attract external support and finding opportunities for further growth, for example by bidding for challenging and high-profile assignments.

Academic Background

Situational leadership theory has a complicated history. From its most compelling statement by Hersey and Blanchard (1977), the model has been revised quite a few times, getting weaker and more confusing with each iteration. For example, Blanchard et al. (1985) changed the framework based on their own 'experience' and conversations with friends, instead of offering theoretical arguments.

Major criticisms include the lack of any theoretical foundation, inconsistencies within the model, as well as vague descriptions of leadership style and follower development stages (Graeff, 1997). The problems get worse in later versions of the model, which are more ambiguous and start to arbitrarily rename parts of the framework. It's unclear why these changes were necessary.

Recall that the contingency model we looked at earlier in this chapter provided us with the LPC scale to discover our leadership style and set out in which situations we should use more task- or relationship-focused behaviour, based on reliable evidence. In comparison, situational leadership theory offers no instruments to support its usage; we have no way of finding out followers' level of development except by making an informed guess.

Early attempts to test the model failed, finding no support for the proposed benefits of deploying the four leadership styles at different stages of follower and team development (Blank et al., 1990; Goodson et al., 1989). Later results showed that the 2007 revised framework was an even poorer predictor of followers' performance than the original version (Thompson & Vecchio, 2009).

Overall, there seemed to be very little support for the validity of situational leadership theory and the model was all but abandoned by the academic community.

Recent testing has been more promising. Thompson and Glasø (2015) found that the four prescribed leadership styles are in fact more effective across the stages of follower development, but only when both the leaders and their followers agree on the assessment of their progress.

Previous studies only asked the leaders to rate their followers' progress and it's no surprise that these tests failed; a leader's assessment alone won't give us the full story. Disagreements over followers' progress may have been holding this theory back.

Imagine it from the perspective of followers who have progressed further than their leader can see. They're already competent and committed to their work, but then get directive or coaching leadership behaviour based on a mismatch in that assessment. It will feel like patronising micromanagement and is unlikely to improve performance.

Likewise, followers who are at earlier stages of professional development but may appear more advanced would receive a hands-off leadership approach that will probably leave them feeling underprepared, overwhelmed, and unsupported. It's equally unlikely to improve their performance.

Both leaders and followers must be involved in the assessment of followers' development, diagnosing their competence and commitment, first individually and then together to reconcile any differences and agree on the level of their progress. Only that will accurately inform us how much task- and relationship-focused behaviour would best encourage and enable our followers' performance.

Advantages and Challenges

I've presented my own generous interpretation of situational leadership theory so that we can continue developing our leadership perspective. We haven't yet got enough evidence supporting the model to suggest that we should closely follow its prescribed guidelines, but the latest research seems promising.

The advantages of situational leadership theory are that it's dynamic and follower-centric, explicitly charging leaders with responsibility for supporting their followers' development. The goal of effective leadership is therefore to build people up to be self-directed, to lead themselves, such that successful teams can continue working effectively without direct supervision.

Compared to the contingency model, which provides insights based on a static appraisal of the context, situational leadership theory offers us a dynamic outlook that incorporates followers' professional development over time and suggests specific ways that we can refocus our leadership behaviour at different stages in the process to best support their growth.

Yet unsolved challenges remain. For example, members of senior management teams might need little direct supervision, even at the onset, while frontline workers could expect their leaders to provide extensive training.

Some followers might also progress through the stages of development quickly, building competence and commitment over the span of several days, weeks, or months. Their pace will vary based on the complexity of the task and their pre-existing expertise. The theory offers no guidance about when these changes are likely to happen, or at what point we should transition into the next leadership style.

As individuals within a team progress at their own pace, we could be called on to provide different kinds of leadership behaviour at the same time to multiple followers. A similar situation would arise again whenever new members join established teams.

Situational Leadership Overview

Situational leadership suggests that different followers and contexts are best served by different leadership styles and that no single approach is going to be effective everywhere.

The contingency model matches leadership behaviour with eight different situation types based on the quality of leader–member relations, the degree of structure inherent in the task, and the leader's positional power.

Situational leadership theory suggests that we should adapt our behaviour to our followers' shifting developmental needs, enabling their progress first by directing, then coaching, supporting, and finally delegating.

The two approaches aren't necessarily exclusive, and we can benefit by thinking about both the context and our followers' needs. Good leaders are mindful of these differences and know when and how to moderate their behaviour to best influence others and support their efforts.

Let's look at another theory called servant leadership that puts your followers' needs first.

SERVANT LEADERSHIP

When Greenleaf (1977) came up with the notion of servant leadership he turned our traditional ideas completely upside down. He rejected the primacy of leaders and argued instead that good leaders must first become good servants. It's in stark contrast to other leadership theories that focus on advancing the leader's ambitions or agenda.

The journey into servant leadership begins with the desire to serve other people, and only afterwards do you consciously choose to take on the responsibility of leadership roles so that you can continue to help more and more people.

Eva et al. (2019) define servant leadership as 'an other-oriented approach to leadership manifested through one-on-one prioritising of follower individual needs and interests, and outward reorienting of their concern for self towards concern for others within the organisation and the larger community' (p. 114).

Focusing only on our own best interests, or even the interests of those directly in our charge, isn't enough. As leaders we must concern ourselves with the advancement of the broader society we live in and everyone who has a stake in what we do. That's where servant leadership comes in – it's about adding to the good of the whole and all of those in it by promoting long-term sustainable growth.

Doing what's right by others is necessary for the good of society and it doesn't mean that we've got to sacrifice profitability. Organisations around the world are realising that considering all their stakeholders helps them to create lasting value. Moral leadership isn't incompatible with, but rather essential to, the survival and success of our organisations (Lemoine et al., 2019).

Servant leadership is about enabling others' development, and I don't just mean that in a strictly work-related sense either. Servant leadership blurs the boundaries of work to include your followers' relational, ethical, and emotional needs as well as their professional development, such that they are empowered to grow as people, and not only as human resources.

People sometimes get the wrong idea when they imagine servant leaders, thinking that they're slaves to other people's whims, but there's nothing submissive or servile about servant leadership. Dedicating yourself to altruistic service requires a strong sense of self, determination, and psychological maturity (Eva et al., 2019).

You're taking responsibility for others' welfare and advancement; it's no small thing. Serving your followers' best interests might sometimes mean pushing them to confront their limiting beliefs and self-sabotaging behaviour, to set challenging tasks that will force them to grow past their current capabilities, and to discipline them when necessary, all so that they can achieve their ambitions.

Let's see what specific behaviours enable servant leaders to deliver on these high ideals.

Six Dimensions

Over the years many authors have tried to capture what exactly servant leadership behaviour includes, each coming up with a different set of dimensions (e.g. Liden et al., 2008; Spears, 1995; Van Dierendonck, 2011; and Van Dierendonck & Nuijten, 2011, among others). Our understanding of servant leadership is therefore fragmented, contested, and incomplete.

To give you some perspective, consider that Van Dierendonck (2011) identified over 40 characteristics of servant leaders described in the literature, and Eva et al. (2019) found 16 different ways to measure servant leadership. Many of the proposed servant leadership characteristics overlap, and the academic community at large is yet to agree on a single set of dimensions.

I've extracted from these earlier contributions the following six succinct dimensions of servant leadership: understanding, healing, morality, humility, stewardship, and growth.

Understanding is about becoming aware of how other people experience their lives. It includes learning about what's happened to them in the past, how that's shaped who they are, what's going on in their lives now, and what's most important to them. Servant leaders listen to their followers, empathise with their perspectives, and respond with warmth and compassion to create safe environments where people feel connection and acceptance.

Healing is about helping people to overcome the emotional and psychological barriers that hold us back from achieving our potential. It includes dispelling self-deprecating thoughts, limiting beliefs, and breaking self-sabotaging patterns of behaviour. Servant leaders build up their followers' self-efficacy so that they believe in themselves, helping them to process their emotions, prevail over their fears and limitations, and build long-term supportive relationships.

Morality is about doing what's right by you, those in your charge, and the wider community. It includes being open, honest, and fair in how you interact with others. It means having the courage to sometimes go against what's easy or popular, and challenging conventional ideas. Servant leaders display integrity by fulfilling their promises and doing the right thing even when no one's watching, because they hold themselves and others accountable to high ethical standards.

Humility is about having a modest perspective about how important you are. It includes a degree of self-awareness and vulnerability, accepting and acknowledging your own flaws and the limits of your influence. It means putting your followers first and prioritising their needs above your own. Servant leaders will often interrupt their own work to help others who are facing problems, and then stand back to give them the credit for a job well done.

Stewardship is about taking care of our followers, organisations, and communities. It means responsibly managing resources, focusing on the long term, and holding them in trust for those who come after us. Servant leaders learn from the past and weigh the consequences of their decisions. They've got the conceptual skills, foresight, and organisational knowledge to provide direction by clarifying the will of the group and persuading others towards a consensus for responsible action.

Growth is about empowering the development of people, organisations, and communities. It means encouraging and enabling others to improve themselves and their place in the world. Servant leaders recognise that people have intrinsic value beyond their contributions as human resources and provide mentoring and support to help them progress and succeed in their endeavours, even if it means losing them from their current role in the organisation.

Let's now see how servant leaders can apply these six principles to add value.

Creating Long-Term Value

Servant leaders indirectly improve and sustain organisational performance across the long term by supporting individual employees and teams, and by creating a positive culture, which then enables organisations to expand their reach and achieve their goals. It's not about directing others towards your vision, but rather, enabling others to reach theirs.

Servant leadership isn't just nice: it's effective too, and has tangible benefits for people, companies, and communities. Research evidence from multiple meta-analyses provides ample support for the positive effects of servant leadership on followers and organisations (Lee et al., 2020; Stein et al., 2020). I'm sure you're starting to see how it works.

When leaders focus their energy and attention on supporting their followers' development so that they reach their full potential, empowering them to handle tasks and decisions on their own, and prioritising their well-being and growth, followers are in turn more engaged and effective in their work (Eva et al., 2019).

When leaders humbly place themselves at the service of others, they inspire followers to incorporate similarly supportive attitudes, values, and behaviours (Ebener & O'Connell, 2010).

People start helping each other and, in doing so, create a culture of service across the whole organisation, which is to everyone's benefit (Greenleaf, 1970).

Servant leaders focus on supporting the growth and development of people, so that they can in turn improve their organisations and communities. Achieving organisational goals is therefore only a by-product of a sustained commitment to meeting their followers' developmental needs.

It's good for your leadership career too. Imagine, for example, that I'm leading a team and I focus all my effort on helping my team to be as effective as they can be, making sure that they've got everything they need to excel in their work. Whenever they reach new milestones, I celebrate their progress and applaud their achievements, giving them all the credit.

My team's success will also reflect well on me – after all, I'm now leading a high performing team that's achieving meaningful goals. Before long, my ability to create high performing teams will enable me to take on more senior roles with greater responsibility, where I can continue to help and support more and more people around me in their ambitions.

Servant leaders don't need to boast about their achievements, because key people in the organisation will almost always already know how much they've done to facilitate the success of their colleagues and followers. And that's how good servants end up in senior leadership roles in their communities and organisations, by supporting others and creating long-term value.

It Comes Back to Why You Lead

Greenleaf (1977) makes a sharp distinction between people who are 'servants first', and people who are 'leaders first'. If you find yourself taking on the responsibility of leadership roles because you're trying to help others and to improve your place in the world, you're a servant first.

Others are attracted to leadership roles only because of the personal rewards and benefits afforded by those positions; they're driven towards leadership first and foremost by their desire for material wealth, social status, and positional power; they're not in it to help anyone but themselves.

Of course we're not categorically 'leaders first' or 'servants first'; these are two opposite ends of a broad spectrum. Few of us are entirely altruistic or entirely self-centred, and more likely most of us will be somewhere in between.

What's important here is to consider whether you're pursuing leadership roles for the right reasons. The desire to help others is the key to effective leadership. Cultivate a commitment to the growth of your followers, to the survival and success of your organisations, and a responsibility to your community.

Let's find out how much servant leadership resonates with your approach. The following quiz (Quiz 4.2) will calculate a score based on your answers.

Quiz 4.2
Servant Leadership

Image Alt Text: https://ecuau.qualtrics.com/jfe/form/SV_29vpOyUROUafGHs

Adapted from Liden et al. (2008) and Van Dierendonck and Nuijten (2011).

I often draw on the six dimensions of servant leadership in my work. Academic positions in higher education typically include three core functions: teaching, research, and service: managerial positions are counted as service. Leadership and service thereby become interchangeable; it's the desire to help others that enables you to lead, and being a leader implies that you serve.

I've held service roles throughout my academic career, including some within the university and volunteer positions as a director of a not-for-profit academy and an associate editor of a journal. My time in these roles has been some of the most fulfilling and productive work I've done so far.

Challenges that Remain

As with all theories, servant leadership is not without its limitations. For example, the six dimensions describe such a virtuous and transcendent altruism that servant leaders appear almost superhuman. I'm not convinced that we can be so radically selfless and committed entirely to the welfare and advancement of others, taking only the pleasure of a job well done for ourselves.

It makes more sense therefore to think about servant leadership, and other leadership theories, as describing an ideal that we can aspire towards, a useful guide to better inform our behaviour, even if we sometimes fall short. I hesitate to describe myself as a servant leader, though I often follow its principles to help me navigate certain leadership situations.

Steering an organisation towards its goals also sometimes requires you to be seen; we can't always lead from the back. One of the most critical times is when things go wrong – you cannot hide behind your team. When your team succeeds, give them praise. But when they fail, that's when you have to step forward, take responsibility, and back your team; the fault is always yours.

Servant leadership also lends itself to manipulation. You could imitate servant leadership behaviour and say all the right things at the right times without ever believing in any of it, carefully cultivating a servant leadership façade not to help others, but as a benevolent disguise to ultimately advance your own personal power, wealth, and esteem.

I believe that our intentions matter and will inevitably surface as actions; there will come a breaking point when a selfish wolf in sheep's clothing will let everyone down at a critical moment to advance their own interests. Servant leaders stay true to the group, even when the going gets tough and they're tempted to stray.

Next, we'll explore a theory that directly addresses the authenticity of leadership behaviour.

AUTHENTIC LEADERSHIP

Authentic leadership is one of the most recent major advances in leadership theory. The approach has taken both the practitioner and academic communities by storm, and its beneficial outcomes are supported across a proliferation of research. The concept of 'authentic' leadership emerged in response to the colossal leadership failures of our generation.

We've seen a flood of corporate scandals in the last few decades, including Enron (2001), WorldCom (2002), Madoff (2008), Lehman Brothers (2008), Deepwater Horizon (2010), Fukushima Daiichi (2011), Volkswagen (2015), and Wirecard (2020); this list represents only a small selection and unfortunately there have been many others.

Each scandal was caused by catastrophic leadership failure. Leaders who in their greed cut corners, sacrificed others' welfare, and subverted due process until it all ended in horrible disaster. And after each scandal, we witnessed the unmasking of the leaders responsible on the world stage; many faced criminal charges as they were held to account.

Before long the World Economic Forum (2015) declared that we were in a 'leadership crisis' (p. 14). A well of cynicism grew as companies and countries around the world routinely engaged in 'woke capitalism', promoting their support for social movements to increase revenue while doing nothing to truly address their own harmful contributions. Greenwashing and token mascots from marginalised groups became commonplace.

Outraged by what we saw, many of us started to ask ourselves the real questions: how do we find leaders that we can trust, leaders who we could believe in, leaders we could respect?

We're sick of people who say the right thing at the right time to create the appearance of 'good' leadership, pretending to care about their followers, the environment, communities, social issues, and their customers without any substantive action. And all the while, making the kinds of decisions that lead to an inevitable collapse and such widespread harm.

Authentic leadership appeared as an antidote. George (2003) first proposed that authentic leaders reveal who they really are and show us their true purpose. The idea was then propelled into the academic sphere with a special issue in *The Leadership Quarterly* (Avolio & Gardner, 2005), and quickly grew into a dominant approach to contemporary organisational leadership.

Peus et al. (2012) define authentic leaders as those who 'are guided by sound moral convictions and act in concordance with their deeply held values, even under pressure; they are keenly aware of their views, strengths, and weaknesses, and strive to understand how their leadership impacts others' (p. 332).

Research has been enabled by two instruments, the Authentic Leadership Questionnaire (Walumbwa et al., 2008), and more recently by the improved Authentic Leadership Inventory (Neider & Schriesheim, 2011). Multiple meta-analyses have since revealed that this is one of the most effective leadership theories that we've developed so far (Banks et al., 2016; Hoch et al., 2018).

Let's look at the qualities and behaviour that are representative of authentic leadership.

Four Dimensions

The academic community broadly agrees that authentic leadership is characterised by four dimensions: self-awareness, an internalised moral perspective, balanced processing, and relational transparency.

Self-awareness is about first developing a clear and comprehensive understanding of your own strengths, weaknesses, and values, and then behaving in ways that are consistent with that knowledge. It includes appreciating how your behaviour affects others and learning about their experiences to help improve your interactions, and inviting feedback to see your talents and limitations more clearly. Authentic leaders accept their strengths without hubris and their weaknesses without shame; they're secure in themselves because they know who they are and what's most important to them. Developing self-awareness requires an active and continuous process of reflection; take time out to explore your life story and critical incidents, and derive meaning from your life experiences.

An internalised moral perspective is about deciding for yourself what's right and having the courage to act on your principles. It includes reflecting on your values to consider what's fair in each situation instead of relying on norms, rules, or even outcomes to guide your behaviour. Authentic leaders resist social pressures to conform to doing what's expected, what's been done before, or what will benefit a few select individuals; instead they stay true to their convictions and draw on core beliefs to make decisions. There's often a personal cost to going against entrenched social norms or the interests of those in power, and it can sometimes feel like no good deed goes unpunished, but that's when it matters most to have the moral fortitude to stand up for what you believe.

Balanced processing is about recognising our own biases and working to be more objective. It means impartially analysing relevant information to make decisions instead of relying on flawed heuristics or mental shortcuts. It includes acknowledging that we're imperfect and make mistakes. Authentic leaders are mindful of the limitations of their own cognitive processes and how they affect their decision-making. They seek feedback and input from others to improve their self-knowledge and find better solutions, especially that which will challenge their current beliefs. Encourage others to voice different points of view and listen carefully to their ideas before coming to a decision. Be brave enough to say that you don't know, or that you need help, and be willing to change your mind.

Relational transparency is about being open and honest in your interactions with others, expressing your ideas clearly and saying what you mean. It includes actively sharing parts of your personal life, and that takes enormous courage. We all want a sense of connection but we're afraid to be judged, condescended to, or made to feel ashamed of our faults. Let yourself be vulnerable and open up to people, empowering them to do the same. Authentic leaders promote transparency in their organisations too, insofar as it's appropriate, recognising that full disclosure might sometimes jeopardise their core values or others' welfare. Whenever possible share what you know and your honest perspectives to encourage productive discussions, and own up to your mistakes.

Let's now consider how these authentic leadership behaviours enable better performance.

Your Journey Inspires Others

Authentic leaders improve followers' performance by creating transparent relationships characterised by mutual trust and shared values (Lux et al., 2023). How we feel about our leaders translates into how we feel about our work and organisations in general. Followers who have positive relationships with their leaders are more engaged with their work and more committed to the organisation's goals.

The vulnerability of authentic leaders emboldens people, so that they too feel safe enough to contribute their best ideas and opinions to the advantage of the organisation, even when they're different to their leaders', such that they feel valued and heard. When authentic leaders reveal their true values and beliefs, they inspire people to see meaning in their work beyond the mundane, which drives engagement and productivity.

Organisations succeed when employees are motivated, engaged, and collaborate with each other. Hundreds of studies support the beneficial outcomes of authentic leadership for individuals, teams, and organisations across different countries and industries (Zhang et al., 2021) – everyone can benefit from a more authentic approach.

Developing your authentic leadership is a life-long personal journey. It's not a destination that you can arrive at and declare yourself done. Rather, it's an ongoing process of self-discovery where you continue to strive towards a clearer and more complete version of yourself, aspiring to become your best self at work (Gardner et al., 2011).

Learning, growing, and developing an authentic self is an iterative process of reflection, sense-making, and self-construal. As you explore your past experiences and the critical incidents that have shaped your life, you gain a deeper understanding of yourself, and by choosing how you interpret these experiences you start to decide who you are as a person, and as a leader.

Authentic leadership carries with it a craving for the ideal, it's an expression of our reaching out towards it, and in doing so we give others hope and faith. Authentic leaders openly share their sometimes-painful process of self-discovery, their moral deliberations, and quest for objectivity; there's beauty in the struggle that encourages followers to develop their own authenticity. It's not about turning you into me, but enabling you to become the best version of yourself.

Through the transparent authentic leadership relationship followers start to develop their own self-awareness, balanced processing, and the moral courage to stay true to their convictions, thereby becoming authentic leaders in their own right. The goal of authentic leadership is, then, to be so completely yourself that everyone else around you feels safe enough to be themselves too.

When authentic leaders and followers safely share their core values, and discuss work honestly and frankly, they can then create more fulfilling and productive workplace experiences. Aligning your followers' work with their personal values and beliefs creates intrinsic motivation, because they're now doing what they want and moving towards goals that they believe in; work becomes an expression of who they are and that's highly engaging.

Let's take a quick survey (Quiz 4.3) to see how authentic leadership might correspond with your own approach. The following test will calculate your authentic leadership score based on your answers.

Quiz 4.3

Authentic Leadership

Image Alt Text: https://ecuau.qualtrics.com/jfe/form/SV_a4druwg8er1NtxY

Adapted from Neider and Schriesheim (2011).

Drawing on the four principles of authentic leadership can help you to improve the performance of your team and organisation by forging stronger workplace relationships that will enable your followers' personal growth, work engagement, and commitment.

This might sound easy. It often isn't, and here's why.

Ongoing Controversy

I'd be remiss if I did not acknowledge the significant ongoing controversy that surrounds authentic leadership. The theory is intuitively appealing, but not everyone is convinced and the details are hotly debated in the academic literature (see Alvesson & Einola, 2019; Gardner et al., 2021 for a summary of the arguments). Let's examine a couple of issues.

Authentic leadership suggests a preoccupation with the self. Leaders might sometimes need to be diplomatic and tailor their approach to the context, keeping their moral stances private instead of eagerly expressing the self. The leader's authentic self may well belong in the background as they attend to the tasks at hand, support their followers' needs, and adjust their behaviour to correspond with norms relating to sex, age, and hierarchical roles.

Measuring authentic leadership is a challenge. Current research shows that followers are influenced by their perceptions of authentic leadership, and not by leaders' objective authenticity. It may be sufficient to cultivate an authentic leadership image that demonstrates the four dimensions clearly to followers, rather than genuinely pursuing an open process of self-discovery, particularly if it's less visible to others and therefore less inspiring.

What if my authentic self is undesirable, including, for example, poor social skills, extremist political or religious views, problems with impulse control, social and racial intolerance, and the like? Such behaviours are generally unhelpful, but only reflect a mainstream usage of 'authentic', rather than the academic construct of 'authentic leadership'.

Being an authentic leader doesn't mean that you're perfect, far from it, but what matters the most is that you're striving. It's an aspirational endeavour towards a morally worthy existence through self-awareness, balanced processing, and transparent relationships. Authentic leadership shows us that people would rather connect with your real flawed self, than a false perfect persona.

SUMMARY

Effective leadership behaviour can be taught. But there's no shortcut. Leadership isn't just 'more natural' for some lucky few and becoming a good leader isn't an accident. You have to study, practise and perfect your craft. Great leaders are made, not born, and that's why anyone can aspire to leadership roles, but it's up to you to make the journey and, while some people can help, no one can do it for you.

At the core of leadership there are three entities: the leader, the task to be accomplished, and the followers who invest their efforts. Leaders can focus their behaviour on either the task at hand to improve team performance now, or on developing cohesive relationships that will improve future performance.

Situational leadership suggests that different followers and contexts are best served by different leadership styles and that no single approach is going to be effective everywhere. Good leaders are mindful of these differences and know when and how to moderate their behaviour to best influence others and support their efforts. The contingency model and situational leadership theory are useful analytical tools to guide your behaviour.

Servant leadership is about prioritising your followers' needs and enabling their personal and professional development, such that they're empowered to grow as people, and not only as human resources. It includes understanding, healing, morality, humility, stewardship, and growth. Servant leaders indirectly improve and sustain organisational performance across the long term by supporting individual employees and teams, and by creating a positive culture which then enables organisations to expand their reach and achieve their goals.

Authentic leadership is an aspirational endeavour that includes self-awareness, balanced processing, an internalised moral perspective, and transparent relationships. Authentic leaders improve organisational performance by generating intrinsic motivation and establishing strong relationships characterised by mutual trust and shared values. Authentic leaders' vulnerability inspires followers to develop their own authenticity, as they openly share their process of self-discovery, their moral deliberations, and quest for objectivity.

'The problems we face did not come down from the heavens, they are made by bad human decisions, and good human decisions can change them.'

Bernie Sanders (circa. 2015).

REFERENCES

Alvesson, M., & Einola, K. (2019). Warning for excessive positivity: Authentic leadership and other traps in leadership studies. *The Leadership Quarterly*, *30*(4), 383–395. https://doi.org/10.1016/j.leaqua.2019.04.001

Avolio, B. J., & Gardner, W. L. (2005). Authentic leadership development: Getting to the root of positive forms of leadership. *The Leadership Quarterly*, *16*(3), 315–338. https://doi.org/10.1016/j.leaqua.2005.03.001

Ayman, R., Chemers, M. M., & Fiedler, F. E. (1995). The contingency model of leadership effectiveness: Its levels of analysis. *The Leadership Quarterly*, *6*(2), 147–167. https://doi.org/10.1016/1048-9843(95)90032-2

Banks, G. C., McCauley, K. D., Gardner, W. L., & Guler, C. E. (2016). A meta-analytic review of authentic and transformational leadership: A test for redundancy. *The Leadership Quarterly*, *27*(4), 634–652. https://doi.org/10.1016/j.leaqua.2016.02.006

Behrendt, P., Matz, S., & Göritz, A. S. (2017). An integrative model of leadership behavior. *The Leadership Quarterly*, *28*(1), 229–244. https://doi.org/10.1016/j.leaqua.2016.08.002

Blake, R. R., & Mouton, J. S. (1964). *The managerial grid*. Gulf Publishing Company.

Blanchard, K. H., Zigarmi, P., & Zigarmi, D. (1985). *Leadership and the one minute manager*. HarperCollins.

Blank, W., Green, S. G., & Weitzel, J. R. (1990). A test of the situational leadership theory. *Personnel Psychology*, *43*(3), 579–597. https://doi.org/10.1111/j.1744-6570.1990.tb02397.x

Braun, M. T., Kozlowski, S. W. J., Brown, T. A., & DeShon, R. P. (2020). Exploring the dynamic team cohesion–performance and coordination–performance relationships of newly formed teams. *Small Group Research*, *51*(5), 551–580. https://doi.org/10.1177/1046496420907157

DeRue, D. S., Nahrgang, J. D., Wellman, N., & Humphrey, S. E. (2011). Trait and behavioral theories of leadership: An integration and meta-analytic test of their relative validity. *Personnel Psychology*, *64*(1), 7–52. https://doi.org/10.1111/j.1744-6570.2010.01201.x

Ebener, D. R., & O'Connell, D. J. (2010). How might servant leadership work? *Nonprofit Management and Leadership*, *20*(3), 315–335. https://doi.org/10.1002/nml.256

Eva, N., Robin, M., Sendjaya, S., Van Dierendonck, D., & Liden, R. C. (2019). Servant leadership: A systematic review and call for future research. *The Leadership Quarterly*, *30*(1), 111–132. https://doi.org/10.1016/j.leaqua.2018.07.004

Fiedler, F. E. (1964). A contingency model of leadership effectiveness. In L. Berkowitz (Ed.), *Advances in Experimental Social Psychology* (Vol. *1*, pp. 149–190). Academic Press.

Fiedler, F. E. (1967). *A theory of leadership effectiveness*. McGraw-Hill.

Fiedler, F. E. (1971). Validation and extension of the contingency model of leadership effectiveness: A review of empirical findings. *Psychological Bulletin*, *76*(2), 128–148. https://doi.org/10.1037/h0031454

Gardner, W. L., Cogliser, C. C., Davis, K. M., & Dickens, M. P. (2011). Authentic leadership: A review of the literature and research agenda. *The Leadership Quarterly*, *22*(6), 1120–1145. https://doi.org/10.1016/j.leaqua.2011.09.007

Gardner, W. L., Karam, E. P., Alvesson, M., & Einola, K. (2021). Authentic leadership theory: The case for and against. *The Leadership Quarterly*, 1–24. https://doi.org/10.1016/j.leaqua.2021.101495

George, B. (2003). *Authentic leadership: Rediscovering the secrets to creating lasting value*. Jossey-Bass.

Goodson, J. R., McGee, G. W., & Cashman, J. F. (1989). Situational leadership theory: A test of leadership prescriptions. *Group & Organization Studies*, *14*(4), 446–461. https://doi.org/10.1177/105960118901400406

Graeff, C. L. (1997). Evolution of situational leadership theory: A critical review. *The Leadership Quarterly*, *8*(2), 153–170. https://doi.org/10.1016/S1048-9843(97)90014-X

Greenleaf, R. K. (1970). *The servant as leader*. Greenleaf Center for Servant-Leadership.

Greenleaf, R. K. (1977). *Servant leadership: A journey into the nature of legitimate power and greatness*. Paulist Press.

Hersey, P., & Blanchard, K. H. (1969). Life cycle theory of leadership. *Training & Development Journal*, *23*(5), 26–34.

Hersey, P. H., & Blanchard, K. H. (1977). *Management of organizational behavior: Utilizing human resources* (3rd ed.). Prentice-Hall.

Hersey, P. H., Blanchard, K. H., & Johnson, D. E. (2012). *Management of organizational behavior: Leading human resources* (10th ed.). Pearson.

Hoch, J. E., Bommer, W. H., Dulebohn, J. H., & Wu, D. (2018). Do ethical, authentic, and servant leadership explain variance above and beyond transformational leadership? A meta-analysis. *Journal of Management*, *44*(2), 501–529. https://doi.org/10.1177/0149206316665461

Lee, A., Lyubovnikova, J., Tian, A. W., & Knight, C. (2020). Servant leadership: A meta-analytic examination of incremental contribution, moderation, and mediation. *Journal of Occupational and Organizational Psychology*, *93*(1), 1–44. https://doi.org/10.1111/joop.12265

Lemoine, G. J., Hartnell, C. A., & Leroy, H. (2019). Taking stock of moral approaches to leadership: An integrative review of ethical, authentic, and servant leadership. *Academy of Management Annals*, *13*(1), 148–187. https://doi.org/10.5465/annals.2016.0121

Liden, R. C., Wayne, S. J., Zhao, H., & Henderson, D. (2008). Servant leadership: Development of a multidimensional measure and multi-level assessment. *The Leadership Quarterly*, *19*(2), 161–177. https://doi.org/10.1016/j.leaqua.2008.01.006

Lux, A. A., Grover, S. L., & Teo, S. T. T. (2023). Reframing commitment in authentic leadership: Untangling relationship–outcome processes. *Journal of Management & Organization*, *29*(1), 103–121. https://doi.org/10.1017/jmo.2019.78

Neider, L. L., & Schriesheim, C. A. (2011). The authentic leadership inventory (ALI): Development and empirical tests. *The Leadership Quarterly*, *22*(6), 1146–1164. https://doi.org/10.1016/j.leaqua.2011.09.008

Peus, C., Wesche, J. S., Streicher, B., Braun, S., & Frey, D. (2012). Authentic leadership: An empirical test of its antecedents, consequences, and mediating mechanisms. *Journal of Business Ethics*, *107*(3), 331–348. https://doi.org/10.1007/s10551-011-1042-3

Spears, L. C. (1995). *Reflections on leadership: How Robert K. Greenleaf's theory of servant-leadership influenced today's top management thinkers*. Wiley.

Stein, A. M., Bell, C. M., & Min, Y. A. (2020). Does 'the servant as leader' translate into Chinese? A cross-cultural meta-analysis of servant leadership. *European Journal of Work and Organizational Psychology*, *29*(3), 315–329. https://doi.org/10.1080/1359432X.2019.1703681

Strube, M. J., & Garcia, J. E. (1981). A meta-analytic investigation of Fiedler's contingency model of leadership effectiveness. *Psychological Bulletin*, *90*(2), 307–321. https://doi.org/10.1037/0033-2909.90.2.307

Thompson, G., & Glasø, L. (2015). Situational leadership theory: A test from three perspectives. *Leadership & Organization Development Journal*, *36*(5), 527–544. https://doi.org/10.1108/LODJ-10-2013-0130

Thompson, G., & Vecchio, R. P. (2009). Situational leadership theory: A test of three versions. *The Leadership Quarterly*, *20*(5), 837–848. https://doi.org/10.1016/j.leaqua.2009.06.014

Van Dierendonck, D. (2011). Servant leadership: A review and synthesis. *Journal of Management*, *37*(4), 1228–1261. https://doi.org/10.1177/0149206310380462

Van Dierendonck, D., & Nuijten, I. (2011). The servant leadership survey: Development and validation of a multidimensional measure. *Journal of Business and Psychology*, *26*, 249–267. https://doi.org/10.1007/s10869-010-9194-1

Walumbwa, F. O., Avolio, B. J., Gardner, W. L., Wernsing, T. S., & Peterson, S. J. (2008). Authentic leadership: Development and validation of a theory-based measure. *Journal of Management*, *34*(1), 89–126. https://doi.org/10.1177/0149206307308913

World Economic Forum. (2015). *Outlook on the global agenda 2015*. World Economic Forum.

Yukl, G. (2012). Effective leadership behavior: What we know and what questions need more attention. *Academy of Management Perspectives*, *26*(4), 66–85. https://doi.org/10.5465/amp.2012.0088

Zhang, Y., Guo, Y., Zhang, M., Xu, S., Liu, X., & Newman, A. (2021). Antecedents and outcomes of authentic leadership across culture: A meta-analytic review. *Asia Pacific Journal of Management*, 1–37. https://doi.org/10.1007/s10490-021-09762-0

Zhang, Y., Waldman, D. A., Han, Y.-L., & Li, X.-B. (2015). Paradoxical leader behaviors in people management: Antecedents and consequences. *Academy of Management Journal*, *58*(2), 538–566. https://doi.org/10.5465/amj.2012.0995

5
CHARISMATIC AND TRANSFORMATIONAL LEADERSHIP

Overview

This chapter introduces you to charismatic leadership and transformational leadership theories. It starts by exploring what exactly charisma is, who has it, and how it relates to leadership. You'll watch Martin Sheen's powerful, impassioned speech at WE Day as a version of charismatic leadership.

We discuss where charisma comes from, including aspects of our appearance, personality traits, general intelligence, behaviour, and context as 'sources' of charismatic leadership. Barack Obama radiates assurance and composure during his Nobel Peace Prize lecture, showing us an entirely different side of charismatic leadership.

Next, we take a behavioural approach to developing charisma, studying what charismatic leaders actually do and the effect that they have on their followers, before considering the dark side of charisma. You'll discover your own charismatic leadership capabilities with a reflective exercise.

The chapter culminates with an overview of transformational leadership, exploring the dimensions it comprises, and the qualities that enable leaders to transform others. You'll learn that it's not just about change – it's about engaging followers' willing participation through their own end values.

Video 5.1: Martin Sheen – WE Day

Video 5.2: Barack Obama – Nobel Peace Prize lecture

Speech 5.1: Martin Luther King Jr – I Have a Dream

Quiz 5.1: Have you got charisma?

Quiz 5.2: Transformational leadership

Charisma is an enigmatic quality long associated with exceptional leadership, and yet it's a concept that's so poorly understood. We have made great progress in recent years to bring charisma out of the shadowy murk of conjecture and into the sober light of day, unriddling its mysteries such that we can all harness and benefit from a more charismatic approach.

In this chapter we'll examine charismatic leadership from a few different angles to get a complete picture of this elusive construct and help guide you to develop your own charisma. Afterwards, we'll consider transformational leadership as an extension of charismatic leadership.

CHARISMA

Charisma has fascinated people throughout the ages, but it's rather difficult to define. We tend to know it when we've experienced it first hand – after interacting with some people, even briefly, we can tell that they're particularly charismatic; we can feel their presence and influence; we're drawn to them somehow.

But it's hard to put into precise words what exactly is happening in those moments when we're interacting with charismatic people. What is it about them, specifically, that leads us to conclude that they're charismatic, or is it is something that they're doing to have this curious effect on others?

Charisma in the ancient Greek translates literally to mean a 'divine gift' (Castelnovo et al., 2017). It stems from classical Greek mythology where the root word *charis* signified many things, including charm, beauty, and grace (Antonakis et al., 2016). And while that's certainly profound, it's not particularly instructive for leadership development.

Throughout history we've often seen charisma attributed to emperors and kings who were bestowed with this divine gift that enabled their reign. Such narratives mirror the religious political arguments used to legitimise sovereign rule, for example, the Mandate of Heaven in China and the Divine Right of Kings in Europe.

Weber (1947, 1968) continued these divine overtones when describing charisma as an extraordinary power that gave people 'the discretion and the means' to impose their will over individuals, groups, organisations, and countries (Sturm & Antonakis, 2015, p. 139). This mystical power is then what makes it possible for monarchs to rule, generals to command, and clerics to inspire.

Today we use charisma to describe the influential politicians, executives, celebrities, and athletes who act as leaders in our modern society (Grabo et al., 2017), and charisma is universally considered a characteristic of effective leadership, even across cultures (Den Hartog et al., 1999).

Charisma is therefore intimately connected with leadership and leadership scholars have studied it extensively over the last 60 years (Banks et al., 2017). But up until very recently charisma wasn't clearly defined or articulated, with most writers referring to it vaguely as a rare talent that some leaders have which allows them to unify followers around a cause (Antonakis et al., 2016).

So, what exactly is charisma from a leadership perspective?

CHARISMATIC LEADERSHIP

House (1977) introduced the first secular notion of 'charismatic leadership' as a distinct style or approach that's grounded in psychology. He argued that this 'divine gift' is more likely a complex interaction between individual leaders' characteristics, their behaviour, the characteristics of their followers, and prevailing situational factors – this was the first breakthrough in our understanding of charismatic leadership.

Unfortunately House (1977) defined charismatic leaders in his seminal work as those who have a strong charismatic effect on their followers. Other scholars followed suit. For example, Yukl (1999) wrote that charismatic leadership is evident in followers' 'attitude of awe and enthusiasm' (p. 294), while Klein and House (1995) continued to describe it in vague terms as 'a fire that ignites followers' energy and commitment, producing results above and beyond the call of duty' (p. 183).

Charismatic leadership has since been defined either in terms of its effects on followers, or else as an unknowable quality or miraculous ability (Banks et al., 2017). I hope you're starting to see why that's unhelpful. Defining charismatic leadership by the outcomes that it's supposed to produce tells us nothing about its actual attributes and functions, and calling it unknowable or miraculous closes the door on all scientific study.

Antonakis et al. (2016) made the second breakthrough by examining charismatic leadership definitions across six decades of research (1954–2014) and extracting a single coherent definition to encompasses the common elements, while keeping the integrity of the core concept.

Charismatic leadership is therefore best defined as 'values-based, symbolic, and emotion-laden leader signaling' (Antonakis et al., 2016, p. 304). Finally we have specific terms to explain the exact nature of those 'complex interactions' alluded to by House (1977). However, Antonakis and colleagues' definition is as elegant as it is complex in itself – what exactly is 'signalling' and how do values, symbols, and emotions feature?

The latest breakthroughs are then made by a collection of works that appear soon after in a special issue of *The Leadership Quarterly* (Antonakis & Gardner, 2017); these contributions apply the signalling-based definition to more comprehensively articulate how charismatic leadership actually works. We'll draw on this body of work to explore charismatic leadership from several different perspectives.

Over the next few sections, we'll start by discussing the emotional basis of charismatic leadership, and then we'll unpack what 'signalling' means, first by understanding how we send signals, and then considering what kind of signals encourage followers to see us as charismatic leaders. We'll discuss aspects of our physical appearance, personality traits, behaviour, and the leadership context as 'sources' of charismatic leadership 'signals'.

Emotional Basis

House (1977) explains that charismatic leaders create intense emotional interactions with their followers, and that it's these strong emotions that then encourage followers' devotion to the leader and action. Charismatic leadership therefore works by influencing followers on an emotional level (Antonakis et al., 2016); we *feel* the effects of charisma and that's what shapes our thoughts and behaviours.

Here's a simplified three-stage outline of how our emotions work (Frijda, 1986; Scherer, 1984). First, we'll have a thought that triggers an emotion, the thought is either a cognitive appraisal of something external that we've perceived with our senses (i.e. sight, hearing, smell, taste, touch). For example, I see a cute cat and I think 'what a beautiful creature' and then feel awe and contentment.

Or else the thought can be part of our internal stream of consciousness as we're making sense of the world around us. For example, I could be reflecting on a colleague engaging me in conversation and think 'my ideas are worth discussing' and then feel fulfilment and pride. Internal thoughts can be unconscious too, so that sometimes we'll trigger emotions without realising why.

Next, we experience the emotion both physiologically and psychologically, which is to say that our bodies and our thoughts change. For example, when we're happy we smile, when we're confident we stand up taller, when we're excited our pupils dilate. We start thinking differently too – for example, when we're scared we start looking for threats, when we're happy we recall other happy memories. Again, you might not even notice that you're doing these things.

The resulting final stage is what we call an 'action tendency' and it's about how we then change our behaviour. For example, when we're angry we might feel an urge to confront the source of our anger, raise our voice, or get aggressive. When we're sad we might want to withdraw from social interactions to seek solitude.

We rapidly and automatically move through these three stages when we experience the six 'basic' emotions: anger, disgust, surprise, happiness, fear, and sadness (Siedlecka & Denson, 2019), whereas our more 'complex' emotions that are a combination of two or more basic emotions (e.g. love, embarrassment, envy, gratitude, guilt, pride, worry, grief, jealousy, or regret) require an active process of reflection and evaluation.

Now, back to charismatic leadership. We can think about our followers' emotions then as the psychological 'mechanism' that translates our charismatic leadership into the specific effects that it has on our followers' thoughts and behaviour. You can use charismatic leadership to influence your followers' behaviour by eliciting different kinds of emotions. For example, Malcolm X often invoked anger, Martin Luther King Jr used pride, love, and compassion, while Steve Jobs alternated between shaming and praise (Sy et al., 2018).

Passionate public speeches are an overt application of charismatic leadership where the speakers trigger intense emotional responses to help connect the audience with their message. Here's one example that epitomises this kind of charismatic approach. The following video (Video 5.1) shows Martin Sheen speaking at WE Day in Vancouver (2010). His message is very interesting, and I want you to pay careful attention to how he delivers it.

Video 5.1

Martin Sheen – WE Day

Summary

Martin Sheen calls for unity by reframing the three basic needs of every human being as freedom, justice, and healing. He condemns the gross inequalities of food, clothing, and shelter as what divides us, and upholds the absolute necessity for freedom, justice, and healing that unites us. His speech is values based, emotion-laden, and symbolic to serve as an example of charismatic leadership.

Image Alt Text: https://www.youtube.com/watch?v=IcYqXI9I4yU

I'm always moved by Martin's speech. Could you feel his charisma? Here's some of what I noticed about the delivery. He shares his values and what he believes to be important. He speaks with passion, changing his tone and volume, and pauses deliberately at specific times. He's expressive with his hands, paces around the stage and then stops at key moments. He uses the story of 'earth as a village' to simplify a complex perspective. The language is more poetry than prose with frequent repetition, juxtaposition, imagery, and meter. And at the end he challenges each member of his audience with personal responsibility to draw us into his message – it's on you, and it's on me.

So which emotions should we entice our followers to feel? Well, that depends on what we want to accomplish.

A skilful charismatic leader can trigger specific emotions to direct their followers' behaviour at a target, which can be a person, an idea, or another group. Depending on whether the target is inside or outside of the charismatic leader's group, and whether the intended behaviour is positive and supportive, or negative and condemning, will dictate which kind of emotions we should elicit.

Sy et al. (2018) propose the following based on four categories of moral emotions identified by Haidt (2003).

Positive behaviour directed at an in-group target can be encouraged by triggering 'other-suffering' emotions which include sympathy and compassion. It's about enticing emotions that will make us want to help or comfort others. For example,

I can highlight how much a colleague is struggling with their work to encourage my followers to support them.

Positive behaviour directed at an out-group target can be encouraged by triggering 'other-praising' emotions which include gratitude, awe, elevation, and admiration. It's about emotions that will make us want to develop beneficial relationships with others. For example, I can highlight how much an external partner has helped us to encourage my followers to connect with them.

Negative behaviour directed at an in-group target can be encouraged by triggering 'self-conscious' emotions which include shame, embarrassment, and guilt. It's about emotions that will make us want to withdraw or apologise to restore our status and repair the relationship. For example, I can highlight how a team member has transgressed our norms or caused harm to encourage my followers to exclude them or seek reparations.

Negative behaviour directed at an out-group target can be encouraged by triggering 'other-condemning' emotions which include anger, contempt, and disgust. It's about emotions that will make us want to be aggressive, seek revenge, or condemn others. For example, I can highlight the injustice of a social system to encourage my followers to attack those who symbolise that system.

Now that we've uncovered emotions as the mechanisms through which charismatic leadership works to affect our followers' behaviour, let's consider how exactly we might trigger these emotions by exploring the concept of 'signalling'.

Signalling

Everything about you, everything you say and do, how you say and do it, and what you don't say and don't do, where, with whom, and at what time, is constantly sending a message to everyone who can observe and receive those messages. These messages are what we call 'signals', and we can think about signals as including everything you do that's visible and in part designed to communicate (Spence, 2002, p. 434).

Signals therefore include all of the possible messages, or 'cues', that you're either actively sending or passively emanating, that can provide a basis for followers to infer ideas about you and your leadership (Reh et al., 2017). Your followers are constantly watching you as their leader and they're picking up on the cues or signals that you're sending.

For example, when I interrupt a colleague who's speaking, I'm signalling to them and anyone else who's watching that I think I'm more important than the speaker I interrupted, among a host of other potential interpretations of that specific interaction.

Signalling then is the process of sending signals or cues to your followers and includes all manner of communication modes. Since these signals that we're sending are messages and contain information that our followers decode, it's essentially a system of language, and therefore includes written, oral, and nonverbal forms (Banks et al., 2017), as well as how we use signs and symbols to convey meaning – for a primer on visual semiotics or the study of signs, see Dunleavy (2020).

For example, if I show up to a meeting in a t-shirt and jeans, I'm signalling that this is a less formal discussion than if I wore a dress shirt and suit. There's a lot of information here that we can interpret: my casual clothing, the context of this meeting, who else is attending, what we'll be discussing, etc. What my followers infer from this signal will then shape their behaviour during the meeting; their comments may be more candid and conversational.

Leaders can therefore influence their followers' behaviour by sending signals that will trigger specific thoughts or emotions (Antonakis et al., 2016). Signals can convey honest information, but they can be actively manipulated too and contrived by leaders to send specific messages (Reh et al., 2017). Our goal in this chapter is then to understand what signals convey a sense of charismatic leadership and how we can use this approach proactively to make ourselves more influential as leaders.

Followers' interpretation of signals is socially embedded, which is to say that we come to understand what things mean through group membership and interaction with others. But we have such diverse backgrounds and experiences that there's plenty of room for misinterpretation.

As leaders we're constantly sending all sorts of different signals to our followers, many of them without us even knowing. Let's now consider what they are, so that we can actively craft ourselves and our leadership approach to be more charismatic. We'll start with our appearance, then look at traits, behaviours, and context.

Stable Appearance

How we appear to followers and other people affects how charismatic they'll think that we are. Let's consider how and why first in terms of our more stable physical characteristics like height, physique, attractiveness, and sex. Later in the chapter when we talk about behaviour, we'll explore aspects of our appearance that are within our immediate control like facial expressions, posture, and fashion, and then move on to consider how we can use our voice.

Physical characteristics are related to charismatic leadership. To understand why, we can take an evolutionary perspective by looking first at how people choose which leaders to follow.

Historically leaders exist to help solve a coordination problem – for example hunting, combat, construction, or group movement (Van Vugt et al., 2008). We decided who we'd follow using a set of automatic mental processes that let us make fast and accurate judgments about the likelihood that a leadership candidate would be successful in coordinating the activities of others.

Physical cues that signal leadership potential include height, attractiveness, formidability, and facial symmetry (Grabo et al., 2017) as evidence of good genes and strong health. We attribute more charisma to leaders demonstrating these characteristics. For example, people who are taller and stronger (Hamstra, 2014), or more physically attractive (Friedman et al., 1988) appear more charismatic to followers.

Our assessments vary depending on the nature of the coordination task that we're facing. For example, people prefer younger looking leaders for situations that demand change, movement, and exploration, while older looking leaders are preferred in times of stability and growth (Spisak et al., 2014). Similarly, we prefer leaders who look more masculine in competitive environments and prefer more feminine looking leaders when cooperation is called for instead (Spisak et al., 2012).

Physical characteristics tend to be less important in signalling leadership potential and charisma when we can directly observe the candidates' performance, and more important when followers have incomplete knowledge about the leaders, or when leaders are more distant (e.g. politicians or senior executives) and their leadership potential is harder to estimate (Antonakis & Jacquart, 2013). That's when we rely more on physical appearance like attractiveness and height to judge leadership competence.

I'm sure you can see why that's far from ideal, and these processes exist from a young age. For example, children aged 5–13 predict presidential elections about as well as adults (Antonakis & Dalgas, 2009) because they're using the same physical cues to pick leaders. The effects are stronger for senior executive roles where physical cues account for around 30% of the effect, compared to 8% for those running for public office (Lawson et al., 2010).

We carry this evolutionary intellectual baggage with us to this day. While it doesn't paint a very inclusive picture for diverse leaders, remember that these mental processes only work before we've got objective performance data. Looks cease to matter when people discover your leadership skills. However, getting physically fit will make your first impression more charismatic by signalling strength, attractiveness, and dedication – that's something we can all work towards.

Personality Traits

Your Big Five personality traits and general intelligence, or 'cognitive ability', are associated with charismatic leadership and can make you seem more or less charismatic. Let's look more closely at which personality dimensions signal charismatic leadership to our followers and how much of a difference they can make.

Banks et al. (2017) found that around 60% of your charismatic leadership can be predicted by a combination of extroversion (25%), agreeableness (20%), and cognitive ability (15%). That's to say that smarter people who are more extroverted and agreeable tend to come across as more charismatic leaders to their followers.

Recall that extroverts are emotionally expressive, assertive, and actively engage in social settings, while more agreeable people are considerate, helpful, generous, and trustworthy. People with these qualities may find it easier to express their emotions, share their values and passions, and consider how their actions affect others, which aligns with the emotion-laden, values-based core of charismatic leadership.

Cognitive ability helps you to scan, assess, and understand complex and fast-changing environments to develop suitable solutions, as well as adapt and respond appropriately in order then to enable and encourage others to engage with your vision. More intelligent people may therefore be better at consciously and intentionally sending relevant charismatic signals to inspire their followers towards specific action.

But more isn't always better and the relationships between traits and charisma are non-linear (Banks et al., 2017). For example, at a certain point an overly agreeable leader will start to come across as an obsequious and fawning sycophant who lacks the determination to pursue their own values, and so they will then cease to be charismatic. Likewise a leader's intelligence, at very high or very low levels, can undermine their charismatic leadership as they either fail to connect with their followers by coming across as arrogant, or else cannot inspire followers' confidence.

Naturally we'll find some overlap between these traits and our next section on behaviour because it's impossible for our followers to directly assess our personality. The mind itself is not observable, and rather, we only infer its attributes from what we can see: our visible behaviour, including for example our actions, expressions, rhetoric, and gestures.

Behaviour

What we do and how we do it can send the strongest charismatic signals and so we'll spend a bit more time studying charismatic leadership behaviour because that's something we can all learn and practise to make ourselves more influential and effective leaders. First, we'll consider what kind of signals we should be sending to appear more charismatic. Then we'll look at how exactly we can send those signals, working our way down to specific behaviours and aspects of appearance that are within our control, including posture, facial expressions, voice, and fashion.

Sources of Charisma

We're interested in sending three kinds of signals – first, those that make us appear more charismatic, which we can think about as 'sources' of our charisma, then the signals that encourage followers to accept us as charismatic leaders which allows us to influence them, and finally signals that enable us to 'use' our charismatic leadership to shape followers' behaviour by triggering specific emotions.

Let's start with our source of charisma. We can appear more charismatic to followers by signalling that we're competent and benevolent (Castelnovo et al., 2017).

We're more likely to trust and defer authority to people who we think are competent. Typical signals of competence are expertise, prestige, and dominance. For example, we're more easily influenced on certain matters by people who have a well-established reputation in the relevant field. We infer from their reputation that they have specialised knowledge and skills; they 'know best', so we're more likely to follow their lead and defer decision-making to their counsel.

But competence alone is not enough; we're wary of being exploited by clever manipulators. For followers to trust us we must also signal our benevolence, indicating that we care about them and their well-being and success. Typical signals of benevolence include making personal sacrifices, generosity, and investing 'costly' resources. For example, time is our most valuable possession, and so we trust leaders who take the time to get to know their followers' needs and then make decisions that support their ambitions.

But you can be charismatic without having any leadership influence whatsoever. For the charismatic effect to occur and for followers to willingly succumb to our influence they must also accept us as charismatic leaders. We can encourage followers' acceptance by demonstrating that we're credible and that we share the followers' values (Antonakis et al., 2016).

Credibility is about whether followers believe in the leader and their signals. It's a function of truth, persuasion, and the audience in context and over time (Self & Roberts, 2019). For example, we're more likely to believe ideas that resemble what we already think is true, or a well-articulated concept over something vague; we're more likely to believe in leaders who are consistent with how they behave across different contexts, with different people, and over time, compared to leaders who are capricious and unpredictable.

Charismatic people cannot become charismatic leaders without credibility. Therefore we must appropriately pitch our leadership behaviour, signals, and ambitions within the scope of our abilities, consistently (Antonakis et al., 2016). Misrepresenting our intentions, saying one thing and doing another, or signalling unrealistic actions risks undermining our credibility and jeopardising the charismatic effect altogether.

Charismatic leaders can be loved but also much loathed by those who do not share in the leader's values – charisma is in the eye of the beholder (Castelnovo et al., 2017). We're enamoured only when, and to the extent that, charismatic leaders' signalling resonates with our values and those of the social in-group where we collectively belong. For example, devout Christians feel that Christian preachers are more charismatic than non-Christian preachers (Schjoedt et al., 2011).

Social groups of every kind coalesce around a collective identity that embodies the 'prototypical' or most essential version of group members (Hogg, 2001). As charismatic leaders we can send the 'right signals' by positioning ourselves as demonstrating key aspects of the ideal social identity and thereby speaking to shared values. Signalling what is right for the collective might seem simple on the surface, but should typically draw upon a keen and detailed analysis of the complex external and internal leadership environment (Banks et al., 2017).

Let's see how we can use charismatic leadership to overcome a challenging situation by signalling competence, benevolence, credibility, and speaking to shared values. In Video 5.2 Barack Obama has just been awarded a Nobel Peace Prize and invited to give a lecture that's broadcast all over the world. The decision was controversial because America was at war with Afghanistan, and Obama defended war in his lecture. I want you to watch the first 12 minutes.

Video 5.2

Barack Obama – Nobel Peace Prize Lecture

Summary

Barack Obama talks about efforts to control the destructive power of war, and to create a lasting peace. He radiates competence and credibility with his knowledge and calm composure, speaking to the imperatives of peace and prosperity as global shared values, and showing benevolence by putting himself to the moral hazard of defending those who rely on him and protecting the rules of law, liberty, and self-determination.

Image Alt Text: https://www.nobelprize.org/prizes/peace/2009/obama/lecture/

I'm fascinated by Obama's mastery of charismatic leadership here. Within minutes I'm ready to accept that Obama knows best, to embrace his political leadership and decision-making, ready to acknowledge that some armed conflict is necessary and even morally justified, and all in the name of peace. It's a frightfully clever persuasion achieved by sending all the right charismatic leadership signals to lull his audience into willing deference.

Now that we know what kind of impression we're trying to make as charismatic leaders, next we'll explore some of the specific things that we can do to send these charismatic signals.

Sending Charismatic Signals

Conger (1999) and Antonakis et al. (2016) explain that sending charismatic signals includes three stages:

First, identifying a bold and desirable vision, direction, or state of affairs that seizes an opportunity or reforms a lamentable issue, while being sensitive to the current environment.

Next, communicating symbolically through speech and behaviour to make the message vivid and clear, while encouraging unity and embodying the values of the collective.

And finally, demonstrating conviction and passion for the mission by personal example, risk-taking, and emotional displays.

We can think about charismatic leaders as skilled actors, working hard to apply specific verbal and nonverbal communication strategies or 'signalling techniques' that allow them to influence their followers (Antonakis et al., 2016). Charismatic leadership is a performance that's carefully designed to persuade an audience and inspire them to act in a particular way towards an intended target (Spencer, 1973). Let's explore some of these techniques so that you can deploy them in your own leadership practice. We'll start with verbal communication which is about how you use language to frame and convey your message.

You can employ the following charismatic communication techniques in your leadership messages to make them more influential (Antonakis et al., 2012). Include metaphors to simplify complex messages and invoke symbolic understanding. Share personal stories to connect with your audience and make your messages more memorable. Draw contrasts to highlight issues and focus attention. Pose rhetorical questions to prompt your audience to engage by considering their own views. Articulate core values and beliefs to clarify your moral stance and show your similarity to the social collective. Set ambitious goals with confidence that they can be achieved to inspire belief.

Let's consider an example from the context of a social movement: Martin Luther King Jr's influential 'I have a dream' speech in August 1963. Listen to the recording or read the transcript (Speech 5.1).

Speech 5.1

Martin Luther King Jr – I Have a Dream

Summary

King outlines the long history of racial injustice in America and encourages his audience to peaceably hold their country accountable to its founding promise of freedom, justice, and equality. His speech demonstrates the verbal signals of charismatic leadership.

Image Alt Text: https://www.npr.org/2010/01/18/122701268/i-have-a-dream-speech-in-its-entirety

---

Reading the transcript, you'll see King deploy many of these verbal techniques to great effect. He uses inclusive language to signal his belonging with the audience: 'I am happy to join with you today.' He repeats the phrase 'One hundred years later' to list the many injustices still faced by his people after the Emancipation Proclamation was signed. He uses a metaphor, referring to the Declaration of Independence as a bank cheque promising rights to life, liberty, and the pursuit of happiness to all Americans, a cheque that's bounced for citizens of colour. And he contrasts their poverty with the 'vast ocean of material prosperity' enjoyed by others, among many other verbal techniques. King's dream resonated as a powerful beacon of hope and inspired sweeping social reforms across the United States (Castelnovo et al., 2017).

Next, we'll explore some of the nonverbal charismatic techniques that we can use.

Nonverbal Charismatic Signals

We gather information from others' body language, as well as from their specific words. When trying to win over an audience, you must realise that you're not only judged on the content you present (Koppensteiner et al., 2015). Charismatic leaders therefore use nonverbal signals and communication techniques to complement and enhance their verbal messages (Antonakis et al., 2012).

We'll focus our attention on the use of posture and hand gestures, facial expressions, gaze and eye contact, voice, and style of dress. We can use these techniques to convey signals of power, competence, and intelligence to make ourselves and our messages more charismatic and influential (Reh et al., 2017).

Adopt an open body posture with arms and legs uncrossed to signal power and status by symbolically occupying more space (Schubert et al., 2011); take an upright posture with your head up, chin parallel to the floor, and shoulders back to signal confidence and intelligence (Murphy et al., 2003).

Use hand gestures to emphasise your verbal message and direct attention; vertical motions punctuate key points and horizontal motions can illustrate movement or progress. More expansive gestures signal dominance (Koppensteiner et al., 2016) and more hand movements overall signal an extroverted personality (Koppensteiner et al., 2015).

Your facial expressions send strong signals of felt emotions and should align with your verbal message. Keep your face relaxed, with eyebrows neutral or lowered to signal power and confidence (Aguinis et al., 1998; Keating et al., 1977); smile to make yourself look more trustworthy (Krumhuber et al., 2007).

Be mindful of your gaze – that is, where you're looking and for how long. Look directly at focal objects and other people, make eye contact, and hold your gaze for longer to signal that you're more powerful (Dovidio & Ellyson, 1982) and intelligent (Murphy et al., 2003).

Vary the volume, tone, pitch, and pace of your voice to create a more passionate delivery. Speak louder to signal your confidence (Kimble & Seidel, 1991), and with a lower pitch to come across stronger and more competent (Klofstad et al., 2015). Adjust your pace, speaking more slowly to signal dominance, faster to show excitement, and use pauses for emphasis (Duez, 1985).

Overall, leaders who display expressive nonverbal behaviour – that is, using gestures, eye contact, variations in tone and the like – appear more charismatic than those who communicate dispassionately (Koppensteiner et al., 2015).

How you navigate the physical environment is important too. Consider that power is a social construct that's inherently tied to our use of physical space (Reh et al., 2017). For example, standing on a podium, in front of a lectern, or sitting behind a large desk signals that whoever occupies this space has more authority.

Now let's talk about fashion. Most people strive to learn and follow social norms of dress, etiquette, and behaviour to fit in and be accepted by their social groups, and to avoid disapproval, ridicule, or exclusion (Cialdini & Goldstein, 2004).

Yet intentional nonconformity actually signals autonomy, higher status, and competence because onlookers infer that you're in a powerful enough position to be immune to the social risks (Bellezza et al., 2014), which is why some wealthy executives can dress *poorgeoisie* in cheap jeans and sneakers – it's a status symbol to be able to not conform.

Add a dash of nonconformity to your appearance to create a more charismatic impression. For example, to work I might wear black jeans with leather dress shoes, a plain t-shirt, and suit jacket with my characteristic silver crow-skull necklace. I'm always well-groomed and professional, but also distinct and memorable.

Cultivate a unique style not only as a healthy and authentic expression of your character, but also as a way of creating an impressive appearance that will make you more charismatic, and therefore more influential as a leader. Be willing to stand out and people will take notice.

Now that we've covered how we can send charismatic signals, let's find out how charismatic you are as a leader. The following quiz (Quiz 5.1) will ask you a series of questions about your behaviour and interactions with others to generate a score.

Quiz 5.1

Have You Got Charisma?

Image Alt Text: https://ecuau.qualtrics.com/jfe/form/SV_efaXjQaDbWgd130

You can work to make yourself a more charismatic leader by practising charismatic verbal and nonverbal communication techniques that will signal to followers your competence, benevolence, credibility, and shared values.

You can also combine a more charismatic approach with any of the other leadership theories that we've discussed. For example, drawing on charismatic communication can enhance a servant or authentic leadership style, making you more effective overall.

Next, let's consider the role of context as another potential source of charismatic leadership.

Context

We can think about charismatic leadership as a set of group processes that emerge as a result of the social context (Calás, 1993). Such charismatic leadership relationships tend to arise during times of crisis, when people are feeling vulnerable and looking for someone who can help them to feel safe and confident again – someone that they can put their faith in.

When we're faced with crises, or situations that are volatile, uncertain, complex, and ambiguous, we can feel out of step with the unknown environment around us, which leaves us feeling afraid, vulnerable, and incompetent. The more uncertain the situation, the more desperately we want to understand what's going on so that we can feel safe and strong again. Castelnovo et al. (2017) call this 'epistemic hunger', which is the need to know and feel secure in that knowledge.

We're driven to understand our environment because that gives us a sense of control; even if the situation is unfavourable, at least we know what to expect. Not knowing what's going on feels like you're losing control over your environment, and that's terrifying. The desperate need to know makes us yearn for the reassuring confidence of the charismatic leader and so we're eagerly willing to accept their influence and authority.

Opinions vary about whether charismatic individuals emerge as leaders during uncertain and challenging times because people are more likely to accept them, or if charismatic leadership is itself socially constructed by people who build up an individual to fulfil that role (Castelnovo et al., 2017). We can revisit Martin Luther King Jr's famous speech as an example of the latter.

For example, Carson (1987) argues that the King 'myth' departs from an accurate historical account because it attributes too much to his qualities as a leader and too little to the social factors that enabled him to address that audience at a pivotal time on a national stage. Our earlier analysis focused only on King's charismatic verbal communication, and by emphasising the individual without considering the wider context of the civil rights movement we exaggerate King's influence and distort his actual significant contribution.

We no longer think of charismatic leaders as saviours who appear to us as role models and objects of identification based on followers' situational needs (cf. House, 1977; Spencer, 1973), and now know that a crisis isn't necessary for charismatic leadership to emerge (Antonakis et al., 2016). However, uncertainty is prevalent in modern organisations and some vulnerabilities like uncertainty can serve as contextual triggers that enable a charismatic approach to be more effective (Banks et al., 2017).

Use this knowledge proactively to first assess when your followers are feeling particularly vulnerable and then see that as an opportunity to best support them with a charismatic approach. Unite your followers around a common cause by signalling both the urgency of the situation and the need for coordinated action to overcome the challenges that you're facing (Grabo et al., 2017).

When you're pitching a charismatic vision for change, be mindful of your audience and the context. You'll need to make a strong connection between the collective 'now' and your articulated future so that you keep representing the values of the group as you advance into the new unknown without crossing the subtle threshold into values that your group won't accept (Castelnovo et al., 2017).

We can think about this values threshold as becoming more lenient in times of strife, when people will readily accept radical change to escape their current predicaments.

Charismatic leaders can equally invoke a threat that isn't real, or exaggerate one that is, to make their audience more receptive to change beyond the normal bounds of their values.

I hope you're starting to see why charismatic leadership can be so dangerous. Let's now consider some of the outcomes of charismatic leadership, before we delve into its fraught and amoral nature.

Outcomes

Charismatic leadership works across all levels of an organisation, from frontline staff to their supervisors and all the way up to chief executives and boards of directors. And not only in business, but in the context of social movements, politics, and religious groups too; it's not tied to an industry or a position and can be used among peers as well as between superiors and subordinates, because it's simply a process of influence (Antonakis et al., 2016).

Meta-analytic review of ample research in organisational settings reveals that charismatic leadership strongly improves the performance of individuals, groups, and firms (Banks et al., 2017). For example, followers' own individual performance improves by 33% and they engage in 28% more organisational citizenship behaviour, which is about willingly going beyond their role requirements to help the organisation succeed; and the overall performance of organisations improves by around 8% on average when leaders adopt a charismatic approach.

The positive effects of charismatic leadership on individual outcomes work across different settings, tasks, and followers. It can operate at a distance too; for example, watching a charismatic leader on video can be almost as effective as seeing them in person, which is particularly relevant to the contemporary leadership challenge of flexible and remote work. Even using a more charismatic verbal communication style alone, with all other factors kept the same, will improve followers' task performance by 17% (Meslec et al., 2020).

Recall from an earlier section that followers' emotions act as the mechanisms that translate our charismatic leadership into the specific effects that it has on their thoughts and behaviour; that's *how* charismatic leadership works to create these positive follower outcomes. You can draw on the various sources of charismatic leadership that are available to you, including your appearance, traits, behaviour, and verbal and nonverbal communication to send signals that will trigger specific emotions and influence your followers.

Learning these techniques will make you more influential as a leader, but what you do with your newfound power is entirely up to you. And so, to conclude our conversation, let's now turn to the 'amoral' nature of charismatic leadership, which isn't to be confused with 'immoral'.

Amorality

Charismatic leadership is one of the few amoral theories in the sense that it does not have an explicit moral component – it provides no guidance at all about what's right and wrong, or how you should and shouldn't use its principles. That's unusual because most contemporary leadership theories take a clear moral stance that your behaviour should contribute positively to the lives of those you lead and to the societies in which you're involved.

Becoming an effective charismatic leader will make you more influential and help you to inspire followers towards your vision, but it doesn't mean that your ambitions will be of any benefit to either your followers or the wider society. You can equally use these same skills to start a suicide cult or rally a militia against the state as set up a charitable organisation or make a for-profit business more socially responsible.

The evolutionary and emotional foundations of charismatic leadership make its effects so powerful that followers may not fully weigh the moral consequences of their behaviour in pursuing the leaders' vision (Popper, 2001). Grabo et al. (2017) describe charisma as 'hijacking' our instincts. When interacting with charismatic leaders, followers even disengage parts of their brain responsible for regulating behaviour, bypassing their rational mind (Schjoedt et al., 2013).

Charisma can be either a blessing or a curse. For every Barack Obama, Martin Luther King Jr, and Nelson Mandela, we've had an Adolf Hitler, Fidel Castro, and Charles Manson. History is full of people who came across as charming and inspiring at first but were only using charismatic leadership to advance their own interests rather than help others. Whether charismatic leaders are likely to have a beneficial or harmful effect on followers and society depends on their goals and motivations as leaders (Bass, 1990).

House and Howell (1992) see charismatic leaders as either more 'socialised' or 'personalised', depending on their priorities. Socialised leaders are empowering and supportive, their behaviour is based on valuing others and inspiring them to strive for prosocial goals beyond self-interest. Personalised leaders are self-promoting and exploitative, their behaviour is based on caring about self as they focus on their own ambitions at the expense of collective interests.

Think carefully about your own leadership motives. Charismatic leadership is probably the most dangerous thing I'll teach you. Please use your newfound power for good, and if you happen to start a cult – don't mention me.

Now let's examine transformational leadership as a natural extension.

TRANSFORMATIONAL LEADERSHIP

Burns (1978) first introduced the concept of transformational leadership by studying the biographies of political leaders. He discovered that those responsible for significant social progress were transformational in that they changed the people and institutions that they interacted with through their leadership.

Burns (1978) defines transformational leadership as a process where 'leaders and followers raise one another to higher levels of morality and motivation beyond self-interest to serve collective interests' (p. 20). Bass (1985) later clarified and expanded on Burns' (1978) political concepts and applied them to organisational contexts. Together these works have been enormously influential and stand as the two foundations of transformational leadership theory (Antonakis et al., 2016).

Transformational leadership is one of the most popular and effective leadership theories that we have; it's embraced by leaders around the world and generates intense research interest (Siangchokyoo et al., 2020). Multiple meta-analyses consistently report the strong positive effects of transformational leadership on followers' performance, engagement, satisfaction, and commitment, among many other desirable outcomes (DeRue et al., 2011; Judge & Piccolo, 2004; Lowe et al., 1996; Wang et al., 2011).

Transformational vs Transactional

Burns (1978) presented transformational leadership in contrast to transactional leadership.

Transactional leaders see themselves as involved in a zero-sum exchange with followers, trading pay for labour, motivation for productivity, and so forth in a give-and-take relationship. They set clear expectations and reward followers for fulfilling them, focusing on short-term goals, self-interest, and reinforcing behaviour through a fair exchange of resources (Wang et al., 2011). The leaders fulfil their followers' basic needs in exchange for acceptable performance (Lowe et al., 1996).

Transformational leadership, in contrast, suggests that both parties can be better off from the experience. Transformational leaders offer followers a purpose that transcends short-term goals and aligns with their followers' intrinsic values, motivating them to look past their own self-interest and work towards a common cause that's bigger than themselves (Judge & Piccolo, 2004).

Burns (1978) believed that all leaders naturally tend towards either a more transactional or transformational style. Bass (1985, 1998) disagreed and argued instead that transformational and transactional leadership each has distinct benefits that can be used to complement one another. A meta-analytic review reveals that transformational leadership outperforms transactional leadership across almost all measures of individual, team, and organisational performance (Wang et al., 2011).

Let's now look at the qualities that enable leaders to transform followers and organisations.

Four Dimensions

Scholars broadly agree that transformational leadership is characterised by the following four dimensions originally proposed by Bass (1985): idealised influence, inspirational motivation, intellectual stimulation, and individualised consideration (cf. Antonakis et al., 2003; Banks et al., 2016; Judge & Piccolo, 2004; Siangchokyoo et al., 2020).

Idealised influence is about charismatic traits and behaviours that create a more influential experience and enable you to transform followers. It includes role modelling the kinds of attitudes and behaviours that support and are consistent with your vision. Transformational leaders draw on charismatic behaviours that signal competence, benevolence, credibility, and speak to shared values to encourage followers to identify with them and embrace their vision. It's about having the respect, confidence, and trust of your team by appearing confident, powerful, and focused on higher ethical ideals. Embody the desirable qualities that you want to see in your team so that your followers will see you as a role model worth emulating.

Inspirational motivation is about developing an ambitious vision that will inspire followers' engagement. It includes first assessing the current situation to clearly appreciate its challenges and opportunities, and then articulating a compelling and more desirable view of the future that draws on and aligns with your followers' values. Transformational leaders motivate followers by appealing to their emotions to create an ambition beyond self-interest. It's about recruiting followers' willing engagement by aligning your vision with their core values, so that their work becomes an extension of who they are. Create a sense of meaning and purpose for followers by connecting their daily tasks with the progress they're making towards the overall vision.

Intellectual stimulation is about challenging followers to think creatively, find solutions to difficult problems, and aspire towards better performance. It includes testing existing assumptions, taking calculated risks, encouraging others to do the same, and inviting followers' input and ideas. Your followers need to feel safe enough with you and on your team to share their ideas and not fear being ridiculed, to try something new and risk failing without feeling like a failure. Transformational leaders motivate followers intrinsically by challenging them to achieve more than they've been able to do before, and supporting them so that they can rise to the challenge. Set the bar high, but also provide all the resources, training, and support that they'll need to get there.

Individualised consideration is about being personally attentive to your followers' needs and tailoring your support to help them progress in their professional development. It includes providing one-on-one mentoring, assigning challenging tasks that will stretch followers' capabilities, and sharing high-profile assignments to reward performance. Transformational leaders listen with empathy and form genuine relationships with followers, working to understand who they are and what's going on for them, so that they can offer personalised support. It's about giving people your time, energy, and attention to show them that they matter to you and building trusting relationships. Treat each follower as a unique individual, invest in their growth, and believe in them to help them reach their potential.

You might have noticed that charismatic leadership is included as the first 'idealised influence' dimension of transformational leadership and overlaps with aspects of 'inspirational motivation' as well. That's intended but incurs its own complications – let's explore the nuances.

Charismatic and Transformational?

Bass (1985) saw charisma as at the core of transformational leadership and wrought the entire concept of charismatic leadership into his first dimension of transformational leadership. Most studies have since measured charismatic leadership by collapsing together the two idealised influence and inspirational motivation dimensions of a transformational leadership scale that's called the MLQ (Banks et al., 2017).

Charismatic leadership is then an essential part of what enables you to transform followers and organisations. We can think of transformational leadership as a natural extension of charismatic leadership theory that goes further to provide more guidance on how to best use your charismatic influence to enlist followers and achieve your vision.

However, not everyone agrees with this approach. Yukl (1999) argues that charismatic and transformational leadership are two distinct concepts. One shouldn't be a dimension of the other and leaders can be transformational without being charismatic. Yet it is unclear whether the first dimension should be removed, reworked, or replaced with something else, since its current form clearly subsumes charismatic leadership and the overall theory has been demonstrably effective.

Recall that early concepts of charismatic leadership were unhelpfully vague and that we only made significant progress towards a clearer understanding from around 2016 onwards. Hazy notions about charisma therefore permeated into foundational transformational leadership texts and we are only now considering how a more modern version of charismatic leadership as signalling reshapes its role in transformational leadership.

Let's now turn our attention to our followers to consider how they're transformed and why that improves their performance.

How are Followers Changed?

Transformational leaders improve overall organisational performance by transforming individual followers to be more productive and engaged in their work. Burns (1978) explains that followers' transformation must be large in magnitude and enduring over time, a permanent and significant expansion of their capabilities and commitment. So how exactly are followers changed?

I build on the work by Siangchokyoo et al. (2020) to propose that followers are changed in five specific ways through transformational leadership interactions.

First, followers' own core values are aligned with the values underpinning the organisational vision such that they are willing to invest their efforts in this shared goal.

Second, followers develop a sense of belonging with the team and organisation and see themselves as part of this collective identity so that they're willing to contribute to the well-being and success of their social group.

Third, followers improve relevant skills through personalised coaching and targeted support to increase the scope of their task-specific capabilities.

Fourth, followers develop a stronger sense of self-efficacy, a belief in their own abilities and potential to accomplish difficult tasks.

Fifth, followers become more autonomous and proactive as well as more analytical and creative problem solvers with the courage to try bold new approaches and to challenge existing ideas.

Transformational leaders therefore promote the growth and professional development of their followers, which enables them to be more productive, and in concert these engaged and high-performing followers collectively improve the overall performance of the organisation (Bass, 1985). Over a hundred studies support these transformative effects and the benefits to individual, team, and organisational performance (Wang et al., 2011).

Now that we've discovered the components, mechanisms, and effects of transformational leadership, let's find out how transformative you are as a leader with a short quiz (Quiz 5.2).

Quiz 5.2

Transformational Leadership

Image Alt Text: https://ecuau.qualtrics.com/jfe/form/SV_7NHlk4KHHTRIUa2

Adapted from the Transformational Leadership Inventory (Podsakoff et al., 1990).

The higher your score, the more your leadership style corresponds with transformational leadership theory. Transformational leadership is particularly relevant today as seismic shifts across the business landscape force organisations to regularly reinvent themselves to remain competitive. Effective transformational leaders excel during times of change and can help their followers and organisations to successfully navigate such turbulent environments.

But the model is not perfect, and some notable limitations bear further scrutiny.

Challenges That Remain

Several major theoretical issues plague transformational leadership in its current form, including how it's defined and the confound with charisma, among others.

Despite the empirical support, the conceptual roots of transformational leadership theory are weak and underdeveloped. Critics suggest that the model is not sufficiently well articulated to allow for empirical testing, and that all of the 'evidence' collected thus far is invalid because the concept itself remains problematically vague (Van Knippenberg & Sitkin, 2013).

Burns' (1978) definition of transformational leadership is compelling, but out of touch with the four dimensions, and Bass (1985) defines it by its outcomes as leadership that 'motivates us to do more than we originally expected to do' (p. 20). Both are therefore unhelpful and the nature of transformational leadership is still unclear (Antonakis et al., 2016).

The conceptual overlap between charismatic and transformational leadership, whether intended or not, remains unresolved (Van Knippenberg & Sitkin, 2013). The issues are exacerbated as the charismatic leadership literature progresses independently of transformational leadership theory. It's unclear if these new ways of thinking about charisma are inherently incorporated into transformational leadership, or if the two now start drifting further apart (Yukl, 1999).

Without solutions to these fundamental problems, academic interest in the concept has started to wane and Siangchokyoo et al. (2020) lament that 'if transformational leadership is not dead, it is surely dying' (p. 14). But I believe that transformational leadership has strong intuitive appeal and compelling empirical support for its positive effects; I remain cautiously optimistic and hope for a revival after the fashion of charismatic leadership in 2016–2017.

SUMMARY

Charisma is universally considered a characteristic of effective leadership that's defined as values-based, symbolic, and emotion-laden leader signalling. Everything you do that's visible and in part designed to communicate sends a message, or 'signal', to everyone who can observe and receive those signals. Certain signals can make us appear more charismatic and influential to our followers.

Sources of charisma include various aspects of our appearance, personality traits, general intelligence, behaviour, and context. Behaviour can send the strongest charismatic signals and we can appear more charismatic to followers by signalling competence, benevolence, credibility, and speaking to shared values.

Charismatic leadership works by influencing followers on an emotional level – we feel the effects of charisma and that's what shapes our thoughts and behaviours. Skilful charismatic leaders can trigger specific emotions to direct their followers' behaviour at a target, which can be a person, an idea, or another group.

We can think about charismatic leaders as skilled actors, working hard to apply specific verbal and nonverbal communication strategies or 'signalling techniques' that allow them to influence their followers. You can also combine a more charismatic approach with any of the other leadership theories – for example to enhance a servant or authentic leadership style, making you more effective overall.

Charismatic leadership is one of the few amoral theories; becoming an effective charismatic leader will make you more influential and help you to inspire followers towards your vision, but it doesn't mean that your ambitions will be of any benefit to either your followers or the wider society. Think carefully about your own leadership motives.

Transformational leadership is about offering followers a purpose that transcends short-term goals and aligns with their intrinsic values, motivating them to look past their own self-interest and work towards a common cause that's bigger than themselves. It includes idealised influence, inspirational motivation, intellectual stimulation, and personalised consideration. Transformational leaders promote the professional development of their followers, which enables them to be more productive and improves organisational performance.

> 'Power tends to corrupt and absolute power corrupts absolutely: great men are almost always bad, even when they exercise influence and not authority.'
>
> Paraphrased from a *Letter to Bishop Mandell Creighton* by Lord John Acton (1887).

REFERENCES

Aguinis, H., Simonsen, M. M., & Pierce, C. A. (1998). Effects of nonverbal behavior on perceptions of power bases. *The Journal of Social Psychology, 138*(4), 455–469. https://doi.org/10.1080/00224549809600400

Antonakis, J., Avolio, B. J., & Sivasubramaniam, N. (2003). Context and leadership: An examination of the nine-factor full-range leadership theory using the Multifactor Leadership Questionnaire. *The Leadership Quarterly, 14*(3), 261–295. https://doi.org/10.1016/S1048-9843(03)00030-4

Antonakis, J., Bastardoz, N., Jacquart, P., & Shamir, B. (2016). Charisma: An ill-defined and ill-measured gift. *Annual Review of Organizational Psychology and Organizational Behavior, 3*(1), 293–319. https://doi.org/10.1146/annurev-orgpsych-041015-062305

Antonakis, J., & Dalgas, O. (2009). Predicting elections: Child's play! *Science, 323*(5918), 1183–1183. https://doi.org/10.1126/science.1167748

Antonakis, J., Fenley, M., & Liechti, S. (2012). Learning charisma: Transform yourself into the person others want to follow. *Harvard Business Review, 90*(6), 127–130.

Antonakis, J., & Gardner, W. L. (2017). Charisma: New frontiers. *The Leadership Quarterly*, *28*(4), 471–472. https://doi.org/10.1016/j.leaqua.2017.06.003

Antonakis, J., & Jacquart, P. (2013). The far side of leadership: Rather difficult to face. In M. C. Bligh & R. E. Riggio (Eds), *Exploring distance in leader–follower relationships: When near is far and far is near* (pp. 155–190). Routledge.

Banks, G. C., Engemann, K. N., Williams, C. E., Gooty, J., McCauley, K. D., & Medaugh, M. R. (2017). A meta-analytic review and future research agenda of charismatic leadership. *The Leadership Quarterly*, *28*(4), 508–529. https://doi.org/10.1016/j.leaqua.2016.12.003

Banks, G. C., McCauley, K. D., Gardner, W. L., & Guler, C. E. (2016). A meta-analytic review of authentic and transformational leadership: A test for redundancy. *The Leadership Quarterly*, *27*(4), 634–652. https://doi.org/10.1016/j.leaqua.2016.02.006

Bass, B. M. (1985). *Leadership and performance beyond expectations*. The Free Press.

Bass, B. M. (1990). Charismatic, charismalike, and inspirational leadership. In B. M. Bass & R. M. Stogdill (Eds), *Bass and Stogdill's handbook of leadership theory: Theory, research and managerial applications* (3rd ed., pp. 184–221). Free Press.

Bass, B. M. (1998). *Transformational leadership: Industry, military, and educational impact*. Lawrence Erlbaum Associates.

Bellezza, S., Gino, F., & Keinan, A. (2014). The red sneakers effect: Inferring status and competence from signals of nonconformity. *Journal of Consumer Research*, *41*(1), 35–54. https://doi.org/10.1086/674870

Burns, J. M. (1978). *Leadership*. Harper & Row.

Calás, M. B. (1993). Deconstructing charismatic leadership: Re-reading Weber from the darker side. *The Leadership Quarterly*, *4*(3/4), 305–328. https://doi.org/10.1016/1048-9843(93)90037-T

Carson, C. (1987). Martin Luther King, Jr.: Charismatic leadership in a mass struggle. *The Journal of American History*, *74*(2), 448–454. https://doi.org/10.2307/1900032

Castelnovo, O., Popper, M., & Koren, D. (2017). The innate code of charisma. *The Leadership Quarterly*, *28*(4), 543–554. https://doi.org/10.1016/j.leaqua.2016.11.003

Cialdini, R. B., & Goldstein, N. J. (2004). Social influence: Compliance and conformity. *Annual Review of Psychology*, *55*, 591–621. https://doi.org/10.1146/annurev.psych.55.090902.142015

Conger, J. A. (1999). Charismatic and transformational leadership in organizations: An insider's perspective on these developing streams of research. *The Leadership Quarterly*, *10*(2), 145–179. https://doi.org/10.1016/S1048-9843(99)00012-0

Den Hartog, D. N., House, R. J., Hanges, P. J., Ruiz-Quintanilla, S. A., Dorfman, P. W., Abdalla, I. A., Adetoun, B. S., Aditya, R. N., Agourram, H., & Akande, A. (1999). Culture specific and cross-culturally generalizable implicit leadership theories: Are attributes of charismatic/transformational leadership universally endorsed? *The Leadership Quarterly*, *10*(2), 219–256. https://doi.org/10.1016/S1048-9843(99)00018-1

DeRue, D. S., Nahrgang, J. D., Wellman, N., & Humphrey, S. E. (2011). Trait and behavioral theories of leadership: An integration and meta-analytic test of their relative validity. *Personnel Psychology*, *64*(1), 7–52. https://doi.org/10.1111/j.1744-6570.2010.01201.x

Dovidio, J. F., & Ellyson, S. L. (1982). Decoding visual dominance: Attributions of power based on relative percentages of looking while speaking and looking while listening. *Social Psychology Quarterly*, *45*(2), 106–113. https://doi.org/10.2307/3033933

Duez, D. (1985). Perception of silent pauses in continuous speech. *Language and Speech*, *28*(4), 377–389. https://doi.org/10.1177/002383098502800403

Dunleavy, D. (2020). Visual semiotics theory: Introduction to the science of signs. In S. Josephson, J. D. Kelly, & K. Smith (Eds), *Handbook of visual communication: Theory, methods, and media* (2nd ed., pp. 155–170). Routledge.

Friedman, H. S., Riggio, R. E., & Casella, D. F. (1988). Nonverbal skill, personal charisma, and initial attraction. *Personality and Social Psychology Bulletin*, *14*(1), 203–211. https://doi.org/10.1177/0146167288141020

Frijda, N. H. (1986). *The emotions: Studies in emotion & social interaction*. Cambridge University Press.

Grabo, A., Spisak, B. R., & Van Vugt, M. (2017). Charisma as signal: An evolutionary perspective on charismatic leadership. *The Leadership Quarterly*, *28*(4), 473–485. https://doi.org/10.1016/j.leaqua.2017.05.001

Haidt, J. (2003). The moral emotions. In R. J. Davidson, K. R. Sherer, & H. H. Goldsmith (Eds), *Handbook of affective sciences* (pp. 852–870). Oxford University Press.

Hamstra, M. R. W. (2014). 'Big' men: Male leaders' height positively relates to followers' perception of charisma. *Personality and Individual Differences*, *56*, 190–192. https://doi.org/10.1016/j.paid.2013.08.014

Hogg, M. A. (2001). A social identity theory of leadership. *Personality and Social Psychology Review*, *5*(3), 184–200. https://doi.org/10.1207/S15327957PSPR0503_1

House, R. J. (1977). A theory of charismatic leadership. In J. G. Hunt & L. L. Larson (Eds), *Leadership: The cutting edge* (pp. 189–207). University Press.

House, R. J., & Howell, J. M. (1992). Personality and charismatic leadership. *The Leadership Quarterly*, *3*(2), 81–108. https://doi.org/10.1016/1048-9843(92)90028-E

Judge, T. A., & Piccolo, R. F. (2004). Transformational and transactional leadership: A meta-analytic test of their relative validity. *Journal of Applied Psychology*, *89*(5), 755–768. https://doi.org/10.1037/0021-9010.89.5.755

Keating, C. F., Mazur, A., & Segall, M. H. (1977). Facial gestures which influence the perception of status. *Sociometry*, *40*(4), 374–378. https://doi.org/10.2307/3033487

Kimble, C. E., & Seidel, S. D. (1991). Vocal signs of confidence. *Journal of Nonverbal Behavior*, *15*(2), 99–105. https://doi.org/10.1007/BF00998265

Klein, K. J., & House, R. J. (1995). On fire: Charismatic leadership and levels of analysis. *The Leadership Quarterly*, *6*(2), 183–198. https://doi.org/10.1016/1048-9843(95)90034-9

Klofstad, C. A., Anderson, R. C., & Nowicki, S. (2015). Perceptions of competence, strength, and age influence voters to select leaders with lower-pitched voices. *PLOS One*, *10*(8), e0133779. https://doi.org/10.1371/journal.pone.0133779

Koppensteiner, M., Stephan, P., & Jäschke, J. P. M. (2015). More than words: Judgments of politicians and the role of different communication channels. *Journal of Research in Personality*, *58*, 21–30. https://doi.org/10.1016/j.jrp.2015.05.006

Koppensteiner, M., Stephan, P., & Jäschke, J. P. M. (2016). Moving speeches: Dominance, trustworthiness and competence in body motion. *Personality and Individual Differences*, *94*, 101–106. https://doi.org/10.1016/j.paid.2016.01.013

Krumhuber, E., Manstead, A. S., & Kappas, A. (2007). Temporal aspects of facial displays in person and expression perception: The effects of smile dynamics, head-tilt, and gender. *Journal of Nonverbal Behavior*, *31*, 39–56. https://doi.org/10.1007/s10919-006-0019-x

Lawson, C., Lenz, G. S., Baker, A., & Myers, M. (2010). Looking like a winner: Candidate appearance and electoral success in new democracies. *World Politics*, *62*(4), 561–593. https://doi.org/10.1017/S0043887110000195

Lowe, K. B., Kroeck, K. G., & Sivasubramaniam, N. (1996). Effectiveness correlates of transformational and transactional leadership: A meta-analytic review of the MLQ literature. *The Leadership Quarterly*, *7*(3), 385–425. https://doi.org/10.1016/S1048-9843(96)90027-2

Meslec, N., Curseu, P. L., Fodor, O. C., & Kenda, R. (2020). Effects of charismatic leadership and rewards on individual performance. *The Leadership Quarterly*, *31*(6), 101423. https://doi.org/10.1016/j.leaqua.2020.101423

Murphy, N. A., Hall, J. A., & Colvin, C. R. (2003). Accurate intelligence assessments in social interactions: Mediators and gender effects. *Journal of Personality*, *71*(3), 465–493. https://doi.org/10.1111/1467-6494.7103008

Podsakoff, P. M., MacKenzie, S. B., Moorman, R. H., & Fetter, R. (1990). Transformational leader behaviors and their effects on followers' trust in leader, satisfaction, and organizational citizenship behaviors. *The Leadership Quarterly*, *1*(2), 107–142. https://doi.org/10.1016/1048-9843(90)90009-7

Popper, M. (2001). *Hypnotic leadership: Leaders, followers, and the loss of self*. Praeger Publishers.

Reh, S., Van Quaquebeke, N., & Giessner, S. R. (2017). The aura of charisma: A review on the embodiment perspective as signaling. *The Leadership Quarterly*, *28*(4), 486–507. https://doi.org/10.1016/j.leaqua.2017.01.001

Scherer, K. R. (1984). On the nature and function of emotion: A component process approach. In K. R. E. Scherer, Paul (Ed.), *Approaches to Emotion* (pp. 293–317). Lawrence Erlbaum Associates.

Schjoedt, U., Sørensen, J., Nielbo, K. L., Xygalatas, D., Mitkidis, P., & Bulbulia, J. (2013). Cognitive resource depletion in religious interactions. *Religion, Brain & Behavior*, *3*(1), 39–55. https://doi.org/10.1080/2153599X.2012.736714

Schjoedt, U., Stødkilde-Jørgensen, H., Geertz, A. W., Lund, T. E., & Roepstorff, A. (2011). The power of charisma – perceived charisma inhibits the frontal executive network of believers in intercessory prayer. *Social Cognitive and Affective Neuroscience*, *6*(1), 119–127. https://doi.org/10.1093/scan/nsq023

Schubert, T. W., Waldzus, S., & Seibt, B. (2011). More than a metaphor: How the understanding of power is grounded in experience. In T. W. Schubert & A. Maass (Eds.), Spatial dimensions of social thought (pp. 153–185). De Gruyter Mouton. https://doi.org/10.1515/9783110254310.153

Self, C. C., & Roberts, C. (2019). Credibility. In D. W. Stacks, M. B. Salwen, & K. C. Eichhorn (Eds), *An integrated approach to communication theory and research* (pp. 435–446). Routledge.

Siangchokyoo, N., Klinger, R. L., & Campion, E. D. (2020). Follower transformation as the linchpin of transformational leadership theory: A systematic review and future research agenda. *The Leadership Quarterly*, *31*(1), 101341. https://doi.org/10.1016/j.leaqua.2019.101341

Siedlecka, E., & Denson, T. F. (2019). Experimental methods for inducing basic emotions: A qualitative review. *Emotion Review, 11*(1), 87–97. https://doi.org/10.1177/1754073917749016

Spence, M. (2002). Signaling in retrospect and the informational structure of markets. *American Economic Review, 92*(3), 434–459. https://doi.org/10.1257/00028280260136200

Spencer, M. E. (1973). What is charisma? *The British Journal of Sociology, 24*(3), 341–354. https://doi.org/10.2307/588237

Spisak, B. R., Grabo, A. E., Arvey, R. D., & Van Vugt, M. (2014). The age of exploration and exploitation: Younger-looking leaders endorsed for change and older-looking leaders endorsed for stability. *The Leadership Quarterly, 25*(5), 805–816. https://doi.org/10.1016/j.leaqua.2014.06.001

Spisak, B. R., Homan, A. C., Grabo, A., & Van Vugt, M. (2012). Facing the situation: Testing a biosocial contingency model of leadership in intergroup relations using masculine and feminine faces. *The Leadership Quarterly, 23*(2), 273–280. https://doi.org/10.1016/j.leaqua.2011.08.006

Sturm, R. E., & Antonakis, J. (2015). Interpersonal power: A review, critique, and research agenda. *Journal of Management, 41*(1), 136–163. https://doi.org/10.1177/0149206314555769

Sy, T., Horton, C., & Riggio, R. (2018). Charismatic leadership: Eliciting and channeling follower emotions. *The Leadership Quarterly, 29*(1), 58–69. https://doi.org/10.1016/j.leaqua.2017.12.008

Van Knippenberg, D., & Sitkin, S. B. (2013). A critical assessment of charismatic–transformational leadership research: Back to the drawing board? *The Academy of Management Annals, 7*(1), 1–60. https://doi.org/10.1080/19416520.2013.759433

Van Vugt, M., Hogan, R., & Kaiser, R. B. (2008). Leadership, followership, and evolution: Some lessons from the past. *American Psychologist, 63*(3), 182–196. https://doi.org/10.1037/0003-066X.63.3.182

Wang, G., Oh, I.-S., Courtright, S. H., & Colbert, A. E. (2011). Transformational leadership and performance across criteria and levels: A meta-analytic review of 25 years of research. *Group & Organization Management, 36*(2), 223–270. https://doi.org/10.1177/1059601111401017

Weber, M. (1947). *The theory of social and economic organization* (A. M. Henderson & T. Parsons, Trans.). Free Press.

Weber, M. (1968). *On charisma and institutional building*. Chicago Press.

Yukl, G. (1999). An evaluation of conceptual weaknesses in transformational and charismatic leadership theories. *The Leadership Quarterly, 10*(2), 285–305. https://doi.org/10.1016/S1048-9843(99)00013-2

6
CULTURE, DIVERSITY, AND INCLUSIVE LEADERSHIP

Overview

This chapter explores how cultural and diversity differences affect leadership outcomes. It starts by defining culture and discussing how cultural practices shape individuals' values and beliefs.

You are then introduced to three well-established cultural value frameworks created by Hall, Hofstede, Trompenaars and Hampden-Turner respectively. In this chapter, you'll work through a series of reflective exercises based on these models to reveal your own cultural profile.

You are then asked to create what you perceive to be the typical cultural profile for the country where you're living, and to consider in what ways your values are most different, and what kind of leadership challenges you may encounter when interacting with others.

The chapter then introduces a new cognitive way to examine cultural differences based on the theory of analytic vs holistic thought that examines the historical roots of how people think. You'll discover your own cognitive tendencies through a reflective quiz.

Next, we explore diversity and inclusion more broadly to consider how multiculturalism plays out across organisations. The chapter concludes with inclusive leadership, a contemporary approach that champions the unique value offered by embracing diversity.

Exercise 6.1: My cultural spheres

Quiz 6.1: Hall, Hofstede, Trompenaars and Hampden-Turner

Exercise 6.2: Cultural value profiles

Quiz 6.2: Holistic cognition scale

Cultural differences may present the single greatest challenge, and opportunity, for contemporary leaders. Individuals today bring a wealth of diverse perspectives, knowledge, and experiences to our organisations. More than ever, we need leaders who appreciate the value of diversity and can enable every follower to contribute their unique talents to the advantage of the group.

In this chapter we will focus primarily on culture and examine a series of different cultural frameworks to develop an understanding of your own 'cultural profile'. Afterwards, we'll consider diversity more generally and discuss what true multiculturalism in organisations looks like. The chapter culminates in an overview of inclusive leadership as an approach that's specifically tailored to harness the considerable benefits of diversity.

GROWING COMPLEXITY

Recall from our discussion of 'contemporary leadership challenges' in Chapter 2 that modern organisations work increasingly on an international stage, with functions distributed across multiple locations. For example, their suppliers, production facilities, distribution networks, headquarters, support offices, and customer-facing outlets may be spread across a dozen countries or more to take advantage of unique benefits offered by different locations. That means we often find ourselves dealing with people in different countries from our own.

International migration has also radically diversified domestic workplaces. On average, up to one-third of the population of developed countries is made up of first-generation migrants who were born overseas themselves and second-generation migrants with at least one parent born abroad. As people move between cities, countries, professions, and social groups, they pick up and share their culture along the way. The interactions create complex 'third culture' identities that mix international heritages and domestic influences (Pollock et al., 2017).

More people today are exposed to, learn about, and embrace cultural differences than ever before. For example, my wife is the quintessential global citizen. Her father's family came from the UK to New Zealand, where he grew up a Kiwi in a small town. He joined the military and ended up in South-East Asia before finding his way into the petroleum industry in the Middle East. Her mother is Malaysian Chinese and was sent to an American boarding school in Singapore from a young age. She grew up with American values and went on to live in Las Vegas, San Francisco, and Hawaii.

They later met back in Singapore, had their first child, my wife, in Abu Dhabi, and then lived on expatriate compounds throughout the Middle East. If you've never seen an American compound before, I assure you that it's a surreal experience. Imagine a walled-in miniature US city laid out with roads and suburban houses in neighbourhoods, complete with schools, shopping malls, movie theatres, restaurants and the like. You wouldn't even know that you were in the Middle East until you stepped outside the security gates and into another world.

After growing up in Abu Dhabi, Qatar, and Saudi Arabia, the family spent some time in Malaysia before sending their daughters to secondary school in New Zealand, where we met. Today my wife looks half-Asian and half-European, sounds American, has some Buddhist beliefs, lives in Australia with me, and has both an Australian and New Zealand passport. Her cultural heritage is a rich tapestry of diverse experiences and perspectives.

That's quickly becoming the norm and individual people are more diverse than ever before. Within organisations it's typical to see heterogeneous constellations of people working together. Appreciate then that every person you're leading has developed a different point of view from a lifetime of experiences, and they'll perceive your leadership rhetoric and behaviour through the unique kaleidoscope of their cultural background.

We'll focus on the complexities that these cultural differences bring to how we understand and practise leadership, and discuss how we can best harness the considerable value that diversity offers our teams and organisations. To get started let's first explore what 'culture' is all about.

CULTURE

The idea of culture stems from the scientific study of humanity known as anthropology, which is a colossal field of academic inquiry that includes domains of human behaviour and biology, societies, linguistics, and culture. Tylor (1871) defines culture as 'that complex whole which includes knowledge, belief, art, morals, law, custom, and any other capabilities and habits acquired by man as a member of society' (p. 1).

So culture is not something that we're born with; rather, it's something that we've learned and picked up through our involvement with other people in society. That includes whatever social groups that we're a part of, including our family, friends, the neighbourhood we grew up in, the schools and universities we've studied at, the cities and countries where we've lived, etc.

As we've interacted with other people in these various social settings we've seen and taken part in a broad array of cultural practices, embracing and embedding some of these behaviours and ideas as aspects of our own identity. We've all been exposed to a radically diverse constellation of customs, traditions, religions, rituals, and heritages that have shaped who we've become – for example, midday prayer, giving each other a high-five, eating with chopsticks, as well as a whole array of celebrations and all the associated rituals, rites, and forms.

Culture is something that's therefore transmitted hereditarily through social interaction, from one generation to the next. You're not born with it, it's not genetic, but you do acquire your unique cultural outlook from others who have come before you, who themselves first learned and then incorporated these cultural practices into their own lives. When we enter the world and begin engaging with other people, we start absorbing aspects of their culture from our social interactions. And there are innumerable discrete cultural practices that people have transmitted down through the ages – for example, Oktoberfest, circumcision, singing Christmas carols, the list goes on.

Now, all these specific things that people do, these cultural practices, influence who we become by shaping our beliefs, moral standards, and behaviour. The practices we engage in teach us about what's important. Each discrete cultural practice has a history, a heritage, that's embedded with specific cultural values that it carries with it. Cultural practices themselves are therefore only the surface manifestations of our underlying cultural values. What we do is only a representation of what we think is important.

But what exactly are these cultural values? Let's dig a little deeper.

CULTURAL VALUES

Cultural values are people's perceptions of and preferences for certain kinds of behaviour, motivations, and ambitions. They're guiding principles that tell us what's appropriate and important in our societies. By being a member of various social circles, we start to understand what people in those groups value, what's expected of us, and what kind of behaviour is appropriate.

Imagine, for example, someone who's raised in a devout Catholic family, where the values around marriage uphold it as a strictly monogamous and lifelong affair. It's unlikely that they'd then consider polygamy or taking on multiple marital partners; that's not a cultural practice that would even enter their realm of possibility. But polygyny is well accepted within certain Islamic faiths and would therefore appear perfectly normal to people embedded in those religious communities.

The same kinds of formative experiences happen across the many social groups that we're involved with. Education offers another good example. If you went to Eton College in the UK where generations of English aristocracy have been groomed, you'd acquire a specific perspective about what society is like, your place in it, and how you should behave. That perspective would likely be very different if you went to a rural school in Pakistan, or an international school in Singapore.

Our cultural values will therefore shape our behaviour, influence what we aspire to, and determine what we think is right and just. More importantly, cultural values will also influence how we see other people's behaviour, motives, and morals. And here's how it starts to affect our leadership interactions.

Leadership Perceptions

You might recall that at the start of Chapter 1 I introduced you to implicit leadership theory (Lord & Maher, 1991), which is your idea of what constitutes effective leadership based on your personal beliefs. House et al. (2004) extend the framework to explain that your ideas about leadership are culturally embedded, and thereby introduced 'culturally endorsed implicit leadership theory'. It's best to think about it as a cultural lens through which we view leadership behaviour.

Followers' cultural leadership perspectives then serve as 'standards that guide what is regarded to be appropriate, desired, and expected of leaders' (Stephan & Pathak, 2016, p. 507). Empirical studies suggest that we're more likely to be endorsed by followers and to succeed as leaders when our behaviour aligns with their cultural leadership expectations (Epitropaki et al., 2013). Our followers' cultural values therefore determine what kinds of leadership behaviour are more or less effective.

Some of our leadership theories might work better or worse with followers who hold certain cultural values, depending on how well those theories align with their values. For example, authentic leadership portrays a certain approach that might not appeal to everyone. Some of our theories may also take on distinct forms across different cultural contexts. For example, the specific behaviours that signal charisma may vary drastically from one cultural frame of interpretation to another. The concept of charismatic leadership could still be just as effective, but enacting it appropriately might require us to alter our approach (cf. Javidan & Carl, 2004).

To be effective leaders in today's diverse organisational contexts we'll first need a clear and coherent understanding of cultural differences, and how they shape our followers' perceptions. We can then work to contextualise our rhetoric and behaviour so that it will be received and experienced exactly as intended. Everything we do as leaders therefore has to be considered from our followers' cultural perspectives.

I hope you're starting to see the challenge. We'll never be able to see perfectly through our followers' eyes, but we must work to develop an informed opinion. Think carefully about how your behaviour might be interpreted and understood.

For example, contemporary organisations across Europe and North America encourage a more egalitarian and participative leadership style, built on an understanding that everyone has something to offer and should be invited to contribute their unique talents. Indeed, most of our conversations so far have been grounded in this perspective, empowering our followers to solve problems themselves, and nurturing feelings of ownership and self-determination in their work.

And yet that's not how everyone, everywhere, believes that their leaders should behave. Attitudes and expectations towards leadership vary considerably. For example, people across Asia tend to prefer that their leaders provide a sense of direction and authority. Followers with different cultural perspectives from us have just as much to offer. But we may need to modify our leadership behaviour to translate these same inclusive ideals into forms that will be interpreted appropriately to have the desired positive effects on diverse followers.

The example above is an over-simplification that serves to introduce you to the concept of adjusting how you lead and interact with culturally diverse followers. You can't rely on naïve ideas about cultural value differences, and it will be a disaster if you get it wrong, such that your leadership behaviour offends rather than uplifts. Let's now consider the different levels or 'spheres' of society where cultural values reside.

Six Layers of Values

We're all part of many spheres of society that influence how we conduct ourselves, as well as our perceptions of and preferences for various behaviours, motivations, and ambitions. We can think about these as different nested levels or 'layers' of cultural values. Figure 6.1 illustrates the six nested layers of cultural values, starting at the global level and drilling down to the individual level.

At the highest level we have the global cultural values of all humankind as a single species. We're all a part of this one world, but we share precious few values and only a handful of concepts are appreciated by everyone. Integrity may be our only true global value; acting consistently with the values you uphold is appreciated by everyone, everywhere, and irrespective of the content of those values.

Within the global level, we then have individual nations and cultural blocs, which are groups of countries that share cultural values – for example, Nordic Europe, the Middle East, Latin America, sub-Saharan Africa (see House et al., 2004). Most cultural studies are at the national level. We can aggregate individual cultural differences to create a coherent idea about the values of each country – for example, Australian, Japanese, Egyptian values.

Global — all humankind as a single species
National — individual countries, and cultural blocs
Societal — industries, regions, religious and ethnic groups
Organisational — companies, organisations, departments, branches
Communal — family, friends, social networks
Individual — your own personal values

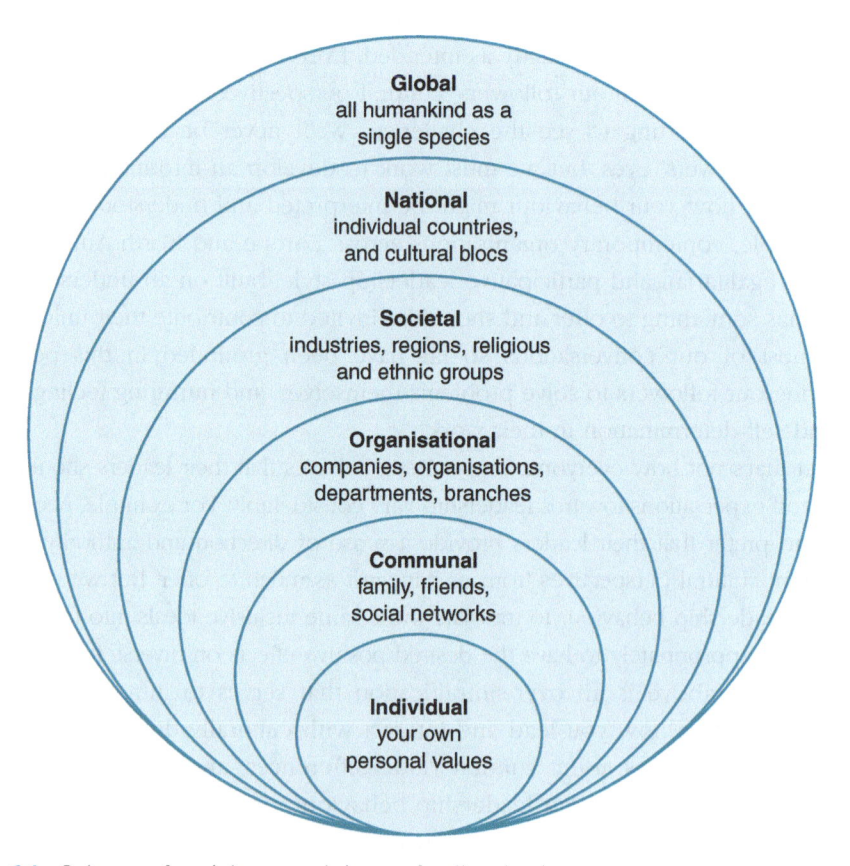

Figure 6.1 Spheres of society as containers of cultural values.

Within the national level, we then have various societal groups, including industries, smaller geographic regions, as well as religious and ethnic groups. For example, people working in the higher education sector have a set of shared values that are different to those in healthcare, agriculture, and mining. The same applies to distinct regions within countries – for example, north and south India; religious groups such as the denominations of Christian, Islamic, and Hindu faiths; and ethnic groups like the Han Chinese, French Canadians, African Americans, or Indigenous peoples.

Within the societal level, we then have individual organisations, including businesses, not-for-profit organisations, government departments, churches, schools/universities, social clubs, and the like. For example, I work at Edith Cowan University and we've articulated our shared values as 'integrity, respect, rational inquiry, personal excellence, and courage'; they guide what we do and how we behave. Every organisation has its own way of doing things that is underpinned by a set of cultural values, even if they're not written down. Some companies build a strong positive culture and draw on it as a source of competitive advantage, while others fester as a result of a toxic culture.

Below the organisational level, we have a private communal sphere which includes our family, friends, and closest social network. The people in this inner circle have a strong influence on our cultural values, first guiding our ideas in early childhood as parents, and then coming together as peers to make sense of the world and our place in it, to understand who we are and who we want to become.

At the lowest level we have the individual, our own unique cultural identity that's personal to us and distinct from everyone else on the planet. Your values will include aspects drawn from all the other layers that you interact with, including the global, national, societal, organisational, and communal levels. Understanding your values as a leader is absolutely critical and so I've dedicated a portion of the next chapter to exploring and unpacking what you believe.

The hierarchy that I've depicted between the six layers is an indication only and not strictly representative. Many exceptions readily come to mind: companies can span industries and national borders; social networks bring people together who work in different organisations, have different religious beliefs and ethnicities, and even live abroad.

Appreciate that we acquire and share values from our societal spheres, as do our followers according to their unique group membership, which then shape their preferences for certain kinds of leadership behaviour.

We can imagine these different layers of cultural values operating at the same time to dictate what's appropriate. For example, a girl sat in my classroom this week: she's part of all humankind; she's South-East Asian, from Thailand, presently in Western Australia, enrolled in higher education at Edith Cowan University in the School of Business and Law; she was with friends, and she's her own person. Her behaviour was an authentic blend of these many social influences and norms.

Let's now consider what kinds of cultural value influences you're experiencing at this moment across these six layers. Please work through Exercise 6.1 to explore the sources shaping your cultural values.

―――――― **Exercise 6.1** ――――――

My Cultural Spheres

Image Alt Text: https://ecuau.qualtrics.com/jfe/form/SV_00Su5I4D9Y0ab0q

---

Certain values can take precedence in specific situations, while others take a back seat. How we interact while we're out dancing with friends on the weekend can be quite different to how we'd behave when we're alone, or in a professional setting. Our individual values can of course clash with the other layers of expectation at the organisational, societal, or national level. They're also dynamic and change over time as we grow, learn, and acquire new values.

Now that we've got an outline of what cultural values are and where they come from, let's dispel some of the stereotypes and myths that surround this contentious topic.

Stereotypes and Myths

As leaders we cannot operate on stereotypes of culture and must work to develop an informed perspective based on reliable research. Like leadership itself, we've all absorbed naïve notions about what people from different cultural groups value based on what we've seen and experienced first-hand.

Unfortunately we tend to extrapolate from our small samples to whole populations, over-generalising what we know. With a little logic and a basic understanding for statistics it becomes clear that a handful of experiences with certain people can't represent the entire groups to which they belong.

Having spent an evening with a few of my in-laws in Malaysia, I might feel that I know what all Malaysian people are like, and therefore what kind of leadership style might work best to inspire them. But I'd be wrong. My in-laws are Malaysian Chinese Buddhists and hold very different values from the Islamic Bumiputera Malays who make up over 60% of the population.

There's no shortcut. We must take the time to understand the various cultural differences and then get to know our individual followers. Learning about your followers' cultural values gives you vital insight into how they're likely to perceive specific leadership behaviours, so that you can adapt your approach to be most effective from within their frame of reference.

Before we go any further, let's dispel a popular myth that all our cultures are converging into one homogeneous global community, a transcendent identity across the planet. Proponents support this story with evidence of convergence like how international migration is cross-pollinating values, common languages are stitching together our differences, international institutions help us to find common cause to overcome global issues, and multinational organisations are standardising our experiences across the world.

Pagel (2013) explains that we're wired by evolution to cooperate on an increasingly larger scale to improve our circumstances, and so we can imagine that eventually we'd get to the global level. But as societies reach a peak standard of living, the benefits of cooperation leak away, and resource scarcity encourages governments to safeguard their citizens with protectionist policies.

The evidence suggests that we might share more of the superficial expressions of culture, like jeans, smartphones, and Netflix, but the fundamental cultural value differences remain intact (Minkov & Hofstede, 2011), and individual people are more diverse now than ever before (Stahl & Maznevski, 2021).

Let's stick to the facts. Although culture comes from the vast domain of anthropology, we only have a handful of major studies in organisational contexts, including the works of Hall (1959), Schwartz (1992), Hofstede (1980), Trompenaars and Hampden-Turner (2020), and House et al. (2004). These scholars have all simplified the enormous complexity of culture down to a few dimensions to give us some actionable insights, albeit in slightly different ways.

Over the next three sections we will examine more closely the dimensions identified by Hall, Hofstede, Trompenaars and Hampden-Turner. You will notice that each one is framed as a dichotomy, a continuum between two polar ends, in the same way we examined dimensions of personality in Chapter 3. At the end we'll take a quiz and calculate your scores across each of these dimensions.

Hall

Hall (1959) studied how people communicate and discovered two dimensions of cultural difference – first, that people vary in how they use verbal and non-verbal communication techniques to convey meaning, which he called high- vs low- context communication; and second, that people vary in how they see time and attend to their work, which he called monochronic vs polychronic.

High- vs Low-Context

Meaning is transferred more implicitly in high-context communication. It's not just about what we say, but rather how we say it. Contextual and non-verbal cues convey a significant portion of the message – for example, where we are at the time, how we interact with the surroundings, our posture, gaze or where we're looking, and how we move our bodies. Emotional displays tend to be more subtle and important, often with just the eyes. In high-context communication you might find that many things are left unsaid, but instead are signalled through non-verbal and contextual cues.

Meaning is transferred more explicitly in low-context communication. It's about saying exactly what you mean, how you mean to say it, with little consideration for contextual or non-verbal cues. The intentional use of specific language becomes critical, as well as how jargon and idioms can enhance meaning. The precise words and phrases that we use, and how we structure what we say conveys most of the message. Emotional displays tend to be quite animated with more direct eye contact, and can emphasise important content. You might find that you have to spell it out to get your idea across clearly.

Monochronic vs Polychronic

People who are monochronic tend to do one thing at a time. Time is divided it into small, precise units. For example, you might plan to spend half an hour reading, then go for a quick 15-minute walk, and be done in time to meet a friend for lunch at 12:30pm. Time is therefore a precious resource that must be invested carefully. Creating detailed schedules and plans becomes critical, as well as punctuality and deadlines. When plans are set, people who are monochronic tend to stick with them and avoid 'wasting' time at all costs, their own and others'; arriving late would cause offence.

People who are polychronic tend to do multiple things at the same time. Time is seen in large fluid sections. For example, you might be cooking dinner while watching TV, referring to a recipe, and tending to your child. Time is therefore not discrete or linear and activities can freely overlap. After starting one thing you don't necessarily need to finish it first before starting another. People who are polychronic rarely feel like they're late or behind schedule; they have all the time in the world. Plans are drawn in broad strokes and can easily change as the day unfolds.

Next, we'll turn our attention to Hofstede's model.

Hofstede

Hofstede (1980) analysed over 100,000 surveys from employees working at IBM across the world, and extracted five cultural value dimensions: individualism vs collectivism, power distance, masculinity vs femininity, uncertainty avoidance, and long- vs short-term orientation. Hofstede et al. (2010) later added a sixth dimension, indulgence vs restraint, which has seen limited uptake by the academic community. Hofstede's original work has been enormously influential and supported in hundreds of studies (Kirkman et al., 2017), so we'll explore these five dimensions.

Individualism vs Collectivism

People who are individualistic tend to have loosely knit social ties. They feel responsible primarily for taking care of themselves and their immediate family – for example, their partner, children, siblings, and parents. People who are individualistic value their privacy and independence; they prefer to have their own space and be self-sufficient. In organisational contexts they tend to focus on tasks rather than relationships; they value personal achievement, even when working in a team and may be highly competitive. It's about having autonomy over your life, the choices you make, and how you express yourself. When transgressing social norms you'd feel guilt, which is about not living up to your own expectations.

People who are collectivistic tend to have very strong social ties. They feel deeply connected to their communities and distinguish between in- and out-groups, receiving mutual support for their loyalty. People who are collectivistic value harmony and cohesion, preferring to keep the peace in their social group. In organisational contexts they tend to focus on relationships rather than tasks, taking the time to engage in social activities to build a positive and close personal rapport with colleagues. It's about feeling connected and sharing times of celebration and times of want to support each other. When transgressing social norms you'd feel shame, which is about not living up to others' expectations.

Power Distance

People with low power distance prefer decision-making authority to be more egalitarian and distributed between leaders and followers within organisations and society. They'd expect to be consulted by their supervisor about decisions relating to their work. People with low power distance prefer democratic governments that give individuals voice, licence to question those in authority, and can hold political leaders to account. It's about having a more equal and participative society. For example, older people tend not to be ascribed any additional respect, they're just like anyone else, and parents treat their children as equals.

People with high power distance prefer decision-making authority to be concentrated in their leaders with greater disparity from followers within organisations and society. They'd expect to be told what to do by their supervisor, who should know what needs to be done, when, how, and by whom. High power distance people tend to accept more autocratic government regimes as an unquestionable fact of life. It's about feeling secure knowing that there's someone in charge. For example, older people are respected as elders in their community and have authority beyond any official capacity, and parents teach their children obedience.

Masculinity vs Femininity

People who are masculine prefer a differentiation between gender-based roles in society. They tend to believe that men should be assertive and ambitious, and women should be modest and caring. People who are masculine view work as more important than family life. For example, family life would typically be structured around the breadwinner, their schedule, their career progression, and supporting their needs so that they can in turn provide for the family. Hofstede (2006) explains that 'boys, not girls, should fight' and 'girls, not boys, may cry' (p. 894). More masculine people therefore tend to first give praise to the strong, celebrating their victory and success.

People who are feminine prefer overlapping gender-based roles in society. They tend to believe that both men and women should be modest and caring, and that either can fulfil the different spheres of responsibility in family life. People who are feminine find balance between work and family. For example, men can stay at home and look after the children, while women pursue primary careers depending on each partner's aptitude, preference, and opportunities for success. Hofstede (2011) explains that 'boys and girls may cry, but neither should fight' (p. 12). More feminine people therefore tend to first give sympathy to the weak, appreciating their efforts and challenges.

Uncertainty Avoidance

People with low uncertainty avoidance are more tolerant of ambiguity. They tend to take each day as it comes and find people and ideas that deviate from the norm curious and interesting, and appreciate surprises and getting blown off course into exciting new adventures. People with less uncertainty avoidance also tend to have lower levels of stress and anxiety; they're easy going. At work it's okay for leaders to not know all the answers, or that they don't have enough information to hold an informed opinion. Too many rules and boundaries become restrictive and can feel stifling.

People with high uncertainty avoidance are less tolerant of ambiguity. They prefer to plan carefully and are less accepting of people who deviate from the norm and ideas that go off script. For example, they appreciate doing their research first and being well prepared so that their adventures go according to plan. People with more uncertainty avoidance tend to have higher levels of stress and anxiety; they're highly strung. At work they expect their leaders to have all the answers and it's terrifying if they don't. Rules and boundaries create security because then they know what to expect, and that feels safe.

Long- vs Short-Term Orientation

People with long-term orientation focus on both the past and the future. They tend to value perseverance, temperance, and thrift. For example, they're careful with resources and dedicate themselves to significant goals worth pursuing, making incremental progress towards completion. People with long-term orientation therefore tend to see success and failure as functions of effort: if you're successful, it's because you put in the hard work. Time, resources, and effort should be invested carefully and with restraint for greater rewards in the future. Change is tested prudently with an appreciation for preserving tradition and ensuring ongoing sustainability.

People with short-term orientation focus on the present. They tend to value living each moment to its fullest. For example, they'd rather spend what they have to experience more of the world, with an associated focus on shorter tasks or smaller goals that yield near-instant gratification, praise, and reward. People with short-term orientation therefore tend to see success and failure anchored in chance or good fortune; if you're successful, it's serendipity. Time, resources, and effort should be enjoyed in the present. With a constant focus on the now, traditions are sacrosanct and kept exactly as they are, unchanged and without adaptation.

Now let's consider the framework proposed by Trompenaars and Hampden-Turner.

Trompenaars and Hampden-Turner

Trompenaars and Hampden-Turner (2020) published the first edition of their book in 1993. In the three decades since they've accumulated over 100,000 survey responses from employees in over 140 different countries. They also identified five cultural value dimensions concerning people and relationships: universalism vs particularism, individualism vs communitarianism, neutral vs emotional, specific vs diffuse, and achievement vs ascription.

Note that individualism vs communitarianism is virtually identical to Hofstede's dimension 'individualism vs collectivism'. It's fascinating to see two separate studies come up with the same idea, which suggests that it's a fundamental aspect of our cultural values. I'll skip explaining it again, but let's look at the other four dimensions that Trompenaars and Hampden-Turner identified.

Universalism vs Particularism

People who value universalism tend to believe that the same ideas and practices can be applied everywhere. They don't need to tailor their thinking and behaviour to different contexts because there's an objective reality that's governed by rules, and if they're working within those rules, then they'll be successful. In organisational settings they prefer to 'get down to business' quickly and focus on the work at hand. Universalists value rational and professional arguments that are supported by compelling empirical evidence. Rules serve as ethical standards to guide decision-making and create a sense of fairness.

People who value particularism tend to believe that circumstances dictate how ideas and practices should be applied. They contextualise interactions, adjusting how they think and behave because reality is subjective and exists only as a social construct between people; success comes from forming collaborative relationships. In organisational settings, small talk is a crucial part of relationship-building to first find common ground before discussing work. Particularists welcome diverse opinions and personal experiences. Consultation gives stakeholders a voice in decision-making, while due process and consensus create a sense of fairness.

Neutral vs Emotional

People who are neutral tend to be more reserved with their emotions, holding them in check. They prefer a calm and professional tone to their communication, with fewer and more subtle non-verbal cues, which can come across as distant or formal. They're less expressive in their face, they'll smile and frown less, preferring to keep their emotions private. You'll also find that they rarely raise their voice. It may therefore be harder to pick up on how they're interpreting your interaction. People who are neutral tend to avoid physical contact and may actively avoid touching, especially colleagues in a professional context.

People who are emotional tend to be more open and expressive with their emotions. They prefer a more animated and boisterous communication style, with more dynamic body language, gestures, and gaze. Their faces are highly expressive, they'll smile easily and often, and openly reveal what they're feeling. When they're excited, they start talking faster and louder, with more pronounced body language. It's therefore easy to tell how they're responding to your conversation. People who are emotional are comfortable with physical contact and will actively reach out to hug colleagues or touch them on the arm or shoulder as part of normal interactions.

Specific vs Diffuse

People who are more 'specific' tend to keep their public, private, and professional lives separate. They'll have a small private space or inner circle consisting of a handful of their closest confidants that they'll guard carefully. Different spaces are then only shared with certain people. For example, work colleagues will remain separate from social acquaintances, and from family and friends; the three groups might never meet. Individuals who are specific also tend to interact differently in each social space – who they are at work is distinct from who they are in public, or in their homes. These different versions of them stay in their corresponding spaces.

People who are more 'diffuse' tend to have an extensive overlap between their public, private, and professional lives. The three spaces are then of equal size with broader membership from across categories, and they're all equally guarded because entering one of the social spaces also grants entry into the others. For example, it's not unusual for a new business partner to invite you home to have dinner with their family. Individuals who are diffuse also conduct themselves the same way across all three spaces. There are no distinct public, private, and professional versions of them. Connecting with them in one capacity means being welcomed into their whole life.

Achievement vs Ascription

People who value achievement accord more status to others depending on how well they perform certain functions in society. It's about what you have accomplished, how competent you are, and if you've been publicly recognised for your achievements. Higher social status is therefore awarded on the basis of individual merit. Talented hardworking people who excel in their personal or professional endeavours, or are known for their specialised expertise, tend to be awarded more status. Having well proven skills, knowledge, or abilities will garner greater status and respect from people who value achievement.

People who value ascription accord more status to others depending on who they are as individuals within that society. It's about your power and position in society, which is a function of your hierarchical rank and title, level of education, and caste or social class. Higher social status is therefore awarded on the basis of reputation. Men, older people, and those from wealthy or well-respected families in the community tend to be ascribed more status. Having the right pedigree, position, or connections will attract greater status and respect from people who value ascription.

Okay, now let's figure out each of your cultural values and put them all together into an overall 'cultural profile'.

CULTURAL PROFILES

I'd like you to first work through a quiz (Quiz 6.1) that will calculate your scores for each of the different cultural value dimensions. For example, it will ask you a few questions and then work out whether you prefer high-context communication or low, whether you're more monochronic or polychronic with your time, and so on for each of the dimensions that we've discussed above.

Be sure to take note of your results as we'll need to use them for our next exercise.

Quiz 6.1

Hall, Hofstede, Trompenaars and Hampden-Turner

Image Alt Text: https://ecuau.qualtrics.com/jfe/form/SV_74FXoEjfkDo7gtE

Adapted from Hall (1959), Hofstede (1980), and Trompenaars and Hampden-Turner (2020).

You should now have scores that place your values along each of the 11 cultural dimensions that we've extracted from the three frameworks proposed by Hall, Hofstede, and Trompenaars and Hampden-Turner. For example, I prefer low-context communication and choose my words carefully. I'm monochronic and like to focus on one thing at a time.

I'm more individualistic and masculine as I appreciate my autonomy and accept gendered roles. I prefer less power distance so that leaders are accountable, and leadership is inclusive. I tend to avoid uncertainty and prefer the security of structure; even my adventures are well planned. I'm focused on the long term and orient my life around ambitious goals.

I'm a universalist and value rational arguments and empirical evidence. I openly express my emotions, but that varies depending on context because I'm more 'specific' with a small inner circle and a distinct professional identity. I believe that respect should be earned by demonstrating merit or achievement.

We can think about these 11 dimensions as coming together to assemble an overall cultural values profile that will be unique and personal. Let's use your earlier quiz results (Quiz 6.1) to work out yours. Exercise 6.2 will ask you to map out your cultural tendencies across these value dimensions.

Exercise 6.2

Cultural Value Profiles

Image Alt Text: https://ecuau.qualtrics.com/jfe/form/SV_6Rsw3aKg2bKlxem

---

Your unique cultural values profile is a fount of strength. Draw on what you believe to inspire and motivate others. Carefully consider the cultural values that you uphold and align your leadership style to best suit your character. You might now have a bit more of an insight into why some of the leadership theories that we've discussed have resonated with you more, or less – it's about your cultural values.

Next, let's think about others' cultural differences. I'd like you to do the same cultural values profile exercise again. But this time, instead of recording your own results, I want you to identify what you think would be the dominant cultural profile for most people across the country where you live. Are people typically more individualistic, or collectivistic? Are they punctual and focused, or do they take a more polychronic approach?

Try to support your choices for each dimension with an example of commonplace behaviour that you see in the community. For example, Australians have a fairly short-term orientation, and so I tend to see more conspicuous consumption on luxury goods and services, with less emphasis on thrift and savings.

Once you've completed a dominant cultural profile for the country, let's compare it with your own profile. Consider which dimensions are most similar, and different from, people in your country. Think carefully about the kinds of challenges that this could present. For example, people with different cultural values may not interpret your leadership behaviour in the way that you intend. Be mindful of the cultural lens through which others will see your behaviour and tailor your leadership approach to be most effective from their perspective. It's not about denying your own cultural values; it's about appreciating theirs.

I hope that's provided you with a useful perspective about cultural differences. But countries aren't always the best 'containers' of culture. Let's explore a few more contemporary ways to think about where cultural differences reside.

CONTAINERS OF CULTURE

We've traditionally thought of culture as existing within countries and large organisations – for example, Korean, British, or Jamaican culture, and the culture at Google, Toyota, or Starbucks. We can imagine countries and organisations then as distinct 'containers' of culture. Hofstede (1980), Trompenaars and Hampden-Turner (2020), Schwartz (1992), and House et al. (2004) all followed this dominant trend. They identified dimensions of cultural value differences, and then aggregated their findings to the country level to describe national cultures.

The problem is that we now know that 80% of the variation in cultural values exists within countries, and not between them (Taras et al., 2016). For example, I was born in Ukraine, I grew up in New Zealand, and now live in Australia; not one of these countries' values fits me well. It's clear that countries are a poor proxy for culture. But it remains unclear where, if not in countries, that cultural differences are contained. Scholars have only recently started to explore this question.

Taras et al. (2016) revealed through their meta-analysis that it's more appropriate for us to think about professions, socio-economic classes, and free vs oppressed societies as contemporary containers of culture. These social groups each have strong cultural norms that transcend national borders. For example, the wealthy in France have more in common with the wealthy in Japan than they do with the poor in France. Likewise nurses, lawyers, and engineers have more in common with others in their profession around the world than do all the people living in India, Italy, or Iran.

One explanation might be that occupations, for example, train people to think in particular ways, to approach and solve problems with specific sets of cognitive tools. That's why accountants all over the world get along and share similar values – they think the same way. A new perspective on cultural differences is emerging that focuses on how people think instead of what values they uphold. Let's take a look.

CULTURAL COGNITION

So far we've been talking about culture as 'cultural values' by examining what different people think is important, on the basis that these cultural values will then shape their perceptions of and preferences for certain kinds of leadership behaviour. That has been the dominant approach to studying culture since the 1980s (Kirkman et al., 2017). But it's not the only way, and more contemporary approaches explore differences in 'how' we think rather than 'what' we think.

How people tend to collect, and make sense of, information about the world varies across cultures – that is, our cognitive processes are different. One prominent model of cultural cognitive differences is called analytic vs holistic thought. Let's see what it's all about.

Analytic vs Holistic Thought

Nisbett et al. (2001) proposed that how we think today derives from two ancient civilisations: Greece and China.

Between 500 BCE and 200 BCE these two civilisations made great progress in philosophy and moral thought (Jaspers, 1953), and their unique circumstances at the time led to two very different social structures. Ancient Chinese society was complex and hierarchical with an emphasis on harmony and balance, while ancient Greek society was characterised by personal agency with a focus on logic and debate.

Their social structures and philosophical ideologies shaped how people thought by making certain patterns of interaction preferable to others. The cognitive approach used by the ancient Greeks was more analytic, and that of the Chinese was more holistic. These two cognitive patterns have endured into the modern era and manifest in contemporary people.

Choi et al. (2007) developed four dimensions of analytic vs holistic thought that capture our different approaches to attention, causality, contraction, and change.

Attention: Object vs context. Attention is about what we notice in the external environment. Analytic thinkers focus their attention on the primary object and assign it to categories based on its attributes. Holistic thinkers take in the context as a whole and focus on the relationships between objects. For example, when asked to describe a dining table, an analytic thinker might say that it's made of dark wood and can seat six people. Whereas a holistic thinker might say that it's a family space for getting together to share a meal.

Causality: Dispositionism vs interactionism. Causality is about how we understand why events happen. Analytic thinkers focus on the internal 'dispositions', characteristics, or motivations of individuals. Holistic thinkers examine the contextual circumstances and 'interactions' between people. For example, when a child is caught stealing, an analytic thinker might look to their personality and motives – maybe they've got issues with authority, or they were looking for a thrill. A holistic thinker might focus instead on their social circumstances, such as problems at home, or pressure from their peers.

Contradiction: Formal logic vs dialectics. Analytic thinkers take all statements as either true or false, and believe that they cannot be both at the same time. When faced with a contradiction, they choose the most plausible option and reject the least. Holistic thinkers reconcile, accept, and transcend contradiction, understanding that even opposing ideas can both be true. When faced with a contradiction, they seek compromise by finding value in both arguments. For example, when asked at 12 noon if it's day or night, an analytic thinker might say that it's day, whereas a holistic thinker might say that it's both, because it's day here and night on the other side of the planet.

Change: linear vs cyclic. Analytic thinkers see change as a linear process moving through incremental and permanent steps. When contemplating the future they expect gradual progress based on their past experiences. Holistic thinkers see the world as in a constant state of change moving in a series of cycles. When contemplating the future they expect frequent cyclical change of greater magnitude. For example, an analytic thinker might picture a successful career as gradual promotion accompanied by an ever-expanding knowledge base and skillset. A holistic thinker, on the other hand, might picture each promotion as a fresh cycle where you re-learn a new role from the beginning and, once mastered, progress to the next level.

Let's take our next quiz (Quiz 6.2) to discover if you have a more analytic or holistic cognitive approach.

―――― Quiz 6.2 ――――

Holistic Cognition Scale

Image Alt Text: https://ecuau.qualtrics.com/jfe/form/SV_eDmPhIclYTcCu6W

Adapted from Lux et al. (2021).

You've likely found yourself somewhere in the middle, including aspects of both analytic and holistic approaches, with one style that tends to be more dominant. Build strength through complementary diversity on your teams by collaborating with people who have different cultural cognitive approaches.

Okay, now that you've got a good grasp of various cultural differences let's consider diversity and inclusion more broadly.

DIVERSITY AND INCLUSION

Diversity is about recognising that we're all different, and similar, across many intersecting dimensions, including gender, sex, sexuality, race, ethnicity, language, culture, religion, mental and physical ability, socio-economic status, carer responsibilities, and immigration status. These many differences are a source of significant advantage and can improve organisational performance (cf. Smulowitz et al., 2019).

Minority groups are traditionally under-represented in organisations, and especially so in leadership roles. But surface-level differences in gender, ethnicity, or nationality won't necessarily bring greater diversity in knowledge and perspectives if people are well acculturated to the group (Wang et al., 2019). The value comes from divergent beliefs, preferences, and problem-solving styles that broaden the range of knowledge and can generate new ideas and solutions (Stahl et al., 2010). And yet increasing diversity alone doesn't automatically produce benefits; what matters is how our organisations can harness that diversity – and that's why we need inclusion (Ely & Thomas, 2020).

Inclusion is about embracing the different skills, perspectives, and experiences that diversity can offer our organisations. Diverse people must feel safe and valued to be able to contribute these talents, and that requires an inclusive organisational culture. Here's where leadership comes in, it's up to leaders to create that positive and supportive climate that enables diverse people to flourish (Mor Barak et al., 2022).

Next we'll explore how diversity plays out in organisations.

Multiculturalism in Organisations

Cox (1991) created a three-stage framework to illustrate how attitudes towards diversity progress in organisations. He describes organisations as monolithic, plural, or multicultural.

In 'monolithic' organisations employees are homogeneous, often with a large majority of white males. The workforce includes few women, ethnic minorities, or diverse employees. There's high structural segregation, which is to say that where diverse people are employed, they tend to feature in either secretarial or maintenance positions, and not in leadership roles. There's also no integration of diverse employees into informal groups and they're excluded from the social side of the organisation. Diversity is met with prejudice and discrimination in monolithic organisations.

In 'plural' organisations employees are more heterogeneous, with greater participation of women, ethnic minorities, and diverse people. Hiring and promotion strategies may give preference to diverse employees, sometimes setting specific targets or quotas, which includes partial structural integration into leadership roles. Managers often receive training on equity, diversity, and inclusion, cultural sensitivity, and so on to reduce bias. Some diverse employees are included in social groups. Diversity is tolerated throughout plural organisations.

In 'multicultural' organisations employees are heterogeneous in proportion to the local population demographic profile, including women, ethnic minorities, and diverse people. There's complete structural integration so that diverse people are represented throughout leadership tiers, and fully integrated into social networks. Diversity is valued throughout multicultural organisations. Unfortunately, few organisations have managed to achieve these characteristics, but appreciation for diversity and inclusion is growing rapidly across all cultural spheres.

Creating inclusive multicultural work environments is fast becoming a core focus for leaders today. Let's explore how inclusive leadership theory can help.

INCLUSIVE LEADERSHIP

Nembhard and Edmondson (2006) first proposed that leadership should be inclusive to help every employee feel safe enough to fully contribute their talents. Carmeli et al. (2010) expanded the idea into 'inclusive leadership' as a distinct approach that's characterised by leaders who are open, accessible, and available to engage with their followers.

Shore et al. (2011) explain that inclusion is about feeling valued as a member of the group while satisfying our need to belong and be unique. Our need for belonging is about developing and maintaining enduring social relationships (Baumeister & Leary, 1995). And our need for uniqueness is about preserving our distinctive sense of self (Fromkin & Snyder, 1980).

Randel et al. (2018) further developed these ideas to define inclusive leadership as 'a set of positive leader behaviours that facilitate group members perceiving belongingness in the work group while maintaining their uniqueness within the group as they fully contribute to group processes and outcomes' (p. 190).

Followers must feel both belonging and uniqueness to truly be included. That means being accepted as legitimate group members, while also acknowledging individual talents and allowing individuals' voices to be heard and appreciated.

Here's what we can do as leaders to create such inclusive workplace cultures.

Five Dimensions

Randel et al. (2018) proposed five dimensions of inclusive leadership behaviour, including three related to belongingness: supporting group members, ensuring justice and equity, and shared decision-making. Two more related to uniqueness: encouraging diverse contributions and helping group members fully contribute. Al-Atwi and Al-Hassani (2021) empirically validated the model.

Belongingness

Supporting group members is about showing that you care about your followers' needs and feelings. It includes checking in with each person on your team to find out how they're doing, to ask about their well-being and experiences working in the group. Inclusive leaders take the time to get to know each of their followers and appreciate them both as individuals, and as valued members of the team.

Ensuring justice and equity is about treating all of your followers fairly and without personal bias. It includes considering how different followers could be affected, even unintentionally, by your decisions and adjusting practices to make sure that everyone has a comparable experience. Inclusive leaders proactively seek input from each of their followers to help develop equitable systems that reduce the opportunity for prejudice to influence processes and outcomes.

Shared decision-making is about enabling every follower to have their voice heard and to contribute to decisions. It includes actively asking for opinions and perspectives from each of your followers, across different formats where individuals can feel comfortable to offer their ideas – for example, in closed meetings, one-on-ones, or offline conversations over email. Inclusive leaders share power by consulting all the relevant stakeholders before reaching a decision.

Uniqueness

Encouraging diverse contributions is about inspiring your followers to offer new ideas that draw on their unique perspectives. It includes promoting the value of divergent thinking that can challenge conventional solutions and spur innovation; our differences are an asset. We must protect and nurture our followers' uniqueness, so that they can thrive and make the most of their talents. Inclusive leaders constructively incorporate diverse perspectives to improve overall performance.

Helping group members fully contribute is about demonstrating to each of your followers that their input is welcome and needed. It means incorporating a broad range of perspectives and making it clear that every voice must be heard: including lower-level employees, new hires, casual staff, and contractors, as well as women, ethnic minorities, and diverse people. Inclusive leaders show us that everyone has something valuable to offer and can bring their full selves to work.

Everyone can Contribute

Inclusive leaders help create an organisational culture that encourages followers' sense of belonging and uniqueness by role modelling and reinforcing these positive behaviours among other followers as well. It's not only about how our leaders treat us personally, but also how they treat everyone else, and how our colleagues treat each other; it has to be everyone (Randel et al., 2018).

Being included helps us to feel psychologically safe and empowered such that we can best contribute our talents.

Psychological safety is about feeling comfortable to be yourself and employ your unique talents without worrying that it will compromise your self-image, status, or career (Edmondson, 1999; Kahn, 1990). When we don't feel safe, we must spend our energy protecting ourselves by watching for threats and taking steps to reduce our vulnerability. Inclusive leaders enable their followers to focus on being productive and taking healthy risks – for example, by volunteering diverse opinions.

Psychological empowerment is about feeling that you matter and have control over what you're doing (Spreitzer, 1995). When we feel empowered, we tend to take the initiative and get more engaged in our work, which improves our performance. Inclusive leaders empower their followers by showing them that they're valued and have a voice in decisions.

Inclusive leadership therefore improves overall organisational performance by enabling everyone to bring their whole self to work.

Challenges in Practice

Inclusive leadership sounds amazing, but it's not without its challenges in practice.

The first challenge is called 'decoupling' and it means having a gap between your diversity and inclusion policies, and their practical implementation in the organisation. It's when leaders fail to live up to their inclusive rhetoric (Mor Barak et al., 2022). The greater the discrepancy between what's said and what really happens, the less likely that followers will see their workplace as truly inclusive.

The second challenge is about differences in interpretation. Women, ethnic minorities, and diverse people may perceive that inclusive rhetoric is disingenuous, as something that's promoted out of necessity rather than as an articulation of real values. People take note of what you do, and investing your effort into enacting inclusive leadership behaviour will signal your genuine support (Randel et al., 2018).

The third challenge comes from encouraging diverse people to assimilate with the dominant group. Helping diverse people to 'fit in' might seem like a good idea. It's not. Asking them to repress their unique characteristics and become more like the mainstream members of the organisation is not inclusion. We don't need to help diverse people fit in; we need to respect and appreciate their differences. Inclusive leaders champion the value of diversity across all aspects of the organisation.

SUMMARY

Cultural differences may present the greatest challenge, and opportunity, for contemporary leaders. Individual people are more diverse than ever before and bring a wealth of perspectives, knowledge, and experiences to our organisations. Appreciate then that every person you're leading has developed a different point of view from a lifetime of experiences, and they'll perceive your leadership rhetoric and behaviour through the unique kaleidoscope of their cultural background. Leaders cannot operate on stereotypes of culture and must work to develop an informed opinion.

Cultural values are people's perceptions of and preferences for certain kinds of behaviour, motivations, and ambitions. They're guiding principles that tell us what's appropriate and important in our societies. Followers' cultural leadership perspectives then serve as standards that guide what is appropriate, desired, and expected of leaders. Your own unique cultural values profile is also a fount of strength. Draw on what you believe to inspire and motivate others. Carefully consider the cultural values that you uphold and align your leadership style to best suit your character.

Diversity is about recognising that we're all different, and similar, across many intersecting dimensions, including gender, sex, sexuality, race, ethnicity, language, culture, religion, mental and physical ability, socio-economic status, carer responsibilities, and immigration status. These many differences are a source of significant advantage and can improve organisational performance. It's up to leaders to create a positive and supportive climate that enables diverse people to flourish.

Inclusive leadership is about helping followers to feel valued as members of the group by creating a sense of belonging, while also keeping their uniqueness. It includes supporting group members, ensuring justice and equity, shared decision-making, encouraging diverse contributions, and helping group members fully contribute. An inclusive culture enables every follower to feel psychologically safe and empowered such that they can best apply their talents. Inclusive leaders show us that everyone has something valuable to offer and can bring their full selves to work.

> 'There's no way I can single-handedly save the world or, perhaps, even make a perceptible difference – but how ashamed I would be to let a day pass without making one more effort.'
>
> Extract from *The Relativity of Wrong* by Isaac Asimov (1988).

REFERENCES

Al-Atwi, A. A., & Al-Hassani, K. K. (2021). Inclusive leadership: Scale validation and potential consequences. *Leadership & Organization Development Journal*, *42*(8), 1222–1240. https://doi.org/10.1108/LODJ-08-2020-0327

Baumeister, R. F., & Leary, M. R. (1995). The need to belong: Desire for interpersonal attachments as a fundamental human motivation. *Psychological Bulletin*, *117*(3), 497–529. https://doi.org/10.4324/9781351153683-3

Carmeli, A., Reiter-Palmon, R., & Ziv, E. (2010). Inclusive leadership and employee involvement in creative tasks in the workplace: The mediating role of psychological safety. *Creativity Research Journal*, *22*(3), 250–260. https://doi.org/10.1080/10400419.2010.504654

Choi, I., Koo, M., & Choi, J. A. (2007). Individual differences in analytic versus holistic thinking. *Personality and Social Psychology Bulletin*, *33*(5), 691–705. https://doi.org/10.1177/0146167206298568

Cox, T., Jr (1991). The multicultural organization. *Academy of Management Perspectives*, *5*(2), 34–47. https://doi.org/10.5465/ame.1991.4274675

Edmondson, A. C. (1999). Psychological safety and learning behavior in work teams. *Administrative Science Quarterly*, *44*(2), 350–383. https://doi.org/10.2307/2666999

Ely, R. J., & Thomas, D. A. (2020). Getting serious about diversity: Enough already with the business case. *Harvard Business Review*, *98*(6), 114–122.

Epitropaki, O., Sy, T., Martin, R., Tram-Quon, S., & Topakas, A. (2013). Implicit leadership and followership theories 'in the wild': Taking stock of information-processing approaches to leadership and followership in organizational settings. *The Leadership Quarterly*, *24*(6), 858–881. https://doi.org/10.1016/j.leaqua.2013.10.005

Fromkin, H. L., & Snyder, C. R. (1980). The search for uniqueness and valuation of scarcity: Neglected dimensions of value in exchange theory. In K. J. Gergen, M. S. Greenberg, & R. H. Willis (Eds), *Social exchange: Advances in theory and research* (pp. 57–75). Plenum Press.

Hall, E. T. (1959). *The silent language*. Doubleday & Company.

Hofstede, G. (2011). Dimensionalizing cultures: The Hofstede model in context. *Online Readings in Psychology and Culture*, *2*(1), 1–26. https://doi.org/10.9707/2307-0919.1014

Hofstede, G. H. (1980). *Culture's consequences: International differences in work-related values*. Sage Publications.

Hofstede, G. H. (2006). What did GLOBE really measure? Researchers' minds versus respondents' minds. *Journal of International Business Studies*, *37*(6), 882–896. https://doi.org/10.1057/palgrave.jibs.8400233

Hofstede, G. H., Hofstede, G. J., & Minkov, M. (2010). *Cultures and organizations: Software of the mind* (3rd ed.). McGraw-Hill.

House, R. J., Hanges, P. J., Javidan, M., Dorfman, P. W., & Gupta, V. (Eds). (2004). *Culture, leadership, and organizations: The GLOBE study of 62 societies*. Sage Publications.

Jaspers, K. (1953). *The origin and goal of history* (M. Bullock, Trans.). Routledge & Kegan Paul.

Javidan, M., & Carl, D. E. (2004). East meets West: A cross-cultural comparison of charismatic leadership among Canadian and Iranian executives. *Journal of Management Studies*, *41*(4), 665–691. https://doi.org/10.1111/j.1467-6486.2004.00449.x

Kahn, W. A. (1990). Psychological conditions of personal engagement and disengagement at work. *Academy of Management Journal*, *33*(4), 692–724. https://doi.org/10.5465/256287

Kirkman, B. L., Lowe, K. B., & Gibson, C. B. (2017). A retrospective on *Culture's Consequences*: The 35-year journey. *Journal of International Business Studies*, *48*(1), 12–29. https://doi.org/10.1057/s41267-016-0037-9

Lord, R. G., & Maher, K. J. (1991). *Leadership and information processing: Linking perceptions and performance*. Unwin Hyman.

Lux, A. A., Grover, S. L., & Teo, S. T. T. (2021). Development and validation of the holistic cognition scale. *Frontiers in Psychology*, *12*(551623), 1–15. https://doi.org/10.3389/fpsyg.2021.551623

Minkov, M., & Hofstede, G. (2011). The evolution of Hofstede's doctrine. *Cross Cultural Management: An International Journal*, *18*(1), 10–20. https://doi.org/10.1108/13527601111104269

Mor Barak, M. E., Luria, G., & Brimhall, K. C. (2022). What leaders say versus what they do: Inclusive leadership, policy-practice decoupling, and the anomaly of climate for inclusion. *Group & Organization Management*, *47*(4), 840–871. https://doi.org/10.1177/10596011211005916

Nembhard, I. M., & Edmondson, A. C. (2006). Making it safe: The effects of leader inclusiveness and professional status on psychological safety and improvement efforts in health care teams. *Journal of Organizational Behavior*, *27*(7), 941–966. https://doi.org/10.1002/job.413

Nisbett, R. E., Peng, K., Choi, I., & Norenzayan, A. (2001). Culture and systems of thought: Holistic versus analytic cognition. *Psychological Review*, *108*(2), 291–310. https://doi.org/10.1037/0033-295X.108.2.291

Pagel, M. D. (2013). *Wired for culture: Origins of the human social mind*. W. W. Norton & Company.

Pollock, D. C., Van Reken, R. E., & Pollock, M. V. (2017). *Third culture kids: The experience of growing up amongst worlds* (3rd ed.). Nicholas Brealey Publishing.

Randel, A. E., Galvin, B. M., Shore, L. M., Ehrhart, K. H., Chung, B. G., Dean, M. A., & Kedharnath, U. (2018). Inclusive leadership: Realizing positive outcomes through belongingness and being valued for uniqueness. *Human Resource Management Review, 28*(2), 190–203. https://doi.org/10.1016/j.hrmr.2017.07.002

Schwartz, S. H. (1992). Universals in the content and structure of values: Theoretical advances and empirical tests in 20 countries. In M. P. Zanna (Ed.), *Advances in Experimental Social Psychology* (Vol. 25, pp. 1–65). Academic Press. https://doi.org/10.1016/S0065-2601(08)60281-6

Shore, L. M., Randel, A. E., Chung, B. G., Dean, M. A., Holcombe Ehrhart, K., & Singh, G. (2011). Inclusion and diversity in work groups: A review and model for future research. *Journal of Management, 37*(4), 1262–1289. https://doi.org/10.1177/0149206310385943

Smulowitz, S., Becerra, M., & Mayo, M. (2019). Racial diversity and its asymmetry within and across hierarchical levels: The effects on financial performance. *Human Relations, 72*(10), 1671–1696. https://doi.org/10.1177/0018726718812602

Spreitzer, G. M. (1995). Psychological empowerment in the workplace: Dimensions, measurement, and validation. *Academy of Management Journal, 38*(5), 1442–1465. https://doi.org/10.5465/256865

Stahl, G. K., & Maznevski, M. L. (2021). Unraveling the effects of cultural diversity in teams: A retrospective of research on multicultural work groups and an agenda for future research. *Journal of International Business Studies, 52*, 4–22. https://doi.org/10.1057/s41267-020-00389-9

Stahl, G. K., Maznevski, M. L., Voigt, A., & Jonsen, K. (2010). Unraveling the effects of cultural diversity in teams: A meta-analysis of research on multicultural work groups. *Journal of International Business Studies, 41*, 690–709. https://doi.org/10.1057/jibs.2009.85

Stephan, U., & Pathak, S. (2016). Beyond cultural values? Cultural leadership ideals and entrepreneurship. *Journal of Business Venturing, 31*(5), 505–523. https://doi.org/10.1016/j.jbusvent.2016.07.003

Taras, V., Steel, P., & Kirkman, B. L. (2016). Does country equate with culture? Beyond geography in the search for cultural boundaries. *Management International Review, 56*, 455–487. https://doi.org/10.1007/s11575-016-0283-x

Trompenaars, F., & Hampden-Turner, C. (2020). *Riding the waves of culture: Understanding diversity in global business* (4th ed.). McGraw-Hill.

Tylor, E. B. (1871). *Primitive culture: Researches into the development of mythology, philosophy, religion, art, and custom* (Vol. 1). Bradbury, Evans, and Company.

Wang, J., Cheng, G. H. L., Chen, T., & Leung, K. (2019). Team creativity/innovation in culturally diverse teams: A meta-analysis. *Journal of Organizational Behavior, 40*(6), 693–708. https://doi.org/10.1002/job.2362

7
VALUES, INTEGRITY, AND ETHICAL LEADERSHIP

Overview

Values, ethics, and integrity are three vital aspects of good leadership; this chapter builds one upon the other to create a holistic understanding of all three. It starts by interrogating the concept of personal values, exploring how we form our values, and why it's so important that we as leaders know what our values really are.

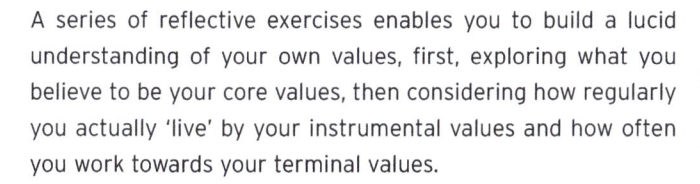

A series of reflective exercises enables you to build a lucid understanding of your own values, first, exploring what you believe to be your core values, then considering how regularly you actually 'live' by your instrumental values and how often you work towards your terminal values.

Next, we consider the different spheres of responsibility that leaders face in the workplace, with particular emphasis on their competing nature: ethical decisions rarely occur in a vacuum and almost always include trade-offs. Understanding our own perspectives prepares us for confronting such ethical dilemmas. You'll work through a reflective exercise to discover how prominent figures in your life have demonstrated integrity.

Exercise 7.1: Your values

Exercise 7.2: Integrity

Quiz 7.1: Ethical leadership

Exercise 7.3: Your perfect life

You are then introduced to ethical leadership and the chapter culminates in a frank discussion about why we as leaders should bother to concern ourselves with ethics and integrity.

To conclude, you are asked to describe a day in your perfect life, and are then challenged to consider whether the core values that you espoused earlier align with this ideal existence – if not, it may be time to have an honest conversation with yourself about who you are and who you want to be.

Positive leadership is impossible to sustain without a clear understanding of ethics. Leaders face a myriad of complex consequences that ripple outwards from their decisions and behaviour. We're rarely faced with simple choices between right and wrong; few of us would knowingly choose 'wrong' if it were that easy. Instead, leaders must carefully navigate the murky grey areas between multiple competing outcomes and responsibilities.

In this chapter we will first explore three essential topics: values, ethics, and integrity, before having a frank conversation about why we should bother burdening ourselves with these additional demands. We will then consider ethical leadership as another approach that's specifically tailored to creating a climate for responsible progress.

VALUES

The notion of 'values' comes from the field of psychology and has a long history. Vernon and Allport (1931) first introduced the concept of personal values as distinct from comparable constructs like personality. Rokeach (1973) then ignited research interest by explaining that our values serve as reference points for the kinds of attitudes that we form and the behaviours that we engage in.

Schwartz and Bilsky (1987) later defined values as 'concepts or beliefs, about desirable end states or behaviours, that transcend specific situations, guide selection or evaluation of behaviour and events, and are ordered by relative importance' (p. 551). Let's now explore what each of these five characteristics means and how they can help us to better understand our own values.

First, your values are the fundamental beliefs you hold about what is important. Values are therefore entirely subjective; they're not facts. They are your personal beliefs and reflect only what you think matters about yourself, others, and the world in general. For example, you might believe that autonomy is important, but that doesn't mean that you are right now entirely independent and unaccountable to anyone else. Rather, it suggests that you'd readily welcome opportunities for autonomy.

Second, values are positively framed and inherently desirable; they describe what you think is good and worthy. Your personal values are therefore often aspirational and describe your ideal self, rather than your actual self (Roccas et al., 2014). For example, you might believe that honesty is important, but that doesn't mean that you always tell the blatant truth to yourself and everyone else in all situations. Rather, it suggests that you're striving towards being honest as much as you can.

Third, values are broad ideals that are relevant throughout many different situations and aspects of life (Schwartz, 1992). They're not constrained to specific contexts and apply across the breadth of experiences including your work, private, social, and public lives. For example, you might believe that achievement is important, and so you'd likely pursue ambitious goals in your personal and professional life, perhaps taking a competitive approach in your career, hobbies, sports, etc.

Fourth, values motivate and shape your attitudes and behaviour. They're the guiding principles in your life that influence how you interact with yourself, others, and the world around you (Rokeach, 1973). What you believe affects your preferences and actions. For example, if you believe that benevolence is important, then you're more likely to help others, supporting colleagues at work who are struggling, volunteering for local charities, and responding with kindness to people around you.

Fifth, values are subjectively ranked based on how important they are. You've got your own hierarchy of value priorities, ranging from values that are extremely important to others that are less so. Your top priority values have the strongest influence as guiding principles in your life (Rokeach, 1973). For example, you might value autonomy, honesty, achievement, and benevolence, but some of these may pull you in different directions, and you'll find that certain values are more important to you and will come first.

Some values are mutually compatible and reflect goals that we can pursue at the same time and with the same kinds of behaviour. Other values conflict with one another and pursuing one might compromise or impede the other. For example, we can pursue two self-enhancing values like power and achievement together, but doing so makes it harder for us to work towards a self-transcendent value like benevolence (Sagiv et al., 2017).

Recognise then that your leadership actions will have trade-offs and that values can guide your decisions and behaviour. To determine what we think is right and wrong, we must first know what is, and isn't, important to us. A lucid understanding of your own personal values is therefore essential to effective leadership, and values are the foundation upon which we build concepts of morality, ethics, and integrity.

But it's hard to embark on a journey of self-discovery when you're faced with an ethical dilemma today. That's why we need to discover and clearly articulate exactly what our values are now, to better prepare us to chart these treacherous waters in the moment. Let's consider two different kinds of values that will help you to better understand what's most important to you now, and in the long run.

Instrumental and Terminal

We can think about values as either instrumental or terminal, sometimes also referred to as intrinsic and extrinsic (Rønnow-Rasmussen, 2015). Instrumental values are those that we use daily to inform how we interact – like good tools, they're means to an end. Instrumental values include, for example, being cheerful, polite, clean, loyal, responsible, courageous, imaginative, logical, forgiving, honest, clever, disciplined, respectful, and hard-working.

Your instrumental values help you navigate the hundreds of little decisions you make all the time about what to do and say, and how to behave. For example, you might arrive to class, work, or social events a few minutes early because you value punctuality. When you see someone throw rubbish in the street, you'd pick it up and put it in a bin because you value cleanliness or looking after the environment. These actions may feel instinctual, rather than deliberate considerations and decisions, but it's your instrumental values that guide you in the minutiae of everyday life.

A good way to discover your instrumental values is to think about the kinds of decisions that you make every day. Look closely at how you behave, alone and with others. What is it that your behaviour and rhetoric are signalling? For example, you might find that you always turn up to university and work engagements, no matter how tired you are, how short on sleep, how busy with other aspects of your life. Think about what that means for you; commitment may be one of your instrumental values then, or discipline, diligence, and hard work.

If you abstain from alcohol, go to bed early, and look after your body well, then perhaps self-care is one of your values. If you're that one friend that everyone in your circle can always count on to show up when there's trouble, then loyalty and responsibility could be important values to you. Pay attention to the details, how you do anything is often how you do everything; if you're careful, patient, and attentive to details when making a cup of coffee, you're probably careful, patient, and attentive to details in your work and social relationships too.

Terminal values are those that reflect life-long ambitions and will guide the major decisions in our lives – like aspirational ideals, they describe desirable outcomes that we pursue. For example, terminal values include freedom, fulfilment, wealth, meaning, recognition, security, wisdom, moral virtue, achievement, happiness, and peace. Imagine your terminal values as describing where you're going, and instrumental values as how you're going to get there.

Your terminal values inform the kinds of careers you pursue, the kinds of life partners that you'll select, whether you'll start a family, where in the world you live and work, and so on. Each of these decisions is a self-selection process that funnels us down specific life paths that echo the values that shape our preferences. Terminal values outline the trajectory and intended destination of our lives.

For example, people working in different occupations tend to prioritise certain values. Knafo and Sagiv (2004) find that managers, bankers, and marketers prioritise achievement and power; social workers, psychologists, and teachers prioritise benevolence; while artists, musicians, and actors prioritise non-conformity. We're drawn to professions that enable us to express our primary values (Arieli et al., 2016), and we're most satisfied when our values align with the nature of our work (Kristof-Brown et al., 2005).

While each of the terminal values that I've listed above sounds important, remember that our values are ordered by our own priorities and that we can't pursue all of them at once. Try, and you'll likely make scant progress towards any of them. That's why you'll need to figure out for yourself what's actually most important to you now, so that everything you do from here onwards will take you closer towards that destination.

But I can't tell you what your values should be. Wealth, achievement, and recognition may go well together – happiness, peace, and moral virtue too – but some will conflict, and you'll need to decide what kind of person you want to be. There's no right or wrong answer to this question. To help you better understand what's shaped you as a person, you also need to find out where your values came from.

Where Values Come From

Values come from a combination of your genetic heritage and exposure to social interactions with your family, education institutions, and broader community. Uzefovsky et al. (2016) estimate that your genetic heritage accounts for around 29% to 47% of the similarity in your values with your biological parents. The remaining 53% to 71% we decide for ourselves based on our experiences.

Our values are formed early on in our lives. By five years old, we can already distinguish between different values and appreciate their conflicts and compatibilities. Children aged 5 to 12 years old demonstrate well-established value hierarchies in their behaviour, even if they're not yet able to articulate the concepts (Döring et al., 2015; Lee et al., 2017).

The particular social and cultural environment in which you grew up therefore has a critical influence on your values. Parents seek to intentionally transmit and reinforce their own values in children, and families are powerful means of value socialisation. Another part of the story is that we also inherently share the same cultural, religious, and economic environment as our parents, and so what we come to believe to be important is often shaped in similar ways by similar social forces (Hitlin & Piliavin, 2004).

When we enter our adolescence from around 10 years old, we start to have more control over our environment by choosing our own friends and social activities, such as hobbies, sports, and preferred pastimes. For example, you might spend much of your free time with a soccer team, or at a library, or skateboarding at a local park. Each of these social institutions then exposes you to different values beyond your family and school that you may or may not choose to incorporate into your own beliefs.

We're constantly looking at the world around us, perceiving, interpreting, and seeking to understand the different ways that people live and interact with the world. All the while we're deciding for ourselves what's right, what's important, what we believe, and how things should be. We're figuring out who we are, who we want to be, and where we fit in.

Sometimes we also develop values in contrast to what we see in the world. You might look out at the world around you and see that there's so much cruelty and selfish materialism. Instead of mimicking these ideals, you might decide that what's really important is what's missing, and develop kindness and generosity as core values in opposition to what you're seeing around you because you've decided that it's wrong and so you'll try to offset that with your own behaviour.

You might see your parents being frugal with their money, rarely spending much of what they make, always saving, working hard, but never enjoying the fruits of their labour. You think that they've wasted their time, that you wouldn't want to come to the end with a fortune in your bank account and no life experiences. So then you might engage in more conspicuous consumption, leisure, and living your life in the moment; you eat cake, take afternoons off, and book that holiday.

We tend to adopt many of our values from significant people in our lives – first our family, then friends and teachers, and close community, but even social media, the news, and so on. The rest is shaped by our own life experiences. We tend to discover what's important to us as we go through the various trials and tribulations of our adolescence. Our values and priorities stabilise during this period of adolescence and then change little in adulthood (Hitlin & Piliavin, 2004). Many studies demonstrate that our adult values are relatively stable over time (e.g. Milfont et al., 2016).

There is, however, a time when our values can and do change significantly after they've been established, and that's during major life-changing events – for example, immigrating to another country, having children, losing loved ones, changing careers, or experiencing significant trauma or illness. It's in these moments that we feel unmoored and adrift in possibility, what we thought about the world before no longer seems to matter, and how we choose to experience these times will reforge us anew.

It can feel like we're discovering our true values for the first time when we're confronted with a life-changing event, or even a near miss. It makes us stop and think about what's actually important. We ask ourselves, if everything was to change today, would we feel proud of the lives we've lived, have we been valuing the right things? Maybe I spent too much time at my desk and not enough time outside, chasing wealth and recognition instead of raising a family, or wallowing in self-indulgence rather than creating something worthwhile. Cataclysmic experiences can awaken us to the real values that perhaps we've been ignoring.

Our individual values exist as one coherent system, and so when you change one part of your value system, it's accompanied by corresponding changes in the rest of your value system (Bardi et al., 2009). For example, after the birth of your first child you may find yourself valuing security and stability more than before, and that will come with reduced emphasis on adventure, discovery, and risk-taking.

Our values are always guiding our choices and behaviour, but it's not always explicitly clear to us what exactly our values are. They're rather like these hidden assumptions that we've absorbed and that exist in the back of our mind. We know what's important to us, but we've rarely had to put it down into specific words before, and so these ideas remain vague and untested.

Discover your Values

We must take time out for introspection to discover our values. I will guide you through a process of reflection to help get you started on this journey. It will require you to be completely honest with yourself. Be warned that self-knowledge is sometimes painful. You might not always like what you see in the mirror, but you cannot hope to grow without first confronting who you are.

We'll next work through an exercise of three parts: I'll ask you first to articulate a few of your most important instrumental and terminal values, then figure out where you've acquired these particular values, and then consider how often you live by and work towards your values.

Your values may be personally held beliefs, but without action – they're just wishful thinking. In Exercise 7.1, I'll ask you to think back over the last two weeks and tell me how often you lived by your instrumental values and how often you worked towards your terminal values. For example, if honesty is one of your instrumental values, how often were you honest with yourself and others in your daily interactions? If financial independence is one of your terminal values, what steps have you taken towards it?

I want you to reflect as deeply as you can on what's really important to you. Be honest with yourself. I'm not going to judge your responses or ask you to share them with anyone; this is just for you to get to know yourself better. It's not until we are in a situation like this where we are asked to articulate our values that we actually come out and say, 'This is what's important to me'.

Exercise 7.1

Your Values

Image Alt Text: https://ecuau.qualtrics.com/jfe/form/SV_2h3MEGyE57JuVKe

---

I hope that this exercise has been enlightening, and helped connect who you are with your life experiences. For example, three of my terminal values are personal transformation, adventure, and making a contribution; they've shaped who I am today and where I'm going next.

Self-Accepting Leaders

Having an honest understanding of your instrumental and terminal values gives you both a direction in life and guidance on how to get there.

For example, if self-expression and creativity are two of your terminal values, they'll inform the kinds of relationships you pursue, the hobbies you engage in, and the professions you feel fit you best. I wager that such a person would rather pursue the arts than become a banker to make more money.

Your instrumental values will inform what you will, and will not, do to reach towards those terminal values. For example, you might value financial independence as a terminal value, but also value kindness and compassion as instrumental values. They'll guide you on that journey and shape your behaviour; you might be less ruthless in your pursuit of wealth compared to others and it could take you longer to build independence, but you might also help many others along the way.

Having that kind of honest relationship with yourself focuses your efforts. There are few things worse than lying to yourself and others about your values – for example, telling yourself that you value generosity and compassion when you really value achievement and recognition. Your actions will inevitably demonstrate that dissonance and the incompatibility of your values such that you'll do both badly because you're not wholly committed to either.

You'd do better to understand what you really want and just go for that wholeheartedly, unashamedly. Don't be afraid to go after what you want; otherwise you'll never get it.

If you can get these two right, you will become a more powerful leader. People will see that consistency in your values and your behaviour, they'll see that self-knowledge of who you are and what you believe about the world. That gives you a position to bring others along on your journey, which is in some ways what leadership is. We're all on a journey. If you have a clear, motivated, powerful purpose, that will attract others to your cause.

This will also prepare you to deal with some of the conflicts and challenges you will face, such as difficult decisions where there is no good choice, just bad and worse choices, and you will need to know what you think is important before you get there.

Now that you've identified a strong foundation of well-articulated values, let's turn our attention to ethics.

ETHICS

Ethics is a branch of philosophy that's concerned with what's right and wrong, based on what's valued. Here you can see the connection to our earlier conversation about values as the foundation of ethics and moral reasoning.

As with leadership itself, people have come up with different ways to think about ethics that are described in various well-known ethical theories or frameworks. Each ethical framework is built upon moral principles or statements about what's most important, which then governs what kinds of behaviours are considered to be right and wrong.

Ethical theories therefore articulate what's valued, by whom, and how valuable it is relative to other considerations, in this way offering guidance about how to weigh our decisions and determine the right course of action.

You may have already heard of one or more ethical theories. We'll consider three – hedonism, stoicism, and consequentialism – to give us a platform to appreciate how ethical theory can inform our leadership decision-making and behaviour.

Hedonism, Stoicism, and Other -isms

The following are broad overviews of three deeply contested concepts within which exist different schools of thought and application. Let them serve as an introduction to our discussion.

The core moral principle of hedonism is that the greatest good is maximising pleasure and minimising pain. We can apply this principle in different ways, either seeking to satisfy our every trifling fancy, or by pursuing a deeper sense of intrinsic fulfilment. We can also consider righteous actions as those that only benefit ourselves irrespective of others, or rather as those actions which will benefit the most people.

The core moral principle of stoicism is that the greatest good is contentment and serenity. Stoicism teaches us to practise self-mastery over our own desires and emotions, so that we may govern how we choose to act, rather than react. We can't always control what happens to us and around us, but we can always control how we internally experience those events. When our will is independent, we have peace of mind and can pursue a virtuous life.

The core moral principle of consequentialism is that the greatest good is in improving our general welfare. Actions are righteous then if they have more positive outcomes than negative. How we get there is of no concern, and so the ends justify the means. Utilitarianism is another version of consequentialism that takes it further to consider everyone equally, and so righteous actions are only those that increase the total happiness and well-being of everyone affected.

Moral Principles

Think of each ethical theory as a separate lens through which we can view behaviour. The moral principles that exist within these frameworks enable us to identify specific decisions, actions, and behaviours as right and wrong.

For example, if someone was to verbally abuse me in the street, it would be wrong, from a stoic perspective, for me to get upset and lash out impulsively in response. Their behaviour does not somehow justify mine and we are each of us responsible for our own actions. As another example, a selfless act of charity that only burdens me and offers me no kind of pleasure would be wrong from an egoic or self-centred reading of hedonism. Altruism is permitted then if I'm only doing it to feel good about myself and thus achieve a deeper sense of pleasure.

Obviously, some ethical theories are better for humankind as a species. We know that if we were all to work together, rather than to satisfy our own individual ambitions, we would progress further in improving our general welfare and moral development.

By being a member of society, you agree to be bound by the moral principles that underpin that society. Some of these principles are explicit, such as the systems of law around the world that include civil law, common law, and religious law. Laws set out what each society has decided is right and wrong, and the consequences for breaking these moral principles.

Some of these principles are unwritten, and we all have implicit moral perspectives that we use to judge what we believe to be right and wrong. For example, many of us might believe that it's wrong to lie. If you asked me on the street for directions, it would be immoral for me to knowingly send you the wrong way for my own amusement.

I've never seen that explicitly written down anywhere, but I'm confident that lying in this manner would be seen as morally wrong, so somehow I've acquired this implicit understanding of what's expected of me in society.

Governments use laws as explicit moral principles that point us in beneficial directions, while our mutually reinforced implicit principles then govern aspects of behaviour that are beyond official control. So far these have been easy examples to get us going. It gets more complicated when we start to think about leadership and organisations. Unfortunately we don't all agree on our implicit morals, and herein lies the challenge.

For example, I might have an employee who's just had their third child. I honour my parental leave obligations as an employer, but when they return to work, they're distracted, overwhelmed by ongoing carer responsibilities, and unable to meet their performance targets. I start the due process for performance management, and after no improvement, I terminate their employment.

In this example I'm perfectly within the explicit ethical framework of Australia – I've followed the laws and regulations. But implicitly, parts of that may feel wrong to some of us, and not others. That's why you need that solid foundation of your own well-articulated individual values, so that you know what's most important to you.

On one hand, I have a moral responsibility to treat my employees fairly, and others having to do more work because of the new parent isn't right. I also have a moral responsibility to ensure the ongoing financial sustainability of the organisation, because if it fails, many others may suffer from sudden unemployment.

On the other hand, my employee is a human being with their own intrinsic worth whom I should respect and support. Their children will soon grow up and may attend day-care such that their carer responsibilities are reduced, and they can return to acceptable levels of performance.

Such are the grey ethical waters that we as leaders must navigate and your values serve as your only guiding compass here. Have no illusions about simple choices between right and wrong; and even doing the right thing by all accounts is no shield against scandal and criticism if someone feels you've been unethical.

So what then, is unethical behaviour? Let's continue to delve deeper.

Unethical Behaviour

Behaviour is unethical when it contradicts the moral principles of a particular society. While it can refer to explicit legal principles, we tend to mean our implicit beliefs.

Plenty of cases readily come to mind. For example, companies including Nike, Adidas, and Apple, among many others have been publicly accused of unethical behaviour for outsourcing their manufacturing to developing world countries with lax labour laws where people routinely work long hours, in poor conditions, for rates far below a living wage.

Others are caught trying to distance themselves from the wrongdoing to deflect blame. For example, Coca-Cola sourced raw ingredients from the Central Izalco sugar mill in El Salvador that is known for using child labour and having poor working conditions.

Often these organisations have not broken any laws or explicit moral principles, and yet we are outraged by the unethical decision-making of their leaders. However, their actions may well be upholding their own personal ethical framework, such as egoic hedonism, and that's where conflicts arise.

Consider global scandals like those involving Lehman Brothers (2008) or Deepwater Horizon (2010), where leaders prioritised what we as a global society felt to be the wrong thing. They took risks in favour of profits, and in the short term leading up to those events, advanced their own standing by generating significant revenue for their firms.

The costs of their selfish actions were borne by others; either by the environment, or by various stakeholders in the communities where those businesses operated. Many people felt that what they did was wrong, they had sacrificed their followers and their stakeholders and our natural environment for their own gain.

In some cases this conduct broke explicit laws, but more than that, they broke our trust by going against our shared implicit understanding about what's right and wrong, and that's what outrages us so.

Ethical Climate

Leaders play a pivotal role in shaping the ethical climate of an organisation. They set the tone for 'how things are done around here', influencing what behaviour is deemed acceptable and appropriate. This influence stems not just from formal directives but from the subtleties of their actions and decisions, which, like a beacon, guide the organisational culture.

In an organisation the leader's actions are under constant scrutiny. Followers look to them for cues on acceptable behaviour, whether they're conscious of it or not. This scrutiny means everything a leader does or says acts as a template for what is considered right and wrong within the organisation. Like sponges, employees absorb these cues, moulding the ethical climate of the team or organisation at large based on what they observe.

If a leader consistently demonstrates a commitment to supporting their team, ensuring they have the necessary tools and information to excel, they signal that these values are paramount. This approach doesn't just foster a positive work environment; it embeds a moral compass within the organisational culture, prioritising ethical conduct and mutual respect.

Conversely when a leader prioritises profit over principles, choosing the easy path over the right one, they set a dangerous precedent. Such actions signal that ethical shortcuts and disregard for consequences are not just tolerated but encouraged. This approach can lead to a toxic ethical climate, where the ends justify the means, regardless of the moral cost.

A leader's ethical stance must be clear and communicated effectively to their team and the wider organisation. It's not enough to have a strong set of ethics; these values must be shared, understood, and seen in practice. Consistency between what a leader claims to value and their actual behaviour reinforces these principles, creating a robust ethical climate.

For example, the case of Lehman Brothers serves as a cautionary tale. The leadership of the company fostered a cut-throat, profit-focused organisational climate, valuing short-term gains over sustainable, ethical practices. This ethos, while financially lucrative in the short run, ultimately contributed to the company's downfall, underscoring the importance of ethical leadership in shaping organisational outcomes.

Leaders are therefore the architects of an organisation's ethical climate. Through their actions, decisions, and the values they espouse, they have the power to cultivate an environment of integrity and respect or, conversely, one of moral ambivalence. It's a profound responsibility, requiring a steadfast commitment to ethical principles and a dedication to embodying these values in every aspect of leadership.

The question then becomes, what kind of ethical climate is desirable? The Lehman Brothers saga illustrates the perils of prioritising short-term gains over sustainable ethical practices. It's a stark reminder that the allure of quick profits can lead to catastrophic outcomes, not just for the organisation but for society at large. Such examples prompt us to reflect on our values and the legacy we wish to leave in our professional endeavours.

A desirable ethical climate is one that aligns with the core values of integrity, respect, fairness, and value for all stakeholders. As leaders, the responsibility lies with us to cultivate an environment that echoes these principles through our words and actions. It's about setting a precedent that goes beyond mere profitability to encompass the welfare of employees, customers, and the broader community. This approach not only fosters a positive organisational culture but also ensures long-term sustainability and success.

Leadership is not just about guiding a team towards achieving business objectives; it's about inspiring a shared vision grounded in ethical practices. As you step into leadership roles, consider the impact of your decisions and behaviours on the ethical climate of your team or organisation. Our actions send powerful messages about what we deem important, shaping the norms and values of our professional environments.

The ethical climate we strive to create within our organisations should reflect our deepest values and principles. It should be an environment where ethical practices are not just encouraged but lived by everyone, from top leaders to every team member. Such a climate fosters trust, respect, and loyalty, contributing to the overall success and longevity of the organisation. As leaders, it's our duty to lead by example, demonstrating that success is not merely measured by financial gains but by the positive impact we have on our teams, our customers, and society at large.

Humans, by our nature, share a desire for fairness, respect, and feeling valued. These universal values can serve as the foundation for building an ethical climate that resonates with everyone. Emphasising respect as a core organisational value, for example, speaks volumes about the kind of culture you aim to cultivate – one in which every individual feels valued and heard.

George (2003) argued that 'we need leaders who lead with purpose, values, and integrity; leaders who build enduring organisations, motivate their employees to provide superior customer service, and create long-term value for shareholders' (p. 9). This vision for leadership and business is antithetical to the approaches seen in cases like Lehman Brothers. It calls for a commitment to transparency, integrity, and a focus on sustainable success.

But what exactly is integrity? Let's discuss that a bit further.

INTEGRITY

Integrity is about more than just being honest. It's about a deep congruence between your values, inner convictions, and your outward actions. For leaders, possessing integrity means you're not just aware of your core values but are also committed to living them out, day in, day out, regardless of the situation or audience.

This concept begins with a thorough self-examination, a journey to discover what you stand for – that is, your moral compass. Once identified, the challenge extends to whether you can, and will, openly share these values. It's about demonstrating vulnerability, allowing others to see your true self and, in doing so, showing the strength of your character.

Having integrity means you don't just hold these values in theory but are prepared to act on them, especially when confronted with situations that test your moral fibre. Are you ready to voice a dissenting opinion when something feels wrong, to stand alone if necessary? This courage to act, even when it's inconvenient or unpopular, is the essence of integrity.

Integrity is reflected not in sporadic acts of virtue but in the steadfast adherence to your values, making them the consistent backdrop of all your decisions and actions. It's about ensuring your behaviour mirrors your claimed values at all times. A single lapse, where actions contradict professed values, can severely undermine a leader's credibility.

Such a breach instantly erodes trust, and it's a long, arduous journey to rebuild what was lost. Integrity, therefore, isn't an attribute you claim but a practice you embody, a relentless pursuit that defines the very essence of effective, respected leadership.

I'd like you to complete our next exercise (Exercise 7.2), which is going to ask you to find someone you know who has integrity.

Exercise 7.2

Integrity

Image Alt Text: https://ecuau.qualtrics.com/jfe/form/SV_3EnYcD3NNd596I0

It takes a certain moral fortitude to consistently demonstrate integrity and I hope that the person you identified can serve as an inspiration for your own leadership journey. Now that you're well equipped with moral compass in hand, let us consider some of the conflicts of responsibility that you'll face as leaders, between multiple competing demands.

Conflicts of Responsibility

Leadership involves navigating a complex web of responsibilities that often intersect and, at times, conflict. Barnard (1958) identified three core types of executive responsibility: personal, organisational, and corporate, each carrying its own unique obligations.

> *Personal responsibilities* entail a leader's duty to uphold ethical standards and legality in their actions. It's about adhering to societal norms, laws, and moral codes, ensuring one's behaviour sets a positive example both within and outside the organisation. This responsibility extends beyond avoiding illegal activities to include fulfilling duties, commitments, and obligations inherent to your role. For leaders, this means not just achieving set key performance indicators (KPIs) and supporting their team but embodying the ethical principles they wish to see reflected in their organisation.
>
> *Organisational responsibilities* are about the collective goals of the business. Leaders are tasked with driving the company towards success, which includes making profits, achieving strategic objectives, and fostering an environment where teams can thrive. This aspect of leadership demands a balance between pursuing ambitious targets and maintaining an ethical approach to business operations.
>
> *Corporate responsibility* is about the role of leaders steering organisations as separate legal entities in their own right, that are capable of moral or immoral

actions. Leaders must ensure that their decisions reflect ethical considerations, avoiding harm to external stakeholders and the environment. For example, a mining company Rio Tinto faced a public outcry in 2020 for destroying two ancient Aboriginal sites in Juukan Gorge, Western Australia. As a result the CEO Jean-Sébastien Jacques and two other executives stepped down for failing to uphold their corporate responsibility. It shows that leaders' decisions directly affect the organisation's moral standing and, by extension, its legal and social obligations.

Navigating these responsibilities requires leaders to constantly balance personal ethics with organisational and corporate objectives. The challenge is in aligning these aspects to ensure that actions at all levels contribute to a positive ethical climate. You must strive to make decisions that not only drive organisational success but also reflect a commitment to societal values and ethical integrity.

At times, these responsibilities will pull you in different directions and you'll need to make sense of where your priorities lie. Let's explore some of the ethical dilemmas you may encounter.

Ethical Dilemmas

Ethical dilemmas in the workplace are situations in which you need to make choices that could compromise your principles or the ethical stance of an organisation. These dilemmas test a leader's ability to balance competing interests and values, often requiring tough decisions that affect both individuals and the wider company.

We'll explore three prominent sources of such dilemmas, including human resources, conflicts of interest, and organisational resources. Each area presents unique challenges, from managing personnel issues with fairness and integrity, reconciling personal gain with organisational benefit, and responsibly allocating company assets. These sections aim to equip you with the insight to handle these complex situations, ensuring that your leadership is both effective and ethically sound.

Human Resources

Human resources are a frequent source of ethical dilemmas for leaders in the workplace. Issues such as privacy, discrimination, harassment, performance evaluation, along with hiring and firing practices, offer ample ground for ethical challenges. Leaders must navigate these issues with care, ensuring their decisions reflect a commitment to fairness, equality, and respect for individual rights.

For example, consider the delicate balance of fostering a multicultural organisation while avoiding tokenism. Leaders are tasked with creating inclusive environments that genuinely reflect societal diversity without reducing individuals to mere representatives of their ethnicity or gender. Similarly, addressing harassment requires leaders to cultivate a culture where such behaviours are unequivocally unacceptable, ensuring the workplace is safe and respectful for all.

Privacy protection, especially in an age where data breaches are commonplace, demands stringent safeguards to secure employees' personal information. Leaders must question the legal implications of their data policies and the ethical considerations of how information is protected, accessed, and shared, by whom and for what purposes. The responsibility requires investment in digital security literacy to shield employees and stakeholders from the risks associated with data vulnerability.

In each of these areas, leaders must exercise ethical judgment, balancing organisational objectives with a steadfast commitment to upholding ethical standards.

Conflicts of Interest

Conflicts of interest arise when our objectivity is compromised – for example, where our personal and professional interests clash. These conflicts challenge the very core of leadership integrity, testing a leader's commitment to objectivity and ethical conduct. When personal relationships intersect with professional duties, they muddy the water, making it hard to see clearly and posing dilemmas that demand careful navigation.

Consider managing a close relative or partner within the same organisation. The dual roles blur the lines between personal affection and professional obligation. Would you really prioritise organisational performance over a personal relationship? Having to fire a spouse for under-performance, for example, pits professional responsibility against personal loyalty. The decision becomes not just a matter of organisational policy but a reflection of the leader's ethical stance.

Financial interests introduce another layer of complexity to conflicts of interest. Senior leaders, often with stock options, find their financial fortunes tied to the organisation's performance. This connection can skew decision-making, prioritising short-term gains that boost stock prices over long-term ethical considerations. The temptation to enhance personal wealth can conflict with the duty to uphold ethical standards and make decisions that benefit all stakeholders, not just personal bank accounts.

Navigating these conflicts requires transparency, where potential conflicts are openly acknowledged and managed, and a commitment to ethical decision-making that transcends personal gain. Leaders must cultivate an environment where ethical dilemmas are approached with integrity, ensuring decisions reflect a balance between personal and organisational values.

Organisational Resources

Organisational resources present another complex arena for ethical dilemmas. For example, have you ever used stationery from work for personal reasons? It might seem trivial, but it raises questions about where we draw the line on the use of corporate assets. This dilemma extends to more significant decisions, like expensing a trip with a potential collaborator. On one hand, such an expense could foster strategic alliances that benefit the organisation. On the other, it could be seen as misusing funds for personal gain. Leaders must navigate these grey areas, balancing personal advantages with the broader interests of the organisation.

The use of an organisation's reputation poses another ethical challenge. Branding oneself with the organisation's name could lend credibility, but also carries the weight of representing that entity's values and standing. Misusing this reputation, intentionally or not, can have far-reaching consequences, potentially harming the organisation and its stakeholders.

Leaders must exercise discernment and integrity when managing organisational resources, constantly evaluating their choices against the backdrop of ethical considerations. It's about making transparent decisions, justifiable not just in the eyes of the organisation but within the broader context of societal norms and values. This careful stewardship of resources, balancing personal, professional, and organisational ethics, is crucial in navigating the complex ethical landscape of the modern workplace.

Balancing Act

Leadership, then, is a balancing act. You're constantly juggling three vital responsibilities: doing the right thing, staying true to yourself, and getting the job done. Each of these aspects presents its own set of challenges, and yet together, they define the essence of effective ethical leadership.

Doing the right thing seems straightforward, but is fraught with complexity in practice. It's about making decisions that align with ethical standards and societal expectations, even when such choices may conflict with immediate organisational goals or personal interests. The right thing isn't a static concept either; it evolves with the shifting landscapes of law, society, and morality, requiring you to be adaptable and principled in your decision-making.

Being true to ourselves, on the other hand, calls for a deep introspection and adherence to personal values and beliefs. It's about authentically aligning your actions with your core values to create a leadership style that's both genuine and impactful. And yet, this internal consistency can sometimes clash with external pressures, be they from the organisation or the broader societal context, challenging you to maintain your integrity amidst competing demands.

Getting the job done is about the measurable outcomes of leadership effort, including the achievement of organisational goals, the fulfilment of stakeholder expectations, and the delivery of tangible results. This responsibility is often the most visible aspect of leadership, and so subject to scrutiny and evaluation. But focusing solely on results, without considering the ethical implications or personal values can lead to short-sighted decisions that harm the organisation's long-term health and reputation.

The true test of leadership lies in harmonising these responsibilities, crafting a path that respects ethical imperatives, aligns with personal values, and achieves organisational objectives. This delicate equilibrium is challenged by the reality of instant global accountability, where your every action and decision are scrutinised and can quickly become fodder for public debate. Leaders must navigate this landscape with a keen awareness of the consequences of their actions, not just for immediate outcomes but for the broader impact on society and their own moral standing.

Effective leadership is about embracing the complexity of balancing doing the right thing, being true to yourself, and getting the job done. It's a journey that requires courage, integrity, and a deep commitment to the values that define us as leaders. This path isn't for everyone; it's not for people who are chasing after fancy titles or financial rewards, but for those who genuinely want to make a positive impact. When you walk this path, the rewards are both in your achievements and in the knowledge that you have led with honour, made a difference, and stayed true to your deepest convictions. That's what makes leadership a profoundly rewarding journey.

But these competing demands create immense pressure on leaders to perform.

Pressure Changes Everything

People respond differently to pressure. Some focus and excel, while others fold. The ability to deliver under pressure is a hallmark of leadership readiness. It signals a readiness for senior roles, where the stakes are higher and the decisions tougher. Not everyone thrives under such conditions.

Staying cool under pressure isn't an optional skill for leaders; it's a fundamental necessity. The ability to make tough decisions, particularly when these decisions pull in opposite directions, defines a leader's effectiveness. Every choice has implications, not just for you, but for your team, the organisation, and broader stakeholders.

Leaders are often forced to make these choices under intense scrutiny and tight deadlines, situations that test their ability to summon their best under pressure. This capacity to perform under pressure, to make decisions that are ethical, true to one's values, and effective, is what distinguishes great leaders from good ones.

WHY BOTHER? ISN'T IT HARD ENOUGH

You might wonder why leaders should burden themselves with doing the right thing and being true to themselves, when just getting the job done seems hard enough already. The answer, though it might seem counterintuitive, is somewhat unsurprisingly about profit, along with some societal and personal benefits of course.

Doing the right thing and being authentic aren't only good moral choices, they're strategic business decisions. When leaders act ethically and authentically, they build trust and credibility, not just within their teams but also with customers, investors, and the broader community. This trust translates into loyalty – a valuable commodity. Consider the fallout from organisations caught in unethical acts; their value plummets not only because of potential fines but also from broken trust and damaged reputations.

Being true to yourself fosters a culture of transparency and integrity, which in turn attracts talent and inspires commitment from employees. People want to work for leaders and organisations that stand for something beyond mere profit. In essence, ethical leadership and authenticity are not just about doing good, they're about doing well. They create a virtuous cycle where ethical practices boost employee engagement, customer loyalty, and ultimately, profitability.

So, while juggling these responsibilities adds complexity, it also lays the foundation for sustainable success. Let's take a closer look at followers' commitment.

Followers' Commitment

Followers choose to stay with an organisation for one of three reasons, which Allen and Meyer (1990) described as continuance, normative, and affective commitment.

> *Continuance commitment* arises from an awareness of the costs associated with leaving the organisation. These employees stay because they perceive that there is a high cost attached to leaving, be it financial security, job market concerns, or personal demands like mortgages and family needs. This form of commitment is rooted in necessity rather than desire, with employees calculating the practical implications of departure versus staying.

> *Normative commitment*, on the other hand, stems from a sense of obligation. It reflects a moral or ethical duty to remain with the organisation. Employees who have normative commitment believe that it's the right thing to do, driven by values of loyalty, stability, and responsibility. They feel a deep-seated obligation to their role, their colleagues, and the organisation at large, often fuelled by a belief in the importance of their contribution and a personal responsibility to continue.

> *Affective commitment* is the emotional bond employees form with their organisation. It's marked by a genuine love for their work, a deep alignment with the organisation's mission, and a connection with their colleagues. These employees stay not because they have to, or ought to, but because they want to. This type of commitment is powerful, fostering a workforce that is not only loyal but also highly motivated and engaged. Employees with affective commitment believe in the organisation's purpose and see their own values reflected in its goals and practices.

Of these, affective commitment is the most important outcome of positive leadership; it signifies a workforce that is not just present, but is passionately engaged.

Positive Leadership

Contemporary positive leadership approaches have revolutionised the way organisations operate and succeed. These models, including authentic, servant, and transformational leadership, promote workplaces where employees are not merely present but are deeply committed and emotionally attached to their organisation. This affective organisational commitment is a critical driver in such organisations thriving culturally and outperforming competitors in sustainable profitability.

Organisations led by positive leaders see significant benefits, including better employee performance, lower turnover rates, and more innovation, among many other desirable workplace behaviours and attitudes (e.g. Hoch et al., 2018). Employees committed on an affective level do not merely perform their duties, they seek to excel, contribute to a positive work culture, and drive the organisation towards its strategic goals. This high level of engagement and performance directly contributes to the bottom line, as motivated employees are more efficient, customer-focused, and adaptable to change.

Contemporary positive approaches to leadership not only make work a more fulfilling and inspiring place but also drive tangible business outcomes. Leaders who inspire, serve, and transform, can attract and retain the best talent, and cultivate environments where employees are motivated to contribute their best, propelling the organisation towards its objectives with enthusiasm and dedication. The path to profitability and sustainable success today is paved with the principles of positive leadership.

Let's now explore the ethical leadership model – it will be the last leadership theory that we cover in the text.

ETHICAL LEADERSHIP

Leaders are a central source of ethical guidance for their followers in the workplace, setting the standard for what's right and expected within an organisation. It's about both embodying and promoting actions that align with moral principles, such as honesty, trustworthiness, fairness, and care. Through their example, ethical leaders become credible role models, inspiring their followers to adopt similar values and behaviours.

Brown et al. (2005) define ethical leadership as 'the demonstration of normatively appropriate conduct through personal actions and interpersonal relationships, and the promotion of such conduct to followers through two-way communication, reinforcement, and decision-making' (p. 120).

This form of leadership isn't just about the actions you take; it's equally about how you interact and communicate with your team. It involves engaging in open dialogue, providing feedback that reinforces ethical behaviour, and making decisions that reflect accepted norms. The term 'normatively appropriate' is kept deliberately vague because what's considered appropriate can vary significantly based on the organisation, industry, and cultural context.

Leaders face the challenge of balancing group goals with the broader ethical landscape. Sometimes, this means resisting the urge to prioritise the immediate interests of the group over the rights and well-being of others (Den Hartog, 2015). Ethical leadership demands a commitment to do no harm and to respect all parties affected by decisions, not merely those within the group. It's about making tough choices that uphold ethical standards, even when it means going against the grain. This commitment prevents ethical failures and fosters an environment of trust and respect.

Dual Responsibilities

Ethical leadership involves acting as both a 'moral person' and a 'moral manager' (Lemoine et al., 2019). Being a moral person is about demonstrating integrity, fairness, and honesty in every interaction. It's about being someone your team can trust, knowing their concerns and rights will be respected and considered. This personal ethical foundation sets the stage for genuine leadership, where actions and decisions reflect a deep commitment to ethical principles.

Being a moral manager is about taking that personal commitment to ethics and embedding it into the fabric of your team or organisation. It involves actively promoting and reinforcing ethical behaviour, setting clear ethical standards, and holding everyone accountable. Through role modelling, communication, and the judicious use of rewards and sanctions, you make ethics a tangible part of daily operations.

It's about making ethics visible and actionable, guiding your team not only by the example you set but also by the standards you enforce. This dual responsibility helps create an environment where ethical conduct is both expected and celebrated, shaping a culture that upholds the highest standards of integrity and responsibility.

Four Dimensions

Brown et al. (2005) identified three dimensions of ethical leadership as acting fairly, allowing voice, and accountability, to which Banks et al. (2021) more recently added having prosocial values.

> *Acting fairly* is about making decisions that are balanced and just, ensuring that all actions taken are free from bias and favouritism. A leader who acts fairly is someone who can be trusted, as they consistently demonstrate impartiality and equity in their dealings with team members. This trust forms the foundation of a strong and cohesive team.

> *Allowing voice* is about listening to what employees have to say and fostering an environment where everyone feels valued and heard. By discussing business ethics and values openly, and encouraging dialogue, leaders ensure that the team's collective voice shapes the moral compass of the organisation. This inclusive approach not only empowers employees but also enriches the decision-making process with diverse perspectives.

> *Accountability* is about setting the standard for ethical conduct by disciplining those who violate ethical standards and by living their personal lives as exemplars of integrity. They define success not solely by outcomes but by the ethical manner in which those results are achieved. This commitment to accountability reinforces the expectation that ethical conduct is non-negotiable, both in achieving goals and in everyday actions.

Prosocial values are about having the best interests of everyone at heart, aiming to benefit not just the organisation but also the individuals within it and the broader community. By prioritising the right thing to do and embedding prosocial values into the organisation's culture, leaders ensure that their vision for success includes the welfare and development of all stakeholders.

Together these dimensions create a leadership approach that's not just effective but deeply rooted in ethical principles. It's about leading with a moral compass, guiding teams towards success that is not only achieved ethically but also contributes positively to the well-being of everyone that's involved.

Effects on Followers and Performance

The positive effects of ethical leadership extend to the performance and overall health of the organisation. Employees who perceive their leaders as ethical are more likely to be satisfied with their jobs, view their leaders as effective, and feel encouraged to exert extra effort (Hoch et al., 2018). This is critical in achieving organisational goals and enhancing productivity. The trust and satisfaction promoted by ethical leadership significantly reduce instances of abusive supervision, deviance, and unethical conduct within the workplace.

Ethical leadership promotes a culture of open communication, where employees feel confident in reporting issues. This transparency is vital for identifying and addressing problems before they escalate, ensuring a healthier organisational climate. Ethical leaders, by promoting altruistic attitudes and fostering an environment of mutual respect, contribute to the development of a strong ethical culture that supports ethical decision-making and prosocial behaviour among followers. Research suggests that ethical leadership improves the performance of both individuals and groups (Den Hartog, 2015).

Ethical leadership also helps to safeguard and enhance the organisation's reputation. In a world where reputation can be a significant asset or liability, ethical leadership helps prevent the reputational damage that can arise from unethical practices or toxic workplace cultures. By embedding ethical values into the core of organisational operations, leaders not only prevent potential crises but also position their organisation for long-term success and sustainability. A commitment to ethical leadership therefore enables the development of resilient, reputable, and high-performing organisations.

I'd like you now to take a quiz (Quiz 7.1) that will ask you about your own ethical leadership behaviour, to see how important this is to your unique approach. Let's see how you go.

━━━━ Quiz 7.1 ━━━━

Ethical Leadership

Image Alt Text: https://ecuau.qualtrics.com/jfe/form/SV_a2AzgPDwKKJGbEW

Adapted from Brown et al. (2005).

I hope that you're starting to see some of the benefits of incorporating a robust ethical perspective in your own leadership journey. And yet it's not a perfect solution to avoiding the dilemmas we discussed earlier in this chapter. Let us now consider some of the limitations of ethical leadership theory.

Challenges That Remain

Ethical leadership theory, while robust in guiding leaders towards fostering environments of integrity and trust, comes with its own challenges. One critical limitation is context-dependence; what's considered ethical can vary significantly across different cultural or organisational settings, and so our interpretations of a leader's actions and decisions can be highly subjective (Lemoine et al., 2019). This means that ethical leadership is often evaluated through the lens of individual perceptions, which can vary widely across teams, organisations, and cultural spheres.

Another limitation is the potential for rigidity in upholding company standards and policies. Ethical leaders, in their commitment to fairness and norm compliance, may inadvertently stifle open criticism of organisational norms. This stance, while ensuring adherence to established ethical guidelines, might limit the scope for questioning and potentially improving these very norms. Additionally, the definition of what constitutes 'right' and 'wrong' in ethical leadership, beyond core values like honesty, remains somewhat ambiguous. This vagueness can leave leaders and followers alike unsure about how to navigate more complex ethical dilemmas that extend beyond basic principles.

Lastly, ethical leadership often relies on transactional influence tactics, such as rewards and punishments, to ensure compliance with ethical standards. While effective in certain contexts, this approach may not be as impactful as more nuanced strategies like persuasion in motivating followers to internalise and embody ethical standards genuinely. This reliance on transactional mechanisms highlights a need for ethical leadership to evolve, incorporating more diverse influence strategies to effectively guide followers towards ethical conduct.

YOUR PERFECT LIFE

Alright, let's finish off this chapter with an exercise (Exercise 7.3) that's as enlightening as it is enjoyable. I invite you to reflect on what a day in your 'perfect life' would look like. Picture it: a day that's the pinnacle of your aspirations and desires. Don't hold back; this is a safe space for you to be honest, and there's no obligation to share your thoughts with anyone else.

Are you visualising a day spent basking in the glow of achievement after closing a massive business deal that sets your future alight? Or maybe it's the simpler pleasures you'd seek, like the tranquillity of a morning without alarms, followed by an afternoon trek through beautiful nature. Maybe it's sunbathing on a luxury yacht, casual sex, and substance abuse; remember that nothing desired is peculiar.

In three to four sentences, describe this perfect day. Let your imagination guide you, and don't shy away from saying what your heart truly craves.

Exercise 7.3

Your Perfect Life

Image Alt Text: https://ecuau.qualtrics.com/jfe/form/SV_beH0E1CywVuKm2O

I hope that you've been completely honest with yourself and your desires. Here's why that matters. Now that you've described a day in your perfect life, I want you to consider whether or not this life aligns with the instrumental and terminal values that you articulated at the start of this chapter – would enacting those values lead you towards the perfect life that you really want?

If there isn't an alignment, then it's high time to have an honest conversation with yourself about what you really want out of life, who you want to be as a person, and how you'd like to live. I want you to put yourself on a trajectory that is consistent with what you truly want, so that you can pursue it wholeheartedly, and unashamedly. If you're conflicted about where you're heading, or worse, misleading yourself, then it's unlikely that you'll get to where you want to be.

This reflection isn't intended to be confrontational but illuminating. It's about peeling back the layers to uncover what you genuinely desire and believe in. Remember, leading in accordance with your values isn't just about personal integrity; it's also about inspiring others to do the same.

SUMMARY

Values are the fundamental beliefs you hold about what is important. They are positively framed and broadly applicable ideals, ranked in order of importance, that motivate and shape your attitudes and behaviour. We can think about values as either instrumental or terminal: instrumental values help you navigate the minutiae of your daily life, while terminal values reflect your life-long ambitions and guide major decisions. We inherit a portion of our values, and the rest we decide for ourselves based on our experiences. Discovering and accepting your true values will make you a more powerful leader.

Ethics is a branch of philosophy that's concerned with what's right and wrong, based on what's valuable. Ethical theories, such as hedonism, stoicism, and consequentialism outline a set of moral principles that identify specific decisions, actions, and behaviours as right and wrong. Behaviour is unethical when it contradicts the moral principles of a particular society. Leaders play a pivotal role in shaping the ethical climate of an organisation by role modelling acceptable behaviour.

Integrity is about congruence between your values, inner convictions, and your outward actions. It starts with a thorough self-examination to discover what you stand for, and extends to whether you can, and will, openly share these values. It's about demonstrating vulnerability, allowing others to see your true self and, in doing so, showing the strength of your character.

Contemporary positive approaches to leadership not only make work a more fulfilling and inspiring place but also drive tangible business outcomes. Leaders who inspire, serve, and transform can attract and retain the best talent, and cultivate environments where employees are motivated to contribute their best, propelling the organisation towards its objectives with enthusiasm and dedication.

Leaders are a central source of ethical guidance for their followers in the workplace. Ethical leadership is about both embodying and promoting actions that align with moral principles, such as honesty, trustworthiness, fairness, and care. Ethical leadership involves four dimensions: acting fairly, allowing voice, accountability, and prosocial values. Through their example, ethical leaders become credible role models, inspiring their followers to adopt similar values and behaviours.

'Until you do what you believe in, you don't know whether you believe it or not.'

Extract from *Tolstoy's Letters Volume II 1880–1910* by Graf Lev Tolstoy, published by Reginald Christian (1978).

REFERENCES

Allen, N. J., & Meyer, J. P. (1990). The measurement and antecedents of affective, continuance and normative commitment to the organization. *Journal of Occupational Psychology*, *63*(1), 1–18. https://doi.org/10.1111/j.2044-8325.1990.tb00506.x

Arieli, S., Sagiv, L., & Cohen-Shalem, E. (2016). Values in business schools: The role of self-selection and socialization. *Academy of Management Learning & Education*, *15*(3), 493–507. https://doi.org/10.5465/amle.2014.0064

Banks, G. C., Fischer, T., Gooty, J., & Stock, G. (2021). Ethical leadership: Mapping the terrain for concept cleanup and a future research agenda. *The Leadership Quarterly*, *32*(2), 101471. https://doi.org/10.1016/j.leaqua.2020.101471

Bardi, A., Lee, J. A., Hofmann-Towfigh, N., & Soutar, G. (2009). The structure of intraindividual value change. *Journal of Personality and Social Psychology, 97*(5), 913–929. https://doi.org/10.1037/a0016617

Barnard, C. I. (1958). Elementary conditions of business morals. *California Management Review, 1*(1), 1–13. https://doi.org/10.2307/41165329

Brown, M. E., Treviño, L. K., & Harrison, D. A. (2005). Ethical leadership: A social learning perspective for construct development and testing. *Organizational Behavior and Human Decision Processes, 97*(2), 117–134. https://doi.org/10.1016/j.obhdp.2005.03.002

Den Hartog, D. N. (2015). Ethical leadership. *Annual Review of Organizational Psychology and Organizational Behavior, 2*(1), 409–434. https://doi.org/10.1146/annurev-orgpsych-032414-111237

Döring, A. K., Schwartz, S. H., Cieciuch, J., Groenen, P. J., Glatzel, V., Harasimczuk, J., Janowicz, N., Nyagolova, M., Scheefer, E. R., & Allritz, M. (2015). Cross-cultural evidence of value structures and priorities in childhood. *British Journal of Psychology, 106*(4), 675–699. https://doi.org/10.1111/bjop.12116

George, B. (2003). *Authentic leadership: Rediscovering the secrets to creating lasting value.* Jossey-Bass.

Hitlin, S., & Piliavin, J. A. (2004). Values: Reviving a dormant concept. *Annual Review of Sociology, 30*, 359–393. https://doi.org/10.1146/annurev.soc.30.012703.110640

Hoch, J. E., Bommer, W. H., Dulebohn, J. H., & Wu, D. (2018). Do ethical, authentic, and servant leadership explain variance above and beyond transformational leadership? A meta-analysis. *Journal of Management, 44*(2), 501–529. https://doi.org/10.1177/0149206316665461

Knafo, A., & Sagiv, L. (2004). Values and work environment: Mapping 32 occupations. *European Journal of Psychology of Education, 19*(3), 255–273. https://doi.org/10.1007/BF03173223

Kristof-Brown, A. L., Zimmerman, R. D., & Johnson, E. C. (2005). Consequences of individuals' fit at work: A meta-analysis of person–job, person–organization, person–group, and person–supervisor fit. *Personnel Psychology, 58*(2), 281–342. https://doi.org/10.1111/j.1744-6570.2005.00672.x

Lee, J. A., Ye, S., Sneddon, J. N., Collins, P. R., & Daniel, E. (2017). Does the intraindividual structure of values exist in young children? *Personality and Individual Differences, 110*, 125–130. https://doi.org/10.1016/j.paid.2017.01.038

Lemoine, G. J., Hartnell, C. A., & Leroy, H. (2019). Taking stock of moral approaches to leadership: An integrative review of ethical, authentic, and servant leadership. *Academy of Management Annals, 13*(1), 148–187. https://doi.org/10.5465/annals.2016.0121

Milfont, T. L., Milojev, P., & Sibley, C. G. (2016). Values stability and change in adulthood: A 3-year longitudinal study of rank-order stability and mean-level differences. *Personality and Social Psychology Bulletin, 42*(5), 572–588. https://doi.org/10.1177/0146167216639245

Roccas, S., Sagiv, L., Oppenheim, S., Elster, A., & Gal, A. (2014). Integrating content and structure aspects of the self: Traits, values, and self-improvement. *Journal of Personality, 82*(2), 144–157. https://doi.org/10.1111/jopy.12041

Rokeach, M. (1973). *The nature of human values.* The Free Press.

Rønnow-Rasmussen, T. (2015). Intrinsic and extrinsic value. In I. Hirose & J. Olsen (Eds), *The Oxford handbook of value theory* (pp. 29–43). Oxford University Press.

Sagiv, L., Roccas, S., Cieciuch, J., & Schwartz, S. H. (2017). Personal values in human life. *Nature Human Behaviour*, *1*(9), 630–639. https://doi.org/10.1038/s41562-017-0185-3

Schwartz, S. H. (1992). Universals in the content and structure of values: Theoretical advances and empirical tests in 20 countries. In M. P. Zanna (Ed.), *Advances in Experimental Social Psychology* (Vol. 25, pp. 1–65). Academic Press. https://doi.org/10.1016/S0065-2601(08)60281-6

Schwartz, S. H., & Bilsky, W. (1987). Toward a universal psychological structure of human values. *Journal of Personality and Social Psychology*, *53*(3), 550–562. https://doi.org/10.1037/0022-3514.53.3.550

Uzefovsky, F., Döring, A. K., & Knafo-Noam, A. (2016). Values in middle childhood: Social and genetic contributions. *Social Development*, *25*(3), 482–502. https://doi.org/10.1111/sode.12155

Vernon, P. E., & Allport, G. W. (1931). A test for personal values. *The Journal of Abnormal and Social Psychology*, *26*(3), 231–248. https://doi.org/10.1037/h0073233

8
SELF-AWARENESS AND LEADERSHIP DEVELOPMENT

Overview

Great leaders know what motivates their own behaviour and attitudes, they know how they respond to different situations, and understand how their behaviour affects others. This chapter starts by exploring self-awareness as the gateway to leadership development. The emphasis is on practical application with exercises that enable you to build your self-knowledge base.

Next, you're introduced to two reflective learning tools that enable personal growth: double-loop learning and the reflective journal. Structured exercises guide you through the steps to create learning opportunities – when these reflective processes become automatic, you are set on a leadership development trajectory that will continue to transform you long after this text.

Good leadership is a product of who you are and what you do; leadership development is therefore a journey of personal growth. The chapter concludes with the concept of personal mastery that challenges you to develop a growth mindset and a sense of personal agency. A reflective exercise reveals how you have responded to adversity in the past, and how you might respond differently today.

Exercise 8.1: Strengths, weaknesses, and desires

Exercise 8.2: Double-loop learning

Exercise 8.3: The reflective journal

Exercise 8.4: Personal mastery

Leadership development is anchored in personal growth. A significant part of the journey is getting to know yourself as a leader. In this chapter we'll explore self-awareness, reflective learning, and personal mastery to help you learn more about yourself. You'll therefore find that this chapter is much more personal to you.

There are no right or wrong responses to any of the activities here; what matters most is your genuine and honest engagement with the material. This is your journey, and while I can show you some of the ways, you'll need to choose and walk your own path. The more open and thoughtful you are in your responses, the more valuable it will be for you.

SELF-AWARENESS

Self-awareness is essential to effective leadership and serves as the foundation for positive contemporary leadership theories. That may seem strange at first, when you consider that leadership is primarily about other people. Let's discuss then what self-awareness might mean from a leadership perspective.

Simply put, self-awareness is how well you understand yourself. The idea was introduced in social psychology by Duval and Wicklund (1972) who explained that when we focus our attention inward onto ourselves, we can evaluate and compare our behaviour to our own internal standards and values. Having such an objective perspective enables us to regulate and adjust our behaviour when we find it out of sync with how we'd like to see ourselves.

Self-awareness is therefore about knowing the 'objective' details of your character, such as your strengths, weaknesses, desires, motivations, values, and priorities. Knowing specific aspects of yourself well is critical to becoming an effective leader (for a recent review, see Carden et al., 2022). Self-awareness allows you to make the absolute most of your strengths, and either avoid, delegate, or develop your weaknesses. When you're clear about your talents and limitations, you can deploy your skills to best effect.

For example, I can't sing. I'm not ashamed of it, it's just a fact. So if there's ever a situation in the workplace where it's absolutely critical that someone sings, I'll delegate. Instead of embarrassing myself and letting down my team, I'll ask one of my colleagues who's blessed with that particular gift to take centre stage. Self-awareness can therefore guide our leadership decision-making such that everyone can best contribute to our mutual benefit.

Self-awareness also allows us to focus our efforts. When we're clear about our values and desires, what's important to us, where we want to go, and what we'd like to achieve with our lives, we can then use that information to direct our energy and time towards specific goals and outcomes in ways that are acceptable to us, align with our values, and deliver our ambitions.

However, as leaders there will be tasks that we can't delegate or avoid, because they're solely our responsibility, and we'll need to develop certain skills to enable us to fulfil the duties of our role if we're to succeed – for example, setting a vision. You can, and should, consult other stakeholders to help develop a shared vision that's meaningful to others, but it's up to you as the leader to articulate and energise others to pursue that vision; even servant leaders seek to clarify the will of the group.

Another example is public speaking. If you want to lead others, you'll need to speak up in front of people, sharing your perspectives and inspiring their collective action towards a compelling vision. If, for example, you consider public speaking to be one of your weaknesses, with self-awareness you can figure out whether that's something which is important to you and your ambitions. If it is, with that knowledge you can then dedicate yourself to improving your public speaking skills until they're a strength that you can draw on to reach your goals.

If your weaknesses are tangential to your goals, like singing is for me as a leadership scholar, then you'll know either to avoid such situations, or delegate when they arise – great leaders know when to let others shine. Remember that you often don't have to do everything yourself; reach out to others for help when your weaknesses get in the way of your core leadership role. For example, if you're struggling to find the data you need to make a decision, enlist the support of someone who can quickly get you the relevant information. Don't waste hours searching on your own. Make sure that you're always investing your time and energy in relevant high-value tasks.

That's the real power of self-awareness: knowing when to use your talents, when to step back so that others can take the lead, when to ask for help, and where to focus your professional development efforts.

You're not going to suddenly become self-aware by the end of this chapter; self-awareness is not a destination. Rather, you'll embark on a journey towards a deeper and more comprehensive understanding of who you are as a leader, and what your personal attributes, capabilities, limitations, and motivations are.

Starting down this path, and more importantly continuing your journey, requires a sense of personal ambition. You've got to want to grow and learn to get better, to understand yourself more, to hone your talents, and reach towards your goals. A few activities will serve to create a foundation and teach you the skills you'll need to keep developing; how much you use them will influence how far down this path you get.

Developing your self-awareness doesn't have to be dramatic. You're unlikely to suddenly discover your purpose today and then implement it tomorrow. What's more likely is that you'll start clarifying what you want out of life, and then you start moving towards it incrementally, drawing on your talents and addressing your weaknesses along the way. Life is long; the point isn't to get to the end now, but to keep moving forward.

One of the most useful skills I've ever learned is perseverance. We sometimes imagine that success requires extraordinary circumstances or natural talent – especially when we consider things like developing world-class expertise, getting physically fit, or any other seemingly insurmountable self-directed project – when actually all you need to do is focus and keep working at it, consistently chipping away at it every day, until one day you'll realise you've made it, and, looking back, can see how far you've come.

Self-awareness is like that too. Every time you learn a little more about yourself, you get a little clearer about who you are and what you want out of life. Don't think about it in radical terms, you're not setting out to reach a finish line and triumphantly declare yourself 'self-aware'. It's the process that matters most and its purpose is to motivate you to make incremental improvements.

Self-Concept

Before we proceed any further, let me clarify that self-awareness isn't the same as your self-concept. The notion of a 'self-concept' stems from the field of psychology and it's made up of all the ideas and beliefs you have about yourself; it's what sociologists would call your 'identity' (cf. Haslam et al., 2022).

Markus (1977) refers to the dominant ideas in our self-concept as 'self-schemas' that can include behaviours, personality traits, physical characteristics, and interests. For example, I believe that I'm assertive (behaviour), outgoing (trait), athletic (physical characteristic), and appreciate art (interest). Self-schemas are reinforced by memories of specific events – for example, I readily recall leadership situations in which I was assertive. Contextual cues and cross-cultural contexts can trigger different schemas. For example, you might have schemas about who you are at work that are distinct from your social schemas.

Some of these beliefs include your general self-categorisations, or ways that you come to define yourself, which tend to be specific identifiable categories – for example, ideas like your gender identity, sexual identity, racial identity, and so on. These statements all answer the question: 'Who am I?'. For example, I might categorise myself as educated, male, heterosexual, European, etc. What you believe about yourself strongly affects your intentions and actual behaviour (Kendzierski & Whitaker, 1997).

Self-concepts are also shaped by the various roles we play throughout life. Our experiences as friends, siblings, parents, and in other roles influence how we think and feel about ourselves, and our view of self is then modified by the feedback we receive from others. For example, you might think of yourself as a sister, a father, or an elder in your community, and that will encourage certain kinds of behaviours and interaction patterns.

You might have heard the popular advice to 'show up as your best self', which invokes the notion of multiple self-concepts: some past, some current, and some future potential selves which we can choose to activate. Future selves represent your ideas about who you might become, who you'd like to become, or who you're afraid of becoming. Possible selves can function as incentives for specific behaviour.

Self-schemas can be self-fulfilling prophesies. Once you believe yourself to be something, you start thinking and behaving in ways that are consistent with and reinforce that self-concept or identity. Believing that you are a leader, or even envisioning yourself as a leader in the future, are therefore important steps towards developing an actual leader identity (Zaar et al., 2020). That's why it's so critical that you start seeing yourself as a leader now.

Your self-concept is therefore a fluid construct that you decide for yourself. You can change your mind about these ideas at any moment. Self-awareness then is something else, because your talents and limitations are unlikely to change as readily without considerable effort. For example, I was good at maths yesterday, I'm still good today, and I'll most likely be good at maths tomorrow.

Let's then consider 'self-knowledge' as perhaps a more useful term to guide our discussion.

Self-Knowledge

Self-awareness from a leadership perspective is best defined as the clarity of your self-knowledge – not who you think you are or believe yourself to be, but how well you know specific details about yourself in a much more factual and literal sense.

So, when we're talking about your strengths and weaknesses, do you know right now exactly what you're good at, what your best talents are, and what you struggle with? For the purposes of your professional development, let's focus on leadership-related concepts. For example, one of my leadership talents is negotiation. I have a knack for bridging difficult conversations with multiple stakeholders and competing demands, knowing that I've built aspects of my career around this skill to best leverage my opportunities for success.

My optimism sometimes manifests as a leadership weakness; I can skip right over significant flaws in my logic or planning that are obvious to those with a more critical outlook. I'm loath to part with my optimistic view, and so instead I've developed a process-driven and consultative approach to decision-making that enables me to address potential blind spots in my thinking. Self-knowledge is thus a powerful way for you to hone your leadership capabilities by building on key strengths and mitigating weaknesses.

The same goes for your desires, motivations, and values. Can you articulate in this moment what exactly you're working towards, and why? Can you tell me what excites you, what gets you out of bed in the morning? Setting yourself clear goals helps you to figure out what you might need to do to reach them, and your values will dictate what you are, and are not, willing to do to get there. Remember that some goals may clash with certain values, and so you'll need to decide for yourself whether the ends will justify the means.

Now I'd like you to work through an exercise (Exercise 8.1) that will ask you to identify a few of your most prominent leadership-related strengths, weaknesses, and desires. Don't be shy about your assets or ashamed of your limitations. Allow yourself to be vulnerable, drop all expectations and just be completely honest with yourself. We all have unique talents and challenges. What's most important is that you discover yours so that you can harness them to make yourself the most effective leader you can be. Keep your answers succinct, so that they're easy for you to remember later.

Exercise 8.1

Strengths, Weaknesses, and Desires

Image Alt Text: https://ecuau.qualtrics.com/jfe/form/SV_4Z585kR8GcQfYaO

The strengths, weaknesses, and desires that you've identified in Exercise 8.1 will serve as a good foundation for developing your own unique leadership style. Think carefully about the different leadership theories that we've discussed and draw on those concepts that harness your talents; some may fit better with your character than others.

Self-Aware Leadership

Extending self-awareness into social interactions enables you to become self-aware leaders. Effective leaders seek to understand how their rhetoric, attitudes, and behaviour can affect and influence others; they're mindful of the role that they play and consciously work to bring about desirable outcomes.

I'm sure you can see the appeal of working with a leader who knows where they can add the most value, and when to back off and let others step up; they recognise how certain situations affect their perceptions, emotions, and state of mind; they know when to ask for help and aren't ashamed of their limitations, which lets them admit mistakes and take steps to improve or make amends. It's no surprise that self-aware leaders are more likely to be endorsed and supported by their followers (Steffens et al., 2021).

Self-aware leaders regularly update their self-knowledge so that it's current and relevant. Be ready to critically evaluate your approach and assumptions in light of changing circumstances, and think carefully about your leadership behaviour and how others are experiencing and responding to your actions. Consider if your conduct is appropriate and whether it's taking you and your followers in the right direction, towards your goals.

If any of those answers are no, then be willing to amend and revise where necessary. But having some stability is important too; consistency builds trust as followers start to learn what to expect. The challenge here is in knowing what to change, and what to stay firm on. As a rough guide, stay true to your vision and values, but be flexible in your approach. That way you can continue to learn and adapt your leadership behaviour, while creating stability with your purpose and integrity around a core set of values.

The self-awareness exercise (Exercise 8.1) you did earlier together with the activities that you completed in Chapter 7 have provided you with a platform of baseline self-knowledge from where you can launch your leadership trajectory forward. Think of this as a good snapshot view of yourself right now as a leader, a foundational understanding of your own unique leadership qualities. Now you can start building on it and refining your leadership identity by thinking critically about your past experiences.

Next, we'll explore how you can continue to develop your leadership self-awareness through targeted reflective learning. We'll cover two approaches that can help you to discover more about yourself and enable to you to keep developing your leadership expertise long after you've finished this text.

REFLECTIVE LEARNING

Reflective learning is the process of thinking back on specific things that have happened to you and then applying frameworks that enable you to analyse those experiences and create a learning opportunity.

Personal reflection is at the core of 'transformative pedagogy' (Meyers, 2008) and it's about empowering you to critically examine your beliefs, values, and experiences so that you can develop a reflective self-knowledge base, an appreciation of multiple perspectives, and a sense of personal agency (Ukpokodu, 2009). Transformative learning is about re-envisioning your 'fixed assumptions and expectations […] to make them more inclusive, discriminating, open, reflective, and emotionally able to change' (Mezirow, 2003, p. 58).

Think of the reflective exercises in this chapter, and throughout the text, as a series of targeted interventions (Harackiewicz & Priniski, 2018) specifically tailored to enable your leadership transformation and emergence (Haber-Curran & Tillapaugh, 2015). It's not just about acquiring more knowledge. I've designed these reflective exercises to help you change the way that you think about leadership, about yourself, and your personal and professional development so that you can pursue an identity that's aspirational.

This form of learning has a unique beauty – it's accessible any time, anywhere, and it's free. You can do it in your underwear on the couch at home. And the insights that you'll gain are deeply personal and directly relevant to you, because they're rooted in your experiences, shaped by your perception of the world and your values. No one else can give you this level of personalised insight; only you can give yourself such powerful and profound understanding.

But doing it once isn't enough. The goal is for reflective practice to become an automatic process in your mind, so that you're constantly learning from your every experience. We call this a growth mindset, and it will set you on a trajectory to pursue further education, career advancement, and personal excellence.

I'll next provide you with two reflective tools that you'll need, called double-loop learning and the reflective journal. Let's get started.

Double-Loop Learning

Argyris and Schön (1974) came up with single- and double-loop theories of learning. They originally used it as a way to explore how decisions are made, mistakes corrected, and information transferred within organisations. They called this process 'organisational learning' and defined it as the 'process of detecting and correcting error. Error is for our purposes any feature of knowledge or knowing that inhibits learning' (Argyris, 1977, p. 116). We'll use these theories to learn more about ourselves, others, and the nature of human interactions (Argyris, 2004).

Both single- and double-loop learning include three stages: first an event takes place, then information about the event is processed, and finally corrective action is taken. What's different is how you process the information and what kind of corrective action you take, and that determines whether you're engaging in single- or double-loop learning.

Let's work through an example to illustrate the two concepts. Imagine that one of your employees is consistently arriving late to work; we'll start with a single-loop learning approach.

Single-Loop Learning

Your first instinct might be to correct the employee's behaviour using either a punitive measure or an incentive. You might think, 'If I address the lateness, perhaps by pointing out the importance of punctuality or by issuing a warning, the problem will be solved.' This approach is typical of single-loop learning. It's a familiar process of observing an event, assessing that it is inconsistent with established norms or expectations, and then applying various remedies that will correct the behaviour. Single-loop learning is therefore about making changes to solve problems based on observation and the application of known rules.

But this approach only skims the surface of the issue. It seeks to fix the visible symptom without probing into the deeper causes. What we haven't yet asked is why was the employee late in the first place? We don't know if it's a matter of time management, personal circumstances, or if they're disengaging from their role, and single-loop learning doesn't ask these questions. It assumes the problem is as simple as the observed behaviour deviating from the norm and that correcting this deviation will rectify the issue.

When we stop at single-loop learning we miss the opportunity for deeper insights that could enable a more meaningful change. It's about fixing errors within the confines of current thinking and practices, without challenging or changing the underlying assumptions that led to those errors in the first place.

Let's see how double-loop learning is different.

Double-Loop Learning

Double-loop learning is about recognising that the way a problem is defined and solved can be a source of the problem.

Double-loop learning invites us to embark on a deeper, more reflective problem-solving journey. It's not just about addressing the immediate error; it's about questioning the underlying assumptions and policies that led to the issue in the first place. Let's take the case of an employee who's consistently late. In a single-loop scenario, we might simply enforce stricter punctuality rules. But double-loop learning pushes us further, it asks us to consider why punctuality is an issue for this employee and to explore the broader context.

We'd start by digging into the root causes of the lateness. We'll need to understand if it's a matter of personal circumstances, a misalignment with work hours, disenchantment with the job, or more structural issues with the way that their work is designed. Double-loop learning encourages us to engage with the employee, opening a dialogue that explores these deeper questions. It's about understanding the wider patterns of behaviour and the systemic factors at play.

This approach requires us to also look inward, considering how our own leadership and the organisational culture might contribute to the problem. Are there aspects of our work environment that discourage punctuality or engagement? By reflecting on our own actions and the organisational structures, we can identify changes that might address not just the symptom, but the underlying causes. Consider whether strict work hours are even necessary, or if a more flexible arrangement could help employees to better balance their work and home life.

Implementing double-loop learning means adopting a mindset of curiosity and openness to change. It involves consulting a wide range of information and perspectives, and giving all relevant parties a voice in the solution. This collaborative approach not only addresses the immediate issue but fosters a culture of accountability and continuous improvement.

Double-loop learning transforms your leadership from a directive to a consultative role. It's about creating a space where employees feel empowered to share their challenges and participate in co-creating the solutions. This leads to more sustainable outcomes, as solutions are rooted in a comprehensive understanding of the problem, including the broader organisational context and individual needs.

Learning from Setbacks

Double-loop learning allows you to learn from your setbacks. Accept that at times things will inevitably go wrong; people will let you down, you'll get into fights, and you'll fall short of both your own expectations and those of others. We will each of us face such setbacks, but it's what you do with those setbacks that makes the difference. You can either learn from your setbacks, or else repeat the same mistakes again and again, and again, getting no further.

I want you to see every one of your setbacks, the ones that have already happened to you, and the ones that are still to come, as opportunities to grow. Every setback offers a powerful learning opportunity. The more you can understand about why it happened, what role you played in it, and what you could do differently, the stronger you'll become.

Let's work through Exercise 8.2. It will ask you to describe a past setback and then guide you through a series of questions to challenge your thinking. Focus on your own behaviour, values, and beliefs, as well as your assumptions and expectations.

Exercise 8.2
Double-Loop Learning

Image Alt Text: https://ecuau.qualtrics.com/jfe/form/SV_b76SATy9QM30bD8

I hope you're starting to see how powerful it can be to challenge the way we see problems, rather than immediately trying to fix things with solutions that may only serve to further entrench dysfunctional underlying assumptions.

When we hide from, or ignore, probing deeper into our setbacks, we encourage single-loop learning with unhelpful cycles of 'corrective' action that can take us no further in our development. Instead, embrace your failures and devour them as troves of valuable self-knowledge. Analyse both your behaviour (single-loop), and whatever you assumed was necessary or appropriate at the time, to test whether that's actually true, or a self-limiting belief that's holding you back (double-loop).

Now let's explore the other reflective learning tool that you'll need, the reflective journal. It's probably a bit different to what you might imagine.

Reflective Journal

Reflective journals have long been used for education and learning (Bean & Melzer, 2021). It's not enough to have an experience in order to learn; you have to reflect on that experience to make personal sense out of the rich, complex, and sometimes confusing information (Schön, 1983), and to thus discover generalisable learning that will enable you to face new situations more effectively (Gibbs, 1998).

Reflective writing encourages the critical appraisal of self-relevant knowledge (Jasper, 2005) and is therefore particularly relevant for leadership development (Choi et al., 2022). We tend to see journalling as impromptu writing that chronicles your experiences, but instead we'll approach it as a structured exercise that will create a learning opportunity in a similar way to loop learning.

Except this time our focus will be a bit different; whereas with double-loop learning we studied our behaviour and assumptions, with the reflective journal we'll focus on our emotional experiences. For your reflective journal, you'll write about an event, your reaction, reflection, and your realisation. Let's take a closer look at what each of these four guiding questions is all about.

Event

First recall and describe an incident that was emotionally charged and had either a negative or a surprising outcome – for example, a performance review with a supervisor who highlights areas of your work that are lacking; a tense conversation with a team in crisis over a project that has fallen far behind schedule; a disagreement with a close colleague over the direction of a project. Even an unexpected success, or a commendation from your peers or supervisors for a job well done can be illuminating and fruitful for reflection.

Be brief, but specific and clear, in outlining what happened, who was involved, and how.

Reaction

Now write down how you reacted in the moment. This step isn't about crafting an eloquent justification; it's about raw honesty. I'd expect an emotional statement here, something like: 'I felt confronted, I became angry and defensive.' When faced with a challenging or surprising event, the whirlwind of emotions that ensues – be it anger, joy, shock, or disappointment – offers you a rare glimpse into your inner self.

Say exactly what you felt, clearly and without censorship. Did you feel undermined during a heated discussion? Were you overwhelmed with self-satisfied pride when your ideas were praised? Identifying these emotions with precise labels is key. This introspection might reveal uncomfortable truths about your innate responses to stress, criticism, or praise.

Admitting that you felt defensive, hurt, unwanted, ashamed, or exhilarated at another's downfall isn't always pleasant, but it's a necessary step towards self-awareness. This honesty paves the way for understanding not just your actions but the motives and insecurities driving them. It's a brave act to confront yourself, and will allow you to start unriddling the complexities of your own emotional landscape. Know that without truth, there can be no growth.

Reflection

Now it's time to ask yourself the main question: why? Why did a particular incident stir up such powerful emotions within you? I want you to go beyond just acknowledging your feelings to try and understand their roots. Again, this process will take honesty and courage; you must be ready and willing to uncover the vulnerabilities or insecurities you may otherwise prefer to ignore.

Take, for example, an example where your reaction was more intense than expected. You might discover it wasn't just about the incident itself, but what it represented to you. Perhaps it highlighted a fear of inadequacy or a struggle with self-worth. Such realisations are critical and reveal the deeper layers of your emotional landscape, shaped by personal values, past experiences, and core beliefs. This stage is about connecting the dots between your initial emotional reaction, and the underlying causes. It's a journey inward, demanding introspection and critical self-appraisal.

Understanding the source of your emotional reaction is crucial. It provides clarity and a path for personal growth. By confronting these truths, you're not only acknowledging your vulnerabilities but also paving the way for meaningful change. This reflective practice is about building resilience, emotional intelligence, and fostering a deeper connection with yourself. It's about recognising that your reactions, though personal and sometimes painful, are gateways to profound self-discovery and transformation.

Realisation

In the final stage of the reflective journal process, you're asked to crystallise your insights into actionable steps for future growth. It's about laying bare the lessons learned and committing to a path of change. This isn't just about acknowledging what went wrong; it's about actively planning how to do better next time. You're drafting a roadmap for personal development, pinpointing the behaviours and responses you aim to modify.

Consider what you've discovered about yourself through this process. You may have identified triggers for certain reactions or realised patterns in your behaviour that don't serve you well. Now's the time to ask: what will I do differently? This could involve developing new strategies for managing time, improving communication, or responding more constructively to criticism. It's about setting intentions for how you'll handle similar situations in the future, equipped with a deeper understanding of your emotional drivers.

This stage is transformative. It's where reflection turns into action, where self-awareness becomes a catalyst for change. You're not just reacting to past experiences; you're using them as a foundation to build a more effective, resilient version of yourself. It's a commitment to growth, to not repeating the same mistakes, and to navigating challenges with greater skill and understanding. Here, you're taking control, deciding not just to react differently, but to be different. This is the essence of learning from reflection; it empowers you to evolve, to make informed choices that align with your values and aspirations. Reflective practice, then, isn't just an exercise; it's a powerful tool for personal and professional development.

I'd now like you to work through the reflective journal Exercise 8.3, this time focusing on your emotions.

Exercise 8.3

The Reflective Journal

Image Alt Text: https://ecuau.qualtrics.com/jfe/form/SV_9yOAuVdrPs6odfw

---

Reflective journalling encourages us to slow down and take an impartial step back, to see what's really going on, and consider how we're going to move forward. I hope that you've made meaningful personal discoveries with this exercise.

So far, we've been reflecting on our past experiences; but we can also reflect 'in action'. Let's see how that's different, and why it might be useful for us as leaders.

Reflection-in-Action

Reflection-in-action is a powerful concept that changes how we approach challenges and opportunities in real time. Schön (1983) proposed it as a continuous loop of observation, reflection, and adjustment as events unfold. It's about being mindful and adaptive, capable of diagnosing and responding to situations with informed and thoughtful action. This dynamic process allows leaders to navigate complex scenarios with agility, applying lessons learned on the fly to improve outcomes (Cattaneo & Motta, 2021).

By practising structured reflective exercises, we lay the groundwork for making reflective processes automatic; I'm training your mind to think critically and reflectively as the default setting. This training involves engaging in deliberate reflection both during and after action, allowing you to integrate theoretical knowledge with practical experience. With repeated practice, reflection will become embedded in your everyday thinking, enabling you to draw on a rich reservoir of insights and strategies in any given moment.

The goal is to develop a reflective habit, where evaluating actions, decisions, and their outcomes becomes as natural as breathing. This habit fosters a mindset of growth and continuous improvement, empowering us to learn from every experience. By consistently applying structured reflection tools to our lives, we not only enhance our ability to reflect in action but also ensure that we're always learning, adapting, and evolving. This approach doesn't just prepare us to handle the challenges we face today; it equips us to anticipate and shape the future.

Progressing from structured reflective exercises to continuous reflection-in-action is about becoming more insightful and responsive leaders. This journey is marked by a commitment to self-awareness, adaptability, and the relentless pursuit of excellence. As you integrate these practices into your daily lives, you will not only become a better leader but also foster environments where learning and growth flourish.

PERSONAL MASTERY

Senge (1990) first articulated the concept of personal mastery as a set of principles and practices that enable a person to learn, create a personal vision, and view the world objectively. Personal mastery is about being in control of your own life (Pearlin et al., 1981), understanding the major forces that shape your experiences, and growing from each encounter. The same way that we'd approach mastering a specific skill, personal mastery is about achieving a level of mastery over your life through consistent practice, reflection, and improvement.

Personal mastery is then a discipline (Senge, 2006), a commitment to a set of principles and practices that become integral to your daily life, and enable you to continuously learn and grow (Garcia-Morales et al., 2007). It's about making an ongoing effort to align your actions with your deepest values and aspirations, ensuring that your growth is both purposeful and concordant with your authentic self.

Embracing personal mastery means embarking on a personal journey towards self-discovery and self-improvement. It's about harnessing your potential to create a life that reflects your highest aspirations. By committing to this path, you'll not only enhance your ability to lead others, but also forge a life of significance and fulfilment. Personal mastery, therefore, is not just a leadership skill but a way of living that will improve your performance, well-being, and self-efficacy (Bui et al., 2013).

Garcia-Morales et al. (2007) explain that personal mastery includes four considerations: articulating a personal vision, seeing our current reality clearly, harnessing the creative tension between the two, and reducing the self-limiting beliefs that prevent us from making progress.

Let's take a closer look at each of these four aspects.

Personal Vision

The first aspect of personal mastery is articulating your personal vision. Life offers each of us endless possibilities for what we might do. Every day you can discover more and more wonderous things, and all of them are interesting if you go into them deeply enough; you might burst with the desire to do everything all at once. But therein lies the trouble, we all have the same 24 hours in a day, and so we must decide for ourselves where it is that we're heading, or else we won't get very far in any direction. And I don't just mean setting a few good goals; it's about crafting a destination for your life that resonates profoundly with your innermost desires and values. Senge (2006) explains that a personal vision is an intrinsic longing for a life of significance and fulfilment; it's not about comparing yourself to others or chasing social affirmation by fulfilling others' perceived expectations. Think about what you want to achieve and who you aspire to become.

This might sound easy; it isn't. One of the challenges is that we often mistake our personal vision for specific goals or objectives, without probing more deeply to understand the motivations behind those goals, or else we frame our vision as avoiding something negative rather than embracing true aspirations. Senge (2006) reminds us that our vision should stem from our own deepest desires and values – it's about what we genuinely yearn for. A personal vision is a potent source of motivation and guidance when it's clearly articulated and accompanied with a profound understanding about why it holds significance for you.

For example, you might declare that your personal vision is to achieve financial independence. It's a commendable goal, but you need to dig a little deeper and figure out why it matters to you. Peel back the layers of your motivations by asking 'why?' until you get to the real reasons. Maybe you're sick of the monotony of your current job and believe that financial independence will provide the freedom to pursue your passions, which may give you a deeper sense of meaning and purpose. So what you're really seeking is a life of meaning and purpose that you feel you can't get from your current conceptualisation of employment. Instead of fixating solely on financial independence as the destination, you could now also explore career avenues that align with your values and bring you a sense of fulfilment, to offer both financial stability and a profound sense of purpose that may better align with your true motives.

As another example, you might say that your personal vision is to travel all over the world. Picture what that might look like: exhilarating at first for sure, always seeing new places, meeting new people, seeing new ways of living, and appreciating the breadth of cultural experiences. But after a year or two of constant travel, you're exhausted. You've had intense, but brief and shallow connections with people, rather than deep, meaningful relationships. You've seen much, but not immersed yourself as a 'local' in any of the lives you've passed through. If you make it to 25 this way, what then do you do with the other 40 years of your career life? Keep asking yourself 'why?' until you figure out what's at the core of this desire: are you running from commitment, or seeking a sense of adventure and exploration, or something else entirely; and is travel really the healthiest way to express this desire?

Our visions can evolve – that's natural – but they must be rooted in clarity and purpose. Sometimes crisis or adversity clarify our personal vision for us, when we suddenly see what we can't live without, what we want to spend our life doing. We chase wealth until we realise that family is priceless. We welcome a child, and suddenly, priorities shift. And that's alright. Our visions can adapt, but we must always understand why we're pursuing them. It's the courage to stand by our visions that sets us on the path to personal mastery (Senge, 2006). Embrace this journey of self-actualisation, armed with a deep understanding of your own intrinsic motivations, and navigate towards your personal visions with steadfast resolve.

Current Reality

The second aspect of personal mastery is seeing our current reality clearly. This means developing an acute awareness of where we stand at this moment, acknowledging the truth about our situation, capabilities, and limitations. I'm not just referring to your physical location or your immediate surroundings. It's about understanding your roles, relationships, and your place in the grand scheme of things. Seeing that clearly requires us to strip away the illusions and self-deceptions that often cloud our self-perceptions and view of the world around us. It may seem simple enough, to know where we stand and who we are right now. But let me tell you, it's not nearly as easy as it seems.

Here's the tricky part – our perceptions are coloured by our biases, or flaws in how we process information (Tversky & Kahneman, 1974). And believe me, we've got plenty. Psychology handbooks provide long lists of cognitive biases, outlining dozens of ways that our thinking goes awry (e.g. Haselton et al., 2015). Most of what we've acquired through evolutionary processes to support our survival and social interactions is rarely helpful in the modern era, and now just clouds our judgment. We'll discuss cognitive biases in more detail in Chapter 10, but for now, let's consider two of the best-known biases that affect the view of our current reality: optimism and pessimism; that is, tending to expect either a positive, or a negative outcome.

Optimism can provide us with motivation and resilience, but it can also skew our view of reality. Being too optimistic we risk overestimating our abilities and underestimating the challenges and negative events that we might face in life. For example, Sharot (2011) explains that optimists underrate their chances of getting divorced, being in a car accident, or suffering from cancer; they also expect to live longer than objective measures would warrant, overestimate their success in the job market, and believe that their children will be especially talented (p. 941). Optimism doesn't just affect our expectations; it can also skew the strategies we devise to navigate our lives and careers. By painting a favourable story, we might neglect the necessary preparation for potential setbacks or fail to develop contingency plans, believing that success is guaranteed.

Pessimism likewise distorts our perception of reality, albeit through a mirror darkly. Where optimists might see a path strewn with opportunities, pessimists expect obstacles at every turn. They brace themselves for failure, convinced that success is an elusive, if not impossible, outcome. Pessimism clouds our judgment, leading at best to a defensive approach towards life and leadership, and at worst, defeatism. And yet a healthy dose of pessimism isn't without its merits; it encourages caution, sober risk assessment, and preparing for setbacks before they arise. But when this caution turns into a fixed outlook, it will hamper growth and innovation. Expecting the worst can be as much a bias as expecting the best.

We're not at the mercy of external forces – we are the architects of our own destiny. By recognising the role of such perceptual biases, we can strive for a more objective understanding of our current circumstances. Trade in unwarranted optimism, or excessive pessimism, and approach each situation with a healthy dose of realism instead. It will require you to critically evaluate your assumptions and embrace uncertainty, recognising that life is a complex interplay of challenges and opportunities. Both good luck, and bad, will eventually run out: take heart, and caution from that. Leaders adept at reading situations accurately are poised to adapt to changing circumstances and better placed to make decisions that are balanced and informed. Commit to seeing the world objectively (Senge, 2006), and it will help you to lead with vision and caution, steering your team and organisation towards success amidst uncertainty.

Creative Tension

The third aspect of personal mastery is about harnessing the creative tension that exists between our personal vision and current reality. Senge (2006) describes this creative tension as a stretched rubber band. At one end, you've got your ultimate goals, the dreams you're chasing. And at the other, that's where you're standing today. This tension isn't just a gap; it's a powerhouse of potential energy that's waiting to be unleashed.

There are only two ways to resolve that tension, and you face a critical choice. You can either pull your current reality forward, step by determined step, until you reach your true aspirations, or in moments of despair, you may be tempted to scale down your dreams, making them seem more 'realistic' and less daunting. But the bigger the dream, and greater the distance from where you are today, the more powerful that creative tension will be. I want you to dream so big that the energy pulling you forward is relentless, and it will keep you going forward long after others would have given up. Embrace the distance as motivation, not as a daunting deterrent. It's this very stretch, this pull, that can propel you forward, driving your progress and turning you into the leader you aspire to be.

Self-Limiting Beliefs

The fourth and final aspect of personal mastery is about reducing the self-limiting beliefs that prevent us from making progress. Senge (2006) talks about self-limiting beliefs as 'structural conflict', or ways that we hold ourselves back. When we're striving towards our vision, we can be our own worst enemies, and the two most harmful beliefs are about our own powerlessness and unworthiness.

Powerlessness is about our self-efficacy, potential, and ability to make meaningful impact. Those nagging thoughts that whisper, 'I can't do this', 'It's too late for me', or that 'I'm not smart enough' aren't just fleeting doubts, they're chains that bind us to our current state, preventing us from reaching out towards our potential. If you believe that you're too insignificant to make a difference or that your voice doesn't matter, you're setting the stage for that to become your reality. You'll likely choose paths that reinforce these beliefs, rather than challenging them, and it will become a self-fulfilling prophesy. Flip the script and you'll see that the world is infinitely malleable, limited only by the choices you make and their consequences. Whether your vision is grand or modest, you have to believe that it's possible for you to achieve it.

Unworthiness is about how we perceive our value in relation to the value of others and what we believe we deserve. Thoughts like 'They won't notice me' or 'I'm not good enough for that opportunity' are based on assumptions about other people's perceptions of us. Beliefs about what others think of us are called our 'metaperceptions' (Elsaadawy et al., 2023) and they're beset with a maze of cognitive biases. The accuracy of our metaperceptions varies wildly and often just reinforces what we already think about ourselves (Elsaadawy et al., 2021). Don't be overly concerned with what others might be thinking of you; focus instead on doing good work and making the right choices. Believe in yourself, as I believe in you, and others too will start to see your potential.

Self-limiting beliefs, like a sense of powerlessness and unworthiness, are conflicting forces pulling you further from your vision. To move beyond these self-limiting beliefs, we must engage in constant self-reflection and challenge our internal narratives. Recognise the power of choice and the role it plays in shaping our reality. Understand that the path to your vision is not fixed but malleable, influenced by your beliefs and actions. By addressing feelings of powerlessness and unworthiness you open the door to a world of possibilities, where your vision is not a distant dream but a tangible destination well within your reach. Remember, leadership and personal mastery are not just about reaching a destination but about the journey of transformation that takes you there.

Let's put these concepts into practice. For Exercise 8.4 I'd like you to think back to a time when you responded to that creative tension between your current reality and your vision.

Exercise 8.4

Personal Mastery

Image Alt Text: https://ecuau.qualtrics.com/jfe/form/SV_1Tauu16z6wrZtcO

If you found yourself moving your life towards your vision, take note of what motivated you, and what held you back, so that you can continue to pare away those ideas that aren't serving you well and reshape your thinking to best enable your progress. If you found that you reigned in your vision, rationalising away your dreams, identify and start dismantling the self-limiting beliefs that prevented you from reaching out towards your goals. Now picture every one of your followers facing the same kinds of internal struggles, albeit with their own unique challenges – it's your role as a leader not only to learn and grow yourself, but to enable others' progress too.

Leading with Mastery

Leading with personal mastery isn't just about acquiring a set of skills; it's about deeply understanding who you are, what drives you, and how you interact with the world around you.

Leading with personal mastery is about having a profound sense of purpose that's behind everything you do. It will require you to ask yourself the tough questions about your ambitions and motivations. It will require a deep dive into your psyche to unearth the real drivers behind your goals. Once you articulate your purpose, you're equipped to tackle almost any challenge that comes your way. Your goals then aren't just ambitious targets, they're expressions of your deepest values and aspirations, and that will attract and energise followers to your cause.

Your current reality, no matter how grim or far from your ideal, isn't an obstacle, it's your starting point. Leaders adept in personal mastery see their situation as a temporary state, a moment in time from which they can advance – it's an empowering perspective. It allows you to engage with your current reality, not as a problem, but as a platform for your growth. You'll learn to appreciate your progress, celebrate your achievements, and yet stay humble to avoid egoic distortions of your self-perception that can hinder any further development.

Cultivate a growth mindset (Senge, 1990) by prioritising constant learning, reflection, and applying the lessons learned. This way of thinking isn't confined to your professional life either; it should permeate through every facet of your existence. Recognise that leadership isn't a fixed trait but a capability that can expand with effort, experience, and perseverance. A growth mindset will also fuel your ability to adapt and innovate in your approach, based on new insights and changing conditions. Your commitment to learning sets a powerful example for your team too, encouraging them to pursue their development paths, to seek out challenges, and to learn from both successes and failures. This creates an environment where team members feel valued and supported in their growth journeys, leading to higher engagement, innovation, and performance.

Be prepared to acknowledge your own ignorance. In an environment where leaders are often expected to appear all-knowing, admitting you don't have all the answers is both radical and liberating. It opens you up to new learning opportunities and shows a strength of character. It's a recognition that your knowledge has limits, which is the first step in expanding those boundaries. This humility is a strength, not a weakness.

Personal mastery requires you to develop a deep belief in yourself. It's not about being arrogant or over-confident. It's about knowing your capabilities and having the faith in yourself to overcome challenges and achieve your goals. Such self-efficacy will both fuel your own ongoing development, and serve as the foundation for you to inspire others. If you're confident in your abilities, that confidence is infectious; and others will start to see you as someone who can lead them through challenges and towards success. To be a leader others follow willingly, you must first convince them of your credibility and capability, and it starts with convincing yourself.

Leading with personal mastery is about aligning your actions with your deepest values, continuously learning and growing, and having the courage to face your limitations and surpass them. It's a journey of self-discovery, requiring honesty, humility, and perseverance. As you embark on this path, remember, the journey is as important as the destination. Your growth as a leader is a testament to your commitment to personal mastery.

You, my readers, are already on this path. By engaging with these ideas, you're taking important steps towards understanding and developing your leadership potential. It's a long road, filled with challenges and opportunities for growth. But remember, the journey to becoming an effective leader, one who leads with personal mastery, starts with a single step: the decision to embark on this path of continuous self-improvement. I believe that you have the potential to transform not only yourselves, but also those around you, for the better.

LEADERSHIP DEVELOPMENT

Leadership development is a process of emergence, and you can't master it in a classroom; it's a journey of personal transformation that prepares you to inspire and guide others. To become an effective leader, commit to a process of continuous learning and growth, focused on developing self-awareness and personal mastery through an iterative process involving education, experience, and reflection.

Self-awareness is about understanding your strengths, weaknesses, values, and the impact of your actions on others. It's about looking in the mirror and asking tough questions. What drives you? What are your values? How do these influence your decisions and leadership style? Self-awareness allows you to lead with authenticity, a quality that fosters trust and respect within your team.

Personal mastery is about taking self-awareness a step further by urging you to constantly seek improvement and excellence in all aspects of your life. It's about setting high standards for yourself and striving to meet them, thereby setting a powerful example for your followers. Leaders who exhibit personal mastery inspire their teams to also pursue their own paths of personal and professional development.

Higher education will be vital to your leadership development. It will provide the theoretical foundation and tools you need to understand and apply leadership principles. Base your leadership on robust, research-informed perspectives. But learning doesn't stop at education and experience will be equally, if not more, important. It's through taking on leadership roles, facing challenges, and reflecting on these experiences that you truly grow. Each experience offers a lesson, an opportunity to refine your leadership approach, and develop resilience.

To continue accumulating leadership experience, you'll have to take the initiative and keep stepping out of your comfort zone. Volunteer for leadership roles or projects that stretch your capabilities. This proactive approach not only accelerates your growth but also demonstrates your willingness to take on responsibility and lead by example. It's in these moments of uncertainty and challenge that you'll discover your potential and develop the confidence to lead. I recommend taking on projects that are just outside your current leadership ability, so that you'll have to grow to deliver on them.

Reflection is a critical component of leadership development. It involves looking back on your experiences, analysing your actions, and learning from them. This reflective practice enables you to identify areas for improvement, understand what works, and adjust your leadership style accordingly. Reflection turns education and experience into actionable personal insight, ensuring that each step forward is informed by lessons learned. I cannot overstate how important this is to leadership development.

Lastly, appreciate that it's an iterative process. Leadership development isn't a one-time event but a continuous cycle of practice, reflection, and growth. As you navigate your leadership journey, remember that the goal isn't to become perfect but to become a more effective, authentic, and inspiring leader. By embracing these principles and dedicating yourself to lifelong learning and self-improvement, you'll not only achieve personal success but also empower those around you to reach their full potential.

Leadership development is about more than just acquiring skills; it's about cultivating an attitude of continuous growth, embracing challenges, and learning from every experience. It's a journey that requires courage, commitment, and a willingness to step into the unknown. But it's also a journey that offers immense rewards, not just for you, but for those you lead. So, take the leap, embrace the process, and become the leader you're meant to be.

SUMMARY

Self-awareness is about how well you know the 'objective' details of your character, such as your strengths, weaknesses, desires, motivations, values, and priorities. Self-awareness is essential to effective leadership and serves as the foundation for positive contemporary leadership theories. Self-aware leaders know where they can add the most value, and when to back off and let others step up; they recognise how certain situations affect their perceptions, emotions, and state of mind; they know when to ask for help and aren't ashamed of their limitations, which lets them admit mistakes and take steps to improve or make amends.

Reflective learning is the process of thinking back on specific things that have happened to you in the past and then applying frameworks to analyse those experiences and create a learning opportunity. It empowers you to critically examine your beliefs, values, and experiences to develop a reflective self-knowledge base, an appreciation for multiple perspectives, and a sense of personal agency. Double-loop learning and the reflective journal are two effective structured exercises that can help you to develop a reflective habit, where evaluating actions, decisions, and their outcomes becomes as natural as breathing.

Personal mastery is a set of principles and practices that enable a person to learn, create a personal vision, and view the world objectively. It's about being in control of your own life, understanding the major forces that shape your experiences, and growing from each encounter. Personal mastery is a discipline that includes articulating your personal vision, seeing your current reality clearly, harnessing the creative tension between the two, and reducing the self-limiting beliefs that prevent us from making progress.

Leadership development, then, is a process of emergence, and you can't master it in a classroom; it's a journey of personal transformation that prepares you to inspire and guide others. To become an effective leader, commit to a process of continuous learning and growth, focused on developing self-awareness and personal mastery through an iterative process involving education, experience, and reflection.

'I am the master of my fate; I am the captain of my soul.'

Extract from *Invictus* by William Henley (1875).

REFERENCES

Argyris, C. (1977). Double loop learning in organizations. *Harvard Business Review*, 55(5), 115–125.

Argyris, C. (2004). *Reasons and rationalizations: The limits to organizational knowledge*. Oxford University Press.

Argyris, C., & Schön, D. A. (1974). *Theory in practice: Increasing professional effectiveness*. Jossey-Bass.

Bean, J. C., & Melzer, D. (2021). *Engaging ideas: The professor's guide to integrating writing, critical thinking, and active learning in the classroom*. John Wiley & Sons.

Bui, H. T. M., Ituma, A., & Antonacopoulou, E. (2013). Antecedents and outcomes of personal mastery: Cross-country evidence in higher education. *The International Journal of Human Resource Management*, 24(1), 167–194. https://doi.org/10.1080/09585192.2012.669781

Carden, J., Jones, R. J., & Passmore, J. (2022). Defining self-awareness in the context of adult development: A systematic literature review. *Journal of Management Education*, 46(1), 140–177. https://doi.org/10.1177/1052562921990065

Cattaneo, A. A. P., & Motta, E. (2021). 'I reflect, therefore I am … a good professional'. On the relationship between reflection-on-action, reflection-in-action and professional performance in vocational education. *Vocations and Learning*, 14(2), 185–204. https://doi.org/10.1007/s12186-020-09259-9

Choi, S., Tian, X., & Stumph, C. (2022). Learning organizational behaviors and leadership through reflective journal writing. *The International Journal of Management Education*, 20(2), 100612. https://doi.org/10.1016/j.ijme.2022.100612

Duval, S., & Wicklund, R. A. (1972). *A theory of objective self awareness*. Academic Press.

Elsaadawy, N., Carlson, E. N., Chung, J. M., & Connelly, B. S. (2023). How do people think about the impressions they make on others? The attitudes and substance of metaperceptions. *Journal of Personality and Social Psychology*, 124(3), 640. https://doi.org/10.1037/pspp0000433

Elsaadawy, N., Carlson, E. N., & Human, L. J. (2021). Who influences meta-accuracy? It takes two to know the impressions we make. *Journal of Personality and Social Psychology*, 121(1), 201. https://doi.org/10.1037/pspp0000376

Garcia-Morales, V. J., Lloréns-Montes, F. J., & Verdu-Jover, A. J. (2007). Influence of personal mastery on organizational performance through organizational learning and innovation in large firms and SMEs. *Technovation*, 27(9), 547–568. https://doi.org/10.1016/j.technovation.2007.02.013

Gibbs, G. (1998). *Learning by doing: A guide to teaching and learning methods*. Further Education Unit.

Haber-Curran, P., & Tillapaugh, D. W. (2015). Student-centered transformative learning in leadership education: An examination of the teaching and learning process. *Journal of Transformative Education*, 13(1), 65–84. https://doi.org/10.1177/1541344614559947

Harackiewicz, J. M., & Priniski, S. J. (2018). Improving student outcomes in higher education: The science of targeted intervention. *Annual Review of Psychology*, 69, 409–435. https://doi.org/10.1146/annurev-psych-122216-011725

Haselton, M. G., Nettle, D., & Andrews, P. W. (2015). The evolution of cognitive bias. In D. M. Buss (Ed.), *The handbook of evolutionary psychology* (pp. 724–746). John Wiley & Sons. https://doi.org/10.1002/9780470939376.ch25

Haslam, S. A., Gaffney, A. M., Hogg, M. A., Rast III, D. E., & Steffens, N. K. (2022). Reconciling identity leadership and leader identity: A dual-identity framework. *The Leadership Quarterly*, *33*(4), 101620. https://doi.org/10.1016/j.leaqua.2022.101620

Jasper, M. A. (2005). Using reflective writing within research. *Journal of Research in Nursing*, *10*(3), 247–260. https://doi.org/10.1177/174498710501000303

Kendzierski, D., & Whitaker, D. J. (1997). The role of self-schema in linking intentions with behavior. *Personality and Social Psychology Bulletin*, *23*(2), 139–147. https://doi.org/10.1177/0146167297232003

Markus, H. (1977). Self-schemata and processing information about the self. *Journal of Personality and Social Psychology*, *35*(2), 63–78. https://doi.org/10.1037/0022-3514.35.2.63

Meyers, S. A. (2008). Using transformative pedagogy when teaching online. *College Teaching*, *56*(4), 219–224. https://doi.org/10.3200/CTCH.56.4.219-224

Mezirow, J. (2003). Transformative learning as discourse. *Journal of Transformative Education*, *1*(1), 58–63. https://doi.org/10.1177/1541344603252172

Pearlin, L. I., Menaghan, E. G., Lieberman, M. A., & Mullan, J. T. (1981). The stress process. *Journal of Health and Social Behavior*, *22*(4), 337–356. https://doi.org/10.2307/2136676

Schön, D. A. (1983). *The reflective practitioner: How professionals think in action*. Basic Books.

Senge, P. M. (1990). *The fifth discipline: The art and practice of the learning organization*. Doubleday/Currency.

Senge, P. M. (2006). *The fifth discipline: The art and practice of the learning organization* (Revised ed.). Doubleday/Currency.

Sharot, T. (2011). The optimism bias. *Current Biology*, *21*(23), 941–945. https://doi.org/10.1016/j.cub.2011.10.030

Steffens, N. K., Wolyniec, N., Okimoto, T. G., Mols, F., Haslam, S. A., & Kay, A. A. (2021). Knowing me, knowing us: Personal and collective self-awareness enhances authentic leadership and leader endorsement. *The Leadership Quarterly*, *32*(6), 101498. https://doi.org/10.1016/j.leaqua.2021.101498

Tversky, A., & Kahneman, D. (1974). Judgment under uncertainty: Heuristics and biases. *Science*, *185*(4157), 1124–1131. https://doi.org/10.1126/science.185.4157.1124

Ukpokodu, O. (2009). The practice of transformative pedagogy. *Journal on Excellence in College Teaching*, *20*(2), 43–67.

Zaar, S., Van den Bossche, P., & Gijselaers, W. (2020). How business students think about leadership: A qualitative study on leader identity and meaning-making. *Academy of Management Learning & Education*, *19*(2), 168–191. https://doi.org/10.5465/amle.2017.0290

9
POWER, INFLUENCE, AND COMMUNICATION

Overview

This chapter first discusses the relationship between power and influence, before identifying the various types of power that leaders can draw on, and considering which influence tactics are most effective. You'll work through activities that reveal your natural tendencies towards these two concepts, discovering as yet untapped sources of power and ways to influence others.

Quiz 9.1: Sources of power

To influence others effectively, we first need to understand the three things that motivate and energise people at work: autonomy, mastery, and purpose. You're then introduced to the concept of psychological empowerment as a contemporary way to drive engagement, building power by giving it away.

Quiz 9.2: Influence tactics

Next, we'll explore what motivates us at work as another way to guide you in influencing others, by aligning your leadership behaviour with your followers' need for autonomy, mastery, and purpose.

Everything we do as leaders to influence others takes place through some form of communication. The chapter concludes by addressing four key communication skills, including written, oral, non-verbal, and active listening, covering both how we convey meaning to others and, more importantly, how we can understand them in return.

Video 9.1: Daniel Pink - The surprising truth about what motivates us

Leading others invariably involves changing their attitudes, behaviours, or emotions in strategic ways that can enable and support progress towards shared goals. Sustained effective leadership therefore requires a clear understanding of power, and how it can be translated into influence through communication.

In this chapter we will first discuss what power is and the sources of power that are available for you to draw on. Next, we'll discuss specific ways that you can use power responsibly to influence people. The chapter concludes with an overview of four communication skills that will be crucial for you to develop in your leadership toolkit.

POWER

Power is a fundamental force in social interactions including amical, romantic, and familial, as well as in political, economic, and media relations (Russell, 1938). Power is pervasive throughout organisations of every kind and is therefore intimately entwined with leadership discourse. Dismiss now any prejudices you may have about power as an inherently immoral concept; like every tool, it can be wielded for good, or for ill.

We'll focus our discussion on the power between individuals, referred to as interpersonal power, and defined as the 'discretion and means to asymmetrically enforce one's will over entities', including people, groups, and organisations (Sturm & Antonakis, 2015, p. 139). Power is therefore the capacity to influence others; it's what allows you to change people's attitudes, behaviours, and emotions.

Leadership is impossible without power, and as leaders, you will need to learn what sources of power are available to you and how you can draw on them to influence people and support their progress towards shared goals.

Power doesn't necessarily have to objectively exist to grant you the capacity to influence the behaviour of other people. What matters is that your followers, or whomever you seek to influence, believe that you have power. As long as they think that you have power, then it's real, and it gives you the capacity to influence them. Power, then, resides in the minds of your followers (Atwater & Yammarino, 1996), and people will therefore perceive your power differently in their own unique and idiosyncratic ways.

Power gives you the capacity to change people's behaviour and influence is the ability to use that power. Influence then is the process of using power to change someone's attitudes, behaviour, emotions. There are of course different ways that you can exercise your power to influence others' behaviour.

Power and influence are therefore deeply interrelated. You first need to have some source of power available for you to draw on, which will then affect how and to what extent you can shape others' behaviour. The sources of power that you choose to employ will also determine what kinds of influence tactics that you can use, and how effective they might be. So let's first consider where power comes from.

French and Raven (1959) initially identified five bases of social power: coercive, legitimate, reward, expert, and referent. Raven (1965) later added information power and

Hersey et al. (1979) added connection power, bringing the total to seven. Coercive, legitimate, reward, information, and connection are positional sources of power because they predominantly stem from your formal role inside organisations and in team structures. Expert and referent are personal sources of power that come from who you are, what you know, and what you can do.

In the following sections we will first explore two main bases of social power: positional and personal, and the seven sources of power within them. You will then work through an exercise that will help you to identify your own preferred power profile. Next, we'll discuss how you can wield your power appropriately, without spilling over into the realms of workplace bullying. Afterwards, I'll introduce you to some of the ways that you can put your power into practice through various influence tactics, before considering empowering others as a more contemporary approach.

Positional Sources of Power

Formal leadership roles, such as team leaders, managers, directors, and executive officers confer various types of power onto the occupant. This is known as positional power, because it exists only because of your formal position in an organisation. Exercise of such power is typically well defined, and its scope primarily encompasses individuals in subordinate positions.

Let's look at a few positional sources of power and see how they offer us the capacity to shape followers' behaviour.

Coercive

Coercive power is your capacity to punish non-compliance. If one of your subordinates doesn't do what you want, you may be able to reprimand them in some way to force them to comply, and not disobey you again in the future. The threat of punishment may be sufficient to motivate their compliance. Coercive power is therefore based on fear and includes physical, social, emotional, political, or economic means.

For example, if you're the service manager of an automotive workshop and one of your mechanics fails to wear appropriate personal protective equipment, you could hit them, ridicule them in front of others, shout at them, or more likely give them a formal warning, impose a fine, reassign them to an undesirable task, reduce their hours, suspend them from work, dismiss them altogether; or else threaten to do any of the above.

The scope of coercive power available to leaders is strictly controlled by employment relations legislation to minimise abuse, and so varies significantly across countries and states.

Legitimate

Legitimate power is your capacity to dictate subordinates' behaviour. The higher your position in the organisational hierarchy, the more legitimate power you have to assign tasks, schedule work, require or prohibit certain kinds of conduct. Your legitimate power extends beyond your immediate subordinates and downwards throughout the hierarchy. It may also spill over organisational borders and enable you to direct external providers, subcontractors, or affiliates, depending on your level.

For example, if you're the general manager of a hotel, you could ask your finance manager, sales manager, HR manager, restaurant manager, etc. to provide you with weekly reports on their activities. You could directly approach a front desk staff member, asking them to stop what they're doing and debrief you on the experiences of specific high-profile guests. You could also reassign a gardener, who may be an external contractor, to focus their attention on another part of the hotel grounds.

Legitimate power is accepted by subordinates who concede an obligation to comply with the formal structures of their organisation that grant superiors the right to influence their behaviour.

Reward

Reward power is your capacity to grant positive outcomes, or remove negative ones. Rewards can be tangible, economic, social, emotional, political, or even spiritual. As with coercive force and the threat of punishment, the promise of future rewards may be sufficient to motivate behaviour, as long as subordinates believe that their compliance will lead to the outcomes. Rewards must be considered valuable by the target followers to have the desired effect, and intrinsic rewards remain more effective in the long term.

For example, if you're a sales manager, to encourage your sales reps you could assign them to a high-profile client or task, give them a bonus for meeting ambitious targets, increase their base salary, promote them into a new role, praise them in front of others, provide more favourable work arrangements or office perks, compliment them, endorse them to other superiors, or else promise to do any of the above.

Rewards should be similar to the desired behaviour itself. For example, offering social praise for subordinates' engagement in pro-social behaviour will better encourage it to continue.

Information

Information power is your capacity to control the dissemination of valuable knowledge that others need or want. Informational power derives from both your formal access to information from meetings, draft policies, organisational strategies, and other internal documents and fora, and informal access through social networks with other relevant internal and external leaders. Releasing, withholding, or amending information, in full or in part, enables you to shape how others will behave in response to that information.

For example, if you're the marketing manager, and you wanted to advance the profile of your social media marketer, you could let them know about a new branding direction before it is made common knowledge or suggest that they upskill in specific competencies that will soon be in high demand based on upcoming changes in organisational strategy. You could withhold relevant information to compromise others' capabilities, or shape the narrative to direct efforts towards specific activities.

Information power can be accumulated by mapping the political terrain and dominant agendas, and it can be used by gatekeeping information and leaking it selectively to relevant parties.

Connection

Connection power is your capacity to sway the opinions and decisions of other powerful leaders. Such connection power can stem from both formal and informal, internal and external networks, as well as your network centrality, which is how close you are to the most powerful person in a particular network (Ibarra, 1993). People will readily cooperate with well-connected leaders to gain favour with their powerful allies or avoid their disapproval.

For example, if you're the manager of a restaurant chain and good friends with the mayor, you could use that as leverage to negotiate better deals with local greengrocers and suppliers who may either want access to your privileged relationship with a key decision-maker in the region to advance their own interests, or else would want to avoid the consequences of their disapproval.

Connection power can be accumulated by building a broad network with strong ties to influential people, and it can be used by swaying decision-makers through informal channels.

Now let's turn our attention to personal sources of power.

Personal Sources of Power

Personal sources of power are inherent in who you are, what you know, what you can do, and how others regard you. There are two personal sources known as expert power and referent power; these exist in addition to, and separate from, any kind of formal leadership role or position within organisations. That's particularly exciting because it means that anyone can work to develop these two sources of power for themselves. You can take them with you wherever you go and use them to influence not only subordinates, but also your peers, colleagues, and superiors, both inside and outside of the organisation.

Let's explore what personal sources of power are available for us to draw on and develop.

Expert

Expert power is your capacity to support others in their work through discipline-specific competence and knowledge. Expert power is based on your expertise in a particular field and includes your knowledge, skills, experience, and talent. Expert power can be demonstrated by reputation, credentials, qualifications, certification, achievements, and directly observed from behaviour. Followers are more likely to comply with the instructions from a leader they believe possesses relevant expertise.

For example, if you're an operational manager at a steel fabrication plant with well-known expertise in weld design, you could draw on your knowledge and experience to convince others to more willingly implement your proposed solutions. Relevant expert power encourages people to trust in your judgment and follow your guidance. Recall that expert power, like any source of power, does not have to objectively exist for it to work; it's the perception of expertise that empowers you. When people believe that you have superior skills or experience, they'll more willingly defer to your leadership.

Expert power tends to have a narrower scope of influence around the specific field of your knowledge and abilities, which can decay over time and must be kept current to remain relevant.

Referent

Referent power is your capacity to garner followers' admiration, respect, or desire to identify with you as their leader. Referent power is based on your personal traits, characteristics, behaviour, charisma, values, the strength of your convictions, and your sense of purpose. Followers more readily comply with leaders who they like, respect, or identify with because they want to be led by them. Followers can base aspects of their self-esteem and sense of accomplishment on a referent leader's approval, which encourages their willing deference.

For example, if you're a software development manager with strong charismatic signals, integrity demonstrated by behaviour that's consistent with your values that are shared by others across the organisation, a compelling purpose behind your work, and desirable personality traits, you would likely have the admiration and respect of those in your professional sphere. You could then draw on that referent power to influence their behaviour, soliciting their support for your ideas, their involvement in projects of your preference, and so on.

Referent power is more susceptible to followers' perceptions, which are difficult to predict and can vary significantly; referent power can therefore be easily lost from a perceived misstep.

Let's now work through the first quiz (Quiz 9.1), which asks you a series of questions about your tendencies to draw on these different sources of power. The results will provide you with a 'power profile' about which kinds of power you prefer to use as a means to influence others.

Quiz 9.1

Sources of Power

Image Alt Text: https://ecuau.qualtrics.com/jfe/form/SV_2bpdNyecj5gJQ7s

Adapted from Hinkin and Schriesheim (1989).

Your overall power profile is not simply reflected by the sum of the power derived from each of the seven types in the profile. Some combinations of power types are more than the sum of their parts and synergise with others, while others work against each other. Referent power, for example, tends to magnify the effect of other types of power as the person being influenced recognises that the influence is coming from a person that they respect. The use of coercive power, however, tends to dilute other power types.

Hopefully this exercise has given you some indication of the sources of power that you're already comfortable using and those that are perhaps as yet underutilised. Think carefully about all the options available to you and, wherever possible, draw on expert and referent power, alone or in combination with other sources, to enhance your overall capacity for influence.

Using Power Appropriately

Effective leadership requires in part the capacity to influence your followers successfully. I trust that by now you're starting to see that power is at play in every interpersonal relationship, and that you've invariably used power yourselves to enable you to influence the people around you. At such times we're often acting on instinct, exerting power naïvely, without fully appreciating exactly what kinds of power are at work, where that power comes from, who has it, at what time, and what it allows them to do. My intention in this chapter is to transform your use of power into intentional and conscious actions that will be far more effective.

Leadership involves a voluntary relationship where followers willingly give up power to the leader (Joullié et al., 2021). Your followers are therefore not subordinate subjects or slaves; they do not obey, but rather agree and choose to follow. Foucault (1980) explains that if people aren't free to choose their own actions, then the relationship is one of violence rather than leadership power. Ironically the more positional power you have as a leader, the harder it is to use (Porter et al., 2004).

So far we've discussed power as something that leaders 'have', which is certainly a helpful perspective, but only scratches the surface of the topic. Consider also that power manifests from a myriad of historic, cultural, and institutional factors (Ladkin & Probert, 2021). Leadership is a social process, and your actions are subject to the expectations and norms inherent in the context.

For example, Ladkin and Probert (2021) discuss the account of Orwell (1970) shooting an elephant in a Burmese village. The beast was rampaging, and Orwell, a police officer with rifle in hand, pursues it to protect life and property. A large group of local onlookers accumulates on the way. When they find it, Orwell is relieved to see that the animal has settled and poses no further threat. But to his dismay he realises that he'll have to shoot the elephant regardless, under the weight of expectation from the immense crowd that's followed him.

Followers authorise their leaders and thereby empower them to act. Exercising your own will as a leader may sometimes be impossible in the face of your followers' expectations, who could otherwise cease to endorse your leadership (Ladkin & Probert, 2021). Stray too far from what your followers believe you should be as their leader, and they'll revoke the power that they've voluntarily vested in you (Van Knippenberg et al., 2004). Power dynamics in leadership relations are therefore often unstable, ambiguous, and reversible (Hindess, 1996). You can push people too far and your followers will rebel if they feel that your leadership threatens their freedom beyond what they've willingly subscribed to (Brehm, 1966).

Seek always to use your leadership power appropriately by having positive effects on people and moving your organisation towards its goals in only ethical, responsible, and lawful ways. At the very least, I counsel you to do no harm. Unfortunately, leaders far too often misuse their power and harm those in their charge, bystanders, and those who stand in their way. Before we go any further, let's discuss workplace bullying as an abuse of leadership power.

Workplace Bullying

Bullying is a form of aggressive behaviour in the workplace that's defined as a systematic pattern of repeated harassment over a prolonged period of time, where the target cannot defend themselves, stop the mistreatment, or escape their situation (Nielsen & Einarsen, 2018). Bullying isn't about a single incident of conflict, but the persistent abuse of a person who's in a vulnerable position relative to the perpetrator (Einarsen, 2000).

Workplace bullying is a global issue with serious negative effects on the mental health of employees and the productivity of organisations. Around 15% of employees around the world, on average, are currently experiencing some level of workplace bullying – that's about one in seven people (Nielsen et al., 2010). And it's not evenly distributed; workplace bullying is more common in poorer countries (Van de Vliert et al., 2013), and in larger, male-dominated, manufacturing organisations (Einarsen & Skogstad, 1996).

Bullying behaviours are most commonly perpetrated by supervisors against their employees, but can also occur between peers, or even by employees against supervisors (Salin, 2003). Bullying is enabled by a power imbalance between the target and the perpetrator, which as we now know, isn't necessarily tied to either party's position or hierarchical status. What matters is that the victims feel subordinate in the situation and thus unable to defend themselves (Einarsen, 2000).

Workplace bullying can take many forms and includes work-related leadership behaviour such as withholding information, social isolation, ignoring input, refusing to communicate, setting unreasonable deadlines, unmanageable workloads, excessive monitoring, assigning meaningless work, or no work (Einarsen et al., 2020). I trust that you're now starting to see parallels between workplace bullying and the abuse of positional power.

Please be mindful of how you wield leadership power and consider carefully how your actions may be affecting the people around you. Whenever possible seek to inspire, include, and empower people to work cohesively towards shared goals, and always be wary of imposing your own will, even when you're convinced that it's the right thing to do.

INFLUENCE

Influence is the process of intentionally changing the attitudes, behaviours, or emotions of another person or group. Power gives you the capacity to affect others, and influence is the action you take to exercise that power and effect change. The specific behaviours, or types of behaviour, that you can use to exert power over others are known as influence tactics.

Various types of influence tactics exist, such as political skills that can help you to secure scarce resources (Munyon et al., 2015), or impression management for building a more positive self-image (Peck & Hogue, 2018). We'll focus our attention on proactive influence tactics that are useful for getting others to follow an immediate request; they're particularly relevant if you have limited authority over your target and positional sources of power are either unavailable or insufficient to secure motivated engagement over and above compliance – for example, when you're influencing peers, superiors, or people outside your organisation.

Yukl et al. (2008) present a dominant classification of proactive influence tactics that is supported by dozens of studies (Lee et al., 2017), and includes rational persuasion, exchange, inspirational appeal, legitimating, apprising, pressure, collaboration, ingratiation, consultation, personal appeals, and coalition. Let's take a closer look at each of these traditional tactics and consider how you could use them to make yourself more influential as a leader.

Traditional Influence Tactics

Rational Persuasion

Rational persuasion is about using logical reasoning and evidence to support a stance or proposition. It involves convincing others that an idea or course of action isn't just sound in theory but is also practically applicable and aligned with overarching goals. Imagine that you're leading a project team and need to shift deadlines to accommodate unforeseen challenges. To use rational persuasion, you'd lay out the facts, project timelines, the nature of the obstacles, and explain how the adjusted deadlines will ensure quality without compromising the project's integrity.

This technique depends on the leader's ability to articulate arguments that are not only compelling but also resonate with the team's or organisation's objectives. It's crucial that these arguments are backed by solid evidence, making the proposed action appear to be the most sensible path forward. For example, when advocating for a new marketing strategy, presenting case studies, market research, and projected outcomes can persuade the team to embrace this change.

Rational persuasion relies on the leader's perceived credibility and trustworthiness. If team members doubt your motives or question your integrity, even the most logical arguments can lose their effects.

Consultation

Consultation is about inviting participation and input from followers in the planning and execution of changes or initiatives. It's a strategy that values the contributions and insights of team members, encouraging them to engage actively in decision-making processes. When leaders adopt a consultative approach, they're not merely seeking endorsement for preconceived plans; they're genuinely interested in the ideas and suggestions of their team.

For example, if you'd like to change the performance targets for your team. Rather than unilaterally imposing the changes, invite the team to discuss the motivations behind the change and to collaboratively define new objectives. This method not only grants team members a voice but also instils in them a sense of ownership over the decisions. As a result, team members are likely to feel more respected and valued, and to support and commit to the changes.

Consultation proves essential when major strategic decisions, like entering a new market, have already been made. Although the broader decision lies beyond the team's control, by involving them in planning and resource allocation, you can foster a shared commitment to the organisation's objectives. With this inclusive tactic you not only gain valuable insights but also cultivate a culture of trust, collaboration, and mutual respect.

Inspirational Appeal

An inspirational appeal draws on the values and ideals that resonate deeply with your team. It's about stirring emotions to inspire your team to work towards a common goal. Imagine that you're leading a project that demands weekend work on rotation among team members to ensure customer access around the clock. When it's a particular member's turn, you might explain that three of their colleagues have already stepped up over the last three weeks, and that it's now their turn. This appeal isn't just a call to action; it's a call to fairness, to shared responsibility, and to honour the commitment shown by their colleagues.

This strategy relies on a clear understanding of your team's values, tapping into what drives them to secure their commitment. Appealing to values that they don't hold salient is unlikely to secure their commitment, and so it's crucial to engage with your team, to listen and learn what they believe. This knowledge allows you to craft messages that not only resonate but also inspire action. Inspirational appeals, when aligned with your team's values, can transform an ordinary request into a compelling call to arms, fostering a sense of unity and purpose.

Collaboration

Collaboration involves offering assistance or necessary resources to encourage someone to agree to carry out a request or approve a proposed change. It's about reducing the associated costs to make the task more manageable. For example, if I wanted you to work on the weekend, I might suggest that we both come in and split the workload on

Saturday and then take Sunday off; that would show that I'm willing to share the burden and actively participate in the task to make it more appealing to you.

As another example, if I asked you to take on more responsibilities, I could also offer to provide you with an assistant or additional resources to ease the workload. Such an approach shows that I'm committed to supporting you, rather than taking advantage of you. Collaboration is a valuable leadership tactic, fostering teamwork and cooperation among team members, and contributes to more positive outcomes and increased willingness to cooperate.

Don't see collaboration as only transactional; it's relational, and builds bonds that can then transcend specific tasks to foster deeper engagement and commitment. By adopting collaboration, you encourage a spirit of teamwork and can help to cultivate an environment where cooperation is the norm.

Apprising

Apprising involves demonstrating how agreeing to your request or proposal will directly benefit the individual or foster their own professional growth. You're presenting a convincing case for why the person should consider your request, emphasising the positive outcomes they stand to gain.

For example, let's say I ask you to work late tonight and spend the weekend writing a report, a considerable commitment that might disrupt your personal plans. To persuade you, I could explain that this will enable you to showcase your skills to our superiors, and may lead to new opportunities for career advancement in the future. Or I could highlight how this effort would allow you to master new tools and techniques, providing an opportunity for skill development. It may also offer you the chance to collaborate with influential colleagues, to expand your professional network.

Apprising is therefore about tailoring the benefits of your request to align with the target's aspirations and desires. It transforms a simple appeal into a compelling proposition that addresses the individual's personal goals and motivations, making them more likely to agree and cooperate willingly. Naturally, you'll need to know about your target's aspirations and desires for this to work.

Ingratiation

Ingratiation is a subtle yet effective influence tactic that involves employing praise as a means to gain the target's cooperation before or during an attempt to influence them. It involves creating a favourable image that encourages others to be more receptive to your requests or proposals.

For example, when you're seeking a colleague's assistance with a task, you might begin by offering them sincere praise for their expertise or capabilities in that area. Alternatively, you could employ self-deprecating humour to make them feel superior, prompting them to step in and help.

Ingratiation can be a powerful tool when used judiciously. When praise is genuine and specific, it can enhance interpersonal relationships and foster goodwill. However, it's important to strike a balance and ensure that ingratiation doesn't come across as manipulative or insincere, as this can erode trust and credibility in the long run.

Personal Appeal

A personal appeal is a straightforward influence tactic that relies on the strength of a personal relationship or friendship to request assistance or support for a proposal. When you have positive, friendly, and collegial relationships with others, it becomes easier to ask them for help or a favour.

For example, in a workplace where you've built strong friendships, you can approach a colleague and say, 'Hey, could you do me a favour?' or 'I need some assistance with this project, and I thought you could help'. The foundation of friendship makes such requests feel natural and fosters a sense of reciprocity.

Personal appeals can be particularly effective when leaders have invested time and effort in building positive relationships with their team members. When team members see their leader as a friend or ally, they are often more willing to support initiatives and work collaboratively, knowing that their leader values the relationship. Building and maintaining positive workplace relationships is therefore an important aspect of effective leadership and influence.

Exchange

An exchange is about leveraging an offer or a promise to elicit compliance or support from your team members. It's a strategic play of give-and-take, anchored in the principle that mutual benefits foster deeper engagement and commitment. Think of it this way: when you propose an exchange, you're not just asking for a favour; you're binding a future commitment that creates a reciprocal bond.

For example, imagine you're at the helm of a pressing project and you need an extra pair of hands. You might approach a team member with an offer: 'If you can lend your expertise here, I'll stand by you in your next big venture.' This not only signals your immediate need, but also cements a partnership that extends beyond the current task. It's a pledge of support that underscores your leadership ethos of mutual progress and shared success.

Leaders who master the art of exchange cultivate a culture of collaboration and mutual respect. They recognise the power of reciprocity in building a cohesive unit where members feel valued and understood. Through these exchanges, leaders set the stage for a symbiotic environment where every contribution is recognised and rewarded, paving the way for a more resilient and adaptive team. This approach not only bolsters team morale but also encourages a spirit of collective achievement.

Legitimising

Legitimising is about establishing that your request is valid, appropriate, and that you have the authority to make it. It's grounded in the belief that for a leader's requests to be followed, they must be seen as legitimate and within the bounds of what's acceptable and expected within an organisation. This tactic draws on established sources of power, such as rules, policies, and job descriptions that form the backbone of organisational structure.

Imagine you need to assign a task that a member of your team believes is beyond their job description. You can legitimise your request by referring to the role requirements outlined in their job description, or other codes of conduct, workplace rules, procedures, guidelines, and so on. Legitimising reinforces that the request is reasonable and valid by grounding it in official work-related agreements.

Legitimising is particularly valuable when you're making an unusual or unexpected request. By referencing established rules or job expectations, you clarify that the request is legitimate and falls within the scope of their responsibilities. Legitimising thereby also ensures that your leadership directives align with established norms of acceptable conduct, which may help alleviate resistance and any sense of wrongdoing.

Pressure

Pressure involves giving people subtle nudges or reminders, checking in on their progress, or even making demands and threats, to encourage them to complete a task or align with a goal. This tactic can vary in intensity, from gentle reminders to more direct and forceful demands. When used with care, pressure can serve as a motivator, pushing individuals towards achieving objectives. But there's a fine line between motivating and coercing.

In its softer form, pressure acts as a nudge towards action. You might remind a colleague about an overdue report with a polite request, highlighting the importance of their contribution. This approach leans on respect and the implicit understanding of shared goals, aiming to inspire action without invoking negative feelings. It's about saying, 'I'm counting on you,' not 'You're failing'. It's a tool for catalysing action, not a weapon for inducing fear.

However, pressure can escalate into a more forceful approach. When urgency is critical, you might say: 'I need that report immediately. Drop everything and get it to me within the next half-hour.' In extreme cases, threats may be used, such as: 'If you don't complete this now, I'll find someone else who can get it done on time.' While pressure can yield short-term compliance, it will invariably damage relationships and harm your reputation if overused in the long term (Reina et al., 2018).

Exercise caution when applying pressure, as an overreliance on this tactic can be perceived as bullying. Effective leadership involves a balance of influence strategies and softer approaches are often more conducive to maintaining positive working relationships.

Coalition

Coalition is about rallying the support of others to sway a target audience or individual towards a specific action or to back a particular idea. It's a strategic move that amplifies your persuasive efforts by leveraging the credibility and respect of those you partner with.

Consider a scenario where you're keen to introduce a groundbreaking project within your organisation. You know the concept is solid, but you also recognise the challenge in gaining widespread acceptance. That's where coalition comes into play. You might team up with a colleague who's highly regarded across departments for their innovative thinking and track record of success. Together, you present your proposal, combining your insights with their influential standing. This partnership doesn't just add weight to your argument; it also broadens the appeal of your proposal, making it more compelling to the wider team.

Coalition thrives on the principle that there's strength in numbers, especially when those numbers include individuals of notable esteem and influence. When you align yourself with others who share your vision and possess their own circles of influence, you create a powerful synergy. This collective force can significantly boost your persuasive power, making it easier to win over sceptics and garner the support needed to bring your ideas to fruition.

It's also about smart alliance-building. The key lies in selecting partners whose expertise, values, and influence complement your own. This strategic selection ensures that your coalition is not just a gathering of voices but a unified front that speaks directly to the interests and respects the concerns of your audience. By presenting a united stance with respected figures, you're not just sharing an idea; you're showcasing a collective belief in its value and potential.

Each of the influence tactics that we've been discussing will be useful at different times, depending on who you're trying influence, what kind of power you're drawing on, what you're trying to achieve, and so on. Consider the vast array of situations that you'll face, from rallying your team around a common goal to navigating complex negotiations. It's not just about what you're asking of your followers, but also how you're asking it and the power dynamics at play.

Leaders must be adept at navigating through a spectrum of strategies, tailoring their approach to the unique context and individuals they're guiding. To be consistently effective across different contexts, you'll need to learn to draw on the full array of influence tactics at your disposal.

Now I'd like you to work through Quiz 9.2 that will ask you a series of questions about all the different influence tactics, and the extent to which you use them consciously to shape others' behaviour.

Quiz 9.2

Influence Tactics

Image Alt Text: https://ecuau.qualtrics.com/jfe/form/SV_dmLn44fulWPQjiu

Adapted from Yukl et al. (2008).

The higher you scored on this assessment, the more influential you probably are as leaders. I'm not going to claim that this is a highly valid psychological assessment, but rather your results are signalling that you're aware that these different ways to influence people exist and you're regularly and intentionally using them to influence others.

I encourage you to experiment using the entire array of tactics in different situations. Try all of them, and see which ones speak to you more. Some will come more naturally, and some will be more appropriate in certain contexts with certain people. The more you use these skills, consciously and intentionally, the better your outcomes will be, and the more influential you'll become as leaders.

Psychological Empowerment

Psychological empowerment is a more contemporary approach to influencing behaviour that's about granting individuals the power and autonomy to positively influence themselves (for a review, see Maynard et al., 2012). Instead of using your power to enable traditional influence tactics, empowerment involves sharing authority and responsibility, fostering a sense of ownership among those you seek to influence, such that they engage in desirable behaviours to pursue relevant outcomes of their own volition.

The concept of empowerment emerged in response to the detrimental effects of bullying and intimidation as influence tactics. Aggressive methods erode respect, disengage employees, and result in minimal effort. Empowerment offers a gentler way to achieve desired outcomes.

Psychological empowerment blends power and influence into a dynamic interaction. By delegating decision-making authority and giving individuals ownership over their work, you can instil a sense of empowerment. When people feel empowered, they exhibit strength, capability, and commitment, leading to improved performance. Instead of dictating specific behaviours, you're nurturing their motivation to engage deeper with their work.

Empowerment thereby promotes a sense of ownership, giving individuals the confidence and dedication needed to excel in their roles. Empowering followers forms a solid foundation that can be enhanced by influence tactics that channel and focus their resulting energy and commitment.

Spreitzer (1995) refined earlier frameworks to identify four dimensions of empowerment: meaning, competence, self-determination, and impact. These dimensions provide a framework for us to understand how empowerment works and how it can be harnessed to influence others more effectively. Empowerment isn't just about relinquishing power; it's about guiding and inspiring others to reach their full potential. Let's take a closer look at each of these dimensions.

Meaning

The first dimension of empowerment is about infusing work with meaning. It involves aligning tasks and responsibilities with a deeper sense of value, purpose, and the personal beliefs held by the individuals you aim to empower. By understanding your followers and connecting their work to the promotion of these values, you provide a sense of significance to their roles.

When people perceive that their work aligns with their core beliefs and values, it ignites a profound sense of purpose. This newfound purpose acts as a powerful motivator, energising individuals to perform at their best. For example, if you're passionate about sustainable architecture and believe it can contribute to a healthier planet, instilling this sense of purpose in your design team can inspire them to create innovative, eco-friendly solutions.

When work carries a sense of meaning, individuals are more likely to approach it with enthusiasm and commitment, ultimately leading to improved performance and outcomes. As a leader, appreciate that building a sense of meaning can be a transformative force in motivating and engaging your team.

Competence

The second dimension of empowerment involves fostering a sense of competence in individuals. This means empowering them by ensuring they feel strong and capable when it comes to specific job-related tasks. As a leader, you achieve this by equipping your team members with the necessary tools and skills to excel in their roles.

For example, by providing comprehensive training, guidance, and support, you convey your confidence in their abilities. When individuals are reassured that they have the skills and knowledge required for their responsibilities, they develop a profound sense of competence. This psychological empowerment enhances their commitment and dedication to their work.

When employees or followers believe they possess the competence to perform their tasks effectively, they approach their responsibilities with enthusiasm and a willingness to excel. As a leader, your role is not only to set the vision but also to empower your team by nurturing their confidence and competence in their abilities. This dimension of empowerment plays a pivotal role in motivating and enhancing their performance.

Self-determination

The third dimension of empowerment revolves around self-determination, granting individuals the autonomy to make choices and decisions regarding their work. When leaders provide their team members with the freedom to choose how they approach their tasks, it conveys trust and confidence in their abilities.

For example, if I allow you the flexibility to determine how you complete a particular assignment, it means I trust your competence and judgment. This sense of autonomy empowers you, giving you control over the method, pace, or approach you employ in your work. By offering this self-determination, leaders acknowledge the unique strengths and insights of their team members.

When individuals have a say in how they carry out their responsibilities, they feel more engaged and committed. This dimension of empowerment not only encourages ownership of tasks but also fosters a sense of responsibility and accountability. Leaders who value self-determination enable their team members to lead their working lives with a greater sense of control, ultimately leading to more motivated and empowered individuals.

Impact

The fourth dimension of empowerment is impact, which involves connecting your followers' work to meaningful outcomes and broader effects on society. When individuals see how their efforts can make a difference, it adds a sense of significance to their tasks.

For example, if I take your assignments and explain that I'll use them to create a paper for a conference, reaching a wide audience and sharing your views on future leadership, your work now extends beyond earning a grade. It influences the world and contributes to a larger purpose.

Impact isn't solely defined by organisational performance metrics. It's also about the subtle signals that leaders send through communication, trust-building, and delegation. By signalling that individuals have control over their work and that it holds meaning and will create a broader impact, leaders empower their team members. This empowerment, in turn, leads to stronger commitment and dedication to the work.

Let's consider now what motivates us at work more broadly.

Motivation at Work

Motivation at work is one of the most enduring and compelling topics in organisational psychology (for a review, see Kanfer et al., 2017). Motivation at work is about understanding how workplace structures and personal attributes, such as your desires, traits, and values, affect your purposeful actions, as well as the mechanisms and processes involved.

Work motivation shapes the skills that people will seek to develop, the careers that they'll pursue, and how they'll allocate their resources, including their attention, effort, time, and human and social capital. Motivation also affects the tasks people select, the level of intensity with which they work, and their perseverance to continue.

Effective motivation at work is critical for leaders of every organisation, including public, private, not-for-profit companies, as well as cultural, religious, and social groups. The outcomes determine the success of such organisations and groups, as well as the personal success and well-being of their members.

What motivates us at work has therefore been studied extensively from a vast array of different perspectives. For example, we're motivated to fulfil our needs for justice, achievement, power, and affiliation; unmet needs create physical and psychological tension that energises us to act. As another example, intrinsic motivation compels us to do things because they're interesting and enjoyable, instead of as means for getting extrinsic incentives.

To effectively influence followers' behaviour in the workplace, you'll need to understand what motivates them. Rather than covering each of the myriad approaches taken in the literature, I'd like you to watch a short video by Daniel Pink that provides a modern take on what motivates us at work. Let's see what you make of it.

Video 9.1

Daniel Pink – The Surprising Truth About What Motivates Us

Summary

Daniel explains that people can be motivated with financial incentives to complete simple mechanical tasks, and offering more money yields higher motivation. Complex creative tasks, however, have an inverted U-shaped relationship with financial incentives, where a little bit is necessary, but too much actually decreases motivation. Instead, Daniel suggests that autonomy, mastery, and purpose are the three things that motivate people beyond money.

Image Alt Text: https://www.youtube.com/watch?v=u6XAPnuFjJc

In today's workplaces, people often engage in complex and creative work. Leaders must recognise this shift and adapt their approach accordingly. First, pay people enough so that they're not worrying about money, and are free to focus on the work. And then motivate your people to excel by fostering a sense of autonomy, mastery, and purpose.

Empower your followers to make decisions and take ownership of their work; the autonomy will instil a sense of pride and ownership, motivating your followers to strive for excellence in their work. Provide opportunities for development and encourage their pursuit of personal mastery, and connect their work to a greater cause so that their efforts have meaning beyond the tasks at hand.

Let's now turn our attention to communication to see how we can put the principles of power and influence into action.

COMMUNICATION

Leadership is a co-constructed relationship that survives and disappears through communication between leaders and followers (Joullié et al., 2021). Communication is the vehicle for transferring understanding and meaning from one person to another. It includes everything from the thoughts you hold in your mind to the way you convey them to others. This process is essential for effective leadership, forming the bedrock upon which successful leadership is built.

Communication involves both creating and transmitting messages to intended receivers, to facilitate a shared understanding. Such messages include aural and or visual cues that are exchanged, and both sender and receiver make sense of these cues' meaning based on their past experiences, culture, prior learning, the communication context, and the relationships between the participants, among other factors (Ruben & Gigliotti, 2016).

Leadership communication is not a linear process where you craft a message, send it via specific cues or signals that are then received, decoded, and acted upon. Meaning is co-constructed from the ongoing interactions between leaders and followers, rather than unilaterally controlled by the leaders, and is often shaped by unplanned cues and unexpected interpretations, rather than as predictable linear events.

Every action, no matter how small, contributes to the overall impression people form of you as a leader. From the moment you say hello to the way you present yourself and your punctuality, every detail matters. These impressions develop quickly, often in the first moments of interaction. For example, arriving sloppily dressed at your first team meeting may signal a lack of seriousness or organisational skills. Similarly, showing up late might imply that you prioritise your time over others' or struggle with time management. Even arriving excessively early can convey nervousness or over-preparation. See everything you do as a form of communication; it's impossible not to communicate (Watzlawick et al., 2011).

Understanding that every action sends a signal about your leadership identity and behaviour is crucial. Communication serves as the conduit through which these signals are conveyed, shaping how others perceive you as a leader. In the upcoming sections we'll explore the various forms of communication, including written, oral, and non-verbal, and discuss how each form contributes to effective leadership.

Written and Oral

Written and oral communication includes everything you might write or say, across every imaginable medium from a report to an email, text message, social media DM, or sticky note, and conversations in person, over the phone, virtually online, pre-recorded or live.

Written communication offers a tangible extension of your leadership. Focus on being clear and coherent. Each sentence you craft should build on the last, moving your reader through your thoughts and ideas with ease. Whether you're drafting an email, a proposal, or a memo, the aim is to leave no room for doubt about your intent. The strength of your written word lies in its ability to stand alone, conveying your message with the same force and clarity as if you were speaking directly to the reader. Rambling or sending mixed messages can dilute the intended impact. Maintain a singular focus and avoid distractions that might detract from the main message; conflicting signals can confuse recipients and hinder effective communication.

Oral communication serves as your immediate connection with your audience, be it your team, peers, or a broader group. Focus on being precise and intentional. When you speak, every word must serve a purpose, whether to inform, inspire, or engage. It's about striking the right chord with your audience through a shared joke, a reference, or simply the language that speaks to them. For example, when sharing information, craft your message to be clear and concise, providing the necessary details without overwhelming the recipients. Conversely, when seeking engagement and participation, present the issues briefly and leave room for others to engage.

Whether you're communicating in written or oral forms, understanding the audience can make all the difference. Take the time to get to know who you're communicating with before you start. A quick online search or a glance at their LinkedIn profile can provide valuable insights into their values, interests, and potential sensitivities. This knowledge empowers you to tailor your message effectively and better influence your audience; a message that resonates is one that's received, understood, and acted upon.

Let's not overlook the importance of the medium. The way you choose to communicate – be it a speech, an email, a report, or a casual conversation – carries with it implications for the tone and formality of your message. Align your chosen medium with the content of your message so that your communication is received as intended and embraced by the target audience. Informal language, such as using a friendly 'hey' when addressing a team, fosters a relaxed and open atmosphere, encouraging transparent and informal responses. On the other hand, a formal salutation like 'Dear Professor' conveys professionalism and requires a similarly formal response.

In both oral and written forms, effective communication requires a balance between clarity and brevity. It's about knowing what to say, how to say it, and when to say it. As leaders, our words are our tools to inspire action, convey vision, and build relationships. They have the power to uplift, motivate, and transform. Effective written and oral communication isn't just an important skill to practise; it's an art to be mastered. It's what will set you apart, enabling you to connect, influence, and lead with impact. Your words have power – use them wisely, and watch as you transform the world around you.

Non-Verbal

Non-verbal communication includes your body language, facial expressions, posture, tone, and even the physical distance you keep in interpersonal interactions. Non-verbal communication shapes how your message is perceived and understood (for a review, see Hall et al., 2019). Studies on non-verbal communication suggest that an estimated 65% to 93% of the message meaning is conveyed through non-verbal cues (Bonaccio et al., 2016). It's therefore critical for leaders to align their non-verbal cues with their verbal message to avoid confusion and minimise misinterpretation.

Face-to-face and video communication offer a rich platform for non-verbal communication. Your facial expressions convey a wealth of information about your emotional state and attitude. When inspiring your team, ensure that your face communicates enthusiasm, energy, and purpose. A lively, confident expression can captivate your audience and make your message more compelling. In contrast, if you appear uninterested, uncertain, or unengaged, your non-verbal cues can signal doubt or indifference, potentially undermining the impact of your message.

Body language is another crucial element of non-verbal communication. The way you carry yourself, your posture, and your movements all contribute to the message you convey. When delivering a message of confidence and strength, maintain an upright posture with shoulders back. This physical stance mirrors your message, enhancing your perceived competence and influence. Conversely, slouching or fidgeting may undermine your message by projecting uncertainty or lack of commitment.

The distance you maintain during interpersonal interactions is also a component of non-verbal communication. It can convey your intention and level of comfort. If you want to establish a close, personal connection, standing closer to someone can signal attentiveness and a willingness to engage at a deeper level. However, it's essential to be aware of personal boundaries and avoid making the other person uncomfortable.

Tone and pitch of voice are integral to non-verbal communication, even in written messages. Your tone can influence how your written words are interpreted. For example, a snippy text message response like 'OK' or 'Fine' might make the recipient feel dismissed, unvalued, or foreshadow an impending confrontation – whether intended, or not. Pay attention to the tone you use in both written and oral communication to ensure that it aligns with, reinforces, and enhances your intended message.

Consistency is paramount in non-verbal communication. To send a clear and impactful message, ensure that what you say aligns seamlessly with how you say it. For example, if you need to reprimand somebody, maintain a stern facial expression, neutral tone, and keep eye contact to enhance the seriousness and impact of the reprimand. An inconsistency between your words and non-verbal cues can send mixed messages that confuse the intent and diminish the impact of your leadership communication.

Effective leaders master the art of combining the right message with appropriate delivery. While the content of your message matters, the way you deliver it can significantly influence how it's received. Be conscious of your non-verbal communication to enhance your leadership influence and facilitate clear and impactful interactions.

Active Listening

Active listening is about how we receive oral information. It's about being present in the moment, giving your complete attention to the speaker, and actively engaging with their message. Listening and being heard create a powerful sense of togetherness (Kluger & Itzchakov, 2022).

Active listening involves maintaining eye contact, not in a creepy or invasive way, but enough to pick up on the non-verbal cues that make up a significant portion of communication. When you look at the speaker, you gain insights from their facial expressions and body language, enriching your understanding of their message. At the same time, it signals to the speaker that you are fully engaged with and value their input. A lack of eye contact can leave the speaker feeling unheard or unimportant, damaging effective communication.

Ask clarification questions when it's appropriate. If you encounter parts of the conversation that are unclear or may need require further elaboration, don't hesitate to ask for more information. It will demonstrate that you are actively engaged with the topic and genuinely want to understand the speaker's perspective. Paraphrasing or summarising what the speaker has said is another technique that can show you're actively processing their message and trying to grasp it fully from within your own frames of reference. These techniques reinforce that you're invested in the conversation and help you to reach a mutual understanding.

Don't interrupt the speaker, even if you're eager to contribute to the discussion. Constant interruptions signal that your voice and opinions take precedence over theirs and convey a lack of respect for their input. Effective leaders refrain from dominating conversations and grant others the opportunity to express themselves fully before responding. Interrupting not only disrupts the flow of the conversation but can also discourage future open communication.

Listening to understand, rather than to formulate a response, is a fundamental principle of active listening. In today's fast-paced world, where multitasking is common, it's crucial to give your full attention to the speaker. Whether you're dealing with trivial concerns or important matters, listening attentively fosters better communication. Even when your time is limited, dedicating a few undistracted minutes to a speaker can significantly enhance their sense of being heard and valued.

As leaders you'll likely face frequent interruptions from your followers, who may come by with work-related questions, new ideas, or to connect over a social chat. It's important for you to respond respectfully. When someone seeks your guidance or input, take a moment to give them your full attention. Acknowledge their presence and let them know you have a few minutes to spare. This brief, but focused, interaction communicates that you respect their need to communicate, even amidst your busy schedule.

For leaders, active listening isn't only about receiving oral messages clearly; it's also about creating an environment where meaningful and effective communication can thrive. How you communicate signals to others what is the appropriate and expected way to interact. By practising active listening, leaders can build trust, foster understanding, and encourage open dialogue within their teams that contribute to stronger relationships and better work-related outcomes.

SUMMARY

Power is a fundamental force in social interactions, including amical, romantic, and familial, as well as in political, economic, and media relations. Leadership is impossible without power, and as leaders, you will need to learn what sources of power are available to you and how you can draw on them to influence people and support their progress towards shared goals. Like every tool, it can be wielded for good, or for ill. We can draw on power from five positional sources: coercive, legitimate, reward, information, and connection; and two personal sources: expert and referent. Effective leaders are aware of the power that's available and use it intentionally and consciously to enable their influence.

Influence is the process of intentionally changing the attitudes, behaviours, or emotions of another person or group. Power gives you the capacity to affect others, and influence is the action you take to exercise that power and effect change. The specific behaviours, or types of behaviour, that you can use to exert power over others are known as influence tactics and include rational persuasion, consultation, inspirational appeal, collaboration, apprising, ingratiation, personal appeal, exchange, legitimising, pressure, and coalition.

Psychological empowerment is a more contemporary approach to influencing behaviour that's about granting individuals the power and autonomy to positively influence themselves. When people feel empowered, they exhibit strength, capability, and commitment, leading to improved performance. Psychological empowerment includes four dimensions – meaning, competence, self-determination, and impact.

Leadership is a co-constructed relationship that survives and disappears through communication between leaders and followers. Communication is the vehicle for transferring understanding and meaning from one person to another; this process is essential for effective leadership, forming the bedrock upon which successful leadership is built.

Communication involves both creating and transmitting messages to intended receivers, to facilitate a shared understanding. Such messages include aural and or visual cues that are exchanged, and both sender and receiver make sense of the meaning of these cues based on past experiences, culture, prior learning, the communication context, and the relationships between the participants.

'Every word has consequences. Every silence, too.'

Jean-Paul Sartre (1945) in *Les Temps Modernes*, *1*(1), p. 5.
Translated by Arthur Hirsh (1982).

REFERENCES

Atwater, L. E., & Yammarino, F. J. (1996). Bases of power in relation to leader behavior: A field investigation. *Journal of Business and Psychology*, *11*, 3–22. https://doi.org/10.1007/BF02278251

Bonaccio, S., O'Reilly, J., O'Sullivan, S. L., & Chiocchio, F. (2016). Nonverbal behavior and communication in the workplace: A review and an agenda for research. *Journal of Management*, *42*(5), 1044–1074. https://doi.org/10.1177/0149206315621146

Brehm, J. W. (1966). *A theory of psychological reactance*. Academic Press.

Einarsen, S. V. (2000). Harassment and bullying at work: A review of the Scandinavian approach. *Aggression and Violent Behavior*, *5*(4), 379–401. https://doi.org/10.1016/S1359-1789(98)00043-3

Einarsen, S. V., Hoel, H., Zapf, D., & Cooper, C. L. (2020). The concept of bullying and harassment at work: The European tradition. In S. V. Einarsen, H. Hoel, D. Zapf, &

C. L. Cooper (Eds), *Bullying and harassment in the workplace: Theory, research and practice* (3rd ed., pp. 3–41). CRC Press.

Einarsen, S. V., & Skogstad, A. (1996). Bullying at work: Epidemiological findings in public and private organizations. *European Journal of Work and Organizational Psychology, 5*(2), 185–201. https://doi.org/10.1080/13594329608414854

Foucault, M. (1980). *Power/knowledge: Selected interviews and other writings 1972–1977* (C. Gordon, L. Marshall, J. Mepham, & K. Soper, Trans.; C. Gordon, Ed.). Pantheon Books.

French, J. R. P., Jr., & Raven, B. H. (1959). The bases of social power. In D. P. Cartwright (Ed.), *Studies in social power* (pp. 150–167). Institute for Social Research, University of Michigan.

Hall, J. A., Horgan, T. G., & Murphy, N. A. (2019). Nonverbal communication. *Annual Review of Psychology, 70*, 271–294. https://doi.org/10.1146/annurev-psych-010418-103145

Hersey, P., Blanchard, K. H., & Natemeyer, W. E. (1979). Situational leadership, perception, and the impact of power. *Group & Organization Studies, 4*(4), 418–428. https://doi.org/10.1177/105960117900400404

Hindess, B. (1996). *Discourses of power: From Hobbes to Foucault.* Blackwell Publishers.

Hinkin, T. R., & Schriesheim, C. A. (1989). Development and application of new scales to measure the French and Raven (1959) bases of social power. *Journal of Applied Psychology, 74*(4), 561. https://doi.org/10.1037/0021-9010.74.4.561

Ibarra, H. (1993). Network centrality, power, and innovation involvement: Determinants of technical and administrative roles. *Academy of Management Journal, 36*(3), 471–501. https://journals.aom.org/doi/abs/10.5465/256589

Joullié, J.-E., Gould, A. M., Spillane, R., & Luc, S. (2021). The language of power and authority in leadership. *The Leadership Quarterly, 32*(4), 101491. https://doi.org/10.1016/j.leaqua.2020.101491

Kanfer, R., Frese, M., & Johnson, R. E. (2017). Motivation related to work: A century of progress. *Journal of Applied Psychology, 102*(3), 338. https://doi.org/10.1037/apl0000133

Kluger, A. N., & Itzchakov, G. (2022). The power of listening at work. *Annual Review of Organizational Psychology and Organizational Behavior, 9*, 121–146. https://doi.org/10.1146/annurev-orgpsych-012420-091013

Ladkin, D., & Probert, J. (2021). From sovereign to subject: Applying Foucault's conceptualization of power to leading and studying power within leadership. *The Leadership Quarterly, 32*(4), 101310. https://doi.org/10.1016/j.leaqua.2019.101310

Lee, S., Han, S., Cheong, M., Kim, S. L., & Yun, S. (2017). How do I get my way? A meta-analytic review of research on influence tactics. *The Leadership Quarterly, 28*(1), 210–228. https://doi.org/10.1016/j.leaqua.2016.11.001

Maynard, M. T., Gilson, L. L., & Mathieu, J. E. (2012). Empowerment – fad or fab? A multilevel review of the past two decades of research. *Journal of Management, 38*(4), 1231–1281. https://doi.org/10.1177/0149206312438773

Munyon, T. P., Summers, J. K., Thompson, K. M., & Ferris, G. R. (2015). Political skill and work outcomes: A theoretical extension, meta-analytic investigation, and agenda for the future. *Personnel Psychology, 68*(1), 143–184. https://doi.org/10.1111/peps.12066

Nielsen, M. B., & Einarsen, S. V. (2018). What we know, what we do not know, and what we should and could have known about workplace bullying: An overview of the literature and agenda for future research. *Aggression and Violent Behavior, 42*, 71–83. https://doi.org/10.1016/j.avb.2018.06.007

Nielsen, M. B., Matthiesen, S. B., & Einarsen, S. V. (2010). The impact of methodological moderators on prevalence rates of workplace bullying. A meta-analysis. *Journal of Occupational and Organizational Psychology, 83*(4), 955–979. https://doi.org/10.1348/096317909X481256

Orwell, G. (1970). Shooting an elephant. In *The collected essays, journalism and letters of George Orwell* (Vol. 1: An age like this 1920–1940, pp. 265–272). Penguin.

Peck, J. A., & Hogue, M. (2018). Acting with the best of intentions ... or not: A typology and model of impression management in leadership. *The Leadership Quarterly, 29*(1), 123–134. https://doi.org/10.1016/j.leaqua.2017.10.001

Porter, M. E., Lorsch, J. W., & Nohria, N. (2004). Seven surprises for new CEOs. *Harvard Business Review, 82*(10), 62–72.

Raven, B. H. (1965). Social influence and power. In I. D. Steiner & M. Fishbein (Eds), *Current studies in social psychology* (pp. 371–381). Holt, Rinehart, & Winston.

Reina, C. S., Rogers, K. M., Peterson, S. J., Byron, K., & Hom, P. W. (2018). Quitting the boss? The role of manager influence tactics and employee emotional engagement in voluntary turnover. *Journal of Leadership & Organizational Studies, 25*(1), 5–18. https://doi.org/10.1177/1548051817709007

Ruben, B. D., & Gigliotti, R. A. (2016). Leadership as social influence: An expanded view of leadership communication theory and practice. *Journal of Leadership & Organizational Studies, 23*(4), 467–479. https://doi.org/10.1177/1548051816641876

Russell, B. (1938). *Power: A new social analysis*. Allen & Unwin.

Salin, D. (2003). Ways of explaining workplace bullying: A review of enabling, motivating and precipitating structures and processes in the work environment. *Human Relations, 56*(10), 1213–1232. https://doi.org/10.1177/00187267035610003

Spreitzer, G. M. (1995). Psychological empowerment in the workplace: Dimensions, measurement, and validation. *Academy of Management Journal, 38*(5), 1442–1465. https://doi.org/10.5465/256865

Sturm, R. E., & Antonakis, J. (2015). Interpersonal power: A review, critique, and research agenda. *Journal of Management, 41*(1), 136–163. https://doi.org/10.1177/0149206314555769

Van de Vliert, E., Einarsen, S. V., & Nielsen, M. B. (2013). Are national levels of employee harassment cultural covariations of climato-economic conditions? *Work & Stress, 27*(1), 106–122. https://doi.org/10.1080/02678373.2013.760901

Van Knippenberg, D., Van Knippenberg, B., De Cremer, D., & Hogg, M. A. (2004). Leadership, self, and identity: A review and research agenda. *The Leadership Quarterly, 15*, 825–856. https://doi.org/10.1016/j.leaqua.2004.09.002

Watzlawick, P., Bavelas, J. B., & Jackson, D. D. (2011). *Pragmatics of human communication: A study of interactional patterns, pathologies and paradoxes*. W. W. Norton & Company.

Yukl, G., Seifert, C. F., & Chavez, C. (2008). Validation of the extended Influence Behavior Questionnaire. *The Leadership Quarterly, 19*(5), 609–621. https://doi.org/10.1016/j.leaqua.2008.07.006

10
PRACTICAL LEADERSHIP SKILLS

Overview

This chapter presents a host of practical leadership skills and techniques that you can use to grow and develop as leaders. It starts by exploring critical thinking, decision-making, and how our cognitive biases affect our ability to make good choices, before moving on to discuss approaches to goal setting and stress management.

You will then examine the ability view of emotional intelligence, to learn how leaders' emotions cascade throughout organisations and influence follower outcomes. A quiz will help reveal your current emotional intelligence capabilities.

Next, you will be introduced to positive psychology, which is about studying the positive aspects of the human experience, those that make life worth living by focusing on improving well-being and fulfilment instead of reducing mental illness, behavioural issues, and negative thinking.

The chapter concludes with a discussion of the power of stories, explaining how we shape behaviour and transfer values and beliefs through the stories that we tell ourselves and others.

Quiz 10.1: Handling stress

Quiz 10.2: Emotional intelligence

Video 10.1: Shawn Achor – The happy secret to better work

Exercise 10.1: Rewire your mind

Video 10.2: Guido Palazzo – The soft power of story telling

Effective leadership requires you to deploy a broad compendium of techniques and approaches to navigate the myriad complexities that are inherent in human interactions and organisational dynamics.

This chapter is your leadership toolkit, packed with techniques to first sharpen your critical thinking, decision-making, goal-setting, and stress management skills. Next, we'll dispel a couple of cognitive biases that can cloud our judgment and explore how emotional intelligence can help us to understand and influence others. Then I'll introduce you to positive psychology and we'll conclude by exploring how the stories we tell can shape behaviours, transfer values, and forge beliefs.

CRITICAL THINKING

To communicate well, you must first be able to think well. Critical thinking is what will enable you to develop compelling ideas that will resonate with followers. You'll need to craft strong arguments and deliver them persuasively so that your audience not only understands, but also embraces your ideas.

So, what exactly is 'critical thinking'? Let's unpack these two concepts one at a time. First, 'critical' denotes the need for an analysis – a careful examination of merits, faults, and limitations. Apply critique throughout every assessment and decision you make, from organisational choices to your leadership style and behaviour.

Critical thinking isn't one-sided; it's about exploring diverse perspectives, considering arguments that challenge your own preconceptions, views, and beliefs, and recognising the limitations of your processes and conclusions. Imagine it as inspecting the edges of your own reasoning to make absolutely sure that you've performed a comprehensive assessment and identified the best possible outcomes.

'Thinking' is the conscious mental processing of information. It's about coming up with ideas, reasoning, solving problems, making judgments, and reaching your own conclusions. The information that you can consider includes everything from organisational documents, published work, and private conversations, to your sensory perceptions – the things you see, hear, and feel, as well as your imagination.

We can combine these two concepts into a cyclical 'critical thinking' framework that can help guide us through these complex processes. Critical thinking involves five stages, starting with identifying, then analysing, reflecting, evaluating, and reasoning. Let's examine each step in a bit more detail.

Identifying

The first step in the critical thinking process is identifying reliable information. It's about determining the value of the information that we encounter. Whenever we engage with any kind of data or information, we must pause to evaluate its worth and reliability, to make informed decisions about how much weight the information should have, and the extent to which we can trust it.

To gauge the reliability of information, we must investigate where it came from and how and why it was created. When making informed decisions, we rely on evidence, and the strength of our decisions rests on the quality of the information at hand. This includes academic literature, such as journal articles, which offer research-informed insights. For example, a journal article may report that transformational leadership improves work engagement, and that provides us with valuable and reliable knowledge that we can then deploy in our own leadership practice.

Our information sources extend beyond academia to also include primary and secondary sources, such as conversations with people and written materials. When consulting these diverse resources, always ask yourself three questions: is the information current, relevant, and reliable?

Information can quickly become outdated, which may either render it irrelevant or worse, give you a false impression that will mislead your judgment. Next, consider whether the information is directly relevant to the issue that you're working on. For example, you may find information that's interesting, accurate, and important, but has little to do with the matter currently at hand. Focus only on what adds value to your work.

Question who created the information, and why. Every piece of data carries a motive, whether it's a political speech designed to sway public opinion, or a commercial advertisement aimed at selling products. Be wary of how others' motives may intentionally shape your perceptions and behaviour through the information you encounter.

Academic work offers us some security here. Scholars seek to advance knowledge for its own sake, with fewer opportunities for direct personal gain. Academic journal articles are therefore more reliable than information supporting a political or commercial agenda, or a sales pitch.

However, even academic research has its limitations, especially in fields where financial interests might influence the results – for example, in medicine and engineering where academic inventions and patents can make fortunes. In the social sciences too, academic reputations and career prospects are determined by research output.

Carefully consider the information that you're consuming and make sure that the information you base your decisions on is current, relevant, and reliable.

Analysing

The second critical thinking step involves analysing information. It is about delving into the data, interpreting it from your perspective, and integrating it into the broader context of your own understanding. Take the information that you've gathered and ponder it. Examine it from various angles to glean insights. Consider its relevance to the bigger picture.

First question whether you've collected enough information. A single article might seem enlightening, but it could represent only one viewpoint among many. It might not reflect the prevailing perspective in the literature. Understanding the extent of the information needed is vital. You don't need to devour every available article; instead, seek the right balance. For small decisions, exhaustive research isn't warranted, while more significant decisions may demand extensive consideration.

Evaluate for yourself whether the evidence supports the conclusions that are presented to you. Information sources typically put forward certain arguments, and substantiate these with evidence, examples, and data. Assess whether these elements logically underpin their conclusions. Scrutinise the balance of their reasoning. Do they provide a comprehensive view of the subject, or do they seem one-sided, potentially leading to biased or motivated conclusions? Be wary of any information that may be leading you down a predetermined path, rather than providing an objective and accurate conclusion.

Every fragment of evidence and information that you gather contributes to your assessment, judgment, and conclusion. As you accumulate these puzzle pieces, your objective is to construct your own interpretation and argument regarding the subject matter. Each piece must fit logically into the sequence, forming a cohesive chain that guides you to your conclusion.

This process isn't just about absorbing information; it's about actively engaging with it, digesting it, and transforming it into your own coherent and rational perspective.

Reflecting

The third step is reflecting. As you interpret information, remember that your unique life experiences shape how you perceive the world. Acknowledge that who you are, your past, and your experiences influence the lens through which you view evidence. Reflect on how your behaviours, actions, and beliefs are shaped by your personal interactions, education, religion, and philosophical ideals. These facets of your life will affect how you interpret the evidence before you.

For example, let's say you read a novel by an author known for expansive writing, and you quickly find it boring and poorly written because it clashes with your preferences. Recognise that your judgment isn't a universal truth about the book's quality. Instead, it reflects how you see the novel through the lens of your personality and past experiences. Your perception, in this case, is influenced by your personal disposition and history.

Consider the influence of your background when analysing information. Are you, consciously or unconsciously, projecting your beliefs and biases onto what you're reading? For example, if you hold strong religious and ideological views that favour authoritative leadership, you might dismiss servant leadership as weak and unimportant. Recognise when your past experiences and beliefs are affecting your judgment and potentially limiting your openness to diverse perspectives.

Reflect also on what you may be overlooking in your search for information. Seeking specific information can create tunnel vision, where you focus too much on one thing and miss out on other valuable insights. Be mindful of your blind spots and think carefully about what you cannot see, and what you're ignoring or choosing not to see.

Be aware of the lens through which you view evidence, and strive to maintain an open and balanced perspective to improve your critical thinking skills.

Evaluating

The fourth step is evaluating. At this stage, you assess all the information you've gathered and understood to make an overall judgment. Whenever you draw a conclusion, it must be precise and well-defined. Clearly state what you're arguing and the context in which it applies. For example, if you claim that a particular leadership style is effective, specify how, in what context, with whom, under what circumstances, and what exactly does it help leaders to achieve.

Your judgments should objectively reflect the evidence that's in front of you. Ensure that your evidence forms a complete narrative that leads to your conclusion. Be wary of logical errors that can compromise the integrity of your judgment and avoid logical fallacies in your reasoning. For example, a false dichotomy presents only two options when more possibilities exist. Straw man arguments misrepresent an opposing view to make it easier to refute. Bandwagon reasoning relies on popular opinion, but popularity doesn't guarantee accuracy. We'll discuss cognitive biases in more detail later in the chapter.

Consider objections or opposing viewpoints. Address these objections with reasoned arguments or provide evidence to demonstrate why they don't apply here. Challenge your own beliefs and be open to the possibility that your initial assumptions may not hold true. Evaluating information requires a commitment to intellectual honesty and a willingness to revise your own position when confronted with contradictory evidence.

Rigorously examine the information to ensure that your claims are well defined and supported by the evidence, address objections, and avoid logical fallacies.

Reasoning

The fifth and final step of the critical thinking process is reasoning, where you argue towards a specific decision. Reasoning is about connecting your evaluations of the evidence from the previous step into strong arguments by linking valid premises to arrive at a logical conclusion.

Let's consider a few examples to show you what I mean. Here's the first argument: 'Most pens have ink. Most ink is black. Therefore, this pen likely has black ink'. It's true that most pens have ink, and that predominantly, ink is black. So, we can deduce that this pen likely has black ink. The two premises are true, and the argument structure is valid, which makes for a strong argument. It's not definitive, as exceptions exist, but it presents a compelling case.

Now for the second argument: 'Most pens have ink. All ink is red. Therefore, this pen has red ink'. Herein lies a flaw: the first premise is still true, but the second isn't because not all ink is red. The logical structure of the argument is valid in the sense that the conclusion is an accurate reflection of the premises. However, the false premise weakens the argument and so we're not convinced by the conclusion.

Here's another example that reveals a common trap: 'Most pens have ink. Some printer ink is red. Therefore, this pen has red ink'. Both premises here are true, but the logical structure of the argument isn't valid – the two premises, if accepted, don't logically lead to the conclusion, and so the overall argument is weak and unconvincing. I often I see these kinds of arguments where true information is presented, but then the conclusion seems to come out of nowhere.

Now let's apply this in a leadership context. Suppose we argue that 'Transformational leadership increases followers' work engagement. This leader's behaviour aligns with the four dimensions of transformational leadership. Therefore, this leader will increase followers' work engagement.' What do you think? Is this argument strong?

Published academic research informs us about the positive effects of transformational leadership theory, including improving followers' work engagement. If our observations of the leader's behaviour align with this theory, we can logically predict such positive outcomes. This argument is strong because it combines consistent logic with true premises.

The more you use the critical thinking process, the more natural and automatic these five steps will become, such that the quality of your reasoning improves across all aspects of your life. Now let's focus on a specific application of critical thinking in leadership contexts: decision-making.

DECISION-MAKING

Decision-making is a fundamental part of effective leadership. Leaders are constantly making choices, and the consequences ripple outwards, affecting countless other people. The higher you are in an organisational hierarchy, the further your sphere of influence extends, such that your decisions affect not only internal stakeholders but also external partners, customers, suppliers, governmental bodies, and not-for-profit organisations.

Leaders' decisions shape the trajectory of their organisations. High-ranking leaders wield significant influence, but the responsibility for sound decision-making reaches all levels of leadership. These choices, no matter how small they might seem, determine an organisation's profitability, customer satisfaction, process efficiency, product quality, and overall sustainability.

The modern business landscape is marked by instant public accountability via the Internet, social media, and online news outlets. Leadership decisions today undergo unprecedented scrutiny. Leaders are expected to act with perfect knowledge, given the vast information readily available, and our decisions are evaluated against this unattainable standard. As leaders, we face impossible odds, and yet we must continue to move forward to the best of our ability, knowing the challenge ahead.

Technological advancements can revolutionise business practices. Leaders must quickly appraise the possibilities, deciding whether to accept the risk of adopting disruptive innovations, lagging behind competitors, or wasting resources on fruitless pursuits. Ethical dilemmas further complicate decision-making as leaders weigh profitability against pro-social and environmental concerns. Leaders are people too, and must balance responsibilities to their families, communities, and organisations, as well as their personal career goals.

Well-informed, intentional decision-making is therefore critical in this complex leadership context. As leaders you'll have to consider each decision, knowing that you may be called on to justify your choices. Careless or impulsive decisions are untenable in a world that demands accountability. Deliberate decision-making practices will help you to navigate the intricate web of responsibilities and ethical dilemmas so that your choices align with your goals and values, as well as those of your organisation.

We'll consider one approach that's called the DECIDE model. Let's take a closer look.

DECIDE Model

The DECIDE mnemonic stands for a six-step decision-making process: define the problem, establish the criteria, consider the alternatives, identify the best option, develop and implement an action plan, and evaluate the solution. You'll notice that the steps aren't complicated, and you probably already follow a version of this process naturally whenever you're making decisions in your everyday life.

The point of this model is to make each step explicit and complete, and to slow down the overall pace of your decision-making. We're all liable to skip steps by taking mental shortcuts and reaching too quickly for solutions, especially in leadership situations where everything can seem urgent all the time. The best approach is to always take the time to think it through the first time round, rather than rushing into a mistake that will take much longer to undo.

Let's take a quick look at each of these six steps.

Define the problem. The first step is to define the problem. That means figuring out both the symptoms and the source of the problem, considering what kind of impact it's had, and whether anything should be done to address it. For example, patient care is suffering at a local hospital A&E/ER. The symptoms may be overcrowding and long wait times, the source may be understaffing and slow internal processes; it makes sense to try and address this problem.

Establish the criteria. Once the problem is known, set the criteria against which you'll assess potential solutions. These criteria form the boundaries within which your solution must fit. Consider factors like cost constraints, alignment with your organisation's mission and values, new advantages that it should offer, existing strengths that should be preserved, and negative consequences to avoid. In our A&E/ER example, criteria could include improved wait times, maintaining high-quality care, and reducing patient attrition.

Consider the alternatives. Next, explore a range of potential solutions, acknowledging the inherent biases that may cloud your judgment. The goal is to consider a variety of alternatives, and to assess the advantages and limitations of each approach. In our example, potential solutions could include expanding the A&E/ER facility, hiring more staff, streamlining procedures, or even diverting patients to other facilities. Assess the advantages, disadvantages, and associated costs for each alternative with an unbiased lens.

Identify the best option. With suitable options now in view, the next step is to select the best solution. Your choice will be informed by experience, intuition and, when possible, experimentation. For our example, a prudent choice may include a combination of measures: such as expanding the A&E/ER facility, separating adult and paediatric patients, and building additional entrances and exits to alleviate congestion.

Develop and implement an action plan. After selecting the best solution, the next step is to develop an action plan and implement the solution. Your plan should outline what needs to be done, how it will be achieved, the necessary resources, and the individuals involved. Set SMART goals that are specific, measurable, achievable, relevant, and time-bound to ensure clarity and accountability. In our example, this step could start with a proposal to the hospital senior leadership team that sets out the problem, solution, and implementation plan.

Evaluate and monitor the solution. The last step is to evaluate and monitor your solution. Compare the achieved outcomes against your predefined criteria to see whether the solution met expectations, exceeded, or fell short in certain areas. Consider your progress at every stage and be ready to adjust your approach where needed. Embrace a spirit of continuous improvement and reflect on the decision-making process itself too.

Following this model will enable you to make better and more responsible leadership decisions, and the reflection cycle will encourage you to further refine and optimise your approach over time. However, one part of the process is still unclear: how do we know when we've identified the best possible solution, and how long should we take trying to assess our options? Let's consider 'maximising' and 'satisficing' as two approaches that can help us to make choices more effectively.

Maximising vs Satisficing

Whenever we're trying to identify the best solution to pursue, as per the fourth step of the DECIDE model, we can use one of two approaches to make the choice: maximising or satisficing.

Maximising is about meticulously exploring and evaluating all the potential alternatives at your disposal, to select the one absolute best option. As you might expect, the maximising approach tends to produce better-quality decisions. However, the process is typically slow and so incurs costs in the form of time. When maximising, you're exposed to a much wider variety of potential solutions and that awareness tends to create uncertainty and self-doubt as you start to question if you've truly found the best alternative, meaning that you're often left less satisfied with your decision.

Satisficing is about looking for alternatives until you find the first one that meets all your criteria. At that point, you stop looking and proceed with that solution. Satisficing typically results in acceptable decisions that might not be as good, but still meet all of the established parameters. The advantage is that you have an acceptable solution and can quickly move forward to implementation. When satisficing, you'll find that you're generally more satisfied with your decisions and the pace with which you can progress.

Both approaches have merit, and so the question is when should you maximise, and when should you satisfice? It's simpler than you might think. If your task is urgent and important, that's when you should satisfice. For example, if you're in a crisis or facing a tight project deadline, you don't have time to investigate every alternative and you're better off to pick the first acceptable option and move forward with a decision quickly.

Satisficing is also the best approach if you're making a decision that's not particularly important – if, for example, you're contemplating where to get lunch today or which toothpaste brand to purchase. Just pick the first choice that satisfies your criteria and quickly move on. Your time is valuable and much better invested elsewhere than in the pursuit of the absolute best toothpaste on the market.

Maximising is useful when you're facing a task or decision that's important, but not urgent. For example, when you're setting the long-term strategic direction of your team or organisation, or working to develop productive relationships with key partners. These are critical endeavours that require careful consideration. Here, you should invest the time and effort to explore and evaluate multiple options, selecting the decisions that best align with your goals and values.

When it comes to maximising, however, be wary of being paralysed by analysis. That's when you spend far too much time scrutinising your options, and either miss your opportunity because of the delay, or fail to make a decision entirely. You're almost always better off taking decisive action, even if it's imperfect, than not making a choice at all, or wasting all of your time deciding while the moment passes you by. Strike a balance between thorough analysis and timely decision-making.

COGNITIVE BIASES

Our decisions are biased whenever we unfairly prefer one option over another, against any logic, evidence, or rational justification. Cognitive biases are systematic errors in our decision-making process. Tversky and Kahneman (1974) introduced the concept and describe them as 'heuristics', or mental shortcuts that people use to reduce the complexity of the task to make decisions.

Simon (1957) introduced the term 'bounded rationality' to explain that people have a finite capacity to process information. The limits of our cognitive ability therefore constrain our decision-making; we simply cannot collect and analyse all the information that's available to us in perfectly rational ways. That's why we've evolved to rely on mental heuristics.

We're often unaware of our cognitive biases and how they may be affecting our judgment. Without interrogating our thought patterns, we tend to over-rely on heuristics, which undermines the rigour of our decision-making and results in suboptimal outcomes. Heuristics are harmless for the most part and help us to navigate our daily lives. However, as a leader you cannot afford to rely on flawed processes when making decisions that will affect your organisation and other people's lives.

Let's explore some of the many ways that our thinking can go awry, so that you're aware of the pitfalls and can mitigate the effects. In the following sections, we'll discuss four cognitive biases that are relevant to leadership situations: confirmation bias, groupthink, attribution asymmetry, and the sunk cost fallacy.

Confirmation Bias

Confirmation bias is the tendency to support our existing beliefs, which shapes the way we look for and interpret information – that is, we generally find what we're looking for. If we're trying to see the best in someone, we'll discover evidence of their virtues, but if we're looking for flaws, we'll find those too.

Confirmation bias is related to the concept of 'cognitive dissonance' (Festinger, 1957), which is an uncomfortable psychological state that we experience when our actions, feelings, ideas, beliefs, or values are inconsistent with our experiences in the external environment. For example, you might believe that the world is a fair and just place, and seeing veterans go homeless would make you feel that uncomfortable cognitive dissonance because it challenges your beliefs.

Confirmation bias affects our decision-making in two ways. First, when we're searching for information. We tend to be selective with what we look for, how we frame our questions, and the kinds of information sources that we draw on. These decisions affect the kinds of information that we're exposed to and typically fit to our pre-existing ideas. Second, in interpreting information when we're faced with evidence that challenges our current views, we try to resolve the discomfort by either ignoring the information or reasoning that it's somehow less reliable so that we can justify dismissing it outright or giving it less weight.

Confirmation bias creates blind spots that undermine the quality of our decision-making. That's why it's so important to actively search for and consider information that challenges our preconceptions. If we already have a particular outcome in mind, our tendency is to construct a narrative and find information that supports our beliefs. It's therefore critical to stop and consider whether we've truly explored options that might not initially appeal to us, and whether we've weighed all the evidence objectively.

Groupthink

Groupthink happens when there's a strong desire for harmony within a group that overrides its members' ability to critically evaluate information. Groupthink often manifests in two distinct contexts.

First, groupthink can happen in highly cohesive groups, where team members share close social connections and strong bonds. People in such tight-knit groups might not want to openly challenge each other question decisions to maintain the friendly atmosphere, or to avoid the unpleasantness of a falling-out. Group decisions can therefore go unexamined, and the advantages of effective teamwork are forfeit, even though the team may appear to have a very positive culture.

Second, groupthink also applies under authoritarian leadership where decisions are not up for debate. For example, when an authoritarian leader announces a decision at the beginning of a meeting, before any discussion can occur, it's likely that followers will align their perspectives with the leader's position or else remain silent, which can be mistakenly interpreted as agreement. This lack of diverse input deprives the group of valuable perspectives and undermines critical evaluation.

In the first case, consensus is the absence of leadership, and a unanimous decision may signal a lack of vision or critical consideration. And in the second case, one person with too firm a belief makes for a majority if others feel unable to contend with the idea. Neither case benefits from the advantages of diverse and collaborative teamwork. It's up to leaders to find the balance between encouraging team cohesion and individual expression to avoid the limitations of groupthink.

Attribution Asymmetry

Attribution asymmetry bias influences how we perceive our own successes and failures compared to those of others. When reflecting on our achievements, we tend to attribute them to internal factors like personal talent, unique abilities, motivation, or ambition. And when we think about our failures, we tend to attribute them to external factors such as bad luck, circumstances, poor timing, or others letting us down.

When we think about others, we do the opposite. When considering others' successes, we often attribute them to external factors, like good luck, strong social networks, or favourable market conditions, and disregard their abilities and effort. And when others fail, we tend to attribute it to internal factors, like their laziness or incompetence. This attribution asymmetry bias misleads the perceptions of our own, and others' abilities and circumstances.

Leadership is about reversing this pattern. Whenever you succeed, give the credit to your team. Recognising and praising the team's contributions is a powerful motivator. Your success as leaders is intrinsically tied to the success of your team, and their victories will reflect positively on your leadership.

On the other hand, when your team is underperforming or fails in their task, that's when you have to take responsibility as their leader, even when you feel it isn't your fault. As the figurehead of the group, having your team's back is what builds trust and respect. Leaders who acknowledge their team's achievements and shoulder responsibility for setbacks create stronger and more productive teams.

Sunk Cost Fallacy

The sunk cost fallacy is when individuals consider costs that have already been incurred and cannot be recovered when making future decisions. The fundamental principle is that these sunk costs should not influence your future choices.

For example, let's consider a scenario in which you've purchased a movie ticket, and after watching 15 minutes of the film, you realise you absolutely hate it. At this point, you face a choice: endure the movie despite hating it or leave and engage in a more enjoyable activity. The cost of the ticket is a sunk cost – money already spent and irrecoverable. The decision should be simple: opt for the more enjoyable alternative.

However, human behaviour often complicates matters. We tend to avoid feeling that we're wasting resources, even when it's not rational. In the case of the movie ticket, the sunk cost fallacy might lead us to stay, believing we should commit to the course of action since we've paid for it. In reality, this choice means suffering both the price of the ticket and the unpleasant movie experience.

Another aspect of the sunk cost fallacy is the influence of public perception. When decisions are visible to others, as in leaving a movie early, the fear of embarrassment can cloud our judgment. Overcoming this bias requires the strength to make proactive decisions without undue concern for others' opinions.

Let's consider it in a business context. Imagine your company invests $20,000 in custom software, only to discover it doesn't meet your needs after a week. Your choices are to invest an additional $10,000 to adapt the software or switch to a $5,000 standard option that meets your requirements. The rational decision is clear: opt for the cost-effective standard option. However, business managers often avoid acknowledging a total loss, choosing instead to spend more to salvage the initial investment. This tendency can lead to cost overruns, highlighting the importance of making pragmatic decisions and cutting losses when necessary.

GOAL SETTING

Effective goal setting for yourself and others is a fundamental part of positive leadership. Setting clear and meaningful goals is essential for individuals and teams to motivate performance and align individual tasks with overall objectives.

Goals are specific, personal objectives you aim to achieve. These objectives should be clearly articulated and linked to your personal vision. Start by brainstorming what you aspire to accomplish across various aspects of life, such as your career or relationships. Identify your lifetime goals, which represent your aspirations over the next decade or more. And then, break these down into smaller, measurable goals.

The key to effective goal setting is to use the SMART mnemonic: effective goals are specific, measurable, achievable, relevant, and time-bound. Specificity ensures clarity, measurability enables progress tracking, achievability keeps you motivated, relevance aligns the goal with your vision, and setting timeframes creates a sense of urgency.

Focus on building on your existing skills and talents. Leveraging what you're already good at increases the likelihood of success. Don't hesitate to share your goals with others and seek their support. People often rally to assist those with open ambitions, forging valuable connections along the way.

Creating milestones to monitor your progress is essential, especially for substantial goals. Breaking them down into manageable tasks helps you track your journey and maintain a sense of achievement. But don't overwhelm yourself with too many goals at the same time. Focusing on a maximum of three at a time allows for effective tracking and prevents spreading yourself too thinly. Ensure your goals are realistic and attainable, but a stretch from where you are now, so that you grow to achieve them.

Be cautious about imposing strict personal deadlines. These deadlines should serve as motivation rather than sources of stress. Grant yourself time to develop and adapt as you work towards your objectives. Remember, the journey towards your goals is invaluable in what it can teach you; it's perfectly normal to face challenges along the way; overcoming them is how you progress.

Goal setting is a potent leadership tool that empowers you to define and achieve your objectives. By following the SMART criteria, leveraging your skills, seeking support, and creating milestones you can set yourself on a path to success. Embrace the journey, adapt when necessary, and keep your vision in focus as you work towards your goals. Learning to do this for yourself first will better prepare you for setting goals for your followers to encourage their development.

STRESS

We feel stress when we perceive that the demands placed upon us exceed our capacity to meet them, surpassing our personal and social resources (Ganster & Rosen, 2013). This perception of being overwhelmed triggers what is known as the 'fight or flight' response, a biological instinct deeply ingrained in our evolutionary history. When this response is activated, our bodies undergo significant changes to prepare for action, releasing a surge of hormones and initiating various physiological responses (McCarty, 2016).

While the fight or flight response is great for coping with life-threatening situations, it becomes a problem when it's routinely triggered in our daily lives, often in response to relatively minor stressors. Even seemingly small threats can flood our systems with stress hormones, resulting in heightened excitability, anxiety, irritability, and increased jumpiness. Adrenaline courses through our veins, pushing us into a state of high alert.

This physiological reaction, though evolved for survival, can prove counterproductive in the business environment. Rather than promoting effective decision-making and collaboration, it often hinders these processes. Under the influence of stress, we tend to rely on instinct over rationality, impeding our ability to process information objectively. Consequently, it becomes crucial for leaders to manage stress effectively, as it's rarely conducive to successful leadership in most situations.

To navigate the challenges of leadership, it's vital to recognise stress, its triggers, and its effects. By doing so, leaders can work towards maintaining a state of calm, rationality, and social sensitivity, which are far more helpful in organisational leadership. Therefore, understanding and managing stress is a fundamental aspect of becoming an effective leader.

Pressure vs Performance

Understanding the relationship between pressure and performance is vital for effective leadership. Think of pressure as analogous to job demands, goals, or deadlines. In Figure 10.1, the bottom left quadrant represents a state of inactivity, where no pressure exists. In this scenario, there are no goals, no direction, and consequently, no performance. However, as soon as we set objectives, goals, or tasks to achieve, we add pressure, which creates some motivation and initiates performance.

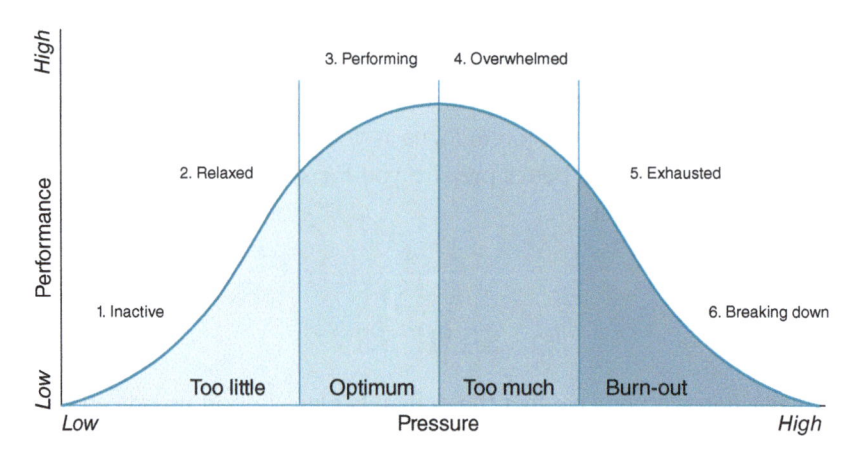

Figure 10.1 Stress - Pressure vs Performance

Adapted from Corbett (2015) and amended to pressure, since stress doesn't improve performance.

Upon entering the workplace, we encounter various projects and deadlines. These job demands create a healthy level of pressure, pushing us towards an optimal stage of performance. At this point, our performance steadily increases as we utilise our available time and resources to meet these demands most productively and efficiently.

However, issues arise when the pressure continues to escalate. As job demands or pressure increase, we reach a tipping point. This transition occurs when we no longer feel we have sufficient resources to handle the growing workload. At this stage, we start to feel overwhelmed and stressed, such that our performance starts to decline.

Many people are constantly in this state, burdened by excessive demands and perpetually behind on commitments. Stress can lead to procrastination, hinder decision-making, and ultimately reduces performance. As pressure continues to mount, people's coping mechanisms start to fail and they court physical and emotional exhaustion. If the pressure continues to increase, they eventually reach a breaking point, where they'll disengage and cease performing altogether.

While some pressure is beneficial, too much can create stress, which is always harmful to performance. After crossing the tipping point, individuals feel threatened, yet lack the capacity and resources to manage the escalating demands effectively. This underscores the importance of stress management in the workplace. It is not only crucial for optimal performance but also essential for individual well-being.

Appreciate the delicate balance between pressure and performance, recognising when job demands are at risk of becoming excessive. Take proactive steps to prevent stress and ensure your teams perform optimally while also taking care of their personal well-being.

Managing Stress

Managing stress – your own stress – is just as important as being mindful of your followers' workload demands and resources. You will be no use to anyone if you cannot manage yourself and learn to successfully navigate the pressures of your role (for a review, see Harms et al., 2017). Let's discuss a few techniques that will help you.

You'll find yourself beset with numerous concurrent demands, and everything might seem urgent and important; it's not. Urgent tasks require your immediate attention; when something is truly urgent, it must be done now, and there are clear consequences if you don't complete these tasks within a certain timeline. Important tasks might not require immediate attention, but they're necessary to achieving your long-term goals.

Prioritise doing what's urgent and important, delegating what's urgent and unimportant, scheduling what's important and not urgent, and avoid wasting your time on anything that's not urgent or important. It's also about knowing when to maximise your productivity, and when to take a step back and recharge; finding this balance is essential, or you'll burn out before achieving your ambitions. Prioritising will require you to get comfortable with saying 'no' – it's not about being uncooperative, but putting your mental health and productivity first.

When you start your day, resist the temptation to dive into low-value tasks like checking emails. Instead, identify the one task that would contribute the most value to your goals, projects, or core organisational objectives, and work on that first. This approach allows you to prioritise high-value tasks over less essential ones like emails or phone calls, which can be dealt with during less productive times of the day. Streamline your workflow and avoid multitasking, which reduces your overall productively (Koch et al., 2018). Focusing on one task at a time ensures you complete it at a higher standard and reduces the stress associated with juggling multiple projects.

Positive thinking significantly impacts how we manage stress (Lightsey, 1994). The lens through which you view your tasks and challenges shapes your experience. Cultivating a mindset that embraces challenges with confidence can dramatically transform your approach to leadership. It's about fostering a belief in your ability to navigate difficulties, which in turn reinforces a cycle of positive outcomes and personal efficacy.

Don't underestimate the power of a social support network (Jolly et al., 2021). Whether it's friends, family members, or colleagues, having people you can confide in offers a release valve for stress. Emotional and moral support plays a vital role in mitigating the pressures that come with leadership. Sharing your challenges not only helps to alleviate stress but also to find solutions you might not have considered.

Regular physical activity is a great way to deal with stress (Lovelace et al., 2007). Even a brief daily walk can markedly reduce stress levels and enhance your overall well-being. Incorporating such physical activity into your routine, particularly outdoors, can also boost your creativity and clear your mind, making you a more effective leader.

Finally, never compromise on sleep. The demands of leadership are high, but sacrificing sleep is counterproductive (Åkerstedt et al., 2002). Aim for at least seven hours of quality sleep each night to ensure you're operating at peak performance. A simple yet effective tip is to avoid screens for at least a half-hour before bedtime to prevent sleep disruption.

Incorporating these strategies into your daily routine as a leader can help to significantly reduce stress. It's not just about enhancing your personal well-being but also about setting a precedent for your team. A leader who manages stress effectively is not only more productive but also more inspiring, creating a positive and resilient work culture.

I'd like you to think back to a leadership situation and then take the following quiz (Quiz 10.1) about stress to see how you handled the experience.

Quiz 10.1

Handling Stress

Image Alt Text: https://ecuau.qualtrics.com/jfe/form/SV_8icBaJYjkL1axim

Adapted from the Kessler et al. (2003) Psychological Distress Scale (K-10).

The higher your score, the more psychological stress you experienced during that leadership interaction. Keeping calm and collected under pressure will serve you well in leadership situations. If you scored in the upper quartile, I encourage you to explore the techniques discussed above to improve your stress management skills, and you'll start to see far better leadership outcomes.

Let's now turn our attention to emotional intelligence and see how it can help us to better understand and influence others.

EMOTIONAL INTELLIGENCE

Emotional intelligence is the ability to manage and express emotions. We can think about leadership as 'emotional labour', where we're constantly working to be aware of, and influence, our own and others' emotions to support individual and collaborative team efforts towards shared goals (Connelly & Gooty, 2015). It serves as the foundation for more effective emotional interactions between leaders and their followers.

Salovey and Mayer (1990) first introduced the concept of emotional intelligence, and then shortly afterwards, Goleman (1995) popularised the idea beyond academic audiences. Mayer and Salovey (1997) later defined emotional intelligence as 'the ability to perceive emotions, to access and generate emotions so as to assist thought, to understand emotions and emotional knowledge, and to reflectively regulate emotions so as to promote emotional and intellectual growth' (p. 5).

In the context of leadership, emotional intelligence affects a host of positive work-related outcomes, such as enhanced managerial skills, increased job satisfaction, and improved performance (Kotsou et al., 2019). Managers, in particular, must adeptly navigate their own emotions and those of their team members to motivate and inspire employees. Similarly, professionals in customer service and healthcare sectors need to effectively manage their inner emotions and outward expressions to provide excellent service to clients or patients while adhering to social and organisational display rules.

Feelings, moods, and emotions play a central role in the leadership process and emotional intelligence contributes significantly to effective organisational leadership (George, 2000). Leaders who underestimate the value of emotional intelligence are likely to encounter major challenges. Those who excel in this aspect can inspire their followers and exceed customer expectations. Effective leaders serve as role models within a group, attentively addressing members' emotions and fostering a positive and supportive environment.

What I've presented here is the 'ability' view of emotional intelligence, which is particularly helpful because you can then work to cultivate and improve your emotional intelligence over time. This perspective includes four emotional intelligence dimensions, or rather, abilities: perceiving emotions, using your emotions, understanding emotions, and managing emotions. These abilities form the basis of emotional intelligence and are essential for effective leadership. Let's take a closer look at them one at a time.

Perceiving Emotions

Perceiving emotions is arguably the most important dimension and involves your capacity to recognise and interpret emotions not only in yourself but also in others, which can be gleaned from their expressions, appearances, voices, and communications. In essence, it's about being able to see and understand the emotional states present in various forms of interaction.

This skill becomes progressively more challenging as we move to modes of communication with lower contextual cues. In a face-to-face conversation it's easier to identify emotions based on body language and facial expressions. However, in an online video call, these cues become less evident. Further still, in a voice call, where only auditory clues are available, the task becomes more demanding. In written forms of communication like emails and text messages, perceiving emotions becomes even more complex due to the absence of visual and auditory context. It's why misunderstandings and conflicts often arise in text-based exchanges as the nuances of emotion can be easily misinterpreted.

The ability to perceive emotions is not limited to understanding others and includes recognising your own emotional state too. This self-awareness is crucial. Are you feeling excited, hungry, bored, or simply eager for a coffee break? Perceiving emotions is the foundation upon which the other aspects of emotional intelligence are built. Identifying both your own emotions and those of others is the first step towards developing your emotional intelligence.

Using Your Emotions

The second dimension of emotional intelligence is using your own emotions. This involves harnessing your emotions to enhance various cognitive activities such as problem-solving, creative thinking, and decision-making. In essence, it's about being in tune with your changing moods throughout the day and your life, and leveraging these emotions to your advantage.

An emotionally intelligent individual possesses the ability to fully utilise their evolving emotional states to suit specific tasks. For example, if you find yourself brimming with frustration and anger, these emotions can be redirected constructively, perhaps through physical exercise like going to the gym or taking a brisk jog. On the other hand, when you're grappling with profound sadness and heartache, these emotions can be channelled into creative pursuits like poetry or painting, allowing you to create meaningful artistic expressions.

Effectively using your emotions means extracting the maximum benefit from them for a particular undertaking. When inspiration strikes, you might find yourself producing some of your best work for a class assignment, demonstrating how emotions can be harnessed to enhance your creative output.

Understanding Emotions

The third dimension of emotional intelligence is understanding emotions. This goes beyond simply recognising emotions and involves delving deeper into their significance. It's about appreciating the meaning behind emotions, their origins, how they evolve, the interconnections among various emotions, and how people express their emotions.

This understanding includes the ability to discern subtle distinctions between emotions that might appear similar at first glance. For example, can you differentiate between someone feeling jealous and someone feeling resentful? Jealousy stems from envy, while resentment stems from hate; these distinct roots give you subtle clues as to how best to respond to the surface emotions.

By exploring tools like an emotions wheel, you can identify core emotions and their various manifestations. Recognising these differences enables you to respond more effectively to emotional situations. Treating jealousy as if it were resentment, for example, would be less effective in addressing the underlying issues.

Emotions are dynamic and constantly change over time. Someone who holds a positive view of you today might exhibit a more reserved demeanour tomorrow. Recognising these subtle shifts and inquiring about the reasons behind them can provide valuable insights into changing emotional states and the factors influencing them, whether it be external events or interpersonal interactions.

Managing Emotions

The fourth dimension of emotional intelligence is managing emotions, and it's the pinnacle of your emotional intelligence abilities. It's about being able to regulate your own emotions and to influence the emotions of others.

Managing your own emotions entails the ability to shift from one emotional state to another, especially when it would be more effective in a particular situation. For example, if you're feeling sad and bored, can you snap out of it and transition to a state of happiness and inspiration? It's about having control over your emotional responses and being able to generate the emotions that are most suitable for a given moment.

This self-regulation extends beyond your own emotions. It also involves understanding how to influence the emotions of others. In conversations, can you choose the right words, tone, and body language to evoke a specific emotion in someone? This skill is crucial for leaders who aim to make others receptive to their influence, foster positive relationships, and create a sense of warmth and security.

In everyday life, we often use this skill without consciously recognising it. Consider situations like competitive sports, where athletes engage in tactics to incite emotions in their opponents. For example, some athletes might use verbal taunts or perform rituals to intimidate their rivals and weaken their performance. In online gaming, players may employ trash-talking to disrupt the focus and emotional equilibrium of their opponents, gaining a competitive edge.

To become proficient in managing emotions, recognise when you're using these techniques, understand their outcomes, and keep a mental record of your successful strategies. The more often you intentionally apply and refine these skills, the better you'll get at using them to your advantage in leadership and interpersonal contexts.

Let's take a short quiz (Quiz 10.2) on emotional intelligence. I want you to try and be as accurate as possible in your responses to how you actually behave, not how you would like to behave. The assessment will give you a score of how emotionally intelligent you are.

Quiz: 10.2

Emotional Intelligence

Image Alt Text: https://ecuau.qualtrics.com/jfe/form/SV_5pch0SXoHbHgDBQ

Adapted from Schutte et al. (1998).

The higher your score, the more emotionally intelligent you are as a leader. But remember that this is a self-report, and we tend to exaggerate our own merits. It's called social desirability bias and it happens whenever we're responding to surveys or interviews; we tend to provide answers we believe will be viewed more favourably by others, rather than giving honest or accurate responses (Reynolds, 1982). Usually that means over-reporting of positive behaviours and under-reporting of negative or socially undesirable behaviours. Whether we're aware of it or not, we're motivated to conform to social norms and expectations, avoid judgment or criticism, and present ourselves in a positive light. I encourage you to be as objective as possible when considering your own abilities, and from that clear perspective you'll be better placed to further develop your skills.

Let's now consider the field of positive psychology to see how it can help us become more effective leaders.

POSITIVE PSYCHOLOGY

Seligman first articulated the concept of positive psychology as the central theme of his presidency at the American Psychological Association in 1998. A special issue in the *American Psychologist* soon followed (Seligman & Csikszentmihalyi, 2000), and the idea then spread rapidly into a major field of research (Seligman et al., 2005). Unlike the well-established field of psychology that we've explored thus far, positive psychology is therefore a relatively recent movement.

This new perspective in psychology focuses on studying the brighter side of our human experience, the elements that infuse life with meaning and joy. Instead of focusing on reducing problems like mental illness, maladaptive behaviour, and negative thinking, positive psychology emphasises improving happiness, well-being, and cultivating a more fulfilling existence. It's about shifting the perspective from trying to fix what's wrong to amplifying what's right, and it's had a profound effect on our approach to leadership.

Positive psychology has since permeated various fields, including organisational behaviour and leadership studies, prompting scholars to reevaluate what effective leadership looks like in the modern workplace (Mills et al., 2013). Over the past two decades, it's reshaped how we think about leadership. In practice, it has translated into an approach where leaders recognise and cultivate the unique strengths of their team members by assigning tasks and responsibilities based on individuals' inherent talents.

Today, forward-thinking organisations look to harness the strengths of their workforce, recognising that each individual has unique abilities that can be maximised for the benefit of both the employee and the organisation. Rather than dwelling on mistakes and offsetting weaknesses, the focus has shifted towards accentuating strengths and recognising achievements. The approach I've taken throughout the present text you'll note is anchored in positive psychology, so that you're ready to embrace this new way of leading.

The result? A happier, more fulfilled, and higher-performing workforce. Positive psychology isn't just a philosophical concept; it's a source of competitive advantage. Organisations that embrace the principles of positive psychology are not only enhancing employee well-being but also bolstering their own reputation. This new way of thinking has ushered in a new era of positive leadership that prioritises building people up, focusing on strengths, and maximising the well-being of everybody in the workplace.

The Happy Secret

I'd now like to share with you a short video by Shawn Achor in which he explains how positive psychology can make us both happier and more successful. He talks like he's ordering a pizza and his phone is on 1% battery – it's as entertaining as it is insightful. Let's see what you think.

Video 10.1

Shawn Achor – The Happy Secret to Better Work

Summary
Shawn challenges conventional perspectives that happiness follows success, arguing that happiness significantly enhances brain function and, by extension, increases productivity, creativity, and success rates. By adopting practices

Image Alt Text: https://www.ted.com/talks/shawn_achor_the_happy_secret_to_better_work

(Continued)

that foster positivity first, such as gratitude exercises, journalling, and acts of kindness, you can rewire you brain to prioritise positivity, which then improves your well-being and work-related performance.

I want you to try the exercise that Shawn recommends at the end of his talk. Write down three things that you're grateful for and one positive experience you've had in the last 24 hours (Exercise 10.1).

Exercise 10.1

Rewire Your Mind

Image Alt Text: https://ecuau.qualtrics.com/jfe/form/SV_9LxigDabr0dGo98

Shawn suggests that if you repeat this exercise every day for 21 days, you'd change how you see the world because your brain would naturally start looking for all of these positive things in life. His 21-day estimate is probably on the optimistic side, but it's within the reported timeframes for how long it takes us to form new habits: 18 to 254 days, depending on complexity (for a review, see Fiorella, 2020). Regardless, I'd encourage you to give it a go, as the effects are well worth the effort.

For now, let's explore the power of storytelling – it will be the last addition to your leadership toolkit in this chapter.

Power of Storytelling

Storytelling can be a potent leadership tool to connect and inspire followers (Auvinen et al., 2013). Crafting narratives that resonate deeply with your team fosters a sense of unity and purpose among followers (Boal & Schultz, 2007). Storytelling is more than just disseminating information; it's about embedding your audience in a shared experience that inspires them towards a specific vision. Through stories, leaders illustrate complex ideas, making them more accessible and compelling (Colville et al., 2012). A well-crafted narrative can bridge gaps between diverse perspectives and unify people around a common cause.

Storytelling in leadership serves as a catalyst for change, encouraging followers to envision possibilities beyond the status quo. Use narratives to exemplify values and ideals, embedding these principles in the collective consciousness of your followers. Draw from personal experiences to lend authenticity and depth to the message. This approach not only conveys information but also stirs emotions, compelling followers to act in alignment with the leader's vision. The emotional resonance of a well-told story can ignite passion and drive in ways that facts and figures alone cannot achieve.

The strategic use of storytelling also allows leaders to present themselves as relatable and human, breaking down the barriers that might otherwise inhibit connection. By sharing your own journeys, including struggles and triumphs, you can foster a sense of empathy and understanding. This vulnerability can strengthen bonds within a team, creating a foundation of trust and mutual respect. Followers, seeing their leader's path, are more likely to embrace their own journey ahead, motivated by the real examples set before them.

Effective leaders recognise the power of narrative to shape culture within an organisation. Stories that highlight collective achievements, exemplify core values, or recount the overcoming of obstacles reinforce a shared identity. This narrative-driven culture cultivates an environment where individuals feel part of something greater, fostering loyalty and a deep commitment to the group's objectives. Storytelling is therefore also a way to perpetuate a legacy, with each narrative layer contributing to the organisation's enduring ethos.

Effective storytelling enables you to inspire, unite, and drive change. You can convey complex ideas, evoke emotional responses, and build stronger connections by crafting strategic narratives. This approach not only enhances your influence as leaders, but also enriches the collective experience by embedding a shared vision that can propel the group forward.

To finish the chapter, I'd like to share with you another video, this one by Guido Palazzo, in which he discusses the power of stories in shaping our behaviour.

Video 10.2

Guido Palazzo – The Soft Power of Story Telling

Summary

Guido explains that stories shape, reinforce, and alter the habits that underpin our decisions. He illustrates the disparity between our intentions and actions, emphasising that this gap does not stem from a lack of information. He suggests that to enact significant change in behaviour, we must target the underlying values and beliefs through compelling stories that are positively framed, include ourselves as direct participants, and illustrate immediate effects on our lives. Such stories have the capacity to resonate with individuals' values, inspiring profound and lasting changes in behaviour.

Image Alt Text: https://www.youtube.com/watch?v=-j7c9b9A2AHc

I hope you're starting to see how powerful stories can be in driving behaviour by reshaping our values and beliefs. Think carefully about your own leadership story, collect those of others, and practise sharing these narratives with your followers – when it's appropriate – to weave a richer tapestry of unifying experiences.

SUMMARY

Critical thinking is about exploring diverse perspectives, considering arguments that challenge your own preconceptions, views, and beliefs, and recognising the limitations of your processes and conclusions. Critical thinking is what enables you to develop compelling ideas that will resonate with followers, and it involves five stages, starting with identifying, then analysing, reflecting, evaluating, and reasoning.

Decision-making is a fundamental part of effective leadership. The DECIDE mnemonic stands for a six-step decision-making process: define the problem, establish the criteria, consider the alternatives, identify the best option, develop and implement an action plan, and evaluate the solution. The point of this model is to make each step explicit and complete, and to slow down the overall pace of your decision-making, so that you take the time to think decisions through the first time round, rather than rushing into a mistake.

The limits of our cognitive ability constrain our decision-making; we simply cannot collect and analyse all the information that's available to us in perfectly rational ways, so that's why we've evolved to rely on mental shortcuts. Cognitive biases are systematic errors in our decision-making process, including, for example, confirmation bias, groupthink, attribution asymmetry, and the sunk cost fallacy, among many others.

We feel stress when we perceive that the demands placed upon us exceed our capacity to meet them, surpassing our personal and social resources. To navigate the challenges of leadership, recognise stress, its triggers, its effects, and work towards a state of calm, rationality, and social sensitivity.

Emotional intelligence is the ability to perceive, manage and express emotions. Leaders are constantly working to be aware of, and influence, our own emotions and the emotions of others to support individual and collaborative team efforts towards shared goals. Emotional intelligence includes four dimensions, or rather, abilities: perceiving emotions, using your emotions, understanding emotions, and managing emotions.

Positive psychology is about improving happiness, well-being, and cultivating a more fulfilling existence. Forward-thinking leaders harness the strengths of their workforce, recognising that each individual has unique abilities that can be maximised for the benefit of both the employee and the organisation. Rather than dwelling on mistakes and offsetting weaknesses, the focus has shifted towards accentuating strengths and recognising achievements.

'All the magic I have known I've had to make myself.'

Extract from *Where the Sidewalk Ends* by Shel Silverstein (1974).

REFERENCES

Åkerstedt, T., Knutsson, A., Westerholm, P., Theorell, T., Alfredsson, L., & Kecklund, G. (2002). Sleep disturbances, work stress and work hours: A cross-sectional study. *Journal of Psychosomatic Research*, *53*(3), 741–748. https://doi.org/10.1016/S0022-3999(02)00333-1

Auvinen, T., Aaltio, I., & Blomqvist, K. (2013). Constructing leadership by storytelling – the meaning of trust and narratives. *Leadership & Organization Development Journal*, *34*(6), 496–514. https://doi.org/10.1108/LODJ-10-2011-0102

Boal, K. B., & Schultz, P. L. (2007). Storytelling, time, and evolution: The role of strategic leadership in complex adaptive systems. *The Leadership Quarterly*, *18*(4), 411–428. https://doi.org/10.1016/j.leaqua.2007.04.008

Colville, I., Brown, A. D., & Pye, A. (2012). Simplexity: Sensemaking, organizing and storytelling for our time. *Human Relations*, *65*(1), 5–15. https://doi.org/10.1177/0018726711425617

Connelly, S., & Gooty, J. (2015). Leading with emotion: An overview of the special issue on leadership and emotions. *The Leadership Quarterly*, *26*(4), 485–488. https://doi.org/10.1016/j.leaqua.2015.07.002

Corbett, M. (2015). From law to folklore: Work stress and the Yerkes-Dodson Law. *Journal of Managerial Psychology*, *30*(6), 741–752. https://doi.org/10.1108/JMP-03-2013-0085

Festinger, L. (1957). *A theory of cognitive dissonance*. Stanford University Press.

Fiorella, L. (2020). The science of habit and its implications for student learning and well-being. *Educational Psychology Review*, *32*, 603–625. https://doi.org/10.1007/s10648-020-09525-1

Ganster, D. C., & Rosen, C. C. (2013). Work stress and employee health: A multidisciplinary review. *Journal of Management*, *39*(5), 1085–1122. https://doi.org/10.1177/0149206313475815

George, J. M. (2000). Emotions and leadership: The role of emotional intelligence. *Human Relations*, *53*(8), 1027–1055. https://doi.org/10.1177/0018726700538001

Goleman, D. (1995). *Emotional intelligence*. Bantom.

Harms, P. D., Credé, M., Tynan, M., Leon, M., & Jeung, W. (2017). Leadership and stress: A meta-analytic review. *The Leadership Quarterly*, *28*(1), 178–194. https://doi.org/10.1016/j.leaqua.2016.10.006

Jolly, P. M., Kong, D. T., & Kim, K. Y. (2021). Social support at work: An integrative review. *Journal of Organizational Behavior*, *42*(2), 229–251. https://doi.org/10.1002/job.2485

Kessler, R. C., Barker, P. R., Colpe, L. J., Epstein, J. F., Gfroerer, J. C., Hiripi, E., Howes, M. J., Normand, S.-L. T., Manderscheid, R. W., & Walters, E. E. (2003). Screening for serious mental illness in the general population. *Archives of General Psychiatry*, *60*(2), 184–189. https://doi.org/10.1001/archpsyc.60.2.184

Koch, I., Poljac, E., Müller, H., & Kiesel, A. (2018). Cognitive structure, flexibility, and plasticity in human multitasking – An integrative review of dual-task and task-switching research. *Psychological Bulletin*, *144*(6), 557–583. https://doi.org/10.1037/bul0000144

Kotsou, I., Mikolajczak, M., Heeren, A., Grégoire, J., & Leys, C. (2019). Improving emotional intelligence: A systematic review of existing work and future challenges. *Emotion Review*, *11*(2), 151–165. https://doi.org/10.1177/1754073917735902

Lightsey, O. R. (1994). 'Thinking positive' as a stress buffer: The role of positive automatic cognitions in depression and happiness. *Journal of Counseling Psychology*, *41*(3), 325–334. https://doi.org/10.1037/0022-0167.41.3.325

Lovelace, K. J., Manz, C. C., & Alves, J. C. (2007). Work stress and leadership development: The role of self-leadership, shared leadership, physical fitness and flow in managing demands and increasing job control. *Human Resource Management Review*, *17*(4), 374–387. https://doi.org/10.1016/j.hrmr.2007.08.001

Mayer, J. D., & Salovey, P. (1997). What is emotional intelligence? In P. Salovey & D. J. Sluyter (Eds), *Emotional development and emotional intelligence: Implications for educators* (pp. 3–31). Basic Books.

McCarty, R. (2016). The fight-or-flight response: A cornerstone of stress research. In G. Fink (Ed.), *Stress: Concepts, cognition, emotion, and behavior* (pp. 33–37). Elsevier. https://doi.org/10.1016/B978-0-12-800951-2.00004-2

Mills, M. J., Fleck, C. R., & Kozikowski, A. (2013). Positive psychology at work: A conceptual review, state-of-practice assessment, and a look ahead. *The Journal of Positive Psychology*, *8*(2), 153–164. https://doi.org/10.1080/17439760.2013.776622

Reynolds, W. M. (1982). Development of reliable and valid short forms of the Marlowe-Crowne social desirability scale. *Journal of Clinical Psychology*, *38*(1), 119–125.

Salovey, P., & Mayer, J. D. (1990). Emotional intelligence. *Imagination, Cognition and Personality*, *9*(3), 185–211. https://doi.org/10.2190/DUGG-P24E-52WK-6CDG

Schutte, N. S., Malouff, J. M., Hall, L. E., Haggerty, D. J., Cooper, J. T., Golden, C. J., & Dornheim, L. (1998). Development and validation of a measure of emotional intelligence. *Personality and Individual Differences*, *25*(2), 167–177. https://doi.org/10.1016/S0191-8869(98)00001-4

Seligman, M. E. P., & Csikszentmihalyi, M. (2000). Positive psychology: An introduction. *American Psychologist*, *55*(1), 5–14. https://doi.org/10.1037//0003-066X.55.1.5

Seligman, M. E. P., Steen, T. A., Park, N., & Peterson, C. (2005). Positive psychology progress: Empirical validation of interventions. *American Psychologist*, *60*(5), 410–421. https://doi.org/10.1037/0003-066X.60.5.410

Simon, H. A. (1957). *Models of man: Social and rational. Mathematical essays on rational human behavior in a social setting*. Wiley.

Tversky, A., & Kahneman, D. (1974). Judgment under uncertainty: Heuristics and biases. *Science*, *185*(4157), 1124–1131. https://doi.org/10.1126/science.185.4157.1124

11
LEADING TEAMS AND MANAGING CONFLICT

Overview

This chapter examines the role of leadership in teamwork, starting with a discussion of the various types of teams and the unique leadership challenges and opportunities offered by each structure.

Next, we move on to explain the stages of team development, with a focus on how the leader's role changes throughout the process, and the different leadership styles that are most appropriate at each stage. You'll reflect on past experiences in teams to consider what enables some groups to overcome conflict during the storming stage, and not others.

Conflict is an inevitable and sometimes desirable part of teamwork. The chapter next explores the nature of constructive and destructive conflict, before moving on to consider five main conflict management strategies: competing, avoiding, accommodating, compromising, and collaborating.

You'll discover your own natural conflict resolution tendencies through a reflective exercise, and the chapter concludes with a discussion about when each of these five approaches is most useful.

Exercise 11.1: Team development

Quiz 11.1: Your conflict modes

Video 11.1: Ralph Kilmann – Leadership and conflict within organisations

The global economy is shifting from traditional industries to knowledge-based economies, which requires us to re-evaluate of how we organise people and work. Teamwork is essential to this new way of working because it fosters collaboration, cross-pollinating ideas, problem-solving, and challenging each other's thinking. Teamwork isn't just about combining individual tasks; it's about creating new synergies and transcends any one person.

Teamwork is integral to modern organisations and exists at all levels from the shop floor to the executive suite. As leaders, you'll invariably be part of a team, and team structures are pervasive throughout all aspects of contemporary organisations (Morgeson et al., 2010). Understanding how to lead them effectively is crucial for achieving shared goals.

GROUPS VS TEAMS

First, let's explore the differences between groups and teams. A group is any number of individuals working together, while a team represents a cohesive unit with a shared purpose. The differences include distinct approaches to leadership, accountability, objectives, performance, and work processes (Fisher & Hunter, 1997).

A designated leader typically holds a strong position of authority in a group and serves to conduct the work of other members, whereas in a team, leadership roles are distributed among members, adapting to the context, expertise, and task at hand (Hoch et al., 2010).

Group members are individually responsible for their own contributions, whereas team members are collectively accountable for their overall objectives. Success and failure are shared among all team members, which fosters a sense of unity and mutual responsibility.

Group objectives typically mirror those of the broader organisation, working towards the same overarching goals, whereas teams can have a specific vision or purpose that may be separate from the organisation's core functions. This unique focus defines the team's existence and sets out what it aims to accomplish.

External parties such as managers or HR professionals typically establish performance goals for groups, imposing specific benchmarks and expectations. Teams, however, have the autonomy to set their own performance targets. While they may receive organisational objectives and guidance, the team decides how to achieve these goals and to what standard.

Groups function solely within the boundaries of the organisation, operating as a subset of the company, whereas teams can transcend organisational borders. They form to address specific issues and the team's distinct vision and purpose may require input from external stakeholders, experts, or professionals.

Group members typically work individually and rely on organised meetings, assigned tasks, and report back on their progress, whereas teams engage in collaborative processes characterised by mutual feedback, problem-solving, constructive challenge, support, and coaching. The interaction among team members is much closer, emphasising their interdependence and the shared pursuit of their common purpose.

TYPES OF TEAMS

There are many different ways that we can organise people into teams (cf. Guzzo & Dickson, 1996), which gives organisations the scope to tailor their approach to specific situations, challenges, or opportunities.

In the following sections, we'll explore four of the most common team structures, which together make up a majority of the teams you will find in organisational settings, including: functional, cross-functional, self-managed, and global or virtual teams. You need to appreciate the nuances of each of these types of teams, and understand your role as leaders in supporting such organisational structures to succeed.

Functional

A functional team structure is the most common and usually features a line manager who oversees several team members who are all experts in a specific domain. Functional teams are often permanent structures within organisations – for example, a group of accountants under the guidance of a senior accounting manager. This alignment streamlines task allocation and enhances the flow of knowledge and support within the team, so it's particularly useful in work contexts that require deep specialisation.

Such teams often share a workspace, fostering an environment ripe for collaboration and immediate communication. The proximity plays a crucial role in building a cohesive unit capable of tackling complex challenges collectively. Despite the inherent advantages, this structure brings a unique set of challenges. The stability, while fostering a strong team identity, can also create a silo effect, isolating the team from the rest of the organisation. This isolation can lead to a narrowed perspective, limiting the team's ability to engage and cooperate with other functional groups within the company.

The heart of a functional team's success lies in a shared vision and a collective commitment to the organisation's objectives. Each member must not only understand their role but also possess the skills required to execute their responsibilities effectively. Skill gaps within the team can disrupt productivity, pushing others to fill these gaps, often at the expense of their own work. As a leader, identify and address these gaps to maintain efficiency and encourage continuous skill development within the team.

Leadership within a functional team involves fostering a culture of mutual learning and knowledge sharing. A leader must champion the idea that success is not solely about individual accomplishments but also about how each member contributes to the team's collective goals. Leaders also serve as the conduit between the team and the rest of the organisation. Functional teams, by nature, rely on other departments to accomplish broader organisational objectives. Therefore cultivating strong relationships and open lines of communication with other teams is essential for seamless collaboration.

To navigate the complexities of leading a functional team, you must appreciate both the inherent strengths and limitations of this structure. The challenge lies in leveraging the team's specialised skills while ensuring that these do not become barriers to broader organisational integration. Effective leadership here means balancing the internal cohesion of the team with its external connections, ensuring that the team not only excels in its domain but also contributes effectively to the overarching goals of the organisation.

Cross-functional

Cross-functional team structures mark a departure from traditional, departmentalised approaches to organisational teamwork. In such setups, individuals from various departments, or even external experts, come together to work towards common goals. This structure is becoming increasingly prevalent and reflects a strategic shift towards enhanced coordination and a holistic customer experience, offering team members a richer, more integrated view of their contributions beyond isolated tasks.

The composition of cross-functional teams varies, ranging from permanent entities like senior management teams, where leaders from different departments collaborate, to temporary, project-specific groups assembled to leverage diverse expertise for organisational initiatives – for example, a c-suite of executives that routinely meet to chart the strategic direction, or a product development team that works from concept to market launch. This flexibility allows companies to adapt and respond to complex challenges and opportunities with agility and innovation.

One defining characteristic of cross-functional teams is the broad range of expertise they encompass. Unlike functional teams, where everyone performs similar tasks, cross-functional team members typically have distinct areas of expertise and strengths. They often represent the best in their respective fields, as they need to cover different aspects of a project or task. This diversity in expertise is both a strength and a challenge. With greater diversity comes a smaller margin for individual error. In functional teams, if one person makes a mistake, others can step in to pick up the slack or fix the issues. However, in cross-functional teams, each member's expertise is unique, and there might not be a safety net to catch mistakes.

Leading a cross-functional team can be more complex because you'll likely lack in-depth knowledge of each team member's field. Instead of a directive and controlling role, your primary focus is facilitation and consultation. Leading as a facilitator and consultant is less hands-on with specific tasks themselves but more about optimising the team's relationships and productivity.

Success in leading cross-functional teams is about creating a collaborative environment where the diverse skills and knowledge of each member are leveraged towards a common goal. This involves not only recognising and valuing the unique contributions of each team member but also ensuring that these contributions are effectively integrated into the team's output. It's about steering the team towards shared objectives, facilitating communication and understanding across different areas of expertise, and resolving conflicts that may arise from diverse perspectives.

Self-managed

Self-managed teams can be either functional or cross-functional, and they work without a direct supervisor. In these teams, decision-making power resides within the team itself. The team has the autonomy to determine how they will carry out their work. Typically, the organisation outlines the mission, scope, and budget, and in some cases, even selects team members; the rest is up to the team to decide. For example, when you need to assess a complex issue like the disruption posed by COVID-19 for your organisation, you might form a self-managed team to investigate it.

The team has the authority to choose its members, giving them the opportunity to assemble a team that possesses the necessary expertise and skills for the task at hand. While the organisation provides the mission and scope, the team operates independently in terms of how they approach the problem. They are not dictated on what to do or how to do it. The organisation may provide a timeframe, budget, and resources to support the team's efforts, such as internal funding, staffing, and office space.

In this format, the team takes on responsibilities that include setting performance goals, defining quality standards, and allocating work among its members. The team is in control of how they solve the problem and what they aim to achieve at each stage of their work. This approach fosters strong commitment among team members because they have a considerable degree of autonomy over their tasks.

Self-managed teams are most effective when composed of experienced and competent employees. Inexperienced or junior employees may struggle to handle such autonomy and responsibility. Self-managed team assignments are best suited to people with the necessary industry and interpersonal skills. For experienced employees, this structure can be highly beneficial, allowing them to leverage their knowledge to the fullest. It's an excellent way to extract the most value from your workforce, especially when they are already experts in their field. Rather than dictating how they should work, this approach empowers them to take the lead and contribute their expertise effectively.

Leaders should act as mentors, offering guidance and support rather than directives. This involves being accessible for consultation, facilitating the acquisition of resources, and helping to remove obstacles that may impede the team's progress. Encouraging open communication and fostering an environment where feedback is freely exchanged are critical. Not everybody thrives when there is a high degree of autonomy and you should be ready to provide additional support for those who may struggle.

Global or Virtual

Many organisations today span multiple geographic locations, encompassing employees from different regions, whether within the same country or internationally. To address the challenges of geographical dispersion, we employ global or virtual teams where team members collaborate without sharing a physical workspace. These dispersed teams may face varying time zones, languages, legal systems, cultures, and customs.

Global or virtual teams stay connected through digital, virtual, and online platforms to overcome the challenges associated with physical distance. Online tools like Microsoft Forms, Google Docs, WhatsApp, and Microsoft Teams facilitate seamless communication, document sharing, and collaborative work, enabling team members to work together efficiently.

Leading a global or virtual team presents unique leadership challenges. It can be more complex than leading a team where face-to-face interactions are the norm. One significant challenge is in building commitment among team members who may never have met in person. When team members receive an email assigning them to a virtual team, they might not feel engaged or connected to a shared purpose beyond themselves. Leaders can build commitment by creating opportunities for collaboration and clarifying how individual members' roles contribute to shared goals.

Another crucial aspect is establishing and maintaining trust among team members who have limited personal interaction. When you haven't met someone face to face, it can be challenging to develop the trust that often naturally occurs through in-person encounters. Leaders should build and sustain trust by fostering open communication, demonstrating reliability, and encouraging transparency within virtual teams.

Communication poses another significant challenge, depending on the preferred mode, as the richness of communication decreases as contextual cues diminish. In face-to-face interactions, you can perceive facial expressions, body language, and tone of voice, which enhance the depth of understanding. However, virtual interactions, whether through video calls, phone calls, emails, or text messages, lack this richness and can lead to miscommunication. Recognise these limitations and, wherever possible, use higher-context modes of communication to mitigate these challenges.

While technology offers solutions, it's important to also consider factors like cost, range, and quality. For small businesses or teams with limited resources, investing in premium communication tools may not always be feasible, but using more accessible platforms can lead to communication issues. Leaders must strike a balance between technology costs and communication effectiveness.

Leading global or virtual teams demands a unique set of leadership skills, including the ability to foster commitment, build trust from a distance, and navigate the nuances of digital communication. Understanding the dynamics of virtual teams is essential for leaders in today's interconnected and geographically dispersed business landscape.

TEAM DEVELOPMENT

When a team first comes together, they embark on a four-stage process: forming, storming, norming, and performing (Tuckman, 1965). You've likely encountered these stages before, and they offer valuable insights into how teams evolve (Bonebright, 2010). As we explore each stage in depth, we'll focus on the role of leadership in guiding teams through these transitions, ultimately enabling them to reach the performing stage efficiently and effectively. Understanding these stages from a leadership perspective equips you with essential tools to facilitate your team's growth and success (for further reading, see Sheard & Kakabadse, 2004, pp. 67–75).

Forming

The first stage of team development is forming, when a group of individuals come together with a sense of uncertainty and a need to establish direction and security. This stage is marked by a lack of clear roles and a vision that may still be hazy. As team members often find themselves in the company of unfamiliar faces, there's a natural self-consciousness, leading to moments of silence and awkwardness.

The role of the team leader during the forming stage involves breaking the ice and fostering introductions among team members. By encouraging individuals to interact and get to know one another, the leader sets the foundation for building trust and collaboration. This process extends beyond work-related expertise and involves understanding each member as a person, their values, and what they consider important.

Addressing questions and concerns is another vital aspect of leadership in this stage. The leader's role here is about clarifying team goals, roles, and expectations. This involves answering fundamental questions such as the purpose of the team, what is expected from each member, the frequency of meetings, and the duration of the team's existence. Effective communication and the establishment of clear norms are essential during this phase.

Leadership in the forming stage often requires a more directive approach. Your role is to actively provide guidance, convey essential information, and help set the norms and boundaries within the team. This involvement and forward presence are essential to guide the team successfully through the initial challenges of forming, paving the way for a more cohesive and productive future.

Storming

Storming is the next stage of team development. After roles have been established, team members begin to feel more at ease in their positions. They actively engage in interactions and work tasks, but this phase is marked by the testing of boundaries. It's a natural human tendency to challenge established norms, and this can lead to conflicts within the team. How these conflicts are addressed will determine the team's ultimate success or failure.

As a team leader during the storming stage, your primary focus should be on processes and relationships. Your role is to guide the team in refocusing on their shared vision and common purpose. Encourage them to work through any relationship challenges that arise and establish clear processes for conflict resolution. If there are legitimate grievances, ensure that they are openly discussed and resolved, aiming for win-win solutions.

In this stage, a more participative leadership style becomes essential. You're no longer dictating tasks or providing constant information. Instead, you're taking a step back and encouraging team members to actively engage, collaborate, and build relationships among themselves. Your leadership becomes more about facilitating the team's interactions and helping them navigate through the conflicts that naturally arise during the storming phase. By fostering open communication and conflict resolution, you can guide the team towards a more cohesive and productive state as they move beyond this challenging stage of development.

Norming

Norming is the next stage of team development. After overcoming initial challenges and reaching a certain stability, team members begin to adhere to the emerging expectations and norms. While some testing and adjustments may still occur, the focus shifts towards goals, performance, and processes. We've laid the groundwork through relationship building, solidified our positions, and gained clarity on our objectives and contributions. It's time to shift our attention towards the actual tasks at hand.

At this point, individual team members' unique strengths and contributions become more evident. Even within a functional team, each member possesses distinct nuances that make them particularly skilled in certain areas. Synergy starts to emerge as we identify who can handle specific tasks most effectively. Perhaps you can take on one responsibility, while I tackle another, and so on.

In the norming stage, the role of the team leader takes on a more consultative and coaching style. You provide feedback to help team members enhance their expertise, especially in areas related to the tasks at hand. Your role is to facilitate role differentiation, recognising who excels in various areas and delegating accordingly. Throughout this process, maintain a clear overall vision and a unifying purpose that reminds the team why they exist and what they aim to achieve.

As a leader, embracing this consultative and coaching approach during the norming stage can empower your team to reach new heights of efficiency and productivity while maintaining a strong sense of unity and purpose.

Performing

The final stage of team development is performing. After successfully navigating through the initial phases, where talent roles are identified, and norms established, your team is now ready for strong performance. In this phase, the primary focus shifts towards continuous improvement. The team is already functioning well, so the question becomes 'How can we do even better?'

It's crucial to understand that you can't reach the performing stage without progressing through the earlier stages. This journey is a sequential process and it's possible to move both forward and backward through these stages. For example, a team that has reached the norming stage may regress into conflict if unresolved issues resurface.

As a team leader in the performing stage, your role takes on a different dimension. You take a step back from the team, giving them some space to excel on their own. Your role becomes about providing support and empowerment. Give your team the autonomy to make decisions, take charge of their tasks, and do the work effectively. Here your role is more about offering ongoing feedback and support as needed. When your team requires assistance, they can approach you for guidance, but your role is no longer about coaching, directing, or mentoring.

During the performing stage, your leadership becomes about trust and empowerment, allowing your team to shine and continue to improve their performance. This stage represents the culmination of effective team development, when your team operates at its peak potential, driven by a shared vision and a commitment to excellence.

Shifting Responsibilities

As you've seen, your leadership role evolves as the team progresses through its life cycle, transitioning from a directive, to a participative, then consultative, and finally an empowering style. The extent of interaction among team members increases as they collaborate more closely, but this also presents opportunities for conflicts to arise. A leader's responsibility is to ensure these conflicts are resolved and the team moves through the stages successfully.

To excel in this role, you must first have a keen understanding of your team's current stage of development. It's essential to recognise that this progression isn't always linear; teams can move both forward and backward through the stages, particularly during the middle phases. Your primary objective is to guide your team to the next stage of development. This involves adapting your leadership style to suit the team's evolving needs (Morgeson et al., 2010).

In the initial forming stage, a directive leadership style is necessary. Leaders establish norms and expectations, providing clear guidance. As the team advances to the storming phase, the focus shifts towards building relationships among team members. While the leader remains central, coaching and facilitating role differentiations become key.

As the team enters the norming stage, the leader's role becomes less central. Instead, they serve as support when needed. Finally, in the performing stage, leaders almost exit the team, becoming peripheral supporting figures. The ultimate goal is for the team to function as a high-performing unit independently, with reduced reliance on the leader (Zaccaro et al., 2001). Effective team leadership is therefore about enabling your team to excel and succeed autonomously; it demands humility and a dedication to the team's success above all else.

I'd like you to now complete our first exercise in this chapter (Exercise 11.1) that will ask you to think back to a teamwork experience. You'll be asked to reflect on your role in the team, and then whether, or how, your team progressed through the various stages of development.

Exercise 11.1

Team Development

Image Alt Text: https://ecuau.qualtrics.com/jfe/form/SV_0Hwoz8ArQQElNfo

---

Getting through the storming stage can be the biggest hurdle for newly established teams, or whenever there's disruption to an existing team. For example, when a new member joins a team that has already been working together for a long time, they will need leadership support to work through the various stages of team development, starting from the beginning again, while the rest of the team is likely to be further along the process. Appreciate that individual team members may have different leadership needs, and you'll need to adapt your approach accordingly to support them and thereby enable the entire team's progress.

TEAM VITAL SIGNS

We can think about teamwork behaviour as illustrating various vital signs that indicate whether the team is constructively progressing through the four stages of development, or if the team is in decline, moving backwards through the stages, and at risk of eventually falling apart altogether. Let's take a closer look at signs of decline first.

Teams in Decline

One clear indicator of a team in decline is when team members avoid sharing negative or uncomfortable information with their leaders. This fear of discussing problems indicates a lack of trust and collaboration. Instead of solving issues together, they paint a false, positive picture for their superiors, allowing problems to fester and grow.

Another alarming sign is when team members engage in heated discussions without factual evidence or logical arguments. Strong opinions without supporting evidence can lead to ideological conflicts, hindering progress. It's essential to encourage evidence-based, constructive conversations to ensure effective problem-solving.

When team members prioritise personal gain over the collective mission, it's a glaring red flag. Such self-interest can undermine the team's shared purpose and harm overall performance. Team members should be aligned with the common goals, not pursuing their individual agendas.

Blame games are also detrimental. When things go wrong, blaming each other rather than addressing issues collectively creates divisiveness. It prevents the team from reaching its potential and resolving conflicts in a healthy manner.

Identifying a team in decline involves recognising signs like a lack of open communication, opinionated heated disputes, a focus on personal rather than collective goals, and blaming each other when things go wrong. By addressing these issues and promoting trust, collaboration, and a shared mission, you can work towards preventing the disintegration of your team.

Teams Progressing

Effective teams demonstrate several key characteristics that indicate their progress and successful development. One crucial aspect is their readiness to confront negative information openly and constructively. Setbacks and challenges are part of any work environment, and an effective team embraces them without fear. When team members promptly bring problems to the group for discussion and input, it signifies a healthy team dynamic focused on problem-solving.

Effective teams also exhibit a commitment to constructive contributions. Members avoid vague or opinion-based statements that lack value. Instead, they engage in discussions with data, logic, and well-reasoned arguments. This approach fosters a collaborative atmosphere where ideas are evaluated based on merit rather than personal attacks or defensive positions.

Effective leadership within the team is another indicator of good progress – for example, when team leaders can constructively challenge the group, and team members respond positively to such challenges. The ability to engage in meaningful discussions without feeling personally attacked reflects a high level of trust and communication within the team.

Acknowledging collective efforts and successes is another great sign. When team members credit each other for success, they reinforce a sense of unity and shared accomplishment. This 'we' mentality fosters a supportive environment, where individual progress is attributed to the collective effort rather than personal achievements.

Unifying behind decisions is a hallmark of an effective team. While not every team member may fully agree with every decision, once a choice is made, it becomes the team's position. Team members uphold and support this decision when interacting with external parties, presenting a united front. Criticising team decisions to outsiders undermines the team's strength and cohesion.

Effective teams are open to negative information, engage in constructive contributions, respond positively to challenges from leaders, credit each other for success, and unify behind their decisions. These characteristics collectively demonstrate a team's developmental progress. As leaders, seek to nurture these qualities within your team to best enable their success.

Every Team is Different

You might well ask why some teams excel while others struggle to perform at the same level. Even if we meticulously replicate team structures, match qualifications and cultural profiles, and even mimic processes across different organisations, the outcomes will still vary. That's because no two tasks, or teams, are truly the same.

Even when seemingly identical on paper, teams differ in subtle and significant ways. Their unique tasks, client interactions, individual strengths, and distinct perceptions all contribute to this diversity. However, one critical factor stands out: the quality of relationships among team members. This is something we cannot replicate or substitute.

Imagine assembling a group of exceptionally intelligent individuals that have no intention of collaborating and don't share a sense of unity, trust, or common purpose. In such an example, their individual potential is squandered. They won't synergise, exchange ideas, or collectively innovate. In contrast, another team that is equally competent but bound by strong bonds of trust and purpose will far outshine them.

Effective teams are not just about brilliant individuals; they are about the synergy that happens when individuals come together with shared commitment and a sense of belonging. It's about fostering an environment where every member feels valued, supported, and empowered to contribute their best. The effectiveness of a team isn't solely determined by its structure or the qualifications of its members, but by the quality of the working relationships and the shared sense of purpose that drives its members to excel together, and that's where we as leaders can offer the most value.

Let's now turn our attention to conflict, and see how we can best navigate its challenges.

TYPES OF CONFLICT

Conflict is a natural part of teamwork. Wall and Callister (1995) define conflict as 'a process in which one party perceives that its interests are being opposed or negatively affected by another party' (p. 517). It's about having differing opinions and being at odds with one another, and it's an integral part of working together effectively. There are different types of conflict (e.g. Jehn, 1995), and we'll consider three for our purposes: task, process, and relationship.

First, we have task conflict. This type of conflict revolves around differences related to your team's goals. It's when people disagree about the team's vision, objectives, or the tasks assigned. Task conflict focuses on where the team is headed and whether everyone is on the same page regarding the destination.

Next, there's process conflict. This type of conflict is about how you reach your destination rather than where you're going. It occurs when team members agree on the team's goals but have differing opinions on the best path to get there. Process conflict is all about the methods and strategies employed to achieve common objectives.

Lastly, we have relationship conflict. This kind of conflict is about the social and interpersonal connections within the team. Even if everyone agrees on the team's overall objectives and the path to reach them, relationship conflicts may still arise due to personality clashes or personal differences. It's about how team members interact and connect with each other beyond the objective aspects of the team's mission.

Each type requires a different approach for resolution and management. As a leader, you'll need to navigate these conflicts to ensure they contribute positively to your team's growth and success. Conflict, when managed constructively, can lead to innovation and improved team dynamics, making it a valuable aspect of leadership to master.

Remember that conflict isn't always bad; it can be constructive as well as destructive. Let's consider how.

Constructive Conflict

Constructive conflict can be a powerful force that drives positive change. When we form teams, we bring together diverse minds, each with its unique perspective and background. Naturally these diverse opinions may not always fit together seamlessly, like a perfect jigsaw puzzle.

Now, conflict arises when these differing opinions clash, and that's where progress can happen. Think of it as a crucible where ideas are forged, tested, and refined. As we work through this diversity of opinion, we can reach a deeper understanding, uncover underlying issues, and approach problem-solving from fresh angles.

Constructive conflict is about disagreement with a purpose – the purpose of growth and improvement. What starts as a clash of ideas can evolve into a far superior solution or a better decision. Through this process, productivity increases, and the team's commitment strengthens.

Embracing constructive conflict can energise and inspire team members. They feel valued when their opinions are heard and respected, even if not everyone agrees. It fosters a culture of open discussion, where multiple viewpoints are encouraged. This environment inspires creativity and motivates people to contribute their best.

Imagine a team where everyone simply nods in agreement without asking questions or challenging ideas. Such complacency stifles innovation. In contrast, constructive conflict encourages people to challenge ideas, propose new approaches, and collectively explore innovative solutions. It's a catalyst for progress, a force that, if harnessed correctly, propels the team towards excellence.

So, if you aim to lead effectively, nurturing constructive conflict within your team is vital. Encourage your team members to voice their opinions, challenge ideas, and engage in meaningful discussions. When handled positively, conflict becomes a powerful tool for growth, creativity, and innovation. It's not about avoiding disagreements but harnessing their potential to drive your team towards greater heights.

Destructive Conflict

Unlike its constructive counterpart, destructive conflict is like a storm that brings turmoil and chaos within a team. It often reveals a lack of common interests among team members. In such situations, individuals may prioritise personal gains over the collective good of the group.

In destructive conflict situations, people tend to fiercely defend their personal opinions or, in some cases, withdraw from the conflict altogether. These conflict resolution methods are usually counterproductive, and drive team members further apart instead of bringing them closer together. Instead of working towards a superior solution by integrating diverse opinions, individuals entrench themselves in their positions, creating a divide.

This division can include forming opposing camps within the group. You'll have those who staunchly support one idea and others who vehemently advocate for another. This polarisation of opinions intensifies the conflict and widens the gap between team members, making it challenging to find common ground.

As destructive conflict takes root, its detrimental effects start to ripple through the team. Productivity drops, commitment wanes, and job satisfaction plummets. No one wants to be part of an organisation or team where such an atmosphere prevails. People seek environments that foster productivity, innovation, and constructive dialogue, where they can contribute without fear of their opinions being dismissed out of hand.

Destructive conflict can take a toll on individuals' well-being. It generates stress and anxiety as interpersonal tensions and disagreements come to the forefront. This constant strife drains people's energy and reduces their engagement. They may find themselves either constantly defending their opinions or disengaging from the conflict altogether, allowing one dominant voice to lead the way. Consequently, creativity suffers, and the team misses out on the synergy that diverse opinions can bring to the table.

Destructive conflict is the antithesis of effective teamwork. It erodes trust, saps energy, and stifles innovation. As a leader, it's crucial to recognise the signs of destructive conflict and take proactive steps to address it. Fostering a culture of open communication, respect, and constructive conflict resolution can help steer your team away from destructive conflict and towards a path of productivity and growth. Remember, as a leader, you have the power to shape the conflict dynamics within your team, for better or for worse (Xin & Pelled, 2003), and steering them towards the constructive end of the spectrum is key to your team's success.

Active vs Passive Conflict

Conflict, whether constructive or destructive, can manifest in both active and passive forms (Winer et al., 2023). Let's explore these variations to gain a deeper understanding.

Constructive Conflict: Active vs Passive

Active constructive conflict involves proactive engagement in resolving disagreements. Perspective taking is a prime example. In this approach, you actively seek to understand others' viewpoints. For example, when faced with a team member's idea you don't fully agree with, you might say: 'I see where you're coming from. Your idea has merits, but here are some concerns I have.' By openly discussing different perspectives, you create room for collaborative solutions.

Expressing emotions can also be a form of active, constructive conflict. Instead of bottling up your feelings, you communicate them honestly. For example, you might say: 'I feel overwhelmed with this project, and I believe my input isn't being considered.' Such openness fosters an environment where emotions are acknowledged, leading to increased productivity as issues are addressed constructively.

Reaching out to others is another active, constructive way to engage in conflict. If you disagree or need assistance, you take the initiative to seek help or initiate a conversation. For example, if you encounter a challenge, you might approach a colleague with a message like: 'I'd like to discuss some concerns I have about our current approach. Can we meet to brainstorm solutions?' Proactively reaching out demonstrates a commitment to collaborative problem-solving.

On the other hand, passive constructive conflict can involve reflective thinking. Rather than immediately expressing disagreement, you take time to contemplate your own perspective and the opposing viewpoint. This reflective approach allows you to assess the merits of both sides and consider potential ways forward.

Delaying your response is another passive, constructive strategy. Instead of reacting impulsively to a conflict situation, you take a moment to cool off and gain clarity. For example, if a colleague presents an idea that leaves you sceptical, you might say: 'I need some time to think about this before I can provide feedback.' This pause allows you to re-evaluate and respond more thoughtfully.

Adapting your approach is also a form of passive constructive conflict. It involves modifying your behaviour or methods to better align with the situation or the team's needs. For example, if you notice that your communication style isn't effectively resolving conflicts within the team, you might adapt by seeking input and feedback from others to improve your approach.

Both active and passive forms of constructive conflict have their place in effective leadership. Active approaches involve direct engagement and communication, while passive approaches emphasise reflection, delayed response, and adaptability. Understanding when to employ each method can help you navigate conflicts and lead your team towards productive resolutions.

Destructive Conflict: Active vs Passive

Active destructive conflict often takes the form of aggression and dominance. One example is the 'all-in-to-win' approach, where people aggressively push their perspective and decisions while disregarding others. They may demean colleagues, belittling their ideas, and displaying anger openly. For example, in a team meeting, someone might say: 'Your proposal is absurd, and you clearly have no idea what you're talking about.' This aggressive behaviour creates a hostile environment and stifles collaboration.

Another active form is retaliating to others' opinions negatively. Instead of engaging in constructive dialogue, individuals respond with aggression or hostility. They might react to differing opinions by attacking them rather than discussing the merits of each viewpoint. This type of behaviour can escalate conflicts and create a toxic atmosphere within the team.

Passive destructive conflict, although less outwardly aggressive, can be equally harmful. One passive response is avoidance, where individuals shy away from confronting issues or people they disagree with. They may avoid discussing critical matters, hoping the problems will disappear on their own. This avoidance can lead to simmering resentment and unresolved issues that fester over time.

Yielding is another passive, destructive behaviour. In this case, people may give in to a decision or course of action without expressing their disagreement. While this may temporarily maintain harmony, it can lead to inner dissatisfaction and frustration. Over time, those who continually yield may feel unfulfilled and disengaged from the team's goals.

Hiding emotions is also a destructive way to handle conflict passively. Instead of openly discussing their feelings, individuals suppress them, which can lead to emotional stress and tension. For example, if you feel overwhelmed or upset but keep these emotions hidden, it can hinder your well-being and prevent you from seeking support or resolution.

Engaging in self-criticism is yet another form of passive, destructive conflict. People may internalise negative thoughts and beliefs about their abilities, leading to self-doubt and reduced self-esteem. For example, if someone repeatedly tells themselves, 'I'm not good enough for this role', it can erode their self-confidence and hinder their performance.

Both active and passive forms of destructive conflict can undermine team cohesion and performance. Active destructive behaviours involve aggression, dominance, and hostility, while passive destructive responses encompass avoidance, yielding, emotion suppression, and self-criticism. Recognising these patterns and addressing them proactively is essential for leaders to create a healthy and productive team environment. Effective leadership involves fostering open communication, constructive conflict resolution, and a culture of mutual respect and support.

CONFLICT RESOLUTION

Thomas and Kilmann (1974) studied how individuals responded to conflict situations. They wanted to understand how different conflict resolution styles affected interpersonal and group dynamics and developed the Thomas-Kilmann Conflict Mode Instrument. It's from their influential work we know people tend to use five different conflict resolution styles, including: competing, avoiding, accommodating, compromising, and collaborating. Let's examine each of these a bit further.

Five Resolution Styles

First, there's the competing style. For example, if you're the team leader, and a disagreement erupts among your team members regarding a critical decision, you assert your perspective forcefully, believing that your way is the only right way. Competitors employ aggressive behaviours and influence techniques to ensure their opinions prevail.

At the opposite end of the spectrum is avoiding. For example, if you're in a team meeting and a heated debate arises over the direction of a project. Rather than jumping into the fray, you choose to remain silent, hoping the conflict will dissipate on its own. Avoiders tend to withdraw, deny, or distance themselves from the conflict, preferring to keep the peace even if it means not addressing the underlying issues.

Next, we have accommodating. Suppose you are part of a cross-functional team and a colleague suggests a different approach that you're not entirely comfortable with. Rather than voicing your concerns, you readily yield and agree to go with their idea. Accommodating is about giving in to others' viewpoints to maintain harmony, even if that means suppressing your own preferences.

We can also seek to compromise, particularly when we're at an impasse. Imagine you're in negotiations with a business partner, and both sides have strong, conflicting demands. To break the deadlock, you agree to make concessions, finding a middle ground that offers partial satisfaction to both parties. Compromisers aim for a balanced solution where both sides give up something to reach an agreement.

Lastly, we can collaborate. For example, imagine that your team is facing a complex problem that requires innovative solutions. Instead of pushing your own ideas or yielding to others, you initiate a collaborative process. You work together with your team members, seeking to understand the root causes of the issue and aiming for a win–win outcome. Collaborators prioritise joint problem-solving over personal agendas, fostering positive outcomes for all parties involved.

While competition, avoidance, and accommodation may have their places in specific situations, they often fall short of delivering optimal conflict resolutions. Compromising strikes a balance, but the gold standard is collaboration. By embracing a collaborative approach, leaders can foster an environment where conflicts are transformed into opportunities for growth and innovative solutions.

Assertive vs Cooperative

Thomas and Kilmann (1974) explain that each of these five conflict resolution styles includes a combination of different levels of assertiveness and cooperation. Let's explore how the styles differ.

Competition is highly assertive but low on cooperation. When using competition, you assertively pursue your own interests, aiming to win at all costs. Cooperation takes a back seat as you prioritise your viewpoint and rights over finding common ground with others.

Avoidance is characterised by low assertiveness and low cooperation. When you avoid conflict, you're usually just ignoring it or postponing the issue. It's a passive approach that shows minimal willingness to engage or cooperate in resolving the conflict.

Accommodation is marked by high cooperation but low assertiveness. Accommodators are inclined to yield to the other party's perspective, even if it means suppressing their own preferences. While they prioritise cooperation, they may lack assertiveness in advocating for their own needs.

Compromise falls somewhere in the middle of competition and accommodation. It combines moderate assertiveness and moderate cooperation. Compromisers are willing to make concessions and find middle ground to reach an agreement. They recognise that it's essential to give up something to resolve the conflict but also expect the other party to do the same.

Collaboration ideally represents a harmonious balance between assertiveness and cooperation. Collaborators actively seek to work together with the other party to delve into the underlying concerns driving the conflict. By eliminating the root causes, they aim for a win–win solution that benefits both parties. Collaboration reflects a high degree of assertiveness and a strong commitment to cooperation.

I'd like you now to work through a short quiz (Quiz 11.1), which asks about your preferred way of handling conflict to determine your score for each of the five styles. The higher your score, the more likely you are to draw on that particular conflict resolution style.

Quiz 11.1

Your Conflict Modes

Image Alt Text: https://ecuau.qualtrics.com/jfe/form/SV_1QZ5US4mCMRpIgq

Adapted from (Rahim, 1983).

As aspiring leaders, understanding these styles and when to employ them can help you navigate conflicts effectively within your teams and organisations. As you've seen from the quiz, some of these approaches will come more naturally to you than others, but you'll need to work on developing a holistic perspective of conflict and draw on each of these styles where appropriate.

WHEN TO USE EACH STYLE

As effective leaders, it's crucial to understand that there's no one-size-fits-all approach to conflict resolution. Instead, you should be adept at using a variety of conflict resolution styles depending on the situation at hand. Each of the five conflict resolution styles – competing, avoiding, accommodating, compromising, and collaborating – has its own strengths and is useful in specific circumstances.

Effective leaders recognise that context matters. They assess the nature and significance of the conflict, the people involved, and the desired outcomes. By employing the appropriate conflict resolution style for each situation, you demonstrate flexibility and adaptability, enhancing your leadership effectiveness.

Let's look at these five conflict resolution styles and consider in which kind of situation each one would be useful for us to draw on as leaders.

Competing

Competing is most effective in specific situations that demand assertiveness, rapid decision-making, and clear direction. Here are some scenarios where the competing style is most appropriate and valuable.

Urgent or critical decisions. Competing is the way to go when you face emergencies or critical situations that require immediate action. Whether it's responding to a crisis, managing a health and safety issue, or handling a public relations disaster, competing ensures that a swift decision is made, reducing potential harm to the organisation.

Unpopular but necessary actions. In situations where you must implement unpopular decisions for the greater good of the organisation, such as cost-cutting measures, downsizing, or enforcing new regulations, the competing style can be effective. It allows you to maintain control and ensure these critical actions are carried out, even if they are met with resistance.

Defending legal or ethical obligations. When compliance with legal requirements or ethical standards is non-negotiable, competing becomes essential. It helps you enforce necessary rules, address discipline issues, and ensure the organisation adheres to its legal and moral responsibilities.

Certainty in decision-making. Competing is suitable when you have concrete evidence and confidence in your decision. In cases where you are certain that your choice is the right one and will significantly benefit the organisation, assertively advocating for your decision through competing is appropriate.

Balancing against persistent competitors. Some individuals habitually use competing to take advantage of passive colleagues. In such situations, employing competing as a leader can level the playing field and ensure that decisions are made based on merits and not solely due to one party's assertiveness.

While competing is a valuable conflict resolution style in these contexts, effective leaders should also recognise when to use other styles, such as collaboration or compromise, to build consensus, foster innovation, and maintain team cohesion. Being adaptable and selecting the most suitable style for each situation demonstrates leadership versatility and enhances overall effectiveness.

Avoiding

You might be surprised how useful avoiding can be as a conflict resolution style for various scenarios. For example, when you're confronted with a conflict over a trivial issue while more significant matters demand your attention, avoiding the minor conflict can be a superior strategy. Remember, you don't have to engage in every skirmish or concern that arises; some can be safely set aside.

If you find no realistic avenue to satisfy your concerns or reach a resolution in a given conflict, it's often wiser to sidestep direct confrontation. Attempting to address such conflicts may only lead to disruption without any foreseeable benefit. Consider whether the disruption caused by the conflict outweighs the potential gains from resolution. If the conflict resolution offers minimal positive outcomes while generating significant drama, maintaining harmony through avoidance may be the better option.

Avoiding conflict can also serve as a valuable tool for allowing individuals involved to cool down and regain perspective. If a confrontation has already occurred, granting people some time to reflect and regain a balanced outlook on the issue can be the right choice. This pause allows both parties to return to the discussion with a more level-headed and rational approach, promoting more constructive dialogue.

Sometimes it's essential to recognise that others might possess superior conflict resolution skills or be better suited to mediate. As leaders, we must acknowledge that we may not always be the best person for the job. If there's someone else more effective at mediating, don't hesitate to delegate the responsibility. While it may seem like avoiding the conflict, it can be an appropriate strategy that leads to more efficient and satisfactory resolution.

Lastly, in situations where the core of the conflict revolves around issues you consider tangential or symptomatic of deeper problems, it's often wiser not to engage in resolving the minor issues. Instead, focus on addressing the underlying and more substantial problems. People might argue about surface-level matters, but the root causes lie elsewhere.

In such cases, avoiding the smaller issues and working towards resolving the deeper problems is a more strategic approach.

Accommodating

One of the best times to accommodate is when you recognise that you are in the wrong. When you discover that your current stance is incorrect, it's a prime opportunity to yield to the other perspective, learn from it, and display your reasonableness as a leader. Demonstrating your willingness to listen and adapt is a hallmark of positive leadership, even when it means not having your way.

If the issue at hand holds significantly more importance for the other party than it does for you, accommodating their viewpoint can be a superior strategy. If you genuinely don't have a strong preference on the matter and you know it carries substantial weight for them, it might be wise to refrain from entering into a conflict altogether. Allowing them to have their way in such cases fosters cooperation and can strengthen working relationships.

Accommodating can also be a strategic move to build social credit for future issues. If you foresee a series of challenges with a team down the line, granting them a few victories in minor conflicts now can position you better to assert your priorities later on. It's a pragmatic approach that acknowledges the value of timing in conflict resolution.

There are times when you might find yourself outmatched in a conflict, even if you still believe you are right. If the opposition has gained a strong foothold and you're losing ground, it may be more sensible to yield in that moment rather than escalating the conflict and potentially facing more significant losses later.

Sometimes the greater good lies in maintaining harmony and stability rather than insisting on being right. In certain situations, accommodating can help preserve a peaceful and cooperative atmosphere, which may be more valuable than proving a point or winning a dispute.

Lastly, as leaders, we can employ the accommodating style to allow our subordinates to make mistakes and learn from them. While we can guide and mentor, there are times when individuals need to experience the consequences of their choices to grow and develop. Allowing them the freedom to pursue their own approaches, even if we foresee potential errors, can lead to valuable learning experiences that contribute to their personal and professional growth.

Compromising

Compromising is particularly effective when the goals in question are important but don't necessarily justify the significant disruption that more assertive conflict resolution modes might entail. In situations where you need to push certain points forward but wish to avoid escalating into a highly confrontational atmosphere, compromising strikes a balance.

Additionally, compromising is helpful when parties with equal power find themselves deeply committed to mutually exclusive goals. For example, if two departments within your organisation are vying for the same set of resources, and their objectives are fundamentally divergent while their size and influence are comparable, compromise often emerges as the most sensible solution. It allows you to attain a middle ground, ensuring that neither party completely dominates the other.

The compromising style can also serve as a means to achieve a temporary settlement or expedite a swift resolution to a complex issue. When you detect a significant conflict brewing, opting for compromise may be a pragmatic choice. It enables you to either temporarily ease the tension and provide a respite from the conflict or swiftly reach a viable solution before the situation escalates beyond control.

You can also compromise as a last resort after considering other conflict resolution strategies like competition or collaboration. If those approaches prove unsuccessful, reverting to compromise can be a strategic move. In such cases, you offer concessions while expecting some in return, aiming to find a middle ground that facilitates progress and cooperation. Mastering when to compromise is essential for maintaining harmony and facilitating progress in complex situations.

Collaborating

Collaboration really shines when both parties' concerns are equally valid, and compromise isn't an option. In such cases, you actively and assertively, yet cooperatively, seek solutions that are truly win–win for all parties involved. It's about finding common ground where everyone benefits, fostering an atmosphere of mutual gain.

Collaborating works exceptionally well when your objective is to learn or develop something mutually beneficial. Instead of settling for a win–lose scenario, it aims to create outcomes where all parties derive value. By combining insights from diverse perspectives, you can arrive at synergistic solutions that harness the collective wisdom of the team.

Collaborating is a potent tool for generating commitment among team members. When individuals have the opportunity to provide input on an issue or participate in decision-making processes related to change initiatives, they begin to feel a sense of ownership and authorship. This shared consensus fosters commitment, as team members appreciate that their voices have been heard and considered.

This style is adept at addressing interpersonal conflicts and emotional tensions in the workplace. When dealing with emotions or personal issues, opting for a collaborative approach is often more effective than competing or engaging in heated confrontations. By working together to understand the root causes of emotional responses and finding collective solutions to alleviate concerns, you can create a more harmonious and productive work environment.

Collaborating is most effective in situations in which both parties are committed to mutual benefit, diverse perspectives can be combined for synergy, creating commitment is most important, and emotional or interpersonal conflicts need to be addressed. Work to encourage collaboration for more positive relationships that enable creativity and promote cohesion.

Next, I want to share with you a video by Ralph Kilmann where he talks about how leaders role model and shape the dominant conflict resolution styles of others throughout the organisation.

Video 11.1

Ralph Kilmann – Leadership and Conflict Within Organisations

Summary

Ralph explains that leaders exert significant influence over the organisational culture through their conflict resolution styles. Their approach to conflict sets the tone for how issues are managed throughout the hierarchy – for example, instilling either a competitive or an avoidant culture. Ralph emphasises that leaders must be conscious of the signals they send through their conflict resolution approach, as these are closely observed and emulated by others within the organisation.

Image Alt Text: https://www.youtube.com/watch?v=qHFTY7_X-kU

Think carefully about what message you want others to get from watching how you handle conflict. Your preferred conflict resolution approach becomes a part of your leadership identity and shows your team: 'This is how it's done around here'.

Note that employees lower in the organisational hierarchy often lean towards avoiding and accommodating conflict. If you aspire for your team to voice their opinions, foster divergent and innovative thinking, and engage in constructive conflict when necessary, then learning to use the different conflict resolution styles can set the stage for such behaviour among your team members. Role modelling positive conflict resolution examples can empower your team to navigate conflicts effectively and best contribute to the organisation's progress.

SUMMARY

There are many different ways that we can organise people into teams, which gives organisations the scope to tailor their approach to specific situations, challenges, or opportunities. The most common team structures in organisational settings include functional, cross-functional, self-managed, and global or virtual teams. The leader's role changes depending on the type of team they're leading.

When a team first comes together, they embark on a four-stage process: forming, storming, norming, and performing. The leader's role evolves as the team progresses through its life cycle, transitioning from a more directive, to a participative, then consultative, and finally an empowering style. Your primary objective is to guide your team to the next stage of development, which means adapting your leadership style to best serve the team's evolving needs.

Effective teams are not just about brilliant individuals; they are about the synergy that happens when individuals come together with shared commitment and a sense of belonging. Therefore, effective team leadership is about fostering an environment where every member feels valued, supported, and empowered to contribute their best.

Conflict is a natural part of teamwork, and is about having differing opinions and being at odds with one another. There are three different types of conflict: task, process, and relationship. Conflict can also be either constructive or destructive, and either active or passive. Constructive conflict can be a powerful force that drives positive change, whereas destructive conflict significantly undermines team members' well-being and performance.

We can resolve conflict with five different conflict resolution styles, including: competing, avoiding, accommodating, compromising, and collaborating. Effective leaders understand that there's no one-size-fits-all approach to conflict resolution. Instead, they're adept at using a variety of conflict resolution styles depending on the situation at hand. Appreciate that each conflict resolution style has its own advantages and is useful in specific circumstances.

> 'I'm not into the culture of complaint. I roll up my sleeves and somehow I get it together.'
>
> Werner Herzog (n.d.).

REFERENCES

Bonebright, D. A. (2010). 40 years of storming: A historical review of Tuckman's model of small group development. *Human Resource Development International, 13*(1), 111–120. https://doi.org/10.1080/13678861003589099

Fisher, S. G., & Hunter, T. A. (1997). Team or group? Managers' perceptions of the differences. *Journal of Managerial Psychology, 12*(4), 232–242. https://doi.org/10.1108/02683949710174838

Guzzo, R. A., & Dickson, M. W. (1996). Teams in organizations: Recent research on performance and effectiveness. *Annual Review of Psychology, 47*(1), 307–338. https://doi.org/10.1146/annurev.psych.47.1.307

Hoch, J. E., Pearce, C. L., & Welzel, L. (2010). Is the most effective team leadership shared? *Journal of Personnel Psychology, 9*(3), 105–116. https://doi.org/10.1027/1866-5888/a000020

Jehn, K. A. (1995). A multimethod examination of the benefits and detriments of intragroup conflict. *Administrative Science Quarterly, 40*, 256–282. https://doi.org/10.2307/2393638

Morgeson, F. P., DeRue, D. S., & Karam, E. P. (2010). Leadership in teams: A functional approach to understanding leadership structures and processes. *Journal of Management*, *36*(1), 5–39. https://doi.org/10.1177/0149206309347376

Rahim, M. A. (1983). A measure of styles of handling interpersonal conflict. *Academy of Management Journal*, *26*(2), 368–376. https://doi.org/10.5465/255985

Sheard, A. G., & Kakabadse, A. P. (2004). A process perspective on leadership and team development. *Journal of Management Development*, *23*(1), 7–106. https://doi.org/10.1108/02621710410511027

Thomas, K. W., & Kilmann, R. H. (1974). *Thomas-Kilmann conflict mode instrument*. Xicom.

Tuckman, B. W. (1965). Developmental sequence in small groups. *Psychological Bulletin*, *63*(6), 384–399. https://doi.org/10.1037/h0022100

Wall, J. A. J., & Callister, R. R. (1995). Conflict and its management. *Journal of Management*, *21*(3), 515–558. https://doi.org/10.1177/014920639502100306

Winer, S., Ramos Salazar, L., Anderson, A. M., & Busch, M. (2023). Resolving conflict in interpersonal relationships using passive, aggressive, and assertive verbal statements. *International Journal of Conflict Management*, *35*(2), 334–359. https://doi.org/10.1108/IJCMA-03-2023-0048

Xin, K. R., & Pelled, L. H. (2003). Supervisor–subordinate conflict and perceptions of leadership behavior: A field study. *The Leadership Quarterly*, *14*(1), 25–40. https://doi.org/10.1016/S1048-9843(02)00185-6

Zaccaro, S. J., Rittman, A. L., & Marks, M. A. (2001). Team leadership. *The Leadership Quarterly*, *12*(4), 451–483. https://doi.org/10.1016/S1048-9843(01)00093-5

12
LEADING PEOPLE THROUGH CHANGE

Overview

This chapter discusses leadership in times of change. It starts by exploring the nature of change, considering what exactly changes, how, why change is necessary, and the role of leaders in both creating and facilitating change.

The chapter starts with change management to explain how change initiatives are planned and implemented within organisations. Two prominent change models are introduced: Kurt Lewin's and John Kotter's. You'll work through a reflective exercise to see how Lewin's force-field analysis can be applied across all leadership interactions.

Next, we unpack the transition cycle to explain how individuals mentally process external change, which enables us to better understand the different roles that leaders need to play at each stage of the transition process. You'll reflect on a past change experience to reveal what kind of support helped you to move through the different stages, and how you might help others to do the same.

Some level of resistance to change is inevitable, and so we consider why people may resist change and what we can do about it as leaders to encourage our followers to embrace change. The chapter concludes with a discussion of the safety climate – to bring your vision to life as a change leader you must create a safe space for your team that promotes trust and cooperation.

Exercise 12.1: Lewin's force-field analysis

Exercise 12.2: Transition cycle

Video 12.1: Simon Sinek – Why good leaders make you feel safe

Change is an inherent part of life, and yet it can be a fraught process when it happens inside organisations. In this chapter we'll first explore change management as a necessary practice for planning and implementing organisational change. We will cover two change models developed by Lewin and Kotter respectively, to consider our role as leaders in facilitating change.

We'll then shift our focus to examine how individual people process and adapt to change, as well as why people might resist change, what that looks like, and how we can help. We'll finish with a discussion about the safety climate of an organisation, and how feeling safe builds the trust, unity, and cooperation necessary to successfully navigate organisational change.

WHAT IS CHANGE?

Heraclitus, an ancient Greek philosopher, said that 'No man ever steps in the same river twice, for it's not the same river and he's not the same man'. His message encapsulates the idea that the river and the individual are both in a perpetual state of transformation.

If we were to cross a river today, our experience would be unique to that specific moment. When we attempt to cross the same river on another day, we'd find ourselves altered, even if just slightly. Likewise, the river itself has evolved too, its flow, patterns, and currents subtly modified. This demonstrates that each moment is distinct, and we cannot recreate any single instance from the past. So, what exactly is changing in this perspective?

Our subjective perspective changes. People change; you and I, we're in a perpetual state of change. What we know today isn't the same as what we'll know tomorrow. As you read this passage, absorbing knowledge, your perspective evolves. While this change may not entirely redefine your identity, it leaves a mark, subtly reshaping your understanding of the world.

Our emotions, too, are in constant flux. How we feel today is different from other days and times in years past; our emotive experience possesses unique qualities and nuances. Our shifting emotions are also further influencing how we perceive and interact with the world around us. Our desires and aspirations are subject to change as well. Today, you may feel drained and want some rest, but tomorrow you might wake up full of energy and excitement, altering your expectations and experiences. This fluidity in our desires impacts how we approach each day and the goals we set.

The objective world itself changes too, much like the ever-changing river Heraclitus spoke of. Time marches forward, and the events that shape our reality are in constant flux. For example, today you find yourself reading this last chapter, but in a few weeks, you'll likely have moved onto something quite different. Events occurring in different corners of the world influence our thoughts and experiences, and even the weather conditions can alter our perception.

So, our subjective perception of the world is continuously evolving, and these changing perspectives act as lenses through which we view and experience reality, shifting with each passing moment. Simultaneously, the objective reality that surrounds us undergoes transformations of its own, as we navigate through it.

This dual process of ever-shifting subjective perceptions and objective reality is what explains the constant dynamism in our existence. As leaders we must embrace this inherent instability, adapt to it, and work to guide our teams through the intricate interplay of personal growth and external change.

That's one perspective. Here's another one from an episode of *House, M.D.* in which Hugh Laurie plays Dr Gregory House and says that 'Time changes everything. That's what people say. It's not true. Doing things changes things. Not doing things leaves things exactly as they were' (Shore & Campanella, 2007). This perspective is quite different; it suggests that unless I start to do something differently, my substantive experiences will remain the same, from one day to the next.

It implies that the passage of time alone does not inherently bring 'real' change, and that it's our actions that can make a meaningful difference. For example, I'm teaching my leadership class on Fridays this semester, and that weekly class occurs because we act to make it happen. If I were to quit my job, this class would cease to exist in its current format. So, meaningful change and impactful experiences result from our deliberate actions, not the mere passage of time.

This viewpoint emphasises our agency and control over our experiences. Rather than feeling passive in the face of constant change, it puts us in the driver's seat. It suggests that the world has a degree of stability, and that our actions shape the course of our lives. By taking deliberate actions, we gain the power to influence and modify our experiences, providing a sense of control over the direction of our lives and the changes we wish to see.

Why do Organisations Need to Change?

Organisations find themselves navigating a volatile, uncertain, complex, and ambiguous environment (Bennett & Lemoine, 2014). It's a landscape marked by frequent revolutionary change. Recall from Chapter 2 that these developments can stem from geopolitical conflicts, technological advancements, and social movements. Emerging new challenges include, increasingly, the real-time interactions, internationalisation, cross-cultural collaboration, accountability and intolerance, an inversion of expertise, and, increasingly flexible and remote work.

Lawler and Worley (2006) advocate for 'built-to-change' organisations that can navigate this dynamic environment. These entities aren't designed as one static, enduring model.

Instead, they are engineered to readily embrace and continuously adapt to change throughout their existence. Such adaptability enables them to stay competitive and seize leadership positions in their respective markets. Conversely, companies failing to adopt this ethos face a path of stagnation, as competitors speed past them in the ever-evolving race.

Organisations typically decline for one of a few main reasons: bad leadership, bad change management, or a toxic organisational culture (Probst & Raisch, 2005). These top the list, though other causes can of course contribute to their demise. By now you should be well on your way to appreciating the kinds of positive leadership approaches that enable productive organisational cultures to thrive, so let's turn our attention to change management.

We'll start by exploring the different types of organisational changes that can take place, and then we'll discuss two change management models, examining the deliberate, process-driven strategies that managers employ within organisations. Afterwards, we'll explore change leadership as a distinct practice that will become clearer as our conversation unfolds. Good change management and change leadership are both necessary for you to successfully navigate the turbulent waters of organisational change.

Four Types of Organisational Change

There are four main types of organisational change, including process change, functional and structural change, culture change, and the redistribution of power within the organisation (cf. Huy, 2001). Each type of change serves a distinct purpose and presents unique challenges and opportunities. Let's take a closer look at each one.

Process

The first type of change is to organisational processes. Processes are the flow of inputs and outputs within an organisation – from the acquisition of raw materials or knowledge from suppliers to the value-adding proprietary processes, such as transforming steel into iPhones. This sequence, encompassing the transformation journey, characterises the essence of organisational operations. When this sequence undergoes alteration, we refer to it as a process change. In essence, process change entails reconfiguring the fundamental procedures by which an organisation operates.

Organisational processes undergo transformation in various ways. For example, consider a manufacturing company shifting from traditional assembly line methods to implementing advanced robotic automation. This change streamlines production, reduces costs, and enhances efficiency. Similarly, in the field of information technology, the transition from manual data entry to sophisticated data management systems exemplifies process change. Such systems improve accuracy, speed, and data accessibility, thereby optimising organisational performance. These examples illustrate how adapting and refining processes can lead to significant enhancements in an organisation's operations and outcomes.

Functional or Structural

The second type of organisational change is functional or structural. This type of change encompasses both horizontal and vertical structures within an organisation. Horizontal structure pertains to how people are organised across various roles and teams, while vertical structure involves the hierarchy from frontline employees to executives. Organisations can have a traditional hierarchy with clear levels of authority or adopt a distributed structure with autonomous, self-managing teams, including virtual teams. Policies and systems dictate the framework of these structures within the organisation.

Any modifications made to these functional and structural aspects represent a significant change for an organisation. These changes can have profound impacts on the company's performance and functionality. For example, a traditional hierarchical structure provides extensive control and oversight, making it suitable for complex, highly regulated industries like aircraft maintenance, where safety and compliance are paramount. In contrast, when creativity and agility are essential, reducing hierarchy and empowering employees to make autonomous decisions become imperative.

Functional and structural changes play a pivotal role in shaping how an organisation operates and responds to evolving business environments. While they may appear easier to implement compared to other types of change, the impact on an organisation's culture, efficiency, and adaptability should not be underestimated.

Cultural

The third type of organisational change is cultural change and it involves altering how people behave within the organisation and the fundamental values that underlie those behaviours. It entails questions such as whether the organisation fosters a friendly and collegial atmosphere, encourages competition, promotes collaboration, or readily engages with external stakeholders. Unlike process or structural changes, influencing cultural change is a more complex endeavour.

Leaders striving to effect cultural change cannot merely draft new policies to mandate desired behaviours. Instead, they must embark on a journey to reshape and influence the values that underpin organisational conduct. Building a culture of cooperation, trust, and collaboration takes time but can have a profound impact on an organisation's performance. A workplace where employees genuinely like each other, work well together, trust one another, and readily share information tends to outperform its counterparts characterised by competitiveness, defensiveness, resistance to change, and a lack of trust.

In many ways, the organisational culture serves as a distinguishing factor between top-performing organisations and those that achieve moderate success in virtually every market. It transcends the product itself, emphasising the critical role of values, behaviours, and the interpersonal dynamics within the organisation in determining overall success. Leaders, therefore, play a crucial role in shaping and nurturing a culture that fosters cooperation, trust, and a commitment to shared values, ultimately contributing to enhanced organisational performance.

Distribution of Power

The fourth category of organisational change is the distribution of power. This aspect is somewhat intertwined with the functional aspects of the organisation, as it involves how power and decision-making authority are allocated among different groups or individuals. While a more hierarchical structure centralises power, this type of change focuses on the social and informal coalitions within the organisation.

For example, consider a large company with functional departments like finance, accounting, marketing, and operations. In such cases, the finance and accounting departments, even though not hierarchically superior, often wield significant influence due to their control over the budget, impacting decision-making and strategy implementation. Another example is a brand-centric company like Nike, where the marketing department may hold substantial power as it manages the organisation's most valuable asset, the brand identity.

In contrast, organisations with IT-based products may see the IT department or algorithm designers exerting substantial influence. Any shifts in the distribution of power within an organisation can profoundly impact its operations and decision-making processes, regardless of hierarchical positions.

CHANGE MODELS

Now let's consider two prominent change models that offer structured frameworks that will help us to navigate organisational change – the first by Lewin (1947) and the second by Kotter (1996). Interestingly, their models share striking similarities, outlining key steps that leaders must master to guide their organisations through the complex process of change. First, let's look at Lewin's model, which starts by explaining how leaders can enable organisational change.

Kurt Lewin

Lewin (1947) believed that change is the result of two opposing forces: driving forces that push for change, and restraining forces that strive to maintain the status quo. Thinking about it in these terms can help us to appreciate what kinds of considerations are encouraging us to change, and what might be preventing us from changing. For reviews of Lewin's work on change management, see the 2017 Special Issue in the *Journal of Change Management* (Burnes & Bargal, 2017) and the review by Burnes (2020).

Driving Forces

Driving forces are catalysts for change that encourage individuals, teams, and organisations towards new objectives and practices. Shifts in the external environment are a source of such driving forces – for example, new technologies, competitive pressures, or regulatory changes. As technological advances emerge, organisations must adapt to stay relevant. Pressure from competitors may demand strategic changes to products, markets, or processes, while new regulations often compel organisations to modify their practices.

Driving forces can also stem from the limitations faced by an organisation – including for example, inefficient processes, poor performance, or outdated systems. Employees and managers might be frustrated with bureaucratic processes that slow down work or cumbersome manual handling that is prone to mistakes. If certain departments or teams consistently fail to meet targets or objectives, there could be a push to change strategies, improve training, or reallocate resources to improve performance. And if current technology isn't keeping pace with industry standards, that may drive an organisation to upgrade its systems.

Career development opportunities and ambitious organisational goals can likewise drive change – for example, offering new training programmes, leadership tracks, or skill development workshops can incentivise employees to initiate and embrace change within the organisation, aiming for personal growth and better career prospects. Setting strategic goals that require innovation, such as sustainability targets or digital transformation objectives, create incentives for departments to change their practices and contribute to broader organisational aims.

Restraining Forces

Restraining forces are barriers to change. Individuals' resistance to change is often rooted in fears about adapting to new practices or structures. Concerns about diminished competence in unfamiliar environments are not unfounded, and transitioning to new ways of working may risk reduced compensation, altered status, performance issues, or job security.

Cultural inertia also poses a significant barrier. When organisational culture is entrenched in specific traditions or workflows, introducing innovations becomes problematic. Employees and management might resist adopting new approaches that do not align with prevailing norms, illustrating how deeply embedded practices can stall progress.

Financial constraints represent another formidable restraining force. Lack of funding to support new technologies, training, or structural changes can halt transformation efforts. This is often the case when organisations face budget constraints or are reluctant to invest in change initiatives.

Time pressures further complicate the situation. The day-to-day demands of operational duties can overshadow efforts to implement new processes. With employees and managers stretched thinly, dedicating time to plan and adapt to new strategies becomes a secondary priority, thus hindering organisational evolution.

Rigid organisational protocols can create a structural inertia that restrains change. Centralised control and multiple layers of hierarchical oversight impede decision-making and can frustrate change initiatives. Additionally, entrenched legacy systems that are integral to daily operations often prove costly and complex to overhaul, which can inhibit technological advancement.

Enabling Change

Leaders can enable change by increasing the driving forces – for example, by introducing performance-based bonuses, role enhancements, or professional development opportunities that motivate employees to adopt new practices.

At the same time, we can encourage change by reducing the restraining forces that impede change – for example, with transparent communication addressing concerns that might cause resistance or anxiety among team members. Providing assurances around job continuity, comprehensive retraining, and increased support can help assuage fears.

Reducing barriers to change is often more effective than increasing the driving forces – putting pressure on people to change often creates more stress than progress, whereas removing obstacles enables people to embrace change. It's about creating environments where change is not only feasible but also less daunting for team members. By removing elements that generate anxiety and fear, and providing necessary resources, leaders can help create safe spaces for more successful organisational change.

Three Phase Process

Lewin's model of organisational change includes three phases: unfreezing, movement, and refreezing. Each stage plays a vital role in the successful transformation of an organisation.

The unfreezing phase is about preparing the organisation for change. It involves challenging existing mindsets and practices. In this stage, leaders need to persuade their teams that change is necessary. The aim is to break down the status quo, allowing people to let go of old habits and consider new ways of working. It's about thawing out rigid ideas and opening up to the possibility of a different approach.

During the movement phase, the actual transition takes place. Here, leaders develop and implement the change plan. This stage encompasses diagnosing the situation, developing strategies, implementing them, and exercising control over the process. It's a period of transition where new methods and practices are put into action.

Finally, the refreezing phase is about solidifying these changes. After implementation, it's crucial to ensure that the new methods become the norm. This phase involves anchoring the new ways of working into the organisation's culture, structure, and policies. Leaders should reinforce the changes by aligning pay structures, rewards, and promotions with the new behaviours. The goal is to ensure that the new practices are maintained and become embedded in the organisation's values and everyday activities.

Lewin's Force-Field Analysis

Now I'd like you to work through Lewin's force-field analysis (Exercise 12.1). This technique encourages you to reflect on a personal change initiative. Think back to an experience where you tried to improve on a skill or achieve a better outcome, like scoring higher in an assessment or any other personal goal.

Start by outlining your vision – that is, your aspirations or what you were trying to accomplish. Next, describe the initial situation or your starting point. And then identify three key driving forces that motivated your change and propelled you forward, and three restraining forces that held you back, discouraged you, or made the journey more challenging.

Exercise 12.1

Lewin's Force-Field Analysis

Image Alt Text: https://ecuau.qualtrics.com/jfe/form/SV_865NkyVzkkLilf0

This basic exercise is a good opportunity for you to identify what motivates you and what holds you back. But appreciating the process is much more important for you as a leader because you can apply this same exercise to developing a better understanding of your team: there will be things that are encouraging them to change and things that are holding them back.

So what we'll do as change leaders is work through this exact same force-field analysis for the individuals working with us, for our teams, and organisations, to see what's enabling them and what's restricting them from moving forward. And then it's our job to reduce those barriers and to incentivise their progress wherever possible.

Let's now take a closer look at Kotter's model, to see what additional insights it can offer us.

John Kotter

Kotter's (1996) model of organisational change refines and extends Lewin's (1947) original three-phase framework, offering more granular insights into each stage of transformation within an organisation. Kotter focuses on large-scale change initiatives, like entering new markets, or cultural shifts that require comprehensive organisational alignment. For a review of Kotter's change model, see Appelbaum et al. (2012).

Kotter (1996) changes the terms, but much of the substance developed by Lewin (1947) remains. In Kotter's version 'unfreezing' becomes 'creating a climate for change', which is about preparing the organisation and its people psychologically, fostering a readiness to adopt novel approaches. 'Movement' becomes 'engaging the whole organisation.'

For Kotter, this stage isn't just about implementing a change plan; it's a call to action for every member of the organisation. It's a strategy to mobilise all stakeholders, ensuring their active participation in the change process.

The final phase, 'refreezing', becomes 'embedding change' in Kotter's framework. This crucial step aims to integrate the changes into the company's very fabric – its culture, structure, and policies – to ensure that these new ways of working endure into the future. What Kotter (1996) contributes, then, is an eight-stage process that fits within this three-phase model. Let's have a closer look.

Eight Stage Process

Kotter's eight-stage model of organisational change offers a robust framework for leaders aiming to implement substantial change within their organisations. The model breaks down the three-phase process into clear, actionable steps, each critical for the success of the overall transformation.

> *Create urgency.* The first stage involves creating a sense of urgency for change. Leaders must convince stakeholders of the immediate need for change, using compelling arguments, influential communication, and various tactics to foster a shared understanding of the urgency.
>
> *Create a guiding team.* Change cannot be a solo endeavour and you will next need to identify a team of champions from across the organisation. This team should consist of individuals respected both officially and socially, representing different groups and functions within the organisation. They are pivotal in communicating and endorsing the vision for change.
>
> *Create the vision.* After establishing the need for change and assembling a guiding team, the next step is to define the vision. This involves detailing what the change entails, why it is necessary, and how it will be implemented. Clarity in the vision is vital to guide the entire change process.
>
> *Share the vision.* Communicate the vision transparently and with full disclosure, addressing how it will impact various roles and teams. Utilise diverse communication channels like global emails, one-on-one meetings, and workshops to engage with and solicit feedback from all levels of the organisation.
>
> *Empower action.* Empowering action involves reducing barriers that hinder movement towards the change. This includes addressing anxieties, providing necessary resources, offering support, and delivering relevant training. Empowerment accelerates the adoption of new behaviours and practices.
>
> *Celebrate early wins.* Recognise and highlight early successes to reinforce the value of the change, motivating others in the organisation and building momentum.

Build momentum. This stage is about leveraging initial successes to initiate more changes, moving people from exploration to commitment. It's a process of demonstrating the path to success and continuously fuelling the momentum of change.

Institute change. The final step is embedding the change into the company's culture, policies, and structure. It's about aligning all organisational systems with the new way of doing things to ensure the change is sustainable and becomes a part of the organisational fabric.

The model not only outlines what needs to be done but also emphasises the how, making it a valuable roadmap for any leader embarking on significant organisational change. Next, we'll discuss organisational change more broadly to see what you can do as leaders to help.

ORGANISATIONAL CHANGE

Organisations typically approach change through structured change plans that are designed to systematically address specific problems the organisation faces. Leaders initiate this process by analysing the current situation, identifying areas for improvement, and devising strategic steps to achieve the desired transformation. This methodical approach ensures a targeted and effective change process, aligning closely with the organisation's overall objectives.

Beware Generic Solutions

Organisations often face similar challenges such as rising labour costs, service and product quality issues, bureaucracy, and a lack of agility. Some leaders are therefore tempted to adopt pre-packaged solutions offered by consultancies that include generic change plans like outsourcing, restructuring, or delayering. These 'solutions' appear attractive because they seem to offer a quick fix to complex issues. For example, outsourcing is often proposed as an answer to high labour costs, suggesting that shifting certain functions to lower-cost regions will reduce expenses.

However, this approach can be problematic. Generic plans might address symptoms – such as high costs or operational inefficiencies – but they often fail to tackle the underlying causes of these issues. For example, restructuring or delayering may seem like effective strategies for streamlining operations, yet they might not address core problems like poor management practices or inadequate technology infrastructure. That's one reason why the vast majority of change initiatives fail (Burnes & Jackson, 2011).

The allure of these generic solutions lies in their simplicity and the promise of immediate results. They become popular as organisations mimic successful implementations by others, often without considering the unique context of their own situation. The result can be a worsening of problems; changes must align with the specific needs and circumstances of the organisation.

To improve an organisation effectively, leaders must first diagnose its unique context, challenges, and circumstances (McFillen et al., 2013). This approach is akin to treating a patient; a doctor wouldn't indiscriminately prescribe medication without understanding the underlying health issue. Similarly, organisational leaders need to delve deep to understand the specific problems that their organisation is facing.

It's not just about identifying surface-level symptoms but uncovering the root causes. This diagnosis forms the foundation for developing a variety of tailored strategies, each addressing different aspects of the issues at hand. A thorough diagnosis ensures that the solutions implemented are not only relevant but also effectively target the core of the issue, leading to sustainable improvement and growth.

Thinking it Through

Organisational change is a process involving many steps, not a sudden shift from 'A' to 'Z'. Successful implementation requires careful planning. Leaders must first appreciate what needs changing and why, ensuring a solid foundation for the change. The next critical phase is determining the 'how' – and not just in broad strokes, but by thinking through the minutiae of the transition from the current state to the desired one.

Consider, for example, implementing new software in a manufacturing organisation's warehouse. The change is not just about swapping old systems for new; it involves understanding the reasons behind the change, such as the limitations of the current system and the advantages of the new one. This understanding must extend to the costs, downtime, and retraining involved. The process also includes preparing the team for the transition: providing training and support; managing the psychological aspects of change, such as resistance and denial; setting up trial platforms; addressing data transfer issues; and ensuring the new system meets current and future requirements.

Leaders must anticipate and plan for potential challenges and hurdles. This preparation is not merely theoretical; it is crucial for convincing the team of the necessity for change, and its feasibility. Without a comprehensive plan, responses to inquiries about the change may breed uncertainty and resistance. By thinking through each step and proactively addressing potential challenges, leaders can craft a robust and effective change plan that guides the organisation through a smooth transition.

Crafting Smart Plans

Crafting smart change plans involves five considerations: purpose, objectives, people, resources, and timeframes. Let's take a closer look at each one.

Purpose

The purpose addresses the core question of why the change is necessary. Understanding the purpose of change initiatives is pivotal for organisations. As a change leader, it is essential to know precisely why a change is necessary and preferable to other options. This clarity of purpose involves a deep comprehension of what the organisation aims to achieve and the reasons underpinning this goal.

It's not enough to adopt new technology or processes because they seem innovative or popular. Leaders must critically evaluate why a specific change is the best solution for their unique situation. This means considering the wider implications of the change – how it will affect stakeholders, other departments, and the overall organisational hierarchy, considering whether it will impose new demands on suppliers and increasing costs, or how consumers may react. For example, when organisations outsourced call centres overseas, many found it led to a decline in service quality, affecting customer satisfaction and brand reputation.

Understanding the purpose helps in navigating the forces that either facilitate or hinder the change. Awareness of these dynamics enables leaders to effectively manage resistance, retraining needs, and potential dips in productivity and confidence. By thoroughly understanding the 'why' behind the change, leaders can strategically plan, anticipate challenges, and guide their teams through the transition, ensuring alignment and maintaining focus on the organisation's overarching goals.

Objectives

The objectives, on the other hand, articulate what the change aims to achieve. These are the tangible targets that the change seeks to hit. Clear objectives transform the abstract concept of change into measurable outcomes. They act as a compass, guiding all decisions and actions throughout the change process. Without well-defined objectives, a change initiative risks becoming directionless or misaligned with the organisation's broader goals.

Consider the decision to implement new software. Leaders must articulate specifically whether the aim is to enhance efficiency, reduce costs, improve customer experience, or something else. These objectives must be clear, measurable, and aligned with the organisation's strategic vision. Objectives provide a benchmark against which the success of the change can be evaluated.

Understanding objectives helps in communicating the change to stakeholders. It allows leaders to explain not just what is changing, but why these changes are crucial. This clarity helps in gaining buy-in from employees, customers, and other stakeholders. It also aids in anticipating and planning for the impacts of change – how it will affect different departments, the workload, and the company culture. Without a deep understanding of the objectives, the organisation might implement changes that are costly or disruptive without achieving meaningful benefits, leading to wasted resources and potential resistance from stakeholders.

People

Change affects not only processes but also the people who operate within these frameworks. Leaders must explain the forthcoming changes, their reasons, and implications to all affected parties. This includes those directly involved in the changed processes, their supervisors, the finance team responsible for budget approvals, and the marketing team, who may perceive the change as impacting brand identity or posing a reputational risk. Externally it's critical to consider how the change will affect customers; engaging with them to gauge their reaction is vital for a successful change implementation.

Assigning clear responsibilities and setting expectations for each team member is another critical aspect of managing people during change. This clarity ensures accountability and aids in monitoring and controlling the process. Leaders should delegate tasks, specifying what needs to be done, by whom, and by when. This approach not only streamlines the change process but also helps in maintaining team morale and productivity during the transition. Understanding and managing these 'people' aspects is a key part of effective leadership in times of change.

Resources

Understanding resource considerations is vital in the development of organisational change plans. Leaders must build a strong business case that encompasses the appropriate allocation and timing of resources. Key questions include whether the necessary budget is available and how to support people through the transition, particularly with training.

Determining who will bear the costs and responsibilities for training is crucial. Will it be an in-house endeavour or will external experts be brought in, perhaps from a software company, to train the team? The selection between in-house and outsourced training has significant implications for both cost and effectiveness.

Effective resource management ensures that the organisation has the necessary financial, human, and material resources to implement the change successfully. It also involves planning for the deployment of these resources in a manner that aligns with the change objectives. By thoroughly considering and planning for resource needs, leaders can mitigate risks of resource shortages and ensure a smoother transition, ultimately contributing to the successful implementation of the change initiative.

Timeframes

Timeframes must be carefully planned and managed to ensure the change process aligns with the readiness and capacity of the organisation. Announcing a change and rushing into training can be counterproductive if people are still grappling with denial and resistance. It's crucial to allow sufficient time for individuals to process and accept the change before moving forward with implementation steps like training; employees need time to familiarise themselves with new approaches. A predictable and realistic timeline helps in managing expectations and maintaining momentum throughout the change process.

Staying on track with timeframes is vital as every element of a change initiative comes with a cost. The assumption is that the investment in change will yield benefits, but if the process is prolonged, costs escalate, and the return on investment diminishes. Constant monitoring and realistic time estimates are essential. Leaders often underestimate the time required for a team to move through various phases of a change, such as denial or acceptance.

External dependencies, like the availability of training providers, must be factored into the planning. Aligning these external schedules with internal needs, such as production cycles, can be challenging and requires diligent coordination. Effective management of timeframes demands experience, flexibility, and a deep understanding of both the change process and the specific dynamics of the organisation and its people.

LEADING CHANGE

So far, we've been talking about change management, which I hope you're starting to realise is something quite different to leading people through change. Change management focuses on the structural aspect of change. It involves planning, implementing, controlling, and diagnosing organisational needs. This process includes designing interventions to facilitate change across the organisation. It's about the mechanics of how change is executed – the strategies, the steps, the methodologies.

Leading people through change, on the other hand, is about the human aspect. It's about inspiring and empowering individuals to embrace and adapt to change. This leadership aspect involves setting a vision, communicating meaning and value in people's work, and providing support throughout the change process. Effective leadership in change is about motivating and guiding individuals to understand and align with the new direction.

For change to be successful, both elements must work in tandem (Gill, 2002). While change management lays out the roadmap for change, leadership ensures that people are willing and able to follow that path. Leaders must not only manage the logistical aspects of change but also lead their teams through the transition, addressing their concerns, fostering their growth, and aligning their efforts with the new vision. This dual focus on structural management and people-oriented leadership is essential for comprehensive and effective change within any organisation.

Personal Change

Organisational change, at its core, is about personal change within the individuals that constitute the organisation. Consider an educational institution like the university where I work; without its staff, from the Vice Chancellor to the cleaners, it would simply be a collection of empty buildings. Therefore, to effect change in an organisation, we must focus on transforming the people within it. Changing the physical aspects, like painting a building blue, might alter its appearance, but it does not fundamentally change the organisation's function or culture.

The real challenge lies in altering the culture and behaviours of people. This requires us to confront uncertainty and the unknown. The current way of operating provides a sense of security and familiarity. When individuals are asked to adopt new methods, they face the unfamiliar, which naturally evokes anxiety and resistance. This reaction is a defence mechanism against perceived threats to safety and comfort.

To successfully navigate this transformation, exceptional leadership is required. Leaders must guide and support their teams through this transition with empathy and understanding. Sudden, large-scale, and forced changes are likely to be met with stiff resistance (Pardo del Val & Martinez Fuentes, 2003). People instinctively resist what they perceive to be unsafe or uncertain. Overcoming this resistance involves gentle persuasion, clear communication, and a demonstration of the benefits and safety of the new way.

The process of leading change begins even before any actual change takes place. It involves careful planning of how the change will be communicated and implemented. This planning must consider the psychological impact on the team members and devise strategies to ease the transition. Successful change leaders understand that change is not just a procedural shift but a journey that affects people on a deep, personal level. They recognise that guiding an organisation through change means guiding its people through a journey of personal transformation, from the familiar to the new, in a way that is supportive, reassuring, and ultimately empowering.

Change vs Transition

Bridges and Bridges (2017) discuss the difference between change and transition. Change refers to an alteration in the external environment or objective situation, such as moving to new premises, introducing new processes, restructuring a department, or shifting organisational strategy. It is tangible and often visible, involving modifications in processes, structures, or technology within an organisation.

Transition, on the other hand, is the internal, psychological process that individuals undergo to adapt to these external changes. It involves the mental steps and emotional journey people experience as they come to terms with new situations. This internal processing is crucial for individuals to accept and embrace the change effectively.

Effective leadership is key in guiding people through this transition. It's not sufficient to simply introduce change; leaders must also support their team through the internal adaptation process. This involves understanding the emotional and psychological responses to change, and providing relevant support. Leaders play a critical role in facilitating a smooth transition by helping their team understand, accept, and adjust to the new reality. This empathetic and supportive approach minimises resistance and prevents disengagement or departure from the organisation.

Transition Cycle Model

We can use the transition cycle model to help us understand how people experience and process change. The model is adapted to organisational change from earlier work by

Kübler-Ross (1969). It's a sequential process with four stages that outline the mental processes people work through when presented with change, starting with denial, then resistance, exploration, and finishing at commitment.

Figure 12.1 maps out these four stages, with time on the horizontal axis and morale and productivity on the vertical axis. Morale and productivity start high, decline slightly at denial, and then plummet as we hit resistance, before coming back up during exploration, and then returning to normal or slightly above at commitment.

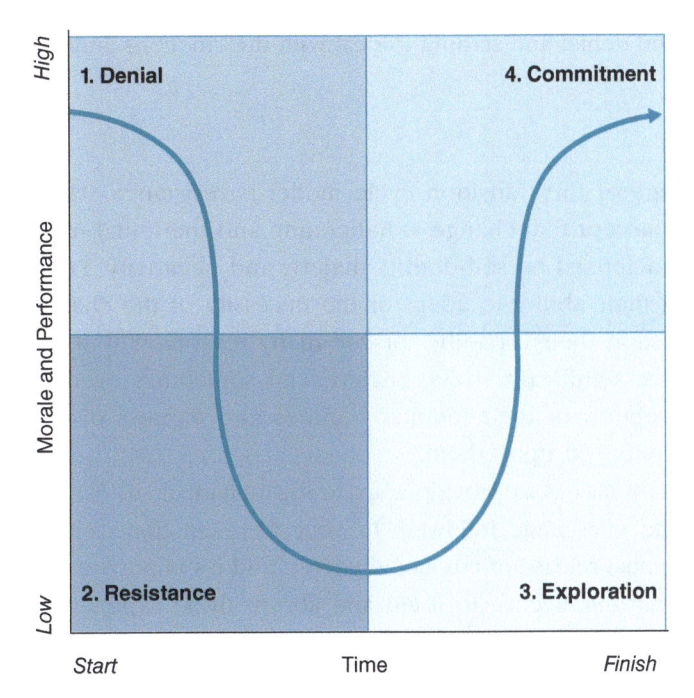

Figure 12.1 Transition cycle model

Adapted from Kübler-Ross (1969).

Let's now consider each stage in a bit more depth to see what we can do as leaders to best support our followers' progress through to commitment.

Denial

The first stage in the transition cycle model is denial. This stage is marked by an initial response of shock and numbness, akin to a deer caught in headlights. When confronted with change, individuals may continue with their daily tasks, behaving as if nothing has changed. This is not just avoidance; it's a psychological mechanism whereby, in their minds, they deny the existence of the change itself. They refuse to acknowledge the need for change, effectively ignoring the new reality.

Leaders' first responsibility is to inform the team about the change. This involves clear communication about the nature of the change, its reasons, and its potential impacts.

However, mere information is not enough. Leaders must also actively seek feedback from their team about the change. This process is not just about gathering insights but also serves a deeper psychological purpose.

By asking for their team's opinions and approaches to the change, leaders encourage them to acknowledge and confront the reality of the situation. This engagement is a subtle yet powerful way to help team members move past denial. It's a shift from merely informing to involving them in the change process. In answering these questions, team members begin to accept that the change is indeed happening, which is a crucial step in moving beyond denial and starting to deal with the emotions and practicalities of the transition.

Resistance

The second stage of the transition cycle model is resistance. This phase starts as soon as people accept that change is happening and the initial numbness of denial fades. It is characterised by self-doubt, anxiety, and negativity. People may express concerns about their ability to adapt or the necessity of the change. For example, they might question their capability or cite many reasons why it's a bad idea. This stage can involve significant stress, anxiety, and sometimes even anger, as people lament the disruption of their familiar routines and express discontent about the changes being imposed upon them.

Leaders' primary task is to provide a space for individuals to express their concerns and feelings, and encourage followers to vent their emotions and fears. This stage involves a substantial release of emotional energy, and it's important for leaders to draw on their emotional intelligence to listen and absorb these expressions without taking them personally or viewing them as definitive assessments of the change itself.

People often do not fully believe everything they say during this stage; rather, they are voicing their stress and anxiety. Leaders must support their team members and give them the space and time to work through these feelings. The leader's role is to remain empathetic, patient, and non-judgmental, understanding that this resistance is a natural part of the change process. Once individuals have expressed their concerns and 'spent' their emotional energy, they are more likely to move towards acceptance and engagement with the change.

Exploration

The third stage in the transition cycle model is exploration. This phase marks a shift from resistance to forward-looking curiosity about the change. Individuals begin to view the change not as a threat but as an opportunity, often experiencing a renewed burst of energy. People start to consider the potential benefits and improvements that the change might bring. This curiosity can manifest as excitement or intrigue about new possibilities and ways of working.

In this stage, there's still a degree of uncertainty. Individuals are not fully convinced yet, but they are open to exploring the change and its implications. They are beginning to see the potential advantages and asking questions about what the change means for them personally and professionally.

As leaders, our role in this exploration stage is critical. We must guide our team members towards the envisioned future but do so gently, without rushing them. It's important to feed their curiosity with information that highlights how the change will benefit them. Focus on improving their experience and demonstrating the practical ways the change will make their work easier or more efficient. Gradually build their confidence and commitment towards the fully implemented version of the change.

Commitment

The final stage in the transition cycle model is commitment. This stage represents the culmination of the change process, where the new way of doing things becomes the new normal. At this point, individuals have fully transitioned from their initial state to complete acceptance embracing the change. They understand and appreciate that the new methods or processes are superior to the old ones and know the reasons why this is the case.

Here the role of leaders transforms significantly; their task now is to empower their employees. Having guided their team through the stages of denial, resistance, and exploration, leaders must now step back and allow their team the autonomy to operate within the new normal. This empowerment is crucial for reinforcing the change and ensuring its sustainability.

Leaders should foster a sense of autonomy, mastery, and purpose among their team members. This approach not only motivates but also cements the commitment to the new ways. At this point, the organisation settles into this new state until the next change initiative arises, which restarts the transition cycle from the beginning.

If change initiatives occur too frequently or overlap significantly, it can lead to 'change fatigue' (Bernerth et al., 2011). This occurs when employees are constantly required to adapt to new changes, moving through the transition cycle repeatedly. Such a scenario can be emotionally taxing and counterproductive. Carefully consider the timing and frequency of change initiatives to ensure that your team can adapt effectively without becoming overwhelmed.

Transition Cycle

Now I'd like you to work through the transition cycle exercise (Exercise 12.2), which asks you to think of a major change that you have faced in your personal or work life. Describe briefly the change – what happened, and how did that affect things for you, and then think about those four stages. Write down how long it took you to get through each of the first three stages. And most importantly, think about the kinds of support that helped you make the transition, because that's going to be really valuable information for you as leaders to consider how you can support others.

Exercise 12.2

Transition Cycle

Image Alt Text: https://ecuau.qualtrics.com/jfe/form/SV_eahl6uoZNhHYA1o

---

When you're helping people transition through change, they'll be experiencing this same process. Knowing this, you can better diagnose where they're at, and know how best to support them towards commitment. Remember, what worked for you might not work for others, so be ready to tailor your approach according to their personal needs and stage in the transition cycle.

RESISTANCE TO CHANGE

Let's first acknowledge that some level of resistance to organisational change is both normal and inevitable (Oreg, 2006). The presence of resistance does not necessarily signify a flaw in the change plan; rather, it's a natural human response to any disruption to the known. Even beneficial changes that promise improved efficiency, increased earnings, or enhanced status can meet resistance, simply because change itself can be intimidating.

Beware that resistance can have a contagion effect, and a single dissenting voice can have a disproportionate impact, potentially undermining an entire change initiative (Sguera et al., 2022). As a leader, expect resistance as an integral part of the change journey. Proactively plan to mitigate potential resistance and address it when it occurs without getting defensive, to transform resistance into constructive engagement (Neves, 2012).

Why do People Resist Change?

Understanding the underlying causes of resistance will better equip us to either avoid it altogether, or else mitigate its harmful effects with constructive approaches. Let's consider some of the main reasons why people might resist organisational change (cf. Erwin & Garman, 2010).

> *Past negative experiences.* Followers may resist change due to negative experiences with past change initiatives. Such legacy issues can create a mindset that change is inherently bad. As a leader, it's important to acknowledge these past experiences

and demonstrate how the current change will be managed differently and more effectively.

Lack of understanding. If followers do not understand the rationale behind the change or fail to see its benefits, they are less likely to support it. Leaders must clearly articulate the reasons for the change, focusing on how it will benefit the team members personally.

Trust issues. If employees don't trust their leaders, they will likely resist change, regardless of its merits. Leaders must build transparent and trusting relationships with their team to facilitate smoother change implementation. When trust is strong, employees are more likely to embrace change, even when it involves uncertainty or personal challenges.

Fear and insecurity. Fear of failure, losing competence, job security, or promotional opportunities can drive resistance. Leaders need to provide emotional support, reassurance, and clear communication about how the change will impact job security and career progression. If followers' job security isn't going to be affected, communicate this early to dispel any apprehension.

Perceived negativity. If followers believe that the change is bad for the organisation or themselves, they will likely resist. It's important for leaders to address these concerns, distinguishing legitimate criticisms from resistance stemming out of fear or misinformation.

Complexity and ambiguity. The more complex and ambiguous the change, the more resistance it is likely to encounter. For example, implementing new reporting standards might be less daunting than adopting a new organisational structure. Leaders should prepare to offer additional support for changes that may push employees out of their comfort zones.

Disruption to social networks. Changes that threaten existing informal networks within the organisation can cause resistance. For example, people may have lunch together, or share a ride into work. Leaders should consider the impact of change on these social structures and seek to preserve useful networks where possible.

Need for stability. Individual openness to experience varies. Some followers may readily embrace change, while others need far more stability. Identifying these differences allows you to tailor your approach, and to be prepared to offer more support to those who might find change more challenging to process.

What Does Resistance Look Like?

When people resist organisational change, it typically involves defensive thinking, resistant behaviour, and emotional resistance (Erwin & Garman, 2010). Let's see what each of these kinds of resistance might include.

Defensive Thinking

Defensive thinking is a socio-cognitive form of resistance to organisational change, often manifesting in cynicism, criticism, and gossip. When employees engage in defensive thinking, they may argue against the change, expressing scepticism and disparaging the competence of management. This can be explicit, with individuals openly criticising the change, or more insidious, involving the spread of rumours or negative perceptions about the initiative.

Such defensive attitudes can create a contagion effect within the organisation. For example, a single employee's cynicism can influence others, leading to the formation of subgroups united in opposition to the change. These groups may reinforce each other's negative views, creating a wave of resistance that spreads throughout the team or department. This dynamic can significantly undermine the change initiative, as it not only hinders acceptance but also fosters a divisive environment, impeding the collective effort needed for successful implementation.

Resistant Behaviour

Resistance to organisational change can manifest in various behaviours, each signalling a different degree of opposition to the new initiatives. Non-compliance is a straightforward form of resistance where employees simply don't follow the new procedures or systems. They continue using old methods despite instructions to change, reflecting a passive but firm resistance.

In some cases, resistance escalates to active disruption. Employees might engage in actions that deliberately counteract or undermine the change efforts. This could range from minor disruptions to significant acts of sabotage that hinder operational efficiency. A more extreme form of resistance is when employees choose to leave the organisation altogether. This often occurs in response to fundamental changes in the organisation's direction, values, or operational methods. When employees feel deeply misaligned with the new path, they might opt out as a form of protest or in discomfort.

Another subtle form of resistance is taking leave during crucial periods of change implementation. Employees may take annual leave during training sessions or rollout phases, thereby passively avoiding engagement with the new systems or processes. Some employees might superficially comply with the change but do so at a minimal, inefficient pace. This 'go-slow' approach is a form of passive resistance, where the outward appearance of compliance masks an underlying reluctance to fully embrace the change.

Prolonged resistance, especially in an environment of constant change, can lead to increased stress and related illnesses. This might manifest as higher rates of sick leave, signs of psychological distress, or reduced performance. It's a signal that the change is impacting employees' mental health, which is a critical workplace issue.

Emotional Resistance

Resistance to organisational change often generates strong emotions, including feelings of fear, uncertainty, irritability, and anger. These emotions are not just confined to employees or subordinates; they can affect anyone within the organisation, including change leaders and managers, who may react to others' interpretations of their change initiatives. Emotions can therefore have a strong contagion effect.

Emotional resistance is particularly potent because of its rapid spread through an organisation. It can influence the overall mood and atmosphere more swiftly than socio-cognitive resistance or behavioural opposition. When individuals express strong emotions like fear or anger about a change, it can resonate with others, creating a ripple effect that amplifies the resistance.

Leaders need to be acutely aware of this emotional dimension. Recognising and addressing these feelings is crucial in managing change effectively, requiring empathetic leadership that acknowledges these emotions, provides support, and fosters an environment where concerns can be openly discussed and addressed. Leaders must not only focus on the logistical aspects of change but also on the emotional well-being of their team, guiding them through the emotional landscape of change with understanding and care.

Leaders Can Resist Change Too

Leaders can resist change too. Frontline and middle managers in particular are in a unique position in the organisational hierarchy that makes them both agents and recipients of change. They are tasked with implementing change initiatives among their teams while simultaneously adapting to directives from higher management. This dual role can lead to a complex relationship with change.

If a leader does not fully understand or agree with the change initiative, it can significantly impact their team. Leaders often serve as role models, and their attitudes towards change are closely observed by their team members. For example, if a leader expresses disagreement or disapproval of a new software system being introduced, their team is likely to mirror these sentiments. This behaviour can create a cascade of resistance, with the leader's negative perception influencing the entire team.

A leader's ability to facilitate change effectively can be hindered by several factors. If a leader is new and hasn't yet established strong relationships of trust and cooperation with their team, presenting and managing change can be challenging. Another critical issue is the lack of resources. Often, leaders are asked to drive change without being provided with the necessary tools and support. This scarcity of resources can lead to frustration and resistance, not just from the leader but also from the team relying on their guidance.

So now that we know why people might resist change, let's see what we can do about it.

Responding to Resistance

Responding effectively to resistance is about empathy, communication, and participation. Let's take a closer look at what that means.

Empathy

Empathy involves understanding and sharing the feelings of others, especially during periods of transition (Hall & Schwartz, 2019). By putting themselves in their followers' shoes, leaders can gain insights into the specific reasons behind the resistance. To effectively employ empathy, leaders must engage in active listening. This approach entails truly hearing and processing what team members are expressing about the change. It's about understanding their concerns, fears, or frustrations.

For example, some may worry about their ability to adapt to new systems or processes, while others might have had negative experiences with past changes. Generic support often doesn't address the unique challenges faced by individual followers, which leaves them feeling alienated and unheard. Once you've understood the specific concerns of your team members, then you can collaborate with them to find suitable solutions. This might involve providing targeted training, offering additional support, or adjusting aspects of the change to better suit their needs.

Communication

Effective communication is particularly useful when you encounter resistance to change. Leaders should embrace full disclosure, providing as much information as possible to their team. In the absence of complete information, followers often fill gaps with rumours and gossip, which can escalate anxiety and create a negative environment. Clear, comprehensive communication about how changes will impact jobs both immediately and in the long term is critical. This approach prevents unnecessary speculation and the spread of misinformation among team members.

Open dialogue not only dispels misconceptions but also builds trust. By being transparent and addressing potential concerns proactively, leaders can mitigate worry and gossip that might otherwise proliferate. This strategy establishes the positive, informed atmosphere that's so crucial to navigating change successfully. Complete and honest communication will therefore help you to guide your teams through transitions and maintain a positive, productive workplace.

Participation

Involving followers in the change process can help reduce their resistance, compared to imposing change on them suddenly. Preparing a change plan is necessary, but you should actively seek input from your team. This can be done by presenting challenges the organisation faces and soliciting ideas from team members, especially in areas where they have expertise. Encouraging followers to share their thoughts and solutions fosters a collaborative environment.

When team members contribute to shaping the change plan, including its execution and methodology, they develop a sense of ownership over the process. This shift in perspective is crucial; they no longer view themselves merely as recipients of change but as architects of it. Participation in the creation process reduces resistance significantly as individuals feel valued and heard. Their contributions and opinions play a direct role in the change, leading to a more harmonious and effective transition. Thus, fostering participation is a key leadership strategy in managing and mitigating resistance to organisational change.

SAFETY CLIMATE

Whether or not people feel safe inside the organisation shapes the overall environment and affects how they'll respond to organisational change. This concept extends beyond physical safety; it's about feeling psychologically safe (Edmondson, 1999), having a sense of belonging, and trust in your leadership.

Creating a safety climate is about establishing a culture where everyone feels secure and protected (Bradley et al., 2012). Organisational change inherently introduces a threat, confronting the unknown and potentially undermining the perceived success and security of employees – so how can we introduce a threat while keeping people safe?

I'd like you to watch this talk by Simon Sinek about why good leaders make you feel safe. Let's see what you make of it.

Video 12.1

Simon Sinek – Why Good Leaders Make You Feel Safe

Summary

Simon argues that leaders must create environments in which their followers feel safe. When we feel secure and supported, we don't have to expend our energy protecting ourselves from each other. Instead we can trust each other and cooperate in facing external threats and seizing opportunities. For Simon, leadership is less about rank and more about the conscious choice to protect and empower those around you. True leaders, Simon says, never sacrifice their people for profit.

Image Alt Text: https://www.youtube.com/watch?v=lmyZMtPVodo

Leaders therefore play a pivotal role in creating a psychological safety climate, especially during times of change. By introducing change, you're essentially bringing a new threat inside the organisation, where your people previously felt safe. That's why you have to work so hard to make sure that the way you design and empower change is supportive, to maintain that sense of security.

The safety climate of an organisation is fundamental for successfully navigating change. It affects not just the immediate response to change but also the long-term viability and success of the organisation. It's about considering the impact of change on the people within the company, their sense of safety, and how this in turn affects trust, unity, and cooperation. As leaders, it's your job to make people feel safe.

SUMMARY

Our existence is defined by a state of perpetual change that's driven by our constantly evolving subjective perspectives and changes to the objective reality around us. Yet substantive change requires us to act.

Organisations must continuously adapt and transform to stay relevant and effective in the face of volatile, uncertain, complex, and ambiguous environments. Four main types of organisational change are process change, functional and structural change, culture change, and the redistribution of power within the organisation.

Lewin (1947) believed that change is the result of two opposing forces – driving forces that push for change and restraining forces that strive to maintain the status quo. Leaders can enable change by increasing the driving forces and reducing the restraining forces. Lewin's model of organisational change includes three phases: unfreezing, movement, and refreezing.

Kotter (1996) then developed an eight-stage change process that fits within Lewin's (1947) three-phase model. It includes first creating urgency, then creating a guiding team, creating a vision, sharing the vision, empowering action, celebrating early wins, building momentum, and concludes with instituting change.

Organisational change processes must first start with a diagnosis of the unique context, challenges, and circumstances. Adopting pre-packaged solutions that include generic change plans like outsourcing, restructuring, or delayering tends to only make things worse.

Leading people through change is about inspiring, empowering, and supporting individuals through change. Transition is the internal, psychological process that people undergo when confronted with external change. The transition cycle model includes four stages: denial, resistance, exploration, and commitment. The role of leaders is to enable their followers to progress through these stages towards commitment.

Some level of resistance to organisational change is both normal and inevitable. Resistance involves defensive thinking, counterproductive behaviour, and negative emotions. Leaders must proactively plan to mitigate potential resistance and address it when it occurs, without getting defensive, to transform resistance into constructive engagement. Creating a climate of psychological safety is therefore particularly important during times of change.

> 'The secret of change is to focus all your energy not on fighting the old, but on building the new.'
>
> Extract from *Way of the Peaceful Warrior* by Dan Millman (1984, p. 113).

REFERENCES

Appelbaum, S. H., Habashy, S., Malo, J. L., & Shafiq, H. (2012). Back to the future: Revisiting Kotter's 1996 change model. *Journal of Management Development*, *31*(8), 764–782. https://doi.org/10.1108/02621711211253231

Bennett, N., & Lemoine, G. J. (2014). What a difference a word makes: Understanding threats to performance in a VUCA world. *Business Horizons*, *57*(3), 311–317. https://doi.org/10.1016/j.bushor.2014.01.001

Bernerth, J. B., Walker, H. J., & Harris, S. G. (2011). Change fatigue: Development and initial validation of a new measure. *Work & Stress*, *25*(4), 321–337. https://doi.org/10.1080/02678373.2011.634280

Bradley, B. H., Postlethwaite, B. E., Klotz, A. C., Hamdani, M. R., & Brown, K. G. (2012). Reaping the benefits of task conflict in teams: The critical role of team psychological safety climate. *Journal of Applied Psychology*, *97*(1), 151–158. https://doi.org/10.1037/a0024200

Bridges, W., & Bridges, S. (2017). *Managing transitions: Making the most of change*. Hachette Books.

Burnes, B. (2020). The origins of Lewin's three-step model of change. *The Journal of Applied Behavioral Science*, *56*(1), 32–59. https://doi.org/10.1177/0021886319892685

Burnes, B., & Bargal, D. (2017). Kurt Lewin: 70 years on. *Journal of Change Management*, *17*(2), 91–100. https://doi.org/10.1080/14697017.2017.1299371

Burnes, B., & Jackson, P. (2011). Success and failure in organizational change: An exploration of the role of values. *Journal of Change Management*, *11*(2), 133–162. https://doi.org/10.1080/14697017.2010.524655

Edmondson, A. (1999). Psychological safety and learning behavior in work teams. *Administrative Science Quarterly*, *44*(2), 350–383. https://doi.org/10.2307/2666999

Erwin, D. G., & Garman, A. N. (2010). Resistance to organizational change: Linking research and practice. *Leadership & Organization Development Journal*, *31*(1), 39–56. https://doi.org/10.1108/01437731011010371

Gill, R. (2002). Change management – or change leadership? *Journal of Change Management*, *3*(4), 307–318. https://doi.org/10.1080/714023845

Hall, J. A., & Schwartz, R. (2019). Empathy present and future. *The Journal of Social Psychology*, *159*(3), 225–243. https://doi.org/10.1080/00224545.2018.1477442

Huy, Q. N. (2001). Time, temporal capability, and planned change. *Academy of Management Review*, *26*(4), 601–623. https://doi.org/10.5465/amr.2001.5393897

Kotter, J. P. (1996). *Leading change*. Harvard Business School Press.

Kübler-Ross, E. (1969). *On death and dying*. Routledge.

Lawler, E. E., & Worley, C. G. (2006). *Built to change: How to achieve sustained organizational effectiveness*. Wiley.

Lewin, K. (1947). Frontiers in group dynamics: Concept, method and reality in social science; social equilibria and social change. *Human Relations*, *1*(1), 5–41. https://doi.org/10.1177/001872674700100103

McFillen, J. M., O'Neil, D. A., Balzer, W. K., & Varney, G. H. (2013). Organizational diagnosis: An evidence-based approach. *Journal of Change Management*, *13*(2), 223–246. https://doi.org/10.1080/14697017.2012.679290

Neves, P. (2012). Organizational cynicism: Spillover effects on supervisor–subordinate relationships and performance. *The Leadership Quarterly*, *23*(5), 965–976. https://doi.org/10.1016/j.leaqua.2012.06.006

Oreg, S. (2006). Personality, context, and resistance to organizational change. *European Journal of Work and Organizational Psychology*, *15*(1), 73–101. https://doi.org/10.1080/13594320500451247

Pardo del Val, M., & Martinez Fuentes, C. (2003). Resistance to change: A literature review and empirical study. *Management Decision*, *41*(2), 148–155. https://doi.org/10.1108/00251740310457597

Probst, G., & Raisch, S. (2005). Organizational crisis: The logic of failure. *Academy of Management Perspectives*, *19*(1), 90–105. https://doi.org/10.5465/ame.2005.15841958

Sguera, F., Patient, D., Diehl, M. R., & Bobocel, R. (2022). Thank you for the bad news: Reducing cynicism in highly identified employees during adverse organizational change. *Journal of Occupational and Organizational Psychology*, *95*(1), 90–130. https://doi.org/10.1111/joop.12369

Shore, D. (Writer), & Campanella, J. J. (Director). (2007). *House, M.D.* Season 3, Episode 12. NBC Universal Television.

AUTHOR'S NOTE

Allow what I've set down in words to serve as a comprehensive introduction to a complex topic. Each section could have been a chapter, and each chapter its own book. I hope that you have found what you've been looking for in these pages: echoes of yourself, and visions of your future.

I'd love to hear from you about your experiences with the text, please feel free to connect with me on LinkedIn.

― LinkedIn ―

Andrei Lux

Image Alt Text: https://www.linkedin.com/in/andrei-lux/

BIOGRAPHY

Dr Andrei Lux is a Lecturer of Leadership and a Research Cluster Lead at the School of Business and Law, Edith Cowan University (ECU) in Western Australia. Andrei's research focuses on authentic leadership and organisational behaviour, with interests in positive follower outcomes such as engagement and commitment, as well as cross-cultural issues such as cognition and values.

Andrei founded the Leadership & People Research Cluster at ECU and has served as an Associate Editor at the Journal of Management & Organization since 2018. Previously, Andrei was a Director, the Treasurer, and Research Committee Chair of the Australian and New Zealand Academy of Management (ANZAM), as well as the ANZAM Conference Chair (2020–2021), Stream Chair of Organisational Behaviour (2018–2022), and the Director of Academic Studies at ECU (2023).

INDEX

Page numbers followed by "f" and "t" indicate figures and tables, respectively.

abusive supervision, 64, 65
accountability, 31–32
achievement, 136
Achor, S., 247–248
active listening, 221–222
active *vs.* passive conflict, 266–268
Adidas, 159
affective commitment, 167
agreeableness, 52–53
Airbnb, 25
Al-Atwi, A. A., 143
Al-Hassani, K. K., 143
Allen, N. J., 167
Allport, G. W., 150
altruism, 157
ambiguity, 27
American Psychological Association, 246
amorality, 111
analytic thought, 139–141
Antonakis, J., 97, 105
Appelbaum, S. H., 287
Apple, 159
apprising, 211
Argyris, C., 183
armed conflict, 24
ascription, 136
attention, 140
attribution asymmetry, 237–238
authentic leadership, 41, 86–87
    balanced processing, 87–88
    controversy, 90
    dimensions, 87–88
    inspiring others, 88–89
    internalised moral perspective, 87
    relational transparency, 88
    self-awareness, 87
Authentic Leadership Inventory, 87
Authentic Leadership Questionnaire, 87
autonomy, 34

balanced processing, 87–88
balancing act, 165–166
Banks, G. C., 102, 169
Barnard, C. I., 162
Bass, B. M., 112, 114, 116
Bastiat, F., 24
Behrendt, P., 70
belongingness, 143
biases *see specific biases*
Big Five personality dimensions, 51–52, 102
    advantages and limitations, 55–56
    agreeableness, 52–53
    conscientiousness, 54
    emotional stability, 53
    extroversion, 52
    openness, 54–55
Bilsky, W., 150
Blanchard, K. H., 77, 79
body language, 220–221
bold leaders, 41
Born This Way Foundation, 15, 16
Bosch, C., 25
bounded rationality, 236
Bridges, S., 294
Bridges, W., 294
Brown, M. E., 168, 169
bullying, workplace, 208
Burnes, B., 284
Burns, J. M., 111–112, 114, 116

Callister, R. R., 264
CANOE acronym, 51
Carmeli, A., 142
Carson, C., 109
Cartwright, E., 25
Castelnovo, O., 109
Castro, Fidel, 111
causality, 140
challenges of leadership

accountability, 31–32
contemporary, 27–36
cross-cultural collaboration, 30–31
flexible and remote work, 33–36
internationalisation, 29
intolerance, 31–32
inversion of expertise, 32–33
overcoming, 37
traditional, 36–37
change, 140, 280–281
leading through, 293
personal change, 293–294
resistance to, 298–303
transition cycle model, 294–298, 295f
transition vs., 294
charisma, 96–97, 108
defined, 96
sources of, 103–105
charismatic leadership, 97–98, 114, 127
amorality, 111
behaviour, 103–108
charismatic signals, nonverbal, 107–108
charismatic signals, sending, 105–106
context, 108–110
defined, 97
emotional basis, 98–100
outcomes, 110
personality traits, 102–103
signalling, 100–101
stable appearance, 101–102
and transformational leadership, 116
charismatic signals
nonverbal, 107–108
sending, 105–106
childhood environment, personality from, 49
Choi, I., 140
Christie, R., 62
coaching leadership, 78, 78f
coalition, 213–215
Coca-Cola, 29, 159
coercive power, 203
cognition, 58–59, 102
Jung, C., 59–60
Myers–Briggs Type Indicator, 60–62
see also cultural cognition
cognitive biases, 235–236
attribution asymmetry, 237–238
confirmation bias, 236
groupthink, 237

sunk cost fallacy, 238
cognitive dissonance, 236
collaboration, 210–211
collectivism, 132–133
commitment
affective, 167
continuance, 167
followers', 167
normative, 167
communication, 218–219
active listening, 221–222
digital, 35–36
face-to-face, 36, 220, 244, 258
during flexible and remote work, 35–36
high- vs. low- context, 131–132
non-verbal, 220–221
oral, 219–220
video, 36
written, 35–36, 219–220
complexity, 27, 124–125
confirmation bias, 236
conflict
active vs. passive, 266–268
armed, 24
constructive, 265–266
destructive, 266
geopolitical, 24–25
of responsibility, 162–163
types of, 264–268
conflict resolution, 268–269
accommodating, 273
assertive vs cooperative, 269–271
avoiding, 272–273
collaborating, 274–275
competing, 271–272
compromising, 273–274
resolution styles, 269
Conger, J. A., 105
connection power, 205
conscientiousness, 54
consequentialism, 157
constructive conflict, 265–266
consultation, 210
contingency model, 73–75, 76t
leadership style, 73–74
situational control, 74–75
continuance commitment, 167
Copeland, N., 16, 17
corporate responsibility, 162–163

courageous leaders, 41
COVID-19 pandemic, 33
Cox, T., Jr., 142
creative tension, 192–193
credibility, 104
critical thinking, 228
   analysing, 229–230
   evaluating, 231
   identifying, 228–229
   reasoning, 231–232
   reflecting, 230–231
cross-cultural collaboration, 30–31
cross-functional teams, 256
cultural cognition
   analytic vs holistic thought, 139–141
   attention, 140
   causality, 140
   change, 140
   contradiction, 140
   holistic cognition scale, 141
cultural differences, 124, 125, 127–128, 130–131, 138–139
cultural diversity, 30–31
cultural profiles, 137–138
cultural values, 128f
   Hall, 131–132
   Hofstede, 132–134
   layers of values, 128–130
   leadership perceptions, 126–127
   stereotypes and myths, 130–131
   Trompenaars and Hampden-Turner, 135–136
culturally endorsed implicit leadership theory, 127
culture, 125–126
   cognition, 139–141
   containers of, 138–139
   cultural values *see* cultural values
   defined, 125
   profiles *see* cultural profiles

Dark Triad personality framework, 62–63
   leadership, 64–65
   means, motive, and opportunity, 63
David, Jacques-Louis, 14f
DECIDE model, 233–234
decision-making, 59, 232–233
   DECIDE model, 233–234
   maximising *vs.* satisficing, 234–235
decoupling, 144
Deepwater Horizon, 86, 159

defensive thinking, 300
delegating leadership, 78, 78f
destructive conflict, 266
developed nations, 25, 38, 40, 42
developing nations, 12, 25, 38–39, 40, 42
digital age, 25
directive leadership, 78, 78f, 261
diversity
   and inclusion, 141–142
   multiculturalism, 142
double-loop learning, 183–186
Dudley, Drew, 8, 17
Dunleavy, D., 101
Duval, S., 178

economic dominance, 39
Edmondson, A. C., 142
emotional basis, 98–100
emotional intelligence, 243
   managing emotions, 245–246
   perceiving emotions, 244
   understanding emotions, 245
   using own emotions, 244
emotional people, 135–136
emotional resistance, 300–301
emotional stability, 53
empathy, 302
Enron, 86
erosion of trust, 25
ethical climate, 159–161
ethical dilemmas
   conflicts of interest, 164
   human resources, 163
   organisational resources, 164–165
ethical leadership, 168
   challenges in, 171
   dimensions of, 169–170
   dual responsibilities, 169
   effects on followers and performance, 170–171
ethics, 156–157
   ethical climate, 159–161
   hedonism, stoicism, and consequentialism, 157
   moral principles, 157–158
   unethical behaviour, 159
Eva, N., 81, 82
everyday leadership, 8, 17, 20
exceptional leadership, 294
exchange, 212

expert power, 205–206
extroversion, 52

face-to-face communication, 36, 220, 244, 258
feeling, 60
femininity, 133–134
Fiedler, F. E., 73–76
fight or flight response, 239
flexible working practices, 33
   advantages, 34, 35
   disadvantages, 34, 35
   leadership challenges, 35–36
followers' commitment, 167
force-field analysis (Lewin), 286–287
Forer effect, 62
Foucault, M., 207
4th Industrial Revolution, 40–41
French, J. R. P., Jr., 202
Fukushima Daiichi, 86
functional teams, 255–256

Garcia-Morales, V. J., 190
Gardner, W. L., 17
Geis, F. L., 62
geopolitical conflicts, 24–25
George, B., 86, 161
Germanotta, Cynthia, 15
Germanotta, Stefani, 15–17
Glasø, L., 79
Global Financial Crisis (GFC) (2008), 10
global teams, 257–258
goal setting, 238–239
Goleman, D., 243
Grabo, A., 111
Greenleaf, R. K., 81, 84
groups, vs. teams, 254
groupthink, 237
growth mindset, 195

Haber, F., 25
Haidt, J., 99
Hall, E. T., 131–132, 137
Hampden-Turner, C., 131, 135–136, 137, 138
Happy secret, 247–248
healing, 82
hedonism, 157
Heraclitus, 280
hereditary genetics, personality from, 48, 61
Hersey, P., 77, 79, 203

heuristics, 235
high- vs. low- context communication, 131–132
Hitler, Adolf, 111
Hofstede, G., 132–134, 137, 138
holistic cognition scale, 141
holistic thought, 139–141
House, R. J., 97, 98, 111, 126, 131, 138
Howell, J. M., 111
humility, 83

idealised influence, 113
immoral behaviour, 12, 63
implicit leadership theory, 2, 126–127
inclusion
   diversity and, 141–142
   multiculturalism, 142
inclusive leadership, 41, 142–143
   belongingness, 143
   challenges in practice, 144–145
   contribution, 144
   dimensions, 143–144
   uniqueness, 143–144
individualised consideration, 113–114
individualism, 132–133
influence, 209
   defined, 18
   idealised, 113
   motivation at work, 217–218
   psychological empowerment, 215–217
   tactics, 209, 223
   traditional influence tactics *see* traditional influence tactics
   see also traditional influence tactics
information power, 204–205
ingratiation, 211–212
inspiration, 19
   inspirational appeal, 210
   inspirational motivation, 113
instrumental and terminal values, 151–153
integrity, 161–162
   balancing act, 165–166
   conflicts of responsibility, 162–163
   ethical dilemmas, 163–165
intellectual stimulation, 113
internalised moral perspective, authentic leadership, 87
internationalisation, 29
intolerance, 31–32

intuition, 59
inversion of expertise, 32–33

Jones, Ben, 15
Journal of Change Management, 284
Jung, C., 59–60

Kahneman, D., 235
Kilmann, R. H., 268, 269, 275
King, Martin Luther, Jr, 106, 109, 111
Klein, K. J., 97
Knafo, A., 152
Kotter, J. P., 284, 287, 288, 304
Kotter's model
   eight stage process, 288–289
   of organisational change, 287–288
Kübler-Ross, E., 295

Ladkin, D., 207
Lady Gaga *see* Germanotta, Stefani
Lawler, E. E., 281
leadership, 2
   academic definitions of, 16–17
   authentic *see* authentic leadership
   challenges of, 7, 8–9 *see also* challenges of leadership
   charismatic *see* charismatic leadership
   coaching, 78, 78f
   crisis, 86
   defined, 3, 13–18, 20
   delegating, 78, 78f
   development, 196–197
   directive, 78, 78f, 261
   ethical *see* ethical leadership
   everyday, 8
   evolution of, 12–13
   exceptional, 294
   fit for context, 75–77
   future leaders, 41
   getting ideas from, 5–6
   leaders with special abilities, 6
   learning about others, 4–5
   management and, 9–10
   modern, 13
   moral, 81
   over-managed and under-led, 11–12
   personality and, 56–58
   positive, 167–168
   relationship-focused, 71–72
   self-aware, 182–183
   servant *see* servant leadership
   sharing ideas, 4–5
   situational *see* situational leadership
   supportive, 78, 78f
   task-focused, 70–71, 72
   on team performance, 72
   transformational *see* transformational leadership
least preferred co-worker (LPC) scale, 73–74
legitimate power, 203–204
legitimising, 212–213
Lehman Brothers, 86, 159, 160
Lewin, K., 284, 287, 304
Lewin's model, of organisational change
   driving forces, 284–285
   enabling change, 286
   Lewin's force-field analysis, 286–287
   restraining forces, 285–286
   three phase process, 286
life cycle of leadership model, 77
long- *vs.* short-term orientation, 134

Machiavelli, N., 12, 13
Machiavellianism, 62, 63
Madoff, 86
management
   defined, 10
   leadership and, 9–10
   over-managed and under-led, 11–12
   scientific, 10
managerial grid, 72
Mandela, Nelson, 111
Manson, Charles, 111
Markus, H., 180
masculinity, 133–134
maximising, *vs.* satisficing, 234–235
Mayer, J. D., 243
McCrystal, S., 27–28, 32, 35
McDonalds, 31
megatrends
   developed nations, 38
   developing nations, 38–39
   economic dominance, 39
   urbanisation, 39–40
metaperceptions, 193
Meyer, J. P., 167
Microsoft, 29
migration, international, 38, 124, 130–131, 141, 145
MLQ scale, 114

monochronic *vs.* polychronic, 132
monolithic organisations, 142
moral emotions, categories of, 99–100
moral leadership, 81
moral principles, of ethics, 157–158
morality, 82–83
motivation
   motivational orientation, 73
   at work, 217–218
multicultural organisations, 142
multiculturalism, 142
Myers–Briggs Type Indicator (MBTI), 60–61
   commercially motivated pseudoscience, 61–62
   limitations of, 61
myths of culture, 130–131

narcissism, 62–63
negative behaviour, 99–100
Nembhard, I. M., 142
Netflix, 25
neuroticism *see* emotional stability
neutral people, 135–136
Nike, 159
Nisbett, R. E., 139
non-verbal communication, 220 221
nonverbal charismatic signals, 107–108
normative commitment, 167

Obama, Barack, 104–105, 111
OCEAN acronym, 51
openness to experience, 54–55
organisational change, 280–281
   careful planning, 290
   cultural, 283
   distribution of power, 284
   functional or structural, 283
   generic solutions, beware of, 289–290
   process, 282
   smart plans, crafting, 290–293
   types of, 282–284
organisational learning, 184
organisational responsibilities, 162
Orwell, G., 207
other-suffering emotions, 99

Pagel, M. D., 131
Palazzo, G., 249
particularism, 135

personal appeal, 212
personal change, 293–294
personal mastery, 189–190
   creative tension, 192–193
   current reality, 191–192
   leading with, 194–195
   personal vision, 190–191
   self-limiting beliefs, 193–194
personal reflection, 3, 7
personal responsibilities, 162
personal vision, 190–191
personality
   from childhood environment, 49
   context matters, 50–51
   from hereditary genetics, 48
   and leadership, 56–58
   from personal choices, 49–50
   profiling, 47–48, 58
   self-development, 56–57
   traits, 46–47, 102–103
   understanding followers, 57–58
   see also Big Five personality dimensions
Peus, C., 87
Pink, D., 218
plural organisations, 142
positional power, 203
positive behaviour, 99–100
positive leadership, 167–168
positive psychology, 246–247
   happy secret, 247–248
   storytelling, power of, 248–250
positive thinking, 242
power, 202–203
   appropriate using of, 207–208
   coercive, 203
   connection, 205
   expert, 205–206
   information, 204–205
   legitimate, 203–204
   personal sources of, 205–207
   positional sources of, 203–205
   referent, 206–207
   reward, 204
   workplace bullying, 208
power distance, 133
powerlessness, 193
pressure, 213
   people's response to, 166
   vs. performance, 240–241, 240f

Probert, J., 207
psychological empowerment, 144
   competence, 216
   impact, 217
   meaning, 215–216
   self-determination, 216–217
psychological safety, 144
psychology
   personality profiling, 47–48
   traits and personality, 46–47
psychopathy, 62, 63, 64–65
public speaking, 179

Randel, A. E., 143
rational persuasion, 209
Raven, B.H., 202
referent power, 206–207
reflection-in-action, 189
reflective journal
   event, 186
   reaction, 187
   realisation, 188
   reflection, 187–188
reflective learning, 183
   double-loop learning, 183–186
   learning from setbacks, 185–186
   reflection-in-action, 189
   reflective journal, 186–188
   single-loop learning, 184
relational transparency, 88
relationship-focused leadership
   cooperation, 71
   coordination, 71
   positive reinforcement, 71
   task-focused leadership *vs.*, 71–72
remote work, 36
resistance, to change, 298
   communication, 302
   defensive thinking, 300
   emotional resistance, 300–301
   empathy, 302
   leader's ability, 301
   participation, 302–303
   reasons for, 298–299
   resistant behaviour, 300
   responding to, 301–303
resistant behaviour, 300
revolutionary change
   geopolitical conflicts, 24–25

   social movements, 26
   technological advancements, 25
reward power, 204
Rio Tinto, 163
Rokeach, M., 150
Rorschach inkblot test, 47

safety climate, 303–304
Sagiv, L., 152
Salovey, P., 243
satisficing, maximising *vs.*, 234–235
Schön, D. A., 183, 189
Schwartz, S. H., 131, 138, 150
scientific management, 10
Seeman, M., 17
self-accepting leaders, 155–156
self-aware leadership, 182–183
self-awareness, 56, 87, 178–180
   self-aware leadership, 182–183
   self-concept, 180–181
   self-knowledge, 181–182
self-care, 152
self-concept, 180–181
self-determination, 127
self-discovery, 88, 89, 90–91, 151, 188, 190, 195
self-knowledge, 7, 20, 181–182
self-limiting beliefs, 193–194
self-managed teams, 257
self-reflection, 7
self-regulation, 51
self-schemas, 180
selfless leaders, 42
Senge, P. M., 189, 190, 192, 193
sensing, 59
servant leadership, 81–82
   challenges, 85–86
   defined, 81
   dimensions, 82–83
   growth, 83
   healing, 82
   humility, 83
   long-term value, creating, 83–84
   morality, 82–83
   stewardship, 83
   understanding, 82
Sharot, T., 192
Sheen, M., 99
Shore, L. M., 142
Siangchokyoo, N., 114, 116

signalling, 100–101
Simon, H. A., 236
Sinek, S., 19, 303
single-loop learning, 184
situational control, 74–75
situational leadership
   contingency model, 73–75, 76t
   fit for context, 75–77
   overview, 80–81
situational leadership theory, 78f
    academic background, 79–80
    advantages and challenges, 80
   leadership styles, 77–79
Slavery Convention (1926), 26
SMART criteria, for goal setting, 239
social desirability bias, 246
social isolation, 34
social media, 31–32, 72, 154, 204, 219, 232
social movements, 26
specific vs diffuse, 136
Spotify, 25
Spreitzer, G. M., 215
stereotypes of culture, 130–131
stewardship, 83
Stogdill, R. M., 17
stoicism, 157
storytelling, power of, 248–250
stress, 239–240
   managing, 241–243
   pressure *vs.* performance, 240–241, 240f
sunk cost fallacy, 238
supportive leadership, 78, 78f
Sy, T., 99

Taras, V., 139
task-focused leadership, 70
   clarifying, 70–71
   facilitating, 71
   motivating, 71
   relationship-focused leadership *vs.*, 71–72
task-related maturity, 77
Taylor, F., 9
team development, 258–259
   forming, 259
   norming, 260
   performing, 260–261
   shifting responsibilities, 261–262
   storming, 259–260
teams
   cross-functional, 256

   functional, 255–256
   global or virtual, 257–258
   groups *vs.*, 254
   self-managed, 257
   types of, 255–258
   vital signs *see* vital signs, team
technological advancements, 25
thinking, 59, 228 *see also* critical thinking
third culture identities, 30, 124
Thomas, K. W., 268, 269
Thomas-Kilmann Conflict Mode Instrument, 268–269
Thompson, G., 79
Toyota, 29
traditional influence tactics
   apprising, 211
   coalition, 213–215
   collaboration, 210–211
   consultation, 210
   exchange, 212
   ingratiation, 211–212
   inspirational appeal, 210
   legitimising, 212–213
   personal appeal, 212
   pressure, 213
   rational persuasion, 209
traits, personality, 46–47, 102–103
transformational leadership, 111–112
   charismatic leadership and, 116
   defined, 112
   dimensions, 112–114
   followers changed, 114–115
   idealised influence, 113
   individualised consideration, 113–114
   inspirational motivation, 113
   intellectual stimulation, 113
   transactional leadership *vs.*, 112
transformative learning, 183
transition, change *vs.*, 294
transition cycle model, 294–298, 295f
   commitment, 297
   denial, 295–296
   exploration, 296–297
   resistance, 296
   transition cycle, 297–298
Trompenaars, F., 131, 135–136, 137, 138
Tversky, A., 235
Tylor, E. B., 125

Uber, 25
uncertainty, 27

uncertainty avoidance, 134
unethical behaviour, 159
uniqueness, 143–144
universalism, 135
unworthiness, 193
urbanisation, 39–40
Uzefovsky, F., 153

vaccinations, 25
values, 150–151
   cultural *see* cultural values
   discovery of, 155
   formation of, 153–154
   instrumental and terminal, 151–153
   long-term, 83–84
   self-accepting leaders, 155–156
Van Dierendonck, D., 82
Vazquez, Carlos, 15f
Vernon, P. E., 150
video communication, 220
virtual teams, 257–258

vital signs, team, 262
   every team is different, 264
   teams in decline, 262–263
   teams progressing, 263–264
volatility, 27
Volkswagen, 86
VUCA environment, 26–27, 37

Wall, J. A. J., 264
Weber, M., 96
Wicklund, R. A., 178
Wirecard, 86
woke capitalism, 86
work–life balance, 34
workplace bullying, 208
World Economic Forum, 40–41, 86
WorldCom, 86
Worley, C.G., 281
written and oral communication, 219–220

Yukl, G., 17, 97, 114, 209